Programming language choice
Practice and experience

Edited by

Mark Woodman
Computing Department
The Open University, UK

INTERNATIONAL THOMSON COMPUTER PRESS
I(T)P An International Thomson Publishing Company

London • Bonn • Johannesburg • Madrid • Melbourne • Mexico City • New York • Paris
Singapore • Tokyo • Toronto • Albany, NY • Belmont, CA • Cincinnati, OH • Detroit, MI

Programming language choice: practice and experience

Copyright © 1996 International Thomson Computer Press

 I(T)P A division of International Thomson Publishing Inc.
The ITP logo is a trademark under licence.

For more information, contact:

International Thomson Computer Press
Berkshire House
168-173 High Holborn
London WC1V 7AA
UK

International Thomson Computer Press
20 Park Plaza
Suite 1001
Boston, MA 02116
USA

Imprints of International Thomson Publishing

International Thomson Publishing GmbH
Königswinterer Straße 418
53227 Bonn
Germany

International Thomson Publishing Asia
221 Henderson Road #05–10
Henderson Building
Singapore 0315

Thomas Nelson Australia
102 Dodds Street
South Melbourne, 3205
Victoria
Australia

International Thomson Publishing Japan
Hirakawacho Kyowa Building, 3F
2-2-1 Hirakawacho
Chiyoda-ku, 102 Tokyo
Japan

Nelson Canada
1120 Birchmount Road
Scarborough, Ontario
Canada M1K 5G4

International Thomson Editores
Campos Eliseos 385, Piso 7
Col. Polenco
11560 Mexico D. F. Mexico

International Thomson Publishing South Africa
PO Box 2459
Halfway House
1685 South Africa

International Thomson Publishing France
1, rue St. Georges
75 009 Paris
France

British Library Cataloguing-in-Publication Data
A catalogue record for this book is available from the British Library

Library of Congress Cataloging-in-Publication Data
A catalog record for this book is available from the Library of Congress

First Printed 1996

ISBN 1-85032-186-5

Cover Designed by Button Eventures
Printed in the UK by Cambridge University Press

Contents

List of figures   xi

List of tables   xiii

List of contributors   xv

1   Introduction – programming language choice   1
    Mark Woodman
    1.1   Background   2
    1.2   Factors influencing choice of programming language   3
    1.3   Organization of the book   4
    1.4   References   6

2   Programming languages: a framework for comparison and choice   7
    Herbert Klaeren
    2.1   Languages, habits, paradigms and culture   7
    2.2   A bit of history   11
    2.3   Literature overview   13
    2.4   Concepts and languages   18
    2.5   The difficulty of language design   20
    2.6   The difficulty of language choice   21
    2.7   Towards a classification schema   23
    2.8   References   25

3   Programming paradigms and culture: implications of expert practice   29
    Marian Petre
    3.1   Introduction – starting from the right notion of paradigm   29
    3.2   How experts use paradigms   30
    3.3   Programming culture and programming style   35
    3.4   Implications for teaching of programming and training of programmers   39
    3.5   Conclusion   41
    3.6   References   42

4   CooL (Combined object-oriented language) – an overview   45
    Martin Weber
    4.1 Introduction   45
    4.2 CooL design criteria   46
    4.3 CooL – the language   48
    4.4 The CooL environment – an overview   60
    4.5 Conclusion   61
    4.6 Postscript   62
    4.7 References   62

5   C++ as an introductory programming language   63
    P. A. Lee and R. J. Stroud
    5.1 Introduction   63
    5.2 Background   64
    5.3 Goals and approach to teaching programming   65
    5.4 Choice of programming languages   67
    5.5 Evaluation of candidate languages   69
    5.6 Why C++?   69
    5.7 Experiences using C++ as an initial teaching language   73
    5.8 Conclusions   78
    5.9 References and annotated bibliography   78
    5.10 Appendix – A stack example   79

6   Using the Turing language across the curriculum   83
    Richard C. Holt, Spiros Mancoridis and David A. Penny
    6.1 Current practice   83
    6.2 A curriculum-cycle approach   84
    6.3 Pedagogical experience   89
    6.4 Language features   90
    6.5 Conclusions   94
    6.6 References and annotated bibliography   95
    6.7 Appendix – Features of the basic Turing language   97
    6.8 Appendix – Additional features of object-oriented Turing   99
    6.9 Appendix – Example: Class structure for workshop   100

7   Modula-2 in the first majors' sequence: five years' experience 107
    Steven C. Cater
    7.1 Introduction   107
    7.2 Modula-2 as the first programming language   108
    7.3 Modula-2 at the University of Georgia   114
    7.4 Conclusions   116
    7.5 References and annotated bibliography   116
    7.6 Appendix – Programming assignments   118

8   Why Ada is for you   125
    Brian Wichmann
    8.1 Introduction   125

8.2 Programming paradigms and applications 126
8.3 ADA 95 128
8.4 Conclusion – Why choose Ada? 132
8.5 References 133

9 About Extended Pascal 135
David Joslin
9.1 History 135
9.2 Why might one choose Extended Pascal? 136
9.3 Implementations 136
9.4 Future developments 137
9.5 Features of Extended Pascal 137
9.6 References 148

10 From ML to C via Modula-3: an approach to teaching programming 149
Peter Robinson
10.1 Introduction 149
10.2 ML 151
10.3 Modula-3 157
10.4 Conclusion 168
10.5 References 169

11 Rationale behind choosing Oberon for programming education at ETH Zürich 171
Josef Templ
11.1 Introduction 171
11.2 Criteria for programming language selection 172
11.3 Language criteria 173
11.4 Operating environment criteria 174
11.5 Examples 177
11.6 Conclusions 179
11.7 References and annotated bibliography 179

12 The suitability of Eiffel for teaching object-oriented software development 181
Ray Weedon
12.1 Introduction 181
12.2 Abstract data types and Eiffel 182
12.3 Programming principles embodied in Eiffel 187
12.4 Eiffel's role in industry 195
12.5 Support for teaching Eiffel 195
12.6 Summary and conclusions 197
12.7 References 197

13 Choosing Smalltalk – a consultant's view   199
    Brian Shearing
    13.1 Introduction: practical and managerial matters   199
    13.2 Technical matters   205
    13.3 Epilogue   214
    13.4 References   214

14 Omega   217
    Günther Blaschek
    14.1 Introduction and overview   217
    14.2 The Omega language   218
    14.3 The programming environment   222
    14.4 The Omega prototype library   226
    14.5 Implementation   226
    14.6 Examples   227
    14.7 Conclusions   233
    14.8 References   233

15 Pride and prejudice: four decades of Lisp   235
    Stuart Watt
    15.1 Introduction   235
    15.2 What is Lisp?   236
    15.3 Why use Lisp?   239
    15.4 What's wrong with Lisp?   250
    15.5 Can I use Lisp in industry?   251
    15.6 What is the future of Lisp?   251
    15.7 Conclusion   252
    15.8 References   253

16 Programming and programming languages   255
    Derek Andrews
    16.1 Architecture is not laying bricks   256
    16.2 Programming versus programming languages   258
    16.3 Feed a person for a day or feed them for life   258
    16.4 A programming language   263
    16.5 A theory of program development   264
    16.6 The rules of programming   265
    16.7 Implications   271
    16.8 A programme for teaching programming   271
    16.9 Other courses   274
    16.10 Summary   274
    16.11 References   275
    16.12 Appendix – Suggested glossary of programming terms   275

17 VDM-SL as a prelude to a language   277
    C. Pronk and P. G. Kluit
    17.1 Introduction   277

17.2 Requirements analysis for a new method   278
17.3 Design model   279
17.4 The new course   281
17.5 The Open University workshop problem   282
17.6 Experiences   288
17.7 Conclusion   289
17.8 References   289

18 Initial programming language choice: a review of the factors   291
    John Traxler
    18.1 Introduction   291
    18.2 What we used to do   293
    18.3 Factors for choosing an initial programming language 294
    18.4 Conclusions   298
    18.5 References   299

19 Programming language choice for distance computing   301
    Mark Woodman and Rob Griffiths
    19.1 Computing courses in the distance mode   301
    19.2 Concepts supported by programming languages   303
    19.3 Non-language criteria   306
    19.4 Conclusion   308
    19.5 References   308
    19.6 Appendix – M206 aims and objectives   309
    19.7 Appendix – Programming language implementation questionnaire   311

20 Standardization and language proliferation   313
    Brian Meek
    20.1 The languages scene   313
    20.2 Partisanship   314
    20.3 Dependence   315
    20.4 Proliferation   315
    20.5 The role of standardization   317
    20.6 Proliferation, standards and choice of languages   318
    20.7 Conclusion   320
    20.8 References   320

21 The role of documentation in programmer training   323
    Johannes Sametinger
    21.1 Introduction   323
    21.2 Conventional documentation   325
    21.3 Literate programming   325
    21.4 Hypertext documentation   327
    21.5 Object-oriented documentation   328
    21.6 Experiences   329
    21.7 Conclusion   330
    21.8 References   330

22 (Re)presenting the p-word: paradigmatic discourse on programming languages 333

Hugh Robinson

22.1 Introduction 333
22.2 The approach 334
22.3 The workshop 335
22.4 The p-word(s) 335
22.5 Pariahs 337
22.6 The unquestioned, the unjustified 339
22.7 The absence of argument 340
22.8 Concluding remarks 342
22.9 References 344

Index 345

Author index 381

List of figures

4.1	COOL concepts	49
4.2	A 'happening' object	50
4.3	'IsA' hierarchy	51
4.4	The COOL environment	60
5.1	Software project stages	65
6.1	A snapshot of the OOT environment	88
7.1	A definition module for stacks of (name, address) pairs	110
7.2	Part of an implementation module for stacks of (name, address) pairs	111
7.3	An implementation module for stacks of (name, address) pairs (cont'd)	112
7.4	A possible definition module for (name, address) pairs	112
12.1	Class hierarchy showing different types of delegate to a workshop	190
13.1	Lexis of SMALLTALK	202
13.2	Concrete syntax of SMALLTALK	203
13.3	Class structure of workshop (attributes in parentheses)	205
13.4	Object model of workshop	206
13.5	Example of data-structure of workshop	207
13.6	Part of typical SMALLTALK class library	209
14.1	Snapshot of an OMEGA session	223
14.2	New Variable dialogue	224
14.3	New Method dialogue	225
14.4	Architecture of the OMEGA system	227
14.5	Creation of the MyStack prototype	228
14.6	The MyStack prototype with the new instance variable content	229
14.7	Persons and roles in the prototype hierarchy	231
15.1	A brief history of LISP	237
15.2	A LISP list structure	239
15.3	Comparison of iterative and sequence versions of the same function	240
15.4	A typical REP loop display	242

15.5 A typical inspector display 243
15.6 Common Graphics code for the evaluation dialogue 248
15.7 The evaluation dialogue display 249

16.1 From specification to code 265
16.2 'Divide and conquer' used to establish a subproblem 267
16.3 Three assignment rules 268
16.4 Case analysis – domain partitioning 269

17.1 The development paradigm 279
17.2 Abstraction and representation functions 280

21.1 Sample literate program 326
21.2 Inherited and overridden methods of a class 328
21.3 Inherited and overridden documentation sections of a class 329

List of tables

5.1   Main features of languages   70
5.2   Overall language comparison   71

12.1 The Stack ADT implemented as the EIFFEL class STACK   186

13.1 Some sources of SMALLTALK   201

14.1 Declarations and their effects   220
14.2 Definitions of prototypes   231

List of contributors

Derek Andrews
Mathematics and Computer Science
University of Leicester
University Road
Leicester
UK LE1 7RH

Steven Cater
Department of Science & Mathematics
GMI Engineering & Management Institute
1700 West Third Avenue
Flint, MI 48504-4898
USA

Ric Holt
University of Toronto
Toronto
Canada

Herbert Klaeren
Universität Tübingen
Wilhelm-Schickard-Institut
Sand 13
D-72076 Tübingen
Germany

Peter Lee
Department of Computing Science
University of Newcastle
Newcastle upon Tyne
UK NE1 7RU

Günther Blaschek
Institut für Informatik Abt Software
Universtät Linz
Altenbergerstraße 69
Linz A-4040
Austria

Rob Griffiths
The Open University
Computing Department
Walton Hall
Milton Keynes
UK MK7 6AA

David Joslin
25 Kader Farm Road
Acklam
Middlesborough
UK TS5 8LJ

Peter Kluit
Delft University of Technology
Fac. of Techn. Math. and Informatics
P.O. Box 356
NL-2600 AJ Delft
Netherlands

Brian Meek
Computing Centre
King's College
Strand
London

Marian Petre
The Open University
Computing Department
Walton Hall
Milton Keynes
UK MK7 6AA

Hugh Robinson
The Open University
Computing Department
Walton Hall
Milton Keynes
UK MK7 6AA

Johannes Sametinger
Institut für Wirtschaftsinformatik
Universtät Linz
Altenbergerstraße 69
Linz A-4040
Austria

Stuart Watt
The Open University
Knowledge Media Institute
Walton Hall
Milton Keynes
UK MK7 6AA

John Traxler
University of Wolverhampton
School of Computing and I.T.
Wulfrana Street
Wolverhampton

Ray Weedon
The Open University
Computing Department
Walton Hall
Milton Keynes
UK MK7 6AA

Mark Woodman
The Open University
Computing Department
Walton Hall
Milton Keynes
UK MK7 6AA

Cornelus Pronk
Delft University of Technology
Fac. of Techn. Math. & Informatics
P.O. Box 356
NL-2600 AJ Delft
Netherlands

Peter Robinson
University of Cambridge
Computer Laboratory
New Museums Site
Pembroke Street
Cambridge
UK CB2 3QG

Brian Shearing
The Software Factory
28 Padbrook
Limpsfield
Oxted
Surrey
UK RH8 ODW

Josef Templ
ETH Zürich
Institut für Computersysteme
ETH-Zentrum
CH-8092 Zürich
Switzerland

Martin Weber
Siemens AG, AUT 3 TA 1
13623 Berlin
Germany

Brian Wichmann
DITC National Physical Laboratory
Queens Road
Teddington
Middlesex
UK TW11 OLW

1 Introduction – programming language choice

Mark Woodman

This book is the result of a workshop on criteria to be used when choosing a programming language whether for use in an academic, a commercial or an industrial setting. The workshop was held at the Open University in September 1993. The book contains both revised and extended versions of papers presented at the workshop and two new contributions which provide a wider context for the topic of programming language choice and which reflect on how we approach it.

The workshop itself arose from a need which my colleagues and I had to understand and prioritize the plethora of criteria for choosing a language for a course we were preparing to develop. At the time, and for most of the period in which this book was being prepared, we had not decided on a syllabus, never mind a language. (We have now: see Chapter 19 for an outline and [Woodman et al., 1996] for details.) The contents of the book, therefore, have not been influenced by my course team's decision, although I have been very influenced by the contributions to the book and by the responses of the workshop delegates to them. However, the emergence of the object-oriented 'paradigm' (see Chapters 3 and 22) has influenced the ordering of chapters.

In this chapter I give the background to the book, my personal views on what can be concluded from it, and a map of its organization. In doing so it is my intention to introduce several ideas about programming language choice that recur frequently in the book; because they appear in many guises this repetition is very necessary.

1

1.1 Background

The past ten to fifteen years have seen significant advances in our understanding of the variety of useful models of software development and of the appropriate technologies to use with these models. We now have a rich set of structured, disciplined, object-oriented, rigorous and formal methods and do not balk at the prospect of comparing them (as in [Sutcliffe, 1991]) or analysing them for their suitability in particular business applications or in particular academic courses. Despite this maturity, both industry and academia frequently fail to maintain their analytical aplomb in the face of programming languages. All too frequently an inappropriate choice of language is due to conflicting language descriptions and inventive implementations which together create confusion for evaluators: perceived deficiencies do not exist, or much-vaunted strengths have an attendant cost in terms of efficiency or security.

However, technical attributes are not the whole story. For industry and commerce, factors such as standards, the variety and quality of implementations and the availability of experienced practitioners matter as much, if not more. For academia, factors such as currency, conceptual power, expressiveness, the availability of textbooks and affordable implementations can matter. Where the development of vocational skills is part of the aims of courses of study, then the needs of industry and commerce will also impinge on academic choice.

The Computing Department at the Open University (OU) has begun a major course development project to replace its introductory course in computing and software development which attracts over 3500 students per year. The issues confronting the course team in choosing a language for this course encompassed those mentioned above as well as the problems of distance teaching, course longevity, industrial relevance and volume-related costs. (The number of software licences to be bought in the first instance is likely to exceed 10 000.) The workshop on programming language choice was therefore organized to assist in the decision-making process, a primary objective of the workshop being to establish selection criteria. (It was the fourth in a serious of workshops on the curriculum, teaching technologies and educational principles held at the OU.)

Hence, the aim of the workshop was to identify criteria and techniques for judging the suitability of languages for particular uses. It was primarily for those involved in higher education but was to be of relevance to practitioners in industry and commerce; the relevance of standards, language implementations and supporting software tools was also explored. Both established and new store–imperative and object-oriented languages were on the agenda, together with mathematically based approaches that might offer the means to diminish the importance of language choice. For neither the workshop nor the book did I set out to exhaustively cover all languages, or even all languages of commercial or theoretical significance. (In practice, evaluators of languages rarely have the luxury of evaluating large numbers of them.) COBOL, FORTRAN and (VISUAL) BASIC are missing; so are APL, PROLOG and MIRANDA; C and classic PASCAL are alluded to, but not discussed in their own rights; and 'new' languages like BETA [Madsen *et al.*, 1993] and SELF are only mentioned – particularly in Herbert Klaeren's survey (Chapter 2). (Many of the 'missing' languages are referenced and can be found via the index.) What I believed to be more important to achieve was coverage in terms of practice, and in terms of the experiences and analyses of the problem of programming language choice. Through reports of these, I believe the factors we need to consider can be exposed. For me, it worked. I trust it will work for you.

1.2 Factors influencing choice of programming language

As many of the contributors observed, many factors are at play when choosing a programming language. Those that come to mind most readily might be termed 'technical': for example, support for abstract data types, speed of compilation, efficacy of run-time semantic checking. (You can observe concern for these factors in all of the chapters on particular languages.)

Other factors might be termed 'managerial' inasmuch as they may be of greater importance to managers: for example, cost, the relationship to legacy code, the availability of trained staff, the support package from a trusted vendor. (Although these were discussed at the 1993 workshop, they are really only aired here by Brian Shearing, who is a consultant.)

More elusive, but no less important, are 'cognitive' factors and 'social' factors. Many claims have been made about the 'naturalness' of languages and associated 'paradigms' but these appear to feature rarely in debates among practitioners. (Marian Petre has addressed the former class of factor and Hugh Robinson the latter; interestingly they concentrate on paradigms in very different ways.)

Before summarizing the factors that I perceived as dominant, I should make some further remarks on what I think the contributors to this work have collectively observed:

- Support for abstract data types is essential; there is no longer any real excuse for anything less than MODULA-2, say.
- Object-oriented facilities are highly desirable; of the languages discussed in any depth, only ML and MODULA-2 had no such facilities.
- Libraries of re-usable program components were desirable, if not essential.
- Suitably powerful programming environments may become a dominant factor when choosing a programming language.
- The availability of textbooks (for students in academia) and training (for professional programmers) is an important issue.
- The perceived needs of the market are important to academics: the apparent availability of people trained in a particular language will determine its longevity within organizations and this will encourage academics to provide the training.
- Unsupported claims of suitability for an application domain, of run-time efficiency, or of productivity can create an impetus in favour of a language.
- Culture (and maybe lethargy) within both academic and commercial departments plays a significant role in programming language choice.

My conclusion is that the main factors that academics have been considering are:

1. the support for ADTs and for object-oriented programming;
2. the availability of textbooks;
3. the ease with which academics can progress from PASCAL.

It is harder to identify separate factors for effecting programming language choice in the commercial and industrial worlds. They tend to combine into one: the likelihood that high-quality, cost-effective programs can be produced on time.

1.3 Organization of the book

The book shares many of the aims of the 1993 workshop; initial versions of many of the chapters in the book were distributed at the conference and the revisions are the result of feedback from the delegates and of interactions in debates that took place. However, the intention of the book is to go further by making the criteria and factors more explicit than they were initially. The reported practices in academia and in commerce and industry are recorded, as are the experiences of individuals. Thus, the practice and experience that reflect and shape the processes involved in choosing a language are emphasized.

Another change from the tenor of the OU workshop is that the academic bias has been lessened a little to make the contributions relevant to colleagues in the software industry.

A survivor from the workshop has been a programming problem I vaguely proposed to the authors – that of a workshop in which presentations were given by presenters, to delegates, and so on. The deliberate vagueness has resulted in many variations on the theme (*cf.* the COOL solution in Chapter 4 and the SMALLTALK solution in Chapter 13). For those who prefer the familiar, the traditional stack ADT frequently appears.

The pragmatic approach of the book should be emphasized. It is not intended to present theoretical arguments about the qualities of languages or their implementations – although Herbert Klaeren's contribution (Chapter 2) does summarize many of the main arguments and cites many of the seminal works for those who wish to pursue this line. (Josef Templ, of ETH Zürich, restates some of the principles of language design in Chapter 11.) The most theoretical treatment of language choice is offered by Derek Andrews in Chapter 16.

Each chapter in the book is self-contained; you can dip into it as you please. However, there is an ordering for those readers who prefer to read the chapters in some coherent sequence. After the next two chapters, the subsequent ones have been organized to allow the reader who is unfamiliar with object-oriented programming to become *au fait* with the main ideas via hybrid languages such as COOL, C++ and object-oriented TURING. Discussions of the 'pure' object-oriented languages – EIFFEL, SMALLTALK and OMEGA – are postponed until Chapters 12–14.

After this introduction the book continues with the chapters by Klaeren and Petre which set the scene for what follows. In Chapter 2 Herbert Klaeren (Universität Tübingen) provides some historical background in which he notes many of the languages that might have been successful (and some would say should have been successful). He also provides a useful review of the literature of programming languages and suggests a classification system. Subsequently, Marian Petre (OU) explores the relationship between technological paradigms and the culture in which they might be used; although she directs her conclusions towards educationists, programmers and their managers will undoubtedly recognize the issues she raises and will readily draw conclusions appropriate to their own contexts.

Then follow the twelve chapters that describe practice and experience of a variety of languages and suggest related criteria for choosing the language. The languages covered include established ones such as C++ (by Pete Lee and R. J. Stroud, University of Newcastle upon Tyne, in Chapter 5) and MODULA-2 (by Steve Cater, GMI Engineering & Management Institute, in Chapter 7) and the modern versions of entrenched ones (such as EXTENDED PASCAL and ADA 95 described by David Joslin and Brian Wichmann respectively in Chapters 8 and 9). Also covered are new languages which have recently been developed for use in commerce and industry (*e.g.* COOL described by Martin Weber, Siemens) and for teaching (*e.g.* TURING, described by Ric Holt and colleagues from the University of Toronto, and OMEGA, described by Günther Blaschek, Johannes-Kepler Universität Linz). ML and MODULA-3 are dealt with by Peter Robinson (University of Cambridge) and EIFFEL is discussed in Chapter 12 by Ray Weedon (OU). Stuart Watt (OU) concludes the sequence with an extensive look at the LISP family.

Following these chapters on particular programming languages are two chapters on formal approaches to programming (and hence to programming languages). In Chapter 16, Derek Andrews (University of Leicester) provides a critical analysis of what is wrong with programming languages from a theoretical, mathematical viewpoint. He also gives some straightforward mathematics that clearly encapsulates the correct ideas and provides comment on what is suitable. In the next chapter, Kees Pronk and Peter Kluit (Technical University of Delft) show how a formal, mathematical notation can be simply used as a prelude to programming. These two chapters take a pragmatic approach to the use of discrete mathematics and will be accessible to most programmers.

Although describing an academic situation, John Traxler's account (in Chapter 18) of how his organization chose programming languages will find resonance with colleagues in commercial and industrial organizations. He clearly demonstrates the importance to the process of choice of the people 'on the ground' – local cultural factors, staff expertise and staff development are all relevant.

I initially wrote Chapter 19 with my colleague, Rob Griffiths, before our syllabus and language had finally been agreed. Having decided on both, we updated the chapter in such a way that we hope the original arguments that arose from the peculiar circumstances of the OU are preserved. However, the reader should be aware that we wholeheartedly went with the tide in favour of object-oriented computing and chose SMALLTALK for good technical reasons, because the number of topics in the syllabus left little time for learning a complex language, for reasons to do with the market, and for reasons of staff development. In short, for all the reasons documented herein.

Programming language standardization is a subject that can divide people. Many software practitioners would argue that standardization inhibits evolution, while others see it as a vital part of software development as an engineering discipline; many approve of the aims but do not use the results. The veteran programming language standardizer, Brian Meek, a computer centre manager (from King's College London), gives his views in Chapter 20 of an area in which he has long been involved.

Tools whose availability is of importance to the use of languages are extremely relevant to language choice. They are represented in this volume in the context of several contributions on particular languages, notably Martin Weber's description of the environment for COOL. In Chapter 21 a documentation tool is described by Johannes

Sametinger (Johannes-Kepler Universität Linz) in an education context, but the tool has obvious application outside it.

The last chapter (22), by Hugh Robinson, provides an analysis of the verbal discourse at the workshop and (indirectly) of the written chapters. This often entertaining chapter shows how software professionals employ a variety of rhetorical devices to forward their arguments, in this case to do with the merits and demerits of programming languages. He provides a quite different view of the ubiquitous term 'paradigm' and certainly questions the common notion that we are engaged in computer 'science' or software 'engineering'. The approach taken in the chapter implies that we should reflect on how we analyse our strategic problems and how we discuss options that address them. It is a provocative note with which to conclude a consideration of the practices and experiences that contribute to programming language choice.

Acknowledgements

Thanks are, of course, due to all the authors of the chapters, not just for the written word but for their reviewing of each other's contributions. Thanks are also due to the delegates at the Open University workshop and to the session chairs, particularly Peter Thomas and Gordon Davies (of the Computing Department at the OU) and Marc Eisenstadt (of the Knowledge Media Institute at the OU).

Trade marks

All trade marks are acknowledged, in particular the following:

> Ada is a registered trade mark of the United States Government, A. J. P. O.
> Unix is a registered trade mark of Novell.
> Sun and SPARC are registered trade marks of Sun Microsystems, Inc.
> Windows, Windows NT and Windows 95 are trade marks of Microsoft Inc.
> Macintosh, Mac OS and A/UX are trade marks of Apple Computer Inc.
> CooL is a registered trade mark.
> IBM and VisualAge are trade marks of International Business Machines.
> SGI and MPS are trade marks of Silicon Graphics Inc.
> NeXT is a trade mark of NeXT Computer Inc.
> Visual Smalltalk, ObjectWorks, Smalltalk/V, Parts and VisualWorks are all trade marks of ParcPlace–Digitalk Inc.
> Teamwork is a registered trade mark of Cadre Technologies.
> Miranda is a trade mark of Research Software Ltd.

1.4 References

Madsen, O.L., Moller-Pedersen, B. and Nygaard, K. (1993), *Object-oriented Programming in the BETA Programming Language*, Addison-Wesley, Reading, MA.

Sutcliffe, A. G. (1991), Object-oriented systems development: survey of structured methods, *Information and Software Technology*, 33(6), 433–42.

Woodman, M., Davies, G. and Holland, S. (1996), The Joy Of Software – Starting With Objects, in *Proceedings ACM SIGCSE, Philadelphia, February 1996*.

2 Programming languages: a framework for comparison and choice

Herbert Klaeren

As its title suggests, this chapter provides a framework for comparing programming languages and choosing among them. It briefly reviews the literature of the area, pointing to seminal works and other valuable sources, and sketches the history of programming languages and their design. The chapter also suggests a classification scheme which should help those who need to choose a programming language.

2.1 Languages, habits, paradigms and culture

Die Grenzen meiner Sprache bedeuten die Grenzen meiner Welt.

L. Wittgenstein, *Tractatus Logico-Philosophicus*, 5.6

We must recognize the strong and undeniable influence that our language exerts on our way of thinking, and in fact defines and delimits the abstract space in which we can formulate – give form to – our thoughts.

N. Wirth *On the Design of Programming Languages* [1974]

A language that doesn't affect the way you think about programming, is not worth knowing.

A. J. Perlis, *Epigrams on Programming*, No.19 [1982]

One certainly undoubted fact in the developmental history of *Homo sapiens* is that humans and tools have shaped each other: humans made tools, tools made humans. For instance, the development of human language can be substantially attributed to the creation of tools for the dissection of food; this allowed the development of far more delicate jaws and in succession enabled humans to produce more diverse, sophisticated sounds. Among the tools humanity created, language seems to be the most powerful one: the whole history of society, philosophy, arts and sciences is hardly imaginable without having language in the first place. Wittgenstein in his famous quote at the beginning of this chapter ('The limits of my language mean the limits of my world') seems to go as far as denying any possibility of thinking – or at least of communicating thoughts to the world – without having a language. Whether we follow his opinion or not, we still have to admit that again the interactions between humanity and its tool apply: we modify our language to better express our thoughts and the modified language leads to new, previously unthinkable thoughts. Slowly, habits and paradigms emerge and a culture is created.

You may ask what all of this has to do with programming languages. Well, it is my view that is has a lot to do with programming – maybe more than we are usually aware. The computing community is in a much better position than most of the other disciplines (except, perhaps, pure mathematics) to create its own language or languages and thus set the limits of its world anew. Perhaps this is the reason why there are so many programming languages. But still the phenomenon described above occurs, as recognized by the quotes of Wirth and Perlis: even a programming language will influence our habits, paradigms and general philosophy about the programming task, so it certainly is important to pay attention to programming languages. It can easily be argued that it is even more important to pay attention to the first language we teach to our students, since this may form habits, paradigms and culture in a way that may be hard to change afterwards.[1]

There are several hundreds of programming languages around,[2] a few dozens of which are really important. The question why there are so many programming languages is obviously tied to the question why a person should design a new programming language instead of using an existing one. For the first high-level languages this question was easily answered: there simply were no existing ones. Nowadays the situation is more complicated. We will leave out of the discussion the considerable fun there is in designing a language as well as other ephemeral reasons.[3] On a more serious scale, there are at least the following points to consider:

Conceptual models: Taking for granted that every program is in some way meant to process information, we must still admit that there may be different views about what information really is, what information processing really means, so there may be different *conceptual models* not only of the application domain but also of the programming process. Of course, this implies different opinions about how programs are best derived and expressed and it may well happen that a new paradigm of program development and notation doesn't fit any of the existing languages.

Application domains: Different application domains seem to call for different languages, and there are new application domains steadily emerging as our technology

---

[1] Paul [1985] says 'No alcohol and BASIC to children below sixteen years'.

[2] For example, see the language list http://cuiwww.unige.ch/langlist

[3] For instance, Stroustrup [1993] tells that he created C++ only because he was educated in SIMULA 67 and thought the language fit for his current task where he only had access to a C compiler.

improves. The straightforward reaction to a new application domain seems to be a new language. POSTSCRIPT, for instance, has been developed for the purpose of high-level descriptions of printed pages with text and graphics.

Deficiencies of known languages: After a fair amount of programming in any language, the programming community becomes aware of certain deficiencies of the language. If these are minor problems, they can be fixed in a sequence of revisions of the language; *cf.* the long history of FORTRAN from the first versions described by Backus [1981] to the present-day language. The new versions may or may not be compatible with the old ones; for example, FORTRAN II was not designed to be compatible with FORTRAN I. The current trend of defining object-oriented extensions to virtually any language except sheer assembler gives a further indication of the trend to adapt older languages to newer trends.[4] If there are larger departures from the culture of a language, if there is no hope for progress within this culture, or if the necessity of mixing several languages arises, a new language is created.

Some of the languages are not much more than variations on a common theme but some have really introduced new *concepts* into programming; these are the more influential ones since they shape the programming culture. It is always amazing to observe how difficult it is to agree on which languages are really important, which ones are good or bad, and which language we should choose for programming education. Perhaps this is just a familiar phenomenon of culture: virtually every culture includes religion – and we all do have rather strong opinions as far as religion is concerned! If we look, for instance, at the frequent 'against/for C++' discussions on UseNet, this certainly bears resemblance to religious wars. Reason doesn't seem to count very much in this discussion; you just have to *believe* that C++ was made by the devil or else that it is the one and only thing that will save your soul. The chapter by Petre in this volume [Petre, 1996] contains much interesting material on programming paradigms and languages. According to her, professional, expert programmers are quite good at *paradigm-switching*; furthermore, despite the fact that some languages have been created, and are marketed, with a specific paradigm in mind, experts don't always use the language that matches their current paradigm.

There are numerous dependencies between theory and practice of programming languages on one hand and software engineering on the other, since the programming language is the most important tool of the software engineer (*cf.* [Ludewig, 1993] and [Klaeren, 1994]). In recognition of this significance of programming languages, there has been a workshop on research issues in the intersection of software engineering and programming language at the 17th International Conference on Software Engineering. Plödereder [1995] summarized the discussions of this workshop by stating that programming languages:

- can minimize the semantic gap between design and implementation;
- establish vocabulary and concepts for programmers and designers;
- in varying degrees support, encourage or enforce software engineering paradigms;
- are today's prime distribution channel for software engineering principles.

He then went on to state that the difficult problem is to *quantify benefits* in such a

---

[4] Alan Perlis, in his wonderful *Epigrams on Programming* [1982], said: 'Some languages manage to absorb change but withstand progress.'

way that a cost/benefit analysis in language choice may be done. Obviously the problem with such quantification of benefits is that it would require *empirical, quantitative research* about programming languages, which has seldom been done.

There are, however, some steps in this direction, for example, the article by Griffiths [1991] comparing safety of programming in MODULA-2 as opposed to C. What Griffiths has done here is to have experienced programmers write some nontrivial programs in MODULA-2 and C. He took snapshots of the sources prior to the first compilation and after the programmers were satisfied with program correctness. The differences between these snapshots were carefully investigated and discussed with the respective programmers who had been asked to only correct errors (not to introduce further changes) and to keep a log of their changes. For every error corrected, the following questions were asked: How was the error found: by the compiler, by a run-time trap or by semantic consideration by the programmer? Did finding the error involve debugger sessions? What would have happened if this error had been made in the other language?[5] Specific attention was paid to errors that needed debugger sessions since these are the really hard ones: here you have to work backwards from wrong results, find out what happened, and take appropriate measures. These are the kind of errors that indicate the (missing) quality of a language. Comparison of the languages was made in both directions. Perhaps not too surprisingly, it turned out that 30 MODULA-2 errors were detected either by the compiler or by run-time traps, none of which would have been reported by the C system, whereas 16 of the 24 errors in C programs that needed debugging would have been caught by the MODULA-2 system. In 3 out of these 24 cases it was simply impossible to commit the C error in MODULA-2. Interestingly enough, Griffiths's original intent was to demonstrate that the extended syntax checks provided by MODULA-2 would only report errors which experienced programmers wouldn't make anyway. The Griffiths paper leaves many questions open but is a step in the right direction. We have to have more controlled experiments in this field, assessing usage properties of languages. This is a point of *programming language pragmatics*, a field which is frequently neglected. Every linguist knows that a language has to be discussed under three aspects:

> *syntax*: dealing with the internal relations of symbols to each other;
>
> *semantics*: dealing with the relations of symbols to the things they denote;
>
> *pragmatics*: dealing with the relations between symbols and their user.

Certainly, the expressivity of programming languages is orders of magnitude lower than that of natural languages; this is mainly a consequence of the intent with which programming languages are constructed. But why shouldn't pragmatics be relevant for programming languages also? Why do computer scientists all too often give the impression that syntax and semantics are all there is to a programming language, even if they are speaking of 'programming linguistics' like Watt [1990]?[6]

---

[5] Of course, the last question is a bit tricky and you have to be careful what you are talking about; certainly, unless 'bilingual' programmers were concerned, it involved a third person familiar with the other language.

[6] A further complication arises from the fact that 'semantics' in computer science usually means explaining one world of formal symbols by another world of formal symbols.

2.2 A bit of history

Software development grew out of mathematical programming, whose practitioners were mathematicians, astronomers, and physicists. They regarded programming as an essentially trivial activity compared to their professional work.

M. Jackson [1994]

He who wants to apprehend the narrowness of his native country should travel; who wants to apprehend the narrowness of his time should study history.

Kurt Tucholsky

I know of no way of judging of the future but by the past.

Patrick Henry (1775)

Much has been said and written about the history of programming (languages); each of the books I review in the next section contains a chapter with historical details. There is neither room nor need to repeat it here. Nevertheless, I do want to stress a few points that may be relevant in the context of the present book and then give some references to the literature.

First of all, we have to realize that programming started as an almost language-less activity: this doesn't contradict the Wittgenstein quote at the beginning of this chapter but merely pays tribute to the fact that the first computers were *fixed-program machines* where the program was connected to the machine by a mechanical operation. It could be contained in punched cards or tapes, switchboards, cables or whatever; in any case, it wasn't 'stored' in the machine in the same way as data was stored. Programming in a certain sense meant wiring the machine. The so-called von Neumann architecture changed this radically: having the program stored in the machine allowed programs to generate programs; this created the abstraction facility needed as a prerequisite to programming languages. It is amazing to see how, at all times, technical developments in the programming field have been smoke-screened by sales talk: even the very first attempts at the use of symbolic instruction codes and addresses instead of bit patterns and octal numbers have audaciously been called 'automatic programming' (see, *e.g.* Backus [1981]). Equally amazing is the fact that sometimes important concepts are invented, forgotten and reinvented with great noise some time later.

Of course, this is a known phenomenon in the history of technology, but in the programming languages field the time scale is much shorter, thus showing in clear daylight the obliviousness of the human race. The most prominent example is object-oriented programming: invented for SIMULA 67 in the late 1960s as a tool for discrete event simulation it was soon seen as an excellent data abstraction facility [Hoare, 1972] and perhaps was the trigger for the occupation with abstract data types within theoretical computer science in the 1970s and 1980s. The current object-oriented trend, frequently connected with heavy advertising for C++, seems to have forgotten both the practical and theoretical roots; as Wirth [1994] remarks, many of the object-oriented programmers in reality only have rediscovered abstract data types. This is one more example for 'The Emperor's Old Clothes' [Hoare, 1987]. There may be a reason for this misunderstanding of SIMULA 67: because object-oriented programming wasn't invented purposefully but only incidentally for the simulation purpose, the concept wasn't designed in a clear, minimal form. Watt [1990] says:

No component of a SIMULA 67 object could be hidden. Furthermore, SIMULA

67 confuses the concept of an object with the independent concepts of *reference* and *coroutine*.

It took some years for the object concept to be laid bare in SMALLTALK. From the conceptual view, the object-oriented discussion should indeed focus much more on SMALLTALK than on C++ which is a sort of a mongrel involving SIMULA 67 and C as ancestors.

It is always dangerous – and perhaps even wrong – to classify historical developments in decades, attaching descriptive labels to them. Some of the textbooks mentioned here have tried this and don't agree too much in their classification. I couldn't resist the temptation to offer my own:

1950s *Early experiments.* The first programming languages aren't designed as such, *i.e.* as languages. Rather, a compiler for a certain class of programs is developed; language is only a by-product of the translating system.

1960s *Decade of syntax.* Beginning with ALGOL-60 (formerly IAL: International Algebraic Language) it is recognized that programming languages really *are* languages. Attention is first paid mainly to syntax, the culmination being the syntactic description of ALGOL-68, which for many practitioners already goes one step too far. PL/I, on the other hand, shows that you shouldn't be too liberal concerning syntax and that it doesn't suffice to provide syntax for semantically unclear and mutually conflicting features.

1970s *Decade of semantics.* This starts with the formal semantics of PL/I[7] which, although clumsy, is a milestone insofar as it makes clear that semantics also has to be rigidly defined. Languages defined in the 1970s show a general awareness of semantic issues (both static and dynamic). Research is carried out on data abstraction and abstract data types, which together with procedural abstraction creates the opportunity for the definition of *virtual machines*; some languages already incorporate these ideas. This decade is best characterized by Wirth, who says that we switched from languages to *in*struct machines to languages to *con*struct machines.

1980s *Decade of software engineering and functional programming.* While the 1970s had already seen languages that were appropriate for large software systems built of separately compiled modules with inter-module syntactic and semantic checks, this is a predominant design objective for ADA and EIFFEL. Programming in the large [DeRemer and Kron, 1976] gets more importance. At the same time, functional programming, which in principle has been present since the days of LISP, is much promoted because of more consistent languages and better implementation techniques.

1990s This decade will in the future perhaps be most closely associated with *object orientation* although today it is still too early for such a prediction.

Turning to the literature now, an obviously important source of information is the proceedings of the ACM conference *History of Programming Languages* [1981] where many designers of programming languages tell their histories. At the time of writing, the proceedings of the second conference on this topic [Lee and Sammet, 1993] is still waiting for its final publication. Much information about older languages can be

---

[7] As a matter of fact, of a subset of PL/I.

found in *Programming Languages: History and Fundamentals* [Sammet, 1969] although this is mainly the raw material on which historical conclusions would still have to be drawn.[8] Also, the collection *A History of Computing in the Twentieth Century* [Metropolis *et al.*, 1980] discuss, among other things, concepts of programming languages; most interesting in this connection is the chapter by Knuth and Pardo [1980] on the early history of programming languages.

2.3 Literature overview

This section is, of course, a personal and certainly biased view of the literature in a field that sometimes is called 'concepts of programming languages', sometimes 'comparative programming languages'. I apologize for any omissions or misrepresentations. Since it is almost impossible to give account of the whole spectrum of publications, we concentrate on textbooks.

As a general remark, it has to be said that most of the books are of a slightly schizophrenic nature: after having discussed general concepts for a while, they most invariably fall into enumerating a catalogue of languages and discussing their properties. The difference between the books is, apart from the quality of the material, in the selection of languages discussed and in the level of detail presented. The usual difficulty is that the reader has to know (or at least be willing to learn to some extent) a substantial number of languages in order to learn about concepts of programming languages; the situation for the authors is made even worse by the fact that some of the languages that really are important from a conceptual point of view, for example, ALGOL-60 and SIMULA 67, play no role at all in present-day practice.

There are two notable exceptions to this mainstream of books: *Essentials of Programming Languages* [Friedman *et al.*, 1992] and *Programming Linguistics* [Gelernter and Jagannathan, 1990], and I want to comment on these first. Friedman *et al.* use a single language (SCHEME) to illustrate essential concepts of programming languages like data and procedural abstraction, parameter-passing mechanisms, run-time organization, exception handling, object orientation, dynamic binding and others. Everything is discussed in terms of interpreters which are much easier to understand than compilers and which are presented as SCHEME programs too. In a sense, this is the most consistent discussion of programming language concepts although many may feel that it has to be complemented by a text presenting examples from different languages.

Gelernter and Jagannathan [1990] (411 pages), after briefly presenting their 'programming linguistics' approach, present their 'Ideal Software Machine' (ISM), a very abstract model of computation. Consisting of recursively nested 'space maps' and 'time maps', the ISM may be hard to get accustomed to, but it allows suitable definitions of scope, block structure, parallel program structure, records, objects, modules, libraries, etc. After 84 pages, the discussion of programming languages begins; every language is related to the ISM. Discussion of languages is organized in historical order because 'only by following the historical record we can track the tidal flows between classical simplicity and rococo extravagance that repeatedly swept over the field'. This organization explains the chapter headings which otherwise would be hard to understand,

---

[8] The earlier paper by Landis [1966] remains influential, but Sammet's 1969 survey is the best starting point.

for example, 'FORTRAN, ALGOL-60 and LISP' and 'APL and COBOL'. Languages treated in the book are ADA, ALGOL-60, ALGOL-68, 60/68, APL, C, COBOL, CSP, FORTRAN, LINDA, LISP, MIRANDA, OCCAM, PASCAL, PL/I, PROLOG, SCHEME, SIMULA 67 and SMALLTALK; even more languages are briefly referenced.

A third book that is a bit unusual is Horowitz's *Programming Languages – A Grand Tour* [1987] (512 pages). What Horowitz has done here is to select and reprint 30 mostly important original articles on programming languages, enriched by a bibliography of roughly 200 references for further reading. The articles are grouped in the following sections: history and good design, the ALGOL family, applicative languages, data abstraction, concurrency, old languages with new faces, more languages for the 1980s. What definitely is missing here is an article on SIMULA 67 in the section on data abstraction.

Now that we have looked at these three exceptions to the rule, the remaining books are discussed in chronological order. The earliest books in this field are Sammet [1969] which is an invaluable source of information mainly about older languages and Wegner [1971]. Sammet [1969] describes in 785 pages about 120 languages originating up to the fall of 1967 with a few 1968 additions in fair detail and with extensive examples, covering practically all relevant languages of the time. In addition, there are introductory chapters on languages in general. Of the languages described, 20 were already dead by that time (so the book is also a contribution towards programming language history) and only 15 were widely implemented and used. You can tell that the Sammet book really is at the beginning of the programming language discussion by noting how much care she takes to argue for the advantage of higher-level programming languages over assembler.

The classic text by Wegner [1971] (401 pages) follows a quite different set of objectives: instead of discussing every (possibly) relevant language, he concentrates mainly on (generic) assembler as an introduction and then on LISP, ALGOL-60 and PL/I with a bit of SIMSCRIPT and SIMULA 67, but he gives much more background information about run-time organization on the one hand and the nature of computation on the other hand. This includes, for instance, discussions of the lambda calculus and the SECD machine.

The next few years see a certain silence in this field, with the exception of books by Pratt and Tucker whose second editions are discussed later. From the 1980s to the present time we then see a growing number of books in this area, which we can safely take as a sign indicating a certain consolidation of programming language theory.

Principles of Programming Languages [Tennent, 1981] has a strong emphasis on PASCAL in its discussion of programming language concepts; other languages are only briefly mentioned where appropriate. The book contains a chapter on formal (mostly denotational) semantics.

Comparing and Assessing Programming Languages [Feuer and Gehani, 1984] (262 pages) is an important collection of 15 individual papers on comparing and assessing programming languages. Willingly restricting themselves to ADA, C and PASCAL, the authors bring together important building blocks for assessing properties of languages and comparing them using objective criteria. Included in the book are also critiques of the three programming languages, some even by their creators. A chapter by Feuer and Gehani themselves gives important hints towards a methodology for comparing programming languages. We shall come back to that in section 2.6.

Programming Languages – Design and Implementation [Pratt, 1984] (583 pages) is the second edition of the book originally published in 1975. The second edition is divided into two parts, the first dealing with concepts and the second with languages. Among the concepts are elementary and structured data types, subprograms and programmer-defined data types, sequence control (including exceptions and coroutines), data control, and operating and programming environments. Further chapters briefly deal with theoretical models in syntax and semantics and with programming language processors, stressing particularly the *virtual machine* aspect. Languages discussed in the second part are ADA, APL, COBOL, FORTRAN 77, LISP, PASCAL, PL/I and SNOBOL4. The language chapters all have the same structure, the sections being: brief overview, annotated example, data types, subprograms, sequence and data control, operating and programming environment, syntax and translation, structure of a virtual computer, references, and suggestions for further reading. Some of the sections are quite short. For FORTRAN, PL/I and PASCAL, the annotated example is the summation of a vector; the ADA chapter consequently generalizes this to a package for vector processing; the other chapters use different examples pertinent to the capabilities of the respective language.

Fundamentals of Programming Languages [Horowitz, 1983] (450 pages) starts with a chapter on the evolution of programming languages, followed by a chapter on the challenge of programming language design and one on syntax definitions. The book in general is quite standard; apart from the usual contents, there is a chapter on exception handling, on concurrency and on data flow languages. Also object-oriented languages are discussed. Horowitz draws quite heavily on ADA; he says in the introduction that 'ADA contains virtually all of the features which are considered essential in a modern programming language'. Other languages are brought in where the subject demands it, so the data abstraction chapter discusses MODULA-2, EUCLID and SIMULA 67, the exception handling chapter PL/I, CLU and MESA, the functional programming chapter LISP, and the object-oriented chapter SMALLTALK.

Sprachen für die Programmierung [Ludewig, 1985] mainly discusses a handful of important languages, almost ignoring concepts in general and not going into very much detail. The book has nevertheless become famous for its nifty cartoons where programming languages are related to car models, together with a slogan that matches both the car and the language. For instance, C is depicted as a Land Rover, with the slogan 'Much flexibility, specifically for down-to-the-earth tasks' and PL/I as a huge American convertible with large tail fins and the slogan 'Much luxury, little security'.

Programming Languages [Tucker, 1986], the second edition of a 1977 book, also is more concerned with discussing specific languages (ADA, APL, C, COBOL, FORTRAN, LISP, MODULA-2, PASCAL, PL/I, PROLOG, SNOBOL) in fair detail but without emphasizing concepts very much. However, 'A major purpose of this text is to describe and apply effective criteria for evaluating and comparing programming languages.' (I shall come back to that in section 2.6.) Interspersed in the programming language discussion are three sections dealing with language design (syntax, semantics, pragmatics). These sections, however, do little more than present some foundations and examples; specifically, they give no guidelines to the design process.

Programming Language Concepts [Ghezzi and Jazayeri, 1987] (428 pages) is the second edition of a 1982 book. The authors claim that 'our purpose is to evaluate programming language concepts in terms of their contribution to the software development process and to develop the criteria needed for such evaluation'. After an introduction including historical remarks and a preview on the evolution of concepts in programming languages (again including historical detail), they have chapters on the structure of programming languages, data types, control structures, and programming in the large [DeRemer and Kron, 1976]. After this, the structuring criteria are changed: the remaining chapters are called functional programming, logic programming, introduction to formal semantics, and language design. In order to study implementation costs for concepts, they present a very simple abstract machine, SIMPLESEM, which is used to explain run-time structures of several classes of languages. Languages used in the main part of the book are ADA, ALGOL-60/68, APL, CLU, COBOL, FORTRAN, LISP, PASCAL, PL/I, PROLOG, SETL, SIMULA 67, SMALLTALK and SNOBOL4; the intent of the authors is to 'emphasize the language that pioneered the concept'. An appendix contains one-page summaries of 21 programming languages, including those mentioned above.

Comparative Programming Languages [Wilson and Clark, 1988] (379 pages) provides just what the title promises; in my view, the comparison is a quite phenomenological one. The book is full of lucid, small examples comparing languages so you can see how certain constructs are expressed in different cultures, but it offers almost no theoretical background. For instance, a program for symbolic differentiation is shown in LISP, LOGO and PROLOG, but the classic *Anatomy of LISP* [Allen, 1978] isn't even listed among the references to the functional programming chapter. Similarly, the chapter on concurrency remains somewhat at the surface: although solutions for the producer/consumer problem are presented using MODULA-2, ADA and OCCAM, there is no detailed discussion of the problems involved and the different ways in which these languages try to address them. The book is ideal for a person wishing to obtain a general overview without being bothered by too much theory. An appendix contains one-page summaries of the most important languages used in the book: ADA, ALGOL-60, ALGOL-68, C, C++, COBOL, FORTRAN 77, LISP, MODULA-2, PASCAL, PL/I, PROLOG and SMALLTALK; as a matter of fact, there are really even more languages used. A further appendix contains an interesting annotated bibliography on a larger class of 26 languages.

A bit outside the family of books discussed here is *Real-time Systems and their Programming Languages* [Burns and Wellings, 1990]; this is mainly a book on real-time systems and therefore deals extensively with synchronization, communication, embedded systems and the like, but in this setting the respective facilities of ADA, MODULA-2 and OCCAM are also discussed and compared.

Programming Languages – Concepts and Constructs [Sethi, 1990] (478 pages) is divided into three parts: introduction (62 pages), concepts and constructs (318 pages), and language description (98 pages). The introduction concentrates on the role of structure in programming and on elements of a programming language with an emphasis on expressions and functions; as a consequence of this approach, this part already contains an introduction to ML. Quoting Sethi himself:

> The chapters in Part II each use two working languages, where possible. The use of two languages allows language design choices to be studied. Thus, control flow and procedures are illustrated using MODULA-2 and C ... Classes, objects, and inheritance are illustrated using SMALLTALK and C++ ... Functional

programming is illustrated by SCHEME ... and Standard ML. Logic programming and PROLOG go hand in hand. Finally, concurrency is treated using ADA.

Part III contains a brief introduction to parse trees and synthesized attributes, a chapter on interpreters, including a SCHEME subset interpreter programmed in SCHEME, and a chapter on static types and the Lambda calculus.

Programming Language Concepts and Paradigms [Watt, 1990] (322 pages) is the first book in a programming languages trilogy, the other books being subtitled 'Syntax and semantics' and 'Processors'. The first book (the only one discussed here) has three parts: elementary concepts (values, storage, bindings, abstraction), advanced concepts (encapsulation, type systems, sequencers, concurrency), and major programming paradigms (imperative, object, functional, concurrent and logic).[9] In the preface, Watt admits that his 'personal highlights were PASCAL, ADA, and ML'; as a matter of fact, most of the book uses examples from these three languages. The programming paradigms chapter obviously also uses other languages for illustration, namely SMALLTALK and PROLOG. A concluding chapter gives some hints on language selection and language design; we will come back to these in the corresponding sections of the present chapter. This is one of the few textbooks that doesn't discuss ALGOL-60/68 (the 20 index entries for these languages only point to text passages like 'such as ALGOL-60' or 'including ALGOL-68'). In general, this book goes deeper than the text by Wilson and Clark; for example, the concurrency chapter gives background information and discusses the inherent problems of this paradigm. Overall, the book seems to be a successful compromise between the 'show everything using a single language' and the 'show all interesting/important languages' approaches.

Comparative Programming Languages – Generalizing the Programming Function [Weiser Friedman, 1991] (578 pages) also contains three parts. The first part, elements of programming languages, gives a short historical introduction but also contains sections on the classification and characteristics of programming languages and on choosing a programming language. A further chapter deals with language processors; the remaining three chapters of Part 1 discuss structure at the data, program and control levels. These chapters are a bit phenomenological in nature and also quite database-oriented. Part 2 is called 'Programming Languages for Information Processing' and starts with a chapter presenting four 'study problems', all operating on an example personal database: bubble sort, sequential file update, multiple lists, binary search tree. The remaining chapters present COBOL, PASCAL, MODULA-2, C, PROLOG and SMALLTALK, each time giving a brief overview, a detailed discussion of the bubble sort program in the respective language, a discussion of language features according to the structure laid out in Part 1, a section on program development and further program texts for the study problems. Part 3 has chapters on program design, fourth-generation productivity tools and expert advisers.

Concepts of Programming Languages [Sebesta, 1992] (497 pages) starts with three chapters containing introduction, brief history of programming languages, and description methods for syntax and semantics. These chapters have a survey character, not going into very much detail. Chapters 4–12 discuss, in a quite logical order, important concepts of programming languages, including coroutines and exception handling.

---

[9] The chapters on functional and concurrent programming have been contributed by Bill Finlay and John Hughes, respectively.

Examples are taken from ADA, ALGOL-60, ALGOL-68, C, CLU, COBOL, FORTRAN, MODULA-2, PASCAL, PL/I and SIMULA 67, wherever appropriate, but also unimplemented languages like Dijkstra's guarded commands are also discussed. The remaining three chapters deal with functional, logic and object-oriented programming languages, introducing LISP, Backus's FP, PROLOG, and SMALLTALK.

The Anatomy of Programming Languages [Fischer and Grodzinski, 1993] (557 pages) definitely is the book with the greatest number of examples (here called 'exhibits'); there are 89 on PASCAL, 66 on C, 35 on ADA, 23 on MIRANDA, 18 on APL, 15 on FORTRAN, 12 on LISP, 12 on FORTH, 11 on PROLOG, 9 on C++, 5 on SCHEME, and 15 on other languages (ALGOL, BASIC, COBOL, DBMAN, PL/I, SNOBOL). These are complemented by 135 exhibits of language-independent concepts. An index of exhibits listed by topics is most helpful for finding a specific example. This alone would already make the book a valuable reference for anybody seeking advice on programming languages, but also the text itself is of superior quality. The book has three parts: 'About Language', 'Describing Computation' and 'Application Modeling'. Coverage of programming language concepts is comparable to Sebesta's.

Except for a typographic problem which makes program code difficult to read, *Programming Languages – Principles and Practice* [Louden, 1993] (641 pages) is in coverage and quality quite comparable to the mainstream of books discussed here. Languages used in the book are, according to the preface, ADA, C, C++, EIFFEL, FORTRAN, MIRANDA, ML, MODULA-2, PASCAL, PROLOG, SCHEME and SMALLTALK, but a closer inspection reveals also some ALGOL-60/68, CLU, SIMULA 67 and other languages.

Programming Languages – Structures and Models [Dershem and Jipping, 1995] (432 pages) is the most recent book I have seen. It covers the main programming paradigms (imperative, functional, logic-oriented, object-oriented, distributed parallel) with a strong emphasis on the imperative paradigm in a quite logical structure, each time giving first an overview chapter and then, similar to Sethi [1990], discussing two languages adhering to this model. An exception is imperative programming where there are additional chapters on data aggregates, procedural abstraction and data abstraction; a second exception is logic programming where there is only PROLOG as a language. The imperative languages are C and MODULA-2, the functional ones SCHEME and ML, the object-oriented languages SMALLTALK and C++, and the distributed parallel languages ADA and OCCAM.

Apart from the textbooks presented here, there are also interesting survey articles that have to be mentioned: Cardelli and Wegner [1985] is probably the best discussion on type systems and polymorphism, and Hudak [1989] gives an excellent introduction to functional programming.

2.4 Concepts and languages

In their interesting paper on conceptual modelling and programming languages, Kristensen and Østerbye [1994] say that 'programming is regarded as a modeling process of some referent system where phenomena and abstractions from this system are expressed in a programming language supporting abstractions based on a general understanding of phenomena and concepts'. In order that a programming language can be successful for a certain application domain, it is therefore essential that it mirrors the concepts of this domain as closely as possible. It is therefore essential to look at the concepts of programming languages.

But what precisely is a *concept* of a programming language? In trying to determine whether a given programming language allows, supports, suggests or enforces a certain concept, we immediately realize that this is a difficult question: most of the time, we do not really see *concepts*, but merely *features* of programming languages, meant to implement certain concepts. Furthermore, our view may be clouded by syntactic similarities. This reminds one of Plato's cave parable where ordinary people see only shadows of things on the wall of a cave but true philosophers are able to 'behold the idea', that is, to grasp an abstract concept. Let us look at an example. Everybody knows the concept of a *for* loop; in abstract syntax, this could be described by

for-loop(index, initial-value, increment, final-value, body)

If we now look at how this concept is implemented using the features of specific languages, we see that in this respect there is no real difference between, say, FORTRAN, BASIC, COBOL and MODULA-2, apart from different syntactic 'sugar'. Note that (classic) PASCAL is different because this language doesn't allow us to specify the increment. While we could still consider this as a sort of projection of the abstract syntax, things get more complicated if we look at FORTH: besides not being able to specify the increment, we also must specify final-value+1 as the value where the loop is finally left. Considering now C, we could go as far as saying that there are no *for* loops in this language, at least none that match the above concept. By contrast, the abstract syntax of what C calls *for* loops is:

for-loop(initial-action, final-condition, loop-action, body)

Obviously we can use this to simulate the *for* loops of the other languages but in reality it isn't a *for* loop at all but rather an initialized *while* loop. Note that we can arbitrarily shift the loop-action to the end of the body or else specify a single-statement body as the loop-action.

This example implies that in order to discuss concepts of programming languages and to assess languages with respect to the concepts they implement we have to:

1. precisely describe the concept in question at the most abstract level possible (the 'idea of the concept' in Plato's terminology), certainly involving abstract syntax and most desirably giving mathematical semantics;

2. relate the relevant part of the concrete language syntax to the abstract form by describing both an appropriate abstraction mapping from the concrete to the abstract syntax and an implementation mapping in the opposite direction; and then

3. evaluate the degree to which the language implements the concept, paying attention both to restrictions and to relaxations of the concept.

This is a crucial step in the comparison of languages which must always precede a choice of a language, but it is also crucial in the classification of languages.

2.5 The difficulty of language design

The language designer should be familiar with many alternative features designed by others, and should have excellent judgement in choosing the best and rejecting any that are mutually inconsistent.

C. A. R. Hoare [1973]

A capable language designer must not only be able to select appropriate features, but must also be able to foresee all effects of their being used in combination.

N. Wirth [1974]

Don't design a new language unless you have a real good reason to do so; there are already too many. The American Humane Society proposes a law against breeding further dogs and kittens (these anyway tend to have a negative price); a similar law for programming languages could also be useful.

F. Brooks [1993]

According to what I have claimed in the introduction about the culture-creating aspect of languages, clearly the design of a programming language is a very important as well as difficult task. Much has been written about this topic; most of the authors use varying amounts of paper and ink to restate what is already implied by the quotes from Hoare and Wirth above, namely that languages should be excellent in every conceivable sense and that therefore language designers have to be excellent too. This precisely matches Brooks's statement [1993] at the History of Programming Languages conference (HOPL-II): 'Great designs come from great designers.' Apart from the suggestion to be excellent, there isn't much advice given to language designers, except perhaps not to be in this business at all; see Brooks above.

Of course, the literature abounds with lists of noble design goals that should be pursued; these very much remind one of lists of software quality marks that are circulated in the software engineering community. While everybody agrees that these are the right goals, nobody can really give advice on how to achieve them. What is also remarkable is that the same lists are occasionally offered as criteria for assessing the quality of languages or language implementations, for example what Wirth [1974] offers as design goals for languages is in [Wirth, 1977] listed as evaluation criteria for 'a language and its documentation'. This isn't necessarily bad but we have to be aware that it opens some trap-doors into which we may finally fall: if we use certain criteria to evaluate already finished languages, it doesn't do any real harm if we are quite aggressive in formulating those criteria; they may even be contradictory in parts. We will then discover that none of the given languages fully satisfies our criteria and we will have to make compromises. There's nothing wrong in doing so. If, on the other hand, we use the same over-ambitious criteria as design goals, we may embark on a hopelessly unsuccessful language design project or, even worse, we may deliver an over-complicated, inconsistent and intractable language. For instance, the Steelman report [Department of Defense, 1978] can be read as a list of criteria that were on the DoD's shopping list for a common high-order programming language. It could in theory have happened that a single existing language satisfied all of these requirements; in that case, DoD would have adopted it. We all know that subsequently the Steelman report was used as a list of design goals for what finally became ADA; and we also know that the programming language experts aren't altogether wholeheartedly singing ADA's praises. Brooks [1993] made an interesting point at the HOPL-II conference: he presented two lists of languages, those with and those without a fan club, and he came to the conclusion that languages *with* a fan club were designed *to please a designer* and those *without* a fan club were designed *to satisfy a set of requirements*. This fits seamlessly into Wirth's suggestion [1974] that one should 'keep the responsibility for the design of the language confined to a single person'.

I cannot conclude this section without giving at least a superficial impression on language design goals found in the literature.

Hoare [1973] lists simplicity, security, fast translation, efficient object code and readability as his proposed design goals.

Wirth [1974] postulates that a programming language should be easy to learn and use, be safe from misinterpretation and misuse, be extensible without change of existing features, have a rigorous mathematical definition which is both self-contained and complete. It should have a convenient notation compatible with established conventions, be machine-independent, be efficiently implemented, have a fast compiler and ready access to program libraries and subprograms written in other languages. The compiler should be adaptable and portable and have minimal development cost. Interestingly enough, he emphasizes that 'Language design is compiler construction', and this a scant 20 years after FORTRAN where, as I have mentioned, compiler construction was language design. How fast do we forget in this business!

Horowitz [1983] distinguishes between essential and desirable goals, the *essential* goals being a well-defined syntactic and semantic description, reliability, fast translation, efficient object code, orthogonality and machine independence. *Desirable* goals are then provability, generality, consistency with commonly used notations, subsets, uniformity and extensibility.

Similar lists are found in most of the books discussed in section 2.3; sometimes they are also split into major and minor goals like in Horowitz above.

2.6 The difficulty of language choice

Assuming that a decision has been made *not* to use assembly language, there is currently no scientific, or even logical, way to choose the best programming language for a particular situation.

J. Sammet [1969]

Of course, making judgements about any programming language is fraught with danger.

G. Booch [1994]

I should like to warn the reader not to interpret this title as an announcement of a general critique of commonly used languages. Although this might be a very entertaining subject, probably all that can be said about it has already been said and heard by those willing to listen. There is no reason to repeat it now.

N. Wirth [1974]

As an aside I would like to insert a warning to those who identify the difficulty of the programming task with the struggle against the inadequacies of our current tools, because they might conclude that, once our tools will be much more adequate, programming will no longer be a problem. Programming will remain very difficult, because once we have freed ourselves from the circumstantial cumbersomeness, we will find ourselves free to tackle problems that are now well beyond our programming capacity.

E. W. Dijkstra [1987]

It should by now have become clear that choice of a language is a difficult task although things may no longer be as bad as back in 1969 when Jean Sammet wrote the sentence quoted above. It should be noted that nevertheless Sammet gives a good description of 'factors in the choice of a language' including very practical and important points. People often aren't aware that the following list of questions may be relevant:

- Who designed the language?
- What were the objectives?
- Who implemented it?
- Who maintains it?
- Is there a national or international standard for the language?
- How much educational effort is involved in introducing it?

Basically, in order to choose a language from several competitors, we have to:

1. set precise criteria for the language to be chosen,
2. assert the respective properties of the languages in consideration, and
3. perform the choice, possibly after weakening the criteria to achieve a compromise.

The difficult part in this is obviously step 2; a further question is whether we really define our own criteria or use general criteria from the literature, for example, from [Wirth, 1977] who defines the following general criteria:

- complete definition without reference to compiler or computer,
- modularization facility,
- size of language,
- conciseness and clarity of description, and
- sound use of language.

Among other things, he claims that:

the definition of a language, comprising its syntax ... and its semantics ... should not extend over more than 50 pages. This primary document should be accompanied by separate documents describing implementations, their limitations, effectiveness, and their reactions to ill-formed programs. The total length of these documents should be not more than 25 pages.

He then goes on to define technical criteria of a general nature for judging a language *implementation* which, of course, we must not confound with the language as such.

The first book which defines and applies a methodology for the comparison of programming languages is [Feuer and Gehani, 1984]. Especially valuable is the chapter by Feuer and Gehani themselves which gives a structured list of detailed questions to be asked in the comparison process. This even includes preliminary considerations such as 'What is the purpose of the comparison? Who is the audience?', the approach to be used and the determination of definitive sources for answers to questions about each language. They go on listing specific technical questions about history and philosophy, syntax, type philosophy and data types, operators and assignment, control flow, routines and scope, concurrent programming facilities, I/O, independent compilation and access to routines in other languages and to the hardware. But they also don't forget to formulate the practical considerations similar to Sammet's questions such as:

- Does a reliable and efficient compiler exist?
- Is it supported?
- Who fixes it if it breaks?
- Is there a standard for the language?
- What about training?
- What about consulting?
- What is the development environment like?

A different method of language evaluation with a view to language choice is described by Tucker [1986]. He presents five 'case studies' (matrix inversion, employee file maintenance, text formatter, 'missionaries and cannibals', job scheduler); the book contains the specifications of the case studies but (of course) not the complete texts of solutions in all of the languages considered. Using the case studies, Tucker assigns grades from 'excellent' to 'poor' in the categories 'expressivity', 'well-definedness', 'data types and structures', 'modularity', 'input–output facilities', 'portability', 'efficiency', 'pedagogy' and 'generality' to the languages. He does not tell, however, how he arrived at the specific grades for any one language. Assuming that this missing part of the documentation exists, Tucker's empirical method isn't bad provided that:

- the case studies are carefully selected to reflect the envisaged use of the language and

- experienced professionals, fluent in the language in question, can be found to program the case studies.

Combined with a controlled experiment in the spirit of Griffiths [1991] this definitely is a scientific way of choosing a language but it has to be complemented by answers to the practical questions given in Feuer and Gehani [1984].

Kristensen and Østerbye [1994] show what care must be taken in comparing languages with respect to given concepts. After having established a model of concepts and phenomena as well as a model of abstraction, they examine two abstraction mechanisms from SMALLTALK (blocks and messages) and set out to 'measure to what extent a given programming language supports conceptual understanding'. Specifically, they compare the abstraction facilities of SMALLTALK, BETA, C++, EIFFEL, CLOS and SELF. Their discussion makes it very clear that this is no easy task, that you have to be careful in doing it, and, above all, that you have to define and clearly state a precise framework in which such comparisons are meaningful.

2.7 Towards a classification schema

In view of what I have argued above, it should be fairly clear that it is by no means easy to present a classification schema and to classify languages accordingly. For instance, if one of the items in the classification were to be the question 'Has it *for* loops?', it would be difficult to give an honest yes/no answer for C (recall the discussion of abstract syntax earlier); we would probably end up with a footnote for this language or else some fine print explaining what precisely we mean by this question.

An early attempt at a classification of programming languages is contained in [Sammet, 1969]. Unfortunately, her taxonomy (procedure-oriented, non-procedural, problem-oriented, application-oriented, special purpose, problem-defining, problem-describing, problem-solving, reference, publication, hardware language) doesn't help very much although she tries to define these categories. One problem is that this classification is too coarse to be meaningful, another is that this seemingly linear list in fact describes overlapping sets of properties.

Rechenberg [1990] makes it clear that no single classification system will be sufficient: classification inevitably leads to a *tree* and there will always be several ways of ordering the levels of this tree. Rechenberg himself proposes two alternative classification schemes and classifies some languages according to them:

1. *Imperative (procedural)*: (a) algorithm-oriented (b) object-oriented	1. *Value-oriented*: (a) algorithmic (b) functional (c) logical
2. *Non-imperative (declarative)*: (a) functional (b) logical	2. *Object-oriented*:

The most elaborate attempts at classification with three separate classification schemes are contained in Weiser Friedman [1991] but these are also the most problematic to use and her classification of known languages will probably raise some discussions. For instance, in the classification by major function, PL/I and ALGOL-68 are classified as 'General purpose/not problem oriented' whereas C and MODULA-2 are classified 'General purpose/problem oriented/systems programming'. Some languages are contained twice in this classification, for example ADA is both 'Not problem oriented' and 'Problem oriented/systems programming'. Other classification schemes are by processing environment and by programming paradigm; for comparison with the schemes by Rechenberg listed above, we shall look at the first two levels of this latter classification:

1. *Process-centred*:   (a)   imperative   (b)   dataflow   (c)   functional
2. *Data-centered*:   (a)   constraint   (b)   rule   (c)   object   (d)   database

Classification of programming languages is still a relatively immature art leaving many problems open and many questions to decide. Also, it doesn't seem completely clear in what sense such classification should be helpful except for the satisfaction of scientists.

2.8 References

Allen, R. (1978), *Anatomy of LISP*, McGraw-Hill, New York.

Backus, J. (1981), The History of FORTRAN I, II and III, in *History of Programming Languages*, R. L. Wexelblat (ed.), Academic Press, New York, 25–44.

Booch, G. (1994), Coming of Age in an Object-Oriented World, *IEEE Computer*, **11**(6), 33–41.

Brooks, F. (1993), Language Design as Design, in *Second ACM SIGPLAN History of Programming Languages Conference, Cambridge, MA*, (not contained in proceedings).

Burns, A. and Wellings, A. (1990), *Real-time Systems and their Programming Languages*, Addison-Wesley, Reading, MA.

Cardelli, L. and Wegner, P. (1985), On Understanding Types, Data Abstraction, and Polymorphism, *ACM Computing Surveys*, **17**, 471–522.

Department of Defense (1978), *STEELMAN Requirements for the DoD High Order Computer Programming Languages*, Technical Report, Department of Defense, Washington, D. C.

DeRemer, F. and Kron, H. K. (1976), Programming in the Large Versus Programming in the Small, *IEEE Transactions on Software Engineering*, **SE-2**(2), 80–6.

Dershem, H. L. and Jipping, M. l. J. (1995), *Programming Languages – Structures and Models*, PWS Publishing / International Thomson Publishing, 2nd edition.

Dijkstra, E. W. (1987), The Humble Programmer, in *ACM Turing Award Lectures – The First Twenty Years*, Addison-Wesley, Reading, MA, 17–31, (first published in *Commun. ACM* 1972).

Feuer, A. R. and Gehani, N. (eds) (1984), *Comparing and Assessing Programming Languages: Ada, C, and Pascal*, Prentice-Hall, Englewood Cliffs, NJ.

Fischer, A. W. and Grodzinsky, F. S. (1993), *The Anatomy of Programming Languages*, Prentice-Hall, Englewood Cliffs, NJ.

Friedman, Da. P., Wand, M. and Haynes, C. T. (1992), *Essentials of Programming Languages*, MIT Press/McGraw-Hill, Cambridge MA/New York.

Gelernter, D. and Jagannathan, S. (1990), *Programming Linguistics*, MIT Press, Cambridge, MA.

Ghezzi, C. and Jazayer, M. (1987), *Programming Language Concepts*, Wiley, New York.

Griffiths, L. (1991), Modula-2 is three times less error prone than C, in *Modula-2 and Beyond, Proc. 2nd International Modula-2 Conference*, 332–8, Loughborough University of Technology, UK.

Hoare, C. A. R. (1972), Proof of Correctness of Data Representations, *Acta Informatica*, **1**, 271–81.

Hoare, C. A. R. (1973), Hints on Programming Language Design, in *Proc. SIGACT/ SIGPLAN Symposium on Principles of Programming Languages*, ACM.

Hoare, C. A. R. (1987), The Emperor's Old Clothes, in *ACM Turing Award Lectures – The First Twenty Years*, Addison-Wesley, 143–61, (first published in *Commun. ACM* **24**(2), 75–83 (1981)).

Horowitz, E. (1983), *Fundamentals of Programming Languages*, Springer-Verlag.

Horowitz, E. (ed.) (1987), *Programming Languages – A Grand Tour*, Computer Science Press, Rockville, MD, 3rd edition.

Hudak, P. (1989), Conception, Evolution, and Application of Functional Programming Languages, *ACM Computing Surveys*, **21**(3), 359–411.

Jackson, M. (1994), Problems, Methods and Specialization, *IEEE Software*, **11**(6), 57–62.

Klaeren, H. (1994), Probleme des Software Engineering. Die Programmiersprache – Werkzeug des Softwareentwicklers, *Informatik-Spektrum*, **17**, 21–8.

Knuth, D. E. and Pardo, L. T. (1980), The Early Development of Programming Languages, in *A History of Computing in the Twentieth Century*, N. Metropolis, J. Howlett and G.-C. Rota (eds), Academic Press, New York, 197–273.

Kristensen, B. B. and Østerbye, K. (1994), Conceptual Modelling and Programming Languages, *SIGPLAN Notices*, **29**(9), 81–90.

Landin, P. J. (1966), The Next 700 Programming Languages, *Commun. ACM*, **9**(3), 157–66.

Lee, J. A. N. and Sammet, J. E. (eds) (1993), *ACM SIGPLAN Second History of Programming Languages Conference*, **28**(3) of *SIGPLAN Notices*, The Association for Computing Machinery.

Louden, K. C. (1993), *Programming Languages – Principles and Practice*, PWS-KENT Publishing Company, Boston.

Ludewig, J. (1985), *Sprachen für die Programmierung*, volume 622 of *Hochschultaschenbücher*, B. I. Wissenschaftsverlag.

Ludewig, J. (1993), Sprachen für das Software-Engineering, *Informatik-Spektrum*, **16**(5), 286–94.

Metropolis, N., Howlett, J. and Rota, G.-C. (eds) (1980), *A History of Computing in the Twentieth Century*, Academic Press, New York.

Paul, D. (1985), Der Computer gehört nicht ins Kinderzimmer, *Computerwoche*, 50–2.

Perlis, A. (1982), Epigrams on Programming, *SIGPLAN Notices*, **17**(9), 7–13.

Petre, M. (1996), Programming Paradigms and Culture: Implications of Expert Practice, in *Programming Language Choice: Practice and Experience*, M. Woodman (ed.), International Thomson Computer Press, London, chapter 3, (this volume).

Plödereder, E. (1995), Report on the Workshop on Research Issues in the Intersection of Software Engineering and Programming Languages, 17th Int. Conf. on Software Engineering, ICSE–17 (not contained in proceedings).

Pratt, T. W. (1984), *Programming Languages – Design and Implementation*, Prentice-Hall, Englewood Cliffs, NJ, 2nd edition.

Rechenberg, P. (1990), Programming Languages as Thought Models, *Structured Programming*, **11**, 105–15.

Sammet, J. E. (1969), *Programming Languages: History and Fundamentals*, Prentice-Hall, Englewood Cliffs, NJ.

Sebesta, R. (1992), *Concepts of Programming Languages*, Benjamin/Cummings.

Sethi, R. (1990), *Programming Languages – Concepts and Constructs*, Addison-Wesley, Reading, MA.

Stroustrup, B. (1993), A History of C++: 1979–1991, in *ACM SIGPLAN Second History of Programming Languages Conference*, J. A. N. Lee and J. E. Sammet (eds), **28**(3) of *SIGPLAN Notices*, 271–97, The Association for Computing Machinery.

Tennent, R. (1981), *Principles of Programming Languages*, Prentice-Hall, Englewood Cliffs, NJ.

Tucker jr., A. B. (1986), *Programming Languages*, McGraw-Hill, 2nd edition.

Watt, D. A. (1990), *Programming Language Concepts and Paradigms*, Prentice-Hall, Hemel Hempstead.

Wegner, P. (1971), *Programming Languages, Information Structures, and Machine Organization*, McGraw-Hill, New York.

Weiser Friedman, L. (1991), *Comparative Programming Languages – Generalizing the Programming Function*, Prentice-Hall, Englewood Cliffs, NJ.

Wexelblat, R. L. (ed.) (1981), *History of Programming Languages*, Academic Press, New York.

Wilson, L. B. and Clark, R. G. (1988), *Comparative Programming Languages*, Addison-Wesley, Wokingham.

Wirth, N. (1974), On the Design of Programming Languages, in *Proc. IFIP Congress '74*, 386–93, North Holland.

Wirth, N. (1977), Programming Languages: What to Demand and How to Assert Them, in *Software Engineering*, R. Perrot (ed.), Academic Press, London. (Reprinted in A. R. Feuer and N. Gehani (eds) *Comparing and Assessing Programming Languages: Ada, C, and Pascal*, Prentice-Hall, 1984.)

Wirth, N. (1994), Gedanken zur Software-Explosion, *Informatik-Spektrum*, **17**(1), 5–10.

3 Programming paradigms and culture: implications of expert practice

Marian Petre

This chapter attempts to align the notion of the programming paradigm with actual, expert practice. It discusses issues such as salesmanship, the relationship between paradigm and language, the role of operational knowledge, reflection, secondary notation and individual skill. The chapter presents an alternative view of programming paradigms as styles or models of reasoning which may be used as frames of reference that evolve from expert practice and are shaped within a programming culture. From that position it considers the implications of programming paradigms especially for the teaching of programming.

3.1 Introduction – starting from the right notion of paradigm

'Paradigm' is one of those wonderful, authoritative words that promises a great deal without making clear exactly what – and this is especially true in the context of programming paradigms. As Tim Rentsch [1982] foresaw for object-oriented programming in 1982:

> Everyone will be in favour of it. Every manufacturer will promote his products as supporting it. Every manager will pay lip service to it. Every programmer will practice it (differently). And no one will know just what it is.

Finding a completely general programming paradigm is computing's search for the philosopher's stone: the cherished notion that the right programming paradigm will be a panacea that leads programmers (even novices) consistently to 'right thinking' and exemplary solutions. What the literature about programming paradigms tends to convey is that language designers everywhere aspire to an ideal of the Kuhnian paradigm [Kuhn, 1962] that paradigms are absolute: complete and exclusive, dominating and defining every aspect of an approach, a set of eyes through which to view the world.

This chapter presents an alternative view of programming paradigms based on studies of expert programmer behaviour: a view of paradigms as selectable reference models that evolve from expert practice and are shaped within a programming culture. Thus, paradigms are styles or models of reasoning used as frames of reference. From that vantage, it considers the implications of programming paradigms which bear on language choice and on the teaching of programming.

This chapter has three main parts. Section 3.2 tries to align the notion of the programming paradigm with actual expert practice. It identifies pertinent issues, such as the relationship between paradigm and language, and the role of operational knowledge, based on expert behaviour. Section 3.3 considers the role of programming culture in defining and nurturing paradigms and in providing a model of practice. Section 3.4 considers the implications of those issues for teaching programming. Evidence and examples will be drawn from a variety of my own investigations of expert programmer behaviour (*e.g.* Petre and Winder [1988], Petre [1991b]) and from the literature.

3.2 How experts use paradigms

3.2.1 Clearing the smokescreen: the role and devices of salesmanship

One thing is clear about programming paradigms: an awful lot has been said, written, broadcast and claimed about them. With so much happening in the computing world – the various population explosions of computers and languages and programmers and publishers, and their accompanying 'information explosion' – and hence with survival at stake, it is no wonder that salesmanship is a factor, and that proponents are selective, or emphatic, or hyperbolic in their portrayal of a 'paradigm'. Nor is it surprising that the programming language literature is fiercely evangelistic, associating 'revolution' and 'religious conversion' with some new programming paradigm. What new paradigms need most is converts: adherents who will nurture a paradigm and attract attention, investment and commitment to it by finding and addressing its shortcomings, by fitting it into real-world contexts, by working through the arguments and issues surrounding its use, by presenting it in public – in short, by providing a 'programming culture'.

A variety of mechanisms (or sales ploys) are employed to distinguish one paradigm from all others, including claims of 'naturalness' (*e.g.* 'Teaching a MIRANDA-like notation first usually can be done quickly and informally, because the notation is quite natural.' Wadler [1987]), disparagement of alternatives (*e.g.* 'BASIC rots the brain.' 'APL – even the name is a contradiction in terms.'), and careful choice of standard examples (*e.g.* Fibonacci series and least common denominator for functional programming).

Yet these devices aren't necessarily just salesmanship; they can have a function in defining the paradigm as well. The claims made for a paradigm can indicate which factors are of particular importance to it. The sneers made against opposing paradigms can indicate what virtues a paradigm boasts – or what it chooses not to address and so dismisses and devalues. The examples chosen as standard can act as a set of fence-posts marking out the terrain of problem types, solution style, and so on, on which the paradigm focuses.

3.2.2 Focus: programming paradigms as lenses, not eyes

A paradigm provides a simple way of dealing with a complex thing; hence, restriction is necessary to the production of a paradigm. A paradigm is a decision about what to see, a kind of formalism, a focus on particular aspects of a problem. It makes some things more accessible by pushing others back. Hence, no one paradigm will suit every problem; no one paradigm will make easier the whole set of problems that people solve with computers.

Expert programmers use a paradigm as a thought-organizer or a discipline or a frame of reference. They collect a repertoire of useful paradigms – of reference models – which offer different views onto which problems can be mapped, and which facilitate different aspects of solution and different virtues.

Thomas Green and I recognized the need to 'escape from formalism' [Petre and Green, 1990] as an essential part of real-life, professional-level design, necessary to cope with things not accessible within a given formalism. Changing paradigm is a mechanism for escape from one formalism – from one set of constraints or values – into an alternative. Expert programmers employ a conscious change of paradigm in order to re-assess a solution or to gain insight. For them, a paradigm is used as a convenient (if temporary) world view, a way of looking at things, a way of doing things – a decision about what the world is, for the moment. But the sense is of a pair of spectacles rather than of the Kuhnian set of eyes – something one can put on, take off, alternate with something of a different hue, like prescription sunglasses, surround with different frames, even combine into bifocals; not necessarily something incorporated permanently and to the exclusion of alternatives.

Constructive switching between paradigms is compatible with the evidence that the programmers who perform best are those who have encountered the most programming languages – *i.e.* whose experience is broadest [Connelly, 1984; Holt *et al.*, 1987] – and with the evidence that experts do not observe language boundaries when constructing solutions but rather borrow useful features across languages or domains [Petre and Winder, 1988].

3.2.3 What motivates the solution: the programmer or the paradigm?

As Brooks [1987] so colourfully stated: 'Sound methodology can empower and liberate the creative mind; it cannot inflame or inspire the drudge.' Programming paradigms don't solve problems; programmers do. The evidence for constructive paradigm-switching shows that programmers use paradigms deliberately to gain insight – that is, they exert a paradigm to reveal the information they know they want or to support the reasoning process they know they need to accomplish. A programming paradigm can provide insight by making obvious the most important information – or it can obscure by emphasizing the wrong information. To overstretch the metaphor used earlier: paradigms are lenses, but the eyes are the programmer's; paradigms change the view, but the vision is the programmer's. The expert treats a programming paradigm as a reasoning tool.

Advocates of paradigms rarely consider what information outside the paradigm is required for its interpretation (even though such information may well be cultivated in the programming culture, as will be discussed later). But 'extra-paradigmatic' information – such as abstraction strategies and program behaviour – may affect a programmer's ability to reason within a paradigm.

3.2.4 The fundamental problems of structuring solutions and managing abstractions

Thomas Green characterizes programming as the building and manipulation of information structures. The hard part – and the one neglected by programming paradigms – is how to decide what structure to impose. Green offers the example of object-oriented programming [Green, 1990]:

> Both anecdotal evidence and observational data [Détienne, 1990] show that programmers have difficulty in deciding which logical entities shall be represented as objects and which as attributes of objects. Object-oriented programming may be effective, but it is certainly not artless: and in that case, it is not natural.

One person's object is another person's attribute. The major problem in programming is not how things are expressed (although that is an issue), but how solutions are conceived.

Part of arriving at a solution is figuring out just what the problem is; many problems are not well-defined. Big solutions require management: identifying a structure within the solution, dividing it up into manageable chunks, and understanding all the implications of one component within a whole system (both the whole program and the program's environment). More recent paradigms have introduced support for building abstractions, but they provide little or no insight into the difficult problems of choosing and managing them. The notion of code re-use doesn't help, because the idea that parts will be 'reusable and interchangeable' [Cox, 1990] assumes too much about solution structure. In fact, it is difficult to build components that are genuinely both useful and reusable, and recent studies suggest that object re-use is too difficult to be common practice.

3.2.5 The problem of predicting behaviour: operational knowledge as an underpinning to other styles of reasoning

One of the critical issues in the real world is time: a program text is static, but the executing system is dynamic. An essential aspect of programming is predicting program behaviour. When people talk about what a program does, they are talking about a program and the device that interprets it – what they mean is 'what does a machine do when instructed by this program'. This is no less true of declarative programs than of procedural ones, even though operational information is outside the paradigm.

Originally, the programming task favoured the machine; programs were fairly direct encodings of machine behaviour. The programmer was left to decide what to do and how it should be done, and how to describe it in terms convenient to the machine. Developments in programming languages and environments have sought to ease the burden of description by hiding the machine behind an intermediate computational model. Instead of translating solutions into machine operations, the programmer describes the solution in the terms of the higher-level, more programmer-oriented model offered by the programming language. (*cf.* Payne's characterization of user and device as 'yoked state spaces' [1987]. In Payne's terms, this is like bringing the device space closer to the user's goal space – albeit only apparently, because actually an additional, intermediate space is yoked: the device space of the language.)

The declarative paradigms and their associated languages attempt to do something more: to ease the burden of decision as well, by removing from the paradigm's view many control or computational issues governing machine behaviour, and by handling them within the language implementation. But declarative programmers do not 'do without' this information; there is evidence (*e.g.* [Petre, 1991a]) that expert programmers have sophisticated operational models, no matter what paradigm they adopt.

In my study [Petre, 1991a] of expert declarative programmers they were asked to give 'declarative readings' of their programs. I found that programmers include operational information even in what they consider wholly declarative readings; they make explicit references to evaluation mechanisms, to the passage of time, and to behaviour. Similarly, Gunnar Moan suggested that declarative reasoning relies on operational competence [Moan, 1987]. Throughout my studies of expert programmers, declarative programmers left traces in their code that showed that they had written operationally. The traces demonstrated that they worked from the language implementation, not exclusively from the language definition. They would take advantage of some discrepancy between the language definition and the language implementation – exploiting some imperative 'hacks' that were needed to make the language work, such as in this Miranda example:

```
leapyear x = True,   x mod 400 = 0
           = False,  x mod 100 = 0
           = True,   x mod 4 = 0
           = False,  otherwise
```

In Miranda, although the order-of-evaluation of guards in a case structure is specifically 'not defined' in the language, the implementation causes a textual-order evaluation. Guards should properly be mutually exclusive, but in many Miranda programs they are progressive.

The emergence of various programming paradigms is a tribute to the difficulty of bridging the space between programmers and machines – and the desirability of making the best use of each. But delivering an alternative paradigm or reasoning model alone may be ineffectual. It must be clear 'how the model works', that is, how a program will behave. In the absence of any more accessible source, experts extract their operational knowledge from the language implementation. Novices find the accommodation more difficult, as evidenced by the studies of novices learning Prolog (*e.g.*

Taylor [1990]). Giving novices some model of operation helps. If they're not given enough information, they borrow (often erroneously) from other models they have.

3.2.6 Evolution, not revolution: paradigms emerge from practice

Despite the persuasive salesmanship that associates 'startling, new' programming paradigms with novel reasoning, revolution and religious conversion, this chapter suggests that programming paradigms are for the most part unstartling and unrevolutionary. With a few notable exceptions, they typically provide a coherent account of something programmers have already been hankering after or attempting via less concerted or direct means. What is 'sold' as revolutionary is often the packaging of ideas that have been pre-figured in practice; the arrival of the 'new' paradigm signals recognition, not revolution.

A paradigm may be codification that emerges from '*post hoc* rationalization'. This view of a programming paradigm as a codification of evolved practice is not unrelated to the sort of *post hoc* rationalization that accounts for the discrepancy between what experts say (especially what they tout) and what they actually do. Notions such as top-down design and the waterfall model of software development are most effective as idealizations or rationalizations, rather than as strict models of practice. Parnas and Clements [1986], for example, make a good argument for faking 'rational' design even though the design process is actually opportunistic, even chaotic. Strictly declarative programming might be viewed as just such a conscious re-assessment instead of a design practice, a rationalized reading which may clarify *post hoc* an imperatively produced program. Extracting the essence out of practice is familiar in mathematics as well. Mathematicians tidy up proofs before they publish them, removing all the detours and blind alleys travelled during the discovery process.

There is evidence from expert programmers that programming paradigms are pre-figured; they are adopted by people who are working that way already, for example by writing programs in a style other than that of the programming language (*e.g.* writing 'structured' assembler, or 'functional' C, or writing a state machine in PROLOG). It is common practice among experts working on large projects to build superstructures or intermediate languages customized for the problem domain onto some crude but effective general-purpose language. In one study [Petre and Winder, 1988], a group of experts had built an object-oriented superstructure for C (although without identifying it in those terms; they still viewed 'object-oriented programming' with some scepticism). Another group had written a schematics-encoding language in LISP.

Paradigms are not language models but reasoning models. A paradigm is more than the language that is deemed to embody it, and a general-purpose programming language is more than a pure instantiation of a single programming paradigm. Certainly, many languages were developed expressly to embody some paradigm. Even so, language and paradigm are not as tightly coupled in practice as they are in theory or in the literature. In [Petre and Winder, 1988] we observed that experts customized languages by adding superstructures that imported an alternative paradigm. Expert programmers needn't change language to change paradigm.

The view I am advancing here, that a paradigm can provide a discipline within which to devise a solution, is a much weaker assertion than those typically advanced by paradigm proponents: those reflect a conviction that programming languages embodying paradigms influence profoundly the sorts of solutions that programmers devise, and that the right language will guide the programmer's thinking and so produce right solutions. Yet I have found no correlation between programming languages and solution strategies; on the contrary, strategies volunteered as typical of one paradigm would often be implemented in a language that fitted within another. The solutions were categorized in terms of paradigms, not languages.

In fact, expert programmers do not observe language or paradigm boundaries when constructing solutions but rather borrow useful features across languages or domains. They don't even program (*i.e.* solve problems) in the target programming language, but rather construct their solution strategies in a personal pseudo-language and subsequently translate into code. Hence, whereas the paradigm may influence strategy, the programming language influences only tactical decisions, the particular implementation choices. A typical programming scenario has an expert switching deliberately between paradigms in order to devise and verify a solution strategy which is then coded in a programming language chosen by the management.

The conditions and criteria that govern an expert's choice of language are not the same as those governing the choice of reasoning strategy [Petre, 1991b]. The choice of language – assuming the programmer is permitted a choice – is usually dominated by practical, social and organizational considerations. Readability and maintenance don't often figure in choice of reasoning strategy, but they certainly affect language choice. Some languages are not genuinely general purpose (*e.g.* the I/O inadequacies of many functional languages) or are inefficient or unpredictable (*e.g.* PROLOG) or don't match existing facilities or products and so are unacceptable on non-paradigm grounds. The overheads for acquiring a new language are high; experts often argue that it is cheaper to know one language intimately and make it 'jump through hoops' than to shop for something new that may or may not be more suitable. And the blacksmith principle applies: experts prefer building their own tools, arguing that it is easier to build up utilities from a low level than to decompose and remodel hidden, built-in, high-level mechanisms. Most professionals are committed to a single language (plus or minus assembler) for the whole of a project or longer.

So, experts can reason variously for expression within a single language, and they can use various languages to express solutions conceived within one paradigm. Given the practicalities, it makes sense to decouple paradigm from language; it provides flexibility of reasoning for the programmer while providing a stable coding medium for the organization. This is not to say that there is no relationship between programming languages and programming paradigms. Clearly particular languages will be more or less suitable for expressing a particular style of solution. But it is a loose association rather than a tight one. The languages probably most closely coupled to paradigm in practice are those arising from solutions: the custom-built intermediate languages or superstructures.

3.3 Programming culture and programming style

Discussions about programming languages are often not just about notations, but about how they should be used. Discussions about programming paradigms are often not just about formalisms, but about how programmers should think. A programming paradigm does not exist in isolation; it is established within the collective experience of a community of users. Where the paradigm provides a reference model, the culture can add a model of practice. The programming culture embraces not just the definition of its paradigm, but the received wisdom of its adherents. A paradigm or a language is altered – both enhanced and limited – by its culture.

3.3.1 Received wisdom: a model of practice

Programming culture extends from typographical and other conventions of expression (*e.g.* the tendency of PASCAL programmers to use long identifiers as opposed to that of C programmers to use short ones) to restrictions on the interpretation of a paradigm. The restrictions have both advantages and disadvantages; sometimes they guide, and sometimes they constrain.

Consider modelling elementary algebra in an object-oriented style, which is often initially misinterpreted by those ingrained in the store–imperative approach. A common mistake is to consider an expression such as x + y inherently asymmetrical in the object-oriented model because the intended effect of the '+ y' message to x is thought to be to change the state of the object referred to by x. On the contrary, the intended effect is to return the sum of the two objects referenced by x and y; thus the expression is symmetric. Apparently, the misunderstanding comes from mixing up the two models by retaining the notion of variables as storage locations (rather than references) and by confusing the use of messages to obtain answers with operations on an ADT that change state.

Another, more constructive, example is the FORTH culture. To outsiders, given the language definition alone, FORTH appears to be a 'write-only' language. But FORTH proponents tout it as an especially 'intelligible' language, because their conventions of use produce a neat structure of definitions which gradually builds up from the messy low-level underpinnings to a surface vocabulary consistent with the problem domain.

Programming culture can be closely and enduringly bound to paradigm. There are plenty of programmers in circulation who grew up in assembly language days who can't write quick-and-dirty solutions in assembler, because the associations of assembler with limited-memory machines (and the culture which that evokes) prompts them to code efficiently.

3.3.2 Local culture: programming style

With a few esoteric exceptions, programming is not a 'pure' activity; it is contaminated by unavoidable contact with reality, with the constraints of time and machines and people. The first program most experts write in an unfamiliar language is one that establishes contact with peripherals: printing HELLO, WORLD.

Inevitably (and particularly for HELLO, WORLD programs), the operating system impinges on the programmer's view, influencing ways of visualizing system interactions and ways of thinking about what a file is and how it is accessed. And programming exists within a broader culture of people working – often together – to solve problems. Portrayals of a paradigm as a *programming style* reflect the infiltration of working programming culture into the notion of paradigm. 'Programming style' takes in not only the reference model (the style of reasoning) but also a model of practice (the style of working), and an *acceptance grammar* that shapes an instantiating language to conform to some standard and to some interpretation of the paradigm (the style of expression).

This notion of local programming culture is manifest in the paradigm subcultures that spring up. Stanford and MIT each developed a LISP community with its own interpretation (and implementation) of the underlying paradigm.

3.3.3 Error-proneness and bad programming

In this chapter I have argued that a paradigm restricts in a particular, useful way; it can provide a discipline within which to devise a solution. Yet it is a vain hope that a programming paradigm itself will provoke good code. Flon's axiom [Flon, 1975] states: 'There does not now, nor will there ever, exist a programming language in which it is the least bit hard to write bad programs.'

Any programming language or raw paradigm is amenable to interpretation and abuse. Moreover, although a paradigm may not drive people into good thinking, there is some evidence that some languages are more error-prone than others, contributing to errors or oversights. For example, in the study cited earlier [Petre and Winder, 1988], stream-oriented SCHEME approaches to various problems caused mishandling of special cases or the failure to include initial elements of a sequence. ADA's abstraction facilities led to complicated, over-generalized solutions which were incomplete. DuBoulay and O'Shea [1981] also suggest that different error types may correlate to particular programming languages. FORTRAN-style parameter-passing (by alignment, unchecked) is a situation in which errors can occur easily. Uncontrolled go-to's are a well-known pitfall; people can write spaghetti, and untutored people do [Sime *et al.*, 1977].

3.3.4 Secondary notation and individual skill

With Thomas Green I introduced the term *secondary notation* [Petre and Green, 1990] to describe the use of layout and typographical cues which are not formally part of the language definition (elements such as indentation, clustering, white space, identifier names) to clarify information (such as structure, function, or relationships) or to give hints to the reader. We found that poor use of secondary notation is one of the things that typically distinguishes a novice's representation from an expert's. Our studies of programming notations (*e.g.* [Petre and Green, 1993]) suggest that experience and personal skill play important roles in the exploitation of secondary notation in both the production and the comprehension of representations. Whereas novices were confused and diverted by surface features, experts matched their comprehension strategies to the structure of the representation.

Similarly, Davies [1989] showed that differences in results between PASCAL and basic C programmers performing a plan-based task were caused by differential training backgrounds: when basic C programmers were taught the precepts of structured programming, the differences disappeared. It appears that 'salience' is influenced by experience, and that what a reader sees is largely a matter of what he or she has learned to look for. Readership is an acquired skill.

It is important to recognize that poor use of secondary notation isn't merely neutral: it can confuse and mislead. Even a well-evolved language is vulnerable to weaknesses in individual expressive skill. On the other hand, skill may help compensate for weakness in a language. Members of programming teams can usually recognize who wrote what by the style 'signature' in the code. Thomas Green [1990] writes about programmers with 'neat' and 'scruffy' habits, and about 'the mystique of cryptic programming'. Neats or scruffies may choose languages appropriate to their preferences, or they may impose their personal style on whatever is available. (Persistent individual style may explain the 'FORTRAN-in-any-language' phenomenon that is usually attributed to the permanent effects of first experience.)

This is where the programming culture plays a role: design conventions which attempt to reinforce meaningful use of secondary notation, although rarely formalized or codified, are consolidated within the culture. The mechanism by which a paradigm is disambiguated, restricted and refined, by which it is associated with a model of practice and a style of expression, by which particular examples emerge as exemplars, by which its weaknesses are avoided, by which newcomers are introduced to (or indoctrinated into) the wisdom, traditions and conventions of the paradigm's local community, is programming culture. Programming culture provides the lore and conventions that can offset error-proneness in a language. The culture can help to smooth out individual variations by providing an 'acceptance grammar' of acceptable practice and usage – and by moulding programmers' expectations.

3.3.5 Reflective v. non-reflective programming – investing in good practice

One of the most enduring effects in empirical studies of programming is individual variation (*e.g.* [Curtis, 1981]). The variability is not just in experience or skill or cognitive style (whatever that may be), but also in what the programmer expects from programming.

There is no doubt that programming has developed and improved over the decades. The early exclusive emphasis on producing machine-readable code soon yielded to the recognition that programs are often read by their human producers (perhaps more often than by the target machines). Notational elements that had nothing to do with efficiency of execution were introduced for the convenience of the programmer. At the extreme, programs were viewed primarily as communications to other programmers, with characters like Dijkstra [1976] publishing programs never intended for machine execution.

Something that distinguishes expert programmers from other programmers is that professionals typically recognize themselves as existing within a programming culture. The professional sees the program as having a potential value in itself; the personal 'corpus of programs' contributes to the professional programmer's reputation and identity. The professional has reason to invest in clear, economical, insightful work for its own sake. To the professional, a program is a communication to another programmer – not just the control of a machine. They reflect on their programs.

In contrast, part-time, non-professional, or casual programmers are usually working independently to write one-off solutions for their own use; if they pass one on, it is as a tool, not as a text. This 'non-reflective' programming is what distinguishes 'part-timers' from full-time professional programmers, even though they may well spend as much time writing code and may create sophisticated applications within their domains. Other, less professional groups of 'part-timers' are similar in this respect; many spreadsheet users address complex problems, but how many people 'read' a spreadsheet?

So, even if the skill and standards of programmers were uniform, their aspirations are not. Paradigms can help smooth differences by providing a common, workable reference model, and cultures can help by promoting shared standards and styles; both can help by minimizing obstacles. But individual differences will persist.

3.4 Implications for teaching of programming and training of programmers

The premise of this chapter has been that, by observing actual practice, we can consider paradigms as they are defined and used in the 'real world', identify the long-term educational target, and, one hopes, avoid misleading paths. By understanding something about how paradigms operate in expert practice, we can hope to understand something about what they are likely – and unlikely – to deliver in teaching. This section interprets the evidence of expert behaviour in the following suggestions for teaching programming and training programmers:

Emphasize programming cultures, not programming languages. When a lecturer assigns a project in, say, ADA, and the student returns a program that causes the lecturer to exclaim 'Holy operating systems! This isn't ADA, this is BASIC!', the problem is not programming language but programming culture. The student's ADA program is syntactically and logically correct, but it doesn't conform to the ADA culture; it doesn't meet the lecturer's expectations about solution strategies and secondary notation. If we want to produce professional (and, ultimately, expert) programmers, teaching and training should emphasize programming cultures, not programming languages.

Support paradigm shifts; teach reasoning styles as selectable tools. The evidence argues for breadth of exposure, for provision of a variety of paradigms, and for support in switching deliberately between paradigms. A paradigm is no panacea, but it can be a powerful tool. Paradigms – styles of reasoning – should be presented as selectable tools. They must be understood as useful views that have both advantages and blind spots.

Cultivate strategy and abstraction skills. Experts sort problems in terms of underlying principles or abstract features (*e.g.* [Chi *et al.*, 1981], [Weiser and Shertz, 1983]), whereas novices rely on surface features. Novices are distracted by syntax; teachers must coax them away from the superficial and show them how to look for structure and strategy. Some teaching appears to emphasize rather than diminish the superficial, categorizing solutions in syntactic terms. Instead, students must learn to think about the semantic structure of solutions, in order to recognize the strategic similarities of different implementations rather than be distracted by tactical differences.

One of the mechanisms modern programming languages have for making structure visible is abstraction, a way of packaging up chunks of program into parcels with locality (with internal scope and a defined interface to other parcels) and generalizing those parcels into program concepts to be used and reasoned about as abstract entities. Although many languages provide tools for building abstractions, neither languages nor paradigms provide much help with choosing or managing abstractions. That must come from the culture. Abstraction building is seductive, even to experts; however, forming generic abstract types can lead into confusing excess of detail and even eclipse the problem itself. Teaching abstraction skills must include teaching how to interpret a solution strategy as a structure of abstractions, how to choose – and to choose the extent of – abstractions, and how to re-build if the abstraction structure fails.

Strategy must be supported by appropriate tactics, and it should be shown that different languages support different tactical or implementation choices. Nevertheless, the emphasis should be on strategic analysis and deep structure, rather than syntactic niceties or surface features.

Decouple solution from coding. Teachers and trainers, like expert programmers, should decouple paradigms from languages. Teaching must aim at the strategic (problem-solving) rather than the tactical (coding) level, providing students with a varied toolkit for reasoning and a reasonable model of practice, rather than a premature allegiance to some single paradigm or language. Paradigms should be presented, not tightly coupled one-to-a-language, but as reasoning models that can be applied across languages (albeit with more or less ease of implementation).

Cultivate readership and reflective programming. Teaching must recognize that being able to read programs is an acquired skill; students must learn perceptual skills, inspection strategies and comprehension strategies – how to look and what to look for. Learning how to read programs is an essential part of programming, and a difficult one.

The 'teaching culture' should encourage students to reflect on their own and others' programs, and to consider their solutions in terms of different paradigms. Experts tend to spend more time than novices planning and evaluating. They tend to consider more fully interactions between functions or components of a system and to form a detailed, abstract, conceptual model. Abstraction skills apply not just to program creation but also to program comprehension, and students must learn to take the time to reflect.

Recognize the importance of secondary notation. A component of readership is the ability to make use of secondary notation, of layout and perceptual clues to meaning. Novices suffer from misreadings and confusions; they are prone to misconceptions about what is important or relevant [Petre and Green, 1993; Davies, 1989]. A poor notation or poor use of a notation can only contribute to the difficulty:

> It is important that the programmer's task not be compounded by an additional layer of complexity from the very tool that is being used to solve the problem.
>
> [Marcotty and Ledgard, 1987]

The programming language should offer conciseness of expression with a clean, uncluttered syntax. It should offer abstraction and structuring tools that facilitate structural visibility. (The literature is littered with examples of elements to avoid: the unnecessary punctuation that clutters LISP and PASCAL; the verbose and repetitive phrasing of COBOL; OCCAM's assignment in both directions, depending on the terms involved; *etc.*)

Provide operational information. Predicting behaviour is an essential part of programming. And it appears that operational knowledge is the underpinning for many styles of reasoning. If teaching fails to explain 'how it works', students will devise their own – usually erroneous or incomplete – operational models. (Recall the misinterpretation of arithmetic in the object-oriented paradigm on page 36.)

Choose a genuinely general-purpose language. Most programmers end up stuck with one language for a project (usually one chosen by management), and so the important skill is to be able to employ the range of reasoning, however the chosen strategy is implemented. Given a commitment to teaching a variety of paradigms, it is reasonable to choose a single programming language, assuming that it is a genuinely general-purpose language with facilities both for abstraction building and for manipulation of low-level details. The choice should respect practical demands as well as algorithmic ones.

If you provide training wheels, remember to take them off. Providing 'scaffolding' in the shape of special environments, protections and tools to support learning is fine – as long as the learning is of generalizable skills, and the student is weaned away from the scaffolding. Programming culture can provide mediocrity management and damage limitation by giving students basic, reliable rules and restrictions until they develop insight.

Foreshadow professional practice. Taught practice should foreshadow actual practice. It makes sense to choose a language that operates in the 'real world' or to choose a subset that scales up to professional practice. Teaching (or training) is counter-productive if it relies on new and different conventions and languages that the student won't meet elsewhere. What is needed is consistency or compatibility with the conventions used in practice by experts.

3.5 Conclusion

This chapter has tried to sort out what a programming paradigm is not (a panacea) and what it is (a tool, a selectable reasoning model) based on how expert programmers use them. The evidence is that expert programmers behave in a variety of ways that differ from programming language theorists' expectations. Expert programmers do not observe language or paradigm boundaries when constructing solutions but rather borrow useful features across languages or domains. They don't even program in the target programming language, but rather construct their solution strategies in a personal pseudo-language and subsequently translate into code, so that the programming language influences only tactical decisions. Expert programmers needn't change language to change paradigm, rather they switch deliberately between paradigms in order to devise and verify a solution strategy which is then coded in some programming language, usually one chosen for reasons having little to do with paradigms. Hence, a paradigm is more than the language that is deemed to embody it, and a general-purpose language, although it may be geared to support one paradigm, can be used to express solutions conceived within other paradigms.

The chapter has argued that a programming paradigm is embedded (perhaps inextricably) in a programming culture that can embrace the collective traditions, wisdom and bigotry of its advocates. Programming culture both enhances and restricts a paradigm or a language: interpreting and disambiguating, providing a model of practice, promoting standards and conventions that establish a style of expression, setting out the 'acceptance grammar' of acceptable usage and practice, sustaining a lore of methods and examples that can minimize obstacles and mould expectations, providing a common ground for communication. The culture can provide a foothold for newcomers and novices.

The chapter has promoted a number of considerations for teaching programming and the further training of programmers:

- emphasize programming cultures, not programming languages;
- support paradigm shifts; teach reasoning styles as selectable tools;
- cultivate strategy and abstraction skills ;
- decouple solution from coding;
- cultivate readership and reflective programming;
- recognize the importance of secondary notation;
- provide operational information;
- choose a genuinely general-purpose language;
- if you provide training wheels, remember to take them off;
- foreshadow professional practice.

In teaching, the choice of programming language is less important than the choice of programming culture and the provision of suitable paradigms. The important thing about paradigms is to provide more than one. A variety of paradigms can be presented via any flexible general-purpose language, so what's needed is a flexible, powerful language with an accessible execution model and a simple, uncluttered syntax.

3.6 References

Brooks, F. (1987), No silver bullet: essence and accidents of software engineering, *IEEE Computer*.

Chi, M. T. H., Feltovich, P. J. and Glaser, R. (1981), Categorization and representation of physics problems by experts and novices, *Cognitive Science*, **5**, 121–52.

Connelly, E. M. (1984), Transformations of software and code may lead to reduced errors, in *Interact '84, First IFIP Conference on Human-Computer Interaction*, Amsterdam, Elsevier Science Publishers.

Cox, B. J. (1990), There is a silver bullet, *Byte*, **15**(10), 209–18.

Curtis, B. (1981), Substantiating programmer variability, *Proceedings of the IEEE*, **69**(7).

Davies, S. P. (1989), Skill levels and strategic differences in plan comprehension and implementation in programming, in *People and Computers V*, A. Sutcliffe and L. Macaulay (eds), Cambridge University Press, Cambridge, England.

Détienne, F. (1990), Difficulties in designing with an object-oriented language: an empirical study, in *Human-Computer Interaction – INTERACT '90*, D. Diaper, D. Gilmore, G. Cockton and B. Shackel (eds), Amsterdam, Elsevier.

Dijkstra, E. W. (1976), *A Discipline of Programming*, Series in Automatic Computation, Prentice-Hall, Englewood Cliffs, N. J.

Du Boulay, B. and O'Shea, T. (1981), Teaching novices programming, in *Computing Skills and the User Interface*, M. J. Coombs and J. L. Alty (eds), Academic Press, London.

Flon, L. (1975), On research in structured programming, *SIGPLAN Notices*, **11**, 16–7.

Green, T. R. G. (1990), The nature of programming, in *Psychology of Programming*, J.-M. Hoc, T. R. G. Green, R. Samurcay and D. J. Gilmore (eds), Academic Press, London, 21–44.

Holt, R. W., Boehm-Davis, D. A. and Schultz, A. C. (1987), Mental representations of programs for student and professional programmers, in *Empirical Studies of Programmers: Second Workshop*, G. M. Olson, S. Sheppard and E. Soloway (eds), Ablex, 33–46.

Kuhn, T. (1962), *The Structure of Scientific Revolutions*, 1st edition, The University of Chicago Press, Chicago.

Marcotty, M. and Ledgard, H. (1987), *The World of Programming Languages*, Springer-Verlag, New York.

Moan, G. (1987), PROLOGraph: a proposed system giving a graphical representation of a PROLOG execution (Manuscript).

Parnas, D. L. and Clements, P. C. (1986), A rational design process: how and why to fake it, *IEEE Transactions on Software Engineering*, **SE-12**(2), 251–7.

Payne, S. J. (1987), Complex problem spaces: modelling the knowledge needed to use interactive devices, in *INTERACT'87*, H.-J. Bullinger and B. Shackel (eds), Elsevier, Amsterdam.

Petre, M. and Green, T. (1990), Where to draw the line with text: some claims by logic designers about graphics in notation, in *Human–Computer Interaction: Interact '90*, D. Diaper, D. Gilmore, G. Cockton and B. Shackel (eds), North-Holland, Amsterdam, 463–8.

Petre, M. and Green, T. (1993), Learning to read graphics: some evidence that 'seeing' an information display is an acquired skill, *Journal of Visual Languages and Computing*, **4**, 55–70.

Petre, M. and Winder, R. (1988), Issues governing the suitability of programming languages for programming tasks, in *People and Computers IV*, Cambridge University Press, Cambridge, England.

Petre, M. (1991), Shifts in reasoning about software and hardware systems: must operational models underpin declarative ones?, in *The Third Workshop of the Psychology of Programming Interest Group, Hatfield, England, January 1991*.

Petre, M. (1991), What experts want from programming languages, *Ergonomics*, **34**(8), 1113–27.

Rentsch, T. (1982), Object oriented programming, *SIGPLAN Notices*, **17**(9).

Sime, M. E., Arblaster, A. T. and Green, T. R. G. (1977), Structuring the programmer's task, *Journal of Occupational Psychology*, **50**, 205–16.

Taylor, J. (1990), Analysing novices analysing Prolog: what stories do novices tell themselves about Prolog?, *Instructional Science*, **19**, 283–309.

Wadler, P. (1987), A critique of Abelson and Sussman – or why calculating is better than scheming, *SIGPLAN Notices*, **22**(3).

Weiser, M. and Shertz, J. (1983), Programming problem representation in novice and expert programmers, *International Journal of Man-Machine Studies*, **19**, 391–8.

4 CooL (Combined object-oriented language) – an overview

Martin Weber

This chapter describes the object-oriented general-purpose language CooL (Combined object-oriented Language). CooL is intended to be used for medium- to large-scale applications, ranging from software development tools to large data-intensive information systems. It combines object-oriented concepts with concepts from procedural languages and from database programming. The design criteria and concepts of CooL are presented and the details given can serve as a basis for the reader to decide whether CooL can be used in a particular environment.

4.1 Introduction

Nowadays a multitude of languages are available to the programmer. It is not always easy to choose the best language for a project. Although many languages are very similar to each other there are also important differences. Languages differ in their concepts – which allow their classification as procedural languages, functional languages, object-oriented languages, logic languages, *etc.*They can also differ in the intended application area – which allows their classification as general-purpose languages, special-purpose languages, languages to support real-time or concurrent applications, *etc.* In addition, their designers might have had different users (programmers) in mind (systems programmers, application programmers, occasional programmers, students, *etc.*). Languages might have been developed to prove or test certain scientific concepts, and different languages may be designed for different project types and sizes (simple *ad hoc* programs, small toy programs, small projects, groupware, large-scale applications).

Languages that are to be used in a wide area of applications are usually compromises between various design goals. Depending on the intended application area and depending on which design goals are stressed you get different languages. So before you can choose a language you have to know about its design criteria, its concepts, the intended application area, *etc.*

In 1989 the ESPRIT project ITHACA[1] started (for a description of the project see [Ader *et al.*, 1990]). The goal of the project was the development of an integrated development environment supporting the whole software development process. A language was needed that could be used by all partners for the various tools of the environment and for the development of applications as well. It had to be a general-purpose language for applications ranging from development tools to large data-intensive information systems. As such it had to be easy enough to understand and use, it had to contain constructs to support readability, maintainability, prototyping, programming in the large [DeRemer and Kron, 1976] and database access, but on the other hand it was not to be too complex. Furthermore it should improve software quality and development productivity. After evaluating various languages it was decided to develop a new language since no available language was sufficient for the project. Today no other publicly available language fulfils these criteria.

The following sections will present the design criteria and concepts of the COOL environment and its language [CooL, 1992]. The intention of this overview is to provide you with a general understanding of the COOL environment. More specifically, this document should help you to:

- understand the system as a whole and become familiar with the system's main principles (*e.g.* its object-orientation);

- gain a clear impression of who should use the system, how you can use the system, and where it can be used.

The outline of the chapter is as follows. The first section explains the criteria used in the design of COOL and relates them, where possible, to the corresponding concepts in COOL. The next section sketches the main language features. The following section describes the functionality of the COOL environment as a whole and lists the major components of the product and outlines their functionality, at the same time showing how the components operate in harmony with one another. The final section contains some concluding remarks regarding where COOL should be used and by whom.

4.2 CooL design criteria

When designing a programming language (and/or a programming environment) the designers should have in mind a number of design criteria. These can be stated explicitly or are, as in many cases, just general rules in the mind of designers. Ideally the language should reflect exactly those explicit and implicit design criteria: all of them, and

---

[1] ITHACA (Integrated Toolkit for Highly Advanced Computer Applications) is a technology integration project funded by the Commission of the European Communities as part of the ESPRIT II programme.

nothing else. Design criteria can range from general rules (*e.g.* 'the language shall have a big market') to rather specific restrictions (*e.g.* 'the language must support graphics programming'). In any case, language design criteria can serve as a starting point to evaluate a language.

The following design criteria were used during the design of COOL; many of them should be (and are) used in the design of other languages or systems as well.

General-purpose language : COOL is designed as a general-purpose language. It can be used in a wide range of application areas, from system programming to complex application systems. It is not designed for real-time or parallel programs (unless supported by the underlying operating system via library facilities).

Support for data-intensive applications : In data-intensive applications up to 40% of the coding effort is used to store and retrieve data. A major goal of COOL is to relieve programmers from coding that part of their applications. In COOL this will be achieved through the use of persistent object types and set-based query language, which have been tested in a prototype version of COOL. They will be part of COOL version 3.0.

Support for large-scale applications : Large-scale programming needs special language support to structure and integrate large programs. In COOL this is done through its object-oriented concepts and the use of modules.

Easy to learn, easy to use : In industry a major obstacle to using a new language is the time necessary to learn it. COOL is designed as a language which is easy to learn. This is especially important in large multi-language projects where programmers have to know more than one language. In COOL this design criterion is reflected by the relatively small number of constructs compared with other languages (*e.g.* C++, ADA). It is also supported by another criterion, namely the orthogonality of concepts (see below), which guarantees that the rules and definitions of language concepts have as few exceptions as possible.

Readability : Experiences during recent decades have shown that usually more time is used in industry for maintaining (debugging, changing, or porting) software than for actually writing it. Therefore it is much more important to be able to read and understand code than write code quickly. This is especially true since new applications are often written by experienced specialists and later maintained by other less experienced programmers. Readability and maintainability are mainly consequences of good design, implementation and documentation of an application. However, a language can support these design goals through carefully chosen syntactic and semantic concepts. In COOL this is done partly through its object-oriented and structuring concepts and partly by choosing an easy abstract and concrete syntax with meaningful keywords.

Object-orientation : Object-oriented programming helps to structure an application into loosely coupled parts which reflect the parts of an application in reality. Object-oriented programming also supports re-use of software components and the ability to change existing components without affecting other components, since objects can only be manipulated through operation of a well-defined interface. In addition, object-orientation supports extending components through the use of inheritance.

Well-defined, orthogonal and integrated concepts : The various concepts of a language should be well defined, they should be orthogonal to each other, and they should be smoothly integrated. Orthogonality and integration of all concepts of a language tend to be a problem whenever some that have not been considered in the initial design of a language are added to it. In COOL all features of this language, including those introduced in COOL 2.0 and COOL 3.0, were carefully designed to get smoothly integrated language with orthogonal concepts. This is reflected by the small number of exceptions which exist in the definition of the language.

Openness : As a general-purpose language COOL covers most programming areas, but there are special problems and application areas where other languages are more appropriate, for instance for low-level systems programming and for real-time applications. Especially large applications combine parts that can well be written in COOL with other parts where other languages are used. In such applications it is important to be able to integrate parts written in different languages into one program. 'Openness' means that integration is possible on a call level at least (you can call functions written in one language from a function written in another language). In COOL openness is reflected by the ability to import and export variables and procedures from and to components written in C or in C-compatible languages.

Reliability : As many errors as possible should be detected automatically before the execution of a program. This criterion led to the strong type system in COOL. In a COOL program it is impossible to get a run-time error because a variable or expression yields an object of a wrong type (with the exception of type ADDRESS which had to be added for efficiency).

Efficiency : Efficiency is not as important as in the 1960s, but with growing programs, data volume and program complexity it is still important to get acceptable response times, run-time behaviour or storage usages. Efficiency is one of the main goals in COOL. It is reflected in the overall language design and in the decision to integrate procedural elements compatible to C into the language. This enables the COOL compiler to generate efficient C code.

4.3 CooL – the language

This section describes the main concepts of the COOL programming language. Examples from a small application are used to illustrate how these concepts are used. The application represents the organization of a workshop. Different object types are used to represent presenters, session chairs, exhibitors, delegates, exhibitions, presentations, tutorials and the workshop itself. The various types representing participants in the workshop have some common state information associated with them. Some of the types have additional information associated with them (*e.g.* a presenter presents a paper). The other types are all happenings, with a name, a location and a time frame associated with them. Again some of them may have additional information (*e.g.* tutorial has participants).

CooL (combined object-oriented language) is an object-oriented general-purpose language with persistent objects (see Figure 4.1). But not everything in COOL has to be an object. And the flow of control is not only represented by messages passed be-

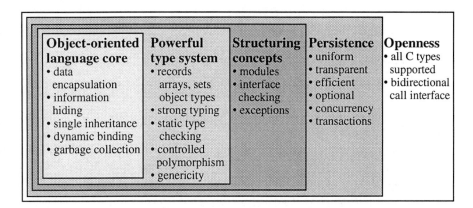

Figure 4.1   CooL concepts.

tween objects. CooL combines object-oriented features with features from procedural languages and data programming.

4.3.1 Types

As basic types CooL supports the types *bool*, *char*, *integer* (including short integer and unsigned integer), *floating point* (including double-precision floating point), *address* and *typed references*. The usual operations are available for basic values (boolean predicates, arithmetic, *etc.*). As structured types CooL offers records, unions, arrays (including open arrays as parameter type in signatures) and strings. Except for the string type, all these types are fully compliant with their C counterparts (*e.g.* CooL records comply with C structs).

However, the most important types in CooL are *object types* which are central to object-oriented facilities in CooL. In general these comply with the Object Management Group (OMG) standards as defined in their Object Management Architecture [Object Management Group, 1992].

4.3.2 Objects and object types

Objects are the basic building blocks of any object-oriented application. An object is an inseparable block of data and operations, where the operations are the only means to manipulate the object's data. The object's data constitutes the memory of the object (sometimes referred to as the object's *state*), while the operations collectively define the object's behaviour. Access to the value of the object's data from outside the object is only permitted by using an appropriate operation, thus ensuring data abstraction. The state of an object is defined by its *instance variables* (data members in C++), while the operations are called *methods* (member functions in C++). Instance variables may be variables of any CooL type.

In CooL, an object must be created explicitly by use of the NEW operation, and it disappears either explicitly by use of the DELETE statement or implicitly when the application program finishes or through garbage collection, when it is no longer accessible.

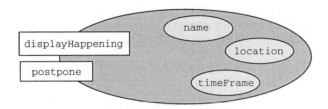

Figure 4.2   A 'happening' object.

For example, consider an object that models the likes of conferences, workshops, exhibitions, *etc.* Since the term 'event' has particular connotations in object-oriented programming, we will call such an object a *happening*. So a *happening* object will consists of the *happening* object's data (name, location and timeFrame) and its methods (displayHappening, postpone). This is depicted in Figure 4.2.

Objects communicate with each other by exchanging messages. A message consists of a selector which specifies the object's method to be executed and a number of parameters (where needed).

Objects with an equal set of methods and an equal set of instances variables are instances of an object type (sometimes also called class).

An object type declaration defines the instance variables and the methods of its objects. The object type declaration consists of an interface, a state and a body. The interface specifies the signatures of public methods accessible by any client of the object type and protected methods accessible only by subtypes of the object type. The state contains declarations for the instance variables of the object type. The body contains the actual code implementing at least the methods listed in the interface.

The following example shows the declaration of an object type Happening. The declaration shows three methods for accessing objects of the type Happening. The first two (displayHappening and postpone) are public methods which can be used by all clients of type Happening, while the the third (getDuration) is a *protected* method which can only be used by subtypes of Happening (see below). The state of every object is defined by the three instance variables declared in the STATE part of the object type definition – (name, location and timeFrame). The first two instance variables have a primitive type (STRING), while the other variable is of another object type – Interval (which is defined somewhere else).

```
TYPE Happening = OBJECT
    METHOD displayHappening();
    METHOD postpone (IN time: Duration);
        ...
PROTECTED
    METHOD getDuration() :   time;
        ...
STATE
    name: STRING; location: STRING;
    timeFrame: Interval;
BODY
    METHOD displayHappening();
    DO
        printf("%s takes place in %s from %s to %s\n",
                name, location, timeFrame.start(), timeFrame.end());
    END DO;
```

```
METHOD postpone (IN time: Duration);
DO
    timeFrame.add(time);
    END DO;
    ...
END OBJECT;
```

An object constitutes a data abstraction which implies that the internal characteristics of an object type are hidden to the outside, and may only be manipulated using appropriate methods. Thus, an object type represents – via its public interface – an abstract data type (ADT) and object-oriented application systems tend to be much more flexible with regard to functional extensions. As long as the interface of an object type remains the same, its internal characteristics may be changed completely. The whole application will be affected by the internal changes.

4.3.3 Inheritance

New object types may be derived from any existing object type by means of a mechanism called *inheritance*. Here, the derived object type is called a *subtype*, while the type it is derived from is called the *supertype*. The subtype inherits all functionality from its supertype. When we have two object types Happening and Presentation, inheritance allows us to:

- define *isA* relationships between similar object types (Presentation *isA* Happening);
- specialize object types (Presentation *isA* specialization of Happening);
- extend object types (Presentation can extend the functionality of Happening);
- re-use code and data structures (Presentation automatically inherits all code and data structures of Happening).

In COOL every type can have only one supertype (single inheritance). A subtype can again be a supertype of other types (see Figure 4.3 for an example of an inheritance hierarchy).

A type inherits that state of its supertype and all public and protected methods declared in the supertype's interface. A subtype can add instance variables, it can add methods, and can redefine the implementation of inherited methods. The following example shows the declaration of two subtypes of Happening (Presentation and Tutorial, which is itself a subtype of Presentation):

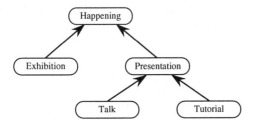

Figure 4.3   'IsA' hierarchy.

```
TYPE Presentation = Happening OBJECT
   ...
   METHOD getPresenter() : Presenter;
STATE
   presenter: Presenter;
BODY
   METHOD getPresenter() : STRING;
   DO
       RETURN  presenter.getName();
   END DO;
END OBJECT;



TYPE Tutorial = Presentation OBJECT
   METHOD addParticipant (IN p: Participant);
   METHOD numberOfParticipants() : INT;
STATE
   participants: SET [Participant];
BODY
   METHOD addParticipant(IN p: Participant);
   DO
      participants.Include(p);
   END DO;
   METHOD numberOfParticipants() : INT;
   DO
       RETURN participants.Cardinality();
   END DO;
END OBJECT;
```

The object type Presentation is a subtype of Happening and, thus, inherits all the methods of Happening (*i.e.* getLocation, putTime and the protected method getDuration) and all its instance variables (name, location and timeFrame), at the same time extending the functionality of Happening by the method getPresenter and the instance variable presenter. The object type Tutorial in turn inherits all methods of Presentation (getLocation, putTime and the protected method getDuration) and all its instance variables (presenter, name, location, time) and adds the method addParticipant and numberOfParticipants and the instance variable participants. Only additional functionality has to be explicitly specified, while the inherited features of an object supertype are provided implicitly.

Until now we have seen how we can inherit and extend functionality from an object type by defining a subtype with the extended functionality. Sometimes, though, it is necessary to change the functionality of an object type in order to re-use it.

In COOL you can change the implementation of an inherited method. Such a method is called a *redefined method*. Let us assume in our example that we want to define an object type Exhibition. An exhibition is a presentation, so we should define Exhibition as a subtype of Presentation. But when we ask who presents the exhibition we are interested in the presenter's name and in the name of their company. So we have to change the method getPresenter. In a redefined method (and in other methods of the subtype) we can still use the original method by preceding the method name with the keyword SUPER, as in SUPER.getPresenter().

```
TYPE Tutorial = Presentation OBJECT
    ...
STATE
    ...
BODY
    REDEFINED METHOD getPresenter() : STRING;
    VAR companyName, presenterName: STRING
    DO
        presenterName := SUPER.getPresenter() ;
        companyName := presenter.getCompany().getName();
        RETURN presenterName + "from" + companyName;
    END DO;
END OBJECT;
```

4.3.4 Dynamic binding and polymorphism

An object in CooL may be assigned to another object if both have the same object type or if the type on the right-hand side is a subtype of the type on the left-hand side. Thus, in our example above a tutorial may be assigned to a presentation (every tutorial is also a presentation) but never the other way around (not every presentation is necessarily a tutorial).

Polymorphism is a concept which allows variables of one object type to hold at different times objects of different types. The *static type* of a variable is the type with which it is declared. The *dynamic type* of a variable is the type of the object to which it currently holds a reference. In CooL polymorphism is restricted in such a way that variables can hold references only to objects of subtypes of their static type.

However, now objects of type Tutorial and of type Presentation both respond to the same message getPresenter but with different method implementations. Dynamic binding is a mechanism to select the method to be executed dynamically. Selection is done at run-time by calling the method of the dynamic type of a variable.

The possibility to redefine methods in subtypes in combination with dynamic binding provides a useful basis for building more generic software. Let us assume that we want to get a list of all presenters in the workshop. In a non-object-oriented programming style this task would be handled by iterating over the set of presentations, checking the type of the presentation and then selecting the corresponding procedure. If, at a later time, a new type of presentation is added, this loop has to be extended to handle the new type as well. In CooL, this application could look like the following fragment.

```
TYPE PresentationList = LIST [Presentation];
    METHOD DisplayPresenters (IN aPresentList: PresentationList);
    VAR aPresentation: Presentation;
    DO
        aPresentation := aPresentationList.first() ;
        print ("We have the following presenters:\n");
        For aPresentation IN 1..aPresentList.NumberOfEntries()
        LOOP
            printf ("%\n", aPresentation.getPresenter());
            aPresentation := aPresentationList.next() ;
        END LOOP;
    END DO;
```

Within the loop, the dynamic type of aPresenter is checked automatically by the run-time system. If the dynamic type is a tutorial then the tutorial-specific method is selected. Otherwise (*e.g.* for talks) the standard getPresenter method is executed.

The type rules in COOL guarantee that no error can occur at run-time due to incorrectly typed expressions. This is mainly done by allowing only methods to operate on objects, which are defined for the static type of the object.

Sometimes it is desirable to find out the dynamic type of an object in order to call special methods of that type. The TYPESELECT statement provides a type-safe way to select the dynamic type of a variable. Without sacrificing strong typing and static type checking this allows you to call methods of the dynamic type of an object, even though the dynamic type is not known at compile-time!

4.3.5 Exceptions

Exception handling is another powerful mechanism to improve software reliability and quality. In practical programming, exceptional situations frequently occur, for example, when opening a file due to missing access rights. In the Unix environment, it is common practice to handle these situations by means of return codes. This depends on the client programmer's discipline and is therefore not really safe. In contrast to the return code approach, an exception handling mechanism allows exceptional situations to be defined, their occurrence trapped, and a correct response made.

An exception has to be declared explicitly and may be signalled via the RAISE statement. Exceptions can be handled within a TRY statement by an exception handler. A TRY statement consists of a statement block and a list of exception handlers. When an exception is raised during the execution of the statement block, the exception handler defined for that exception is executed, and the execution continues after the end of the TRY statement. If the TRY statement does not contain a handler for the exception, it is propagated to the dynamically innermost TRY statement which defines a handler for that exception. If an exception is not handled at all, it is propagated to the COOL run-time exception handler which prints an error message with the exception name and exits the program.

In an earlier example, we wanted to print a set of presentations and their presenters. But what would have happened if we had presentations with no presenter assigned yet? Instead of returning an undefined string, the method getPresenter should raise an exception indicating that nobody has been assigned as presenter yet. This exception can be handled in a TRY statement:

```
EXCEPTION NoPresenter;              -- define the exception

TYPE Presentation = Happening OBJECT
   ...
BODY
   METHOD getPresenter() : STRING;
   DO
      IF presenter = NIL THEN
         RAISE NoPresenter;         -- raise the exception
      ELSE
         RETURN presenter.getName();
      END IF;
   END DO;
END OBJECT
```

```
TYPE PresentationSet = SET [Presentation];

METHOD DisplayPresenters (IN aPresentSet : PresentationSet);
DO
    printf ("We have the following presenters:\n");
    FOR p IN a PresentSet
    LOOP
        TRY                           -- exception can occur here
            printf ("%\n", p.getPresenter());
        EXCEPT
            CASE NoPresenter:         -- handler for NoPresenter
                printf("no presenter for %\n",p.getName());

            OTHERWISE                 -- handler for others
                printf("something went totally wrong\n");
                RERAISE;              -- raise same exception again
        END TRY;
    END LOOP;
END DO
```

4.3.6 Genericity

There is one useful kind of abstraction which cannot be modelled with object types: the *container classes*. Lists, arrays, sets, *etc.* are the COOL container classes. Container classes have the property that the element type is not relevant for the definition of a container class. A stack, for instance, provides the methods push and pop.

A *generic object type* in COOL is a type-safe way to model container classes. A declaration of a generic object type is a template for an object type. Formal type parameters are used as place holders. A generic object type can be instantiated by supplying an actual type for each of the formal type parameters. An instance of a generic object type is an object type and it can be used just like an ordinary object type. The following example shows the definition of a generic stack:

```
EXCEPTION StackOverflow;
EXCEPTION EmptyStack;

TYPE Stack [ElemType] = OBJECT
    METHOD push (IN elem : ElemType);
    METHOD pop() : ElemType;
STATE
    n: INT;
    data: ARRAY[100] OF ElemType;
BODY
    INITIALLY  DO n := 1; END DO;

    METHOD push (IN elem: ElemType);
    DO
        IF n <=100 THEN
            data[n] := elem;
            n := n + 1;
        ELSE
            RAISE StackOverflow;
        END IF;
    END DO;
```

```
METHOD pop() : ElemType;
DO
    IF n>1 THEN
        n := n - 1;
        RETURN data [n]
    ELSE
        RAISE EmptyStack;
    END IF;
END DO;

END OBJECT;
```

Instances of this generic stack can be used for specific stacks, for instance a stack of persons. This is done by defining a variable of type stack[Person]. This variable can then be used just like any other variable of an object type. The instantiated object type provides the interface of the generic Stack, where the formal type paramenter ElemType is replaced by the actual parameter Person:

```
METHOD foo (IN you: Person, IN me:  Person,  OUT who:  Person);
VAR myPersonStack: Stack[Person];
DO
    myPersonStack   := NEW Stack[Person];
    myPersonStack.push (me);
    myPersonStack.push (you);
    who := myPersonStack.pop();
END DO;
```

4.3.7 Persistence

Typically, about 30–40% of the development of data-intensive applications is spent on designing and implementing persistence [Atkinson *et al.*, 1983]. Persistence usually includes:

- an interface to a (relational) database (which can be embedded SQL or a procedural access layer);
- the design of the database schema (including various transformations to normalize the tables);
- operations which transform application objects into database objects;
- retrieval and storage operations;
- concurrency control and transactions (usually, but not always provided by the database system);
- data security (again, usually but not always provided by the database system).

Any object type in COOL can be defined to be persistent. All objects of a persistent object type are persistent, that is they reside in an OODBMS. Instance variables can be declared unique and serve as keys to objects. Complex boolean expressions can be used to retrieve sets of objects. Accesses to the OODBMS are transparent to the user. COOL provides transaction blocks which either commit or abort. CoOMS, as the underlying database system, provides concurrency control and data security. Persistence causes no penalty for transient objects. A declaration of a persistent object type looks very similar to a declaration of a normal object type:

```
TYPE Happening = PERSISTENT OBJECT
   METHOD getLocation: STRING;
   METHOD postpone (IN time: Duration);
   ...

PROTECTED
   METHOD getDuration() : time;
   ...

STATE
   name: STRING
   location: STRING;
   timeFrame: Interval;

UNIQUE
   id = name;

BODY
   METHOD getLocation: STRING;
   DO
       RETURN location;
   END DO;
   ...
END OBJECT;
```

The only differences between the transient declaration and the persistent declaration of Happening are the use of the keyword PERSISTENT and the UNIQUE part which lists unique clauses. A *unique clause* defines a set of instance variables which uniquely identify an instance of an object type. There cannot be two objects with the same values in all instance variables of their unique clause. In our example there cannot be two happenings with the same name.

Persistent objects are manipulated just like transient objects. However, unless they are explicitly deleted they survive the end of a program and are stored automatically in CoOMS, the OODBMS used to store persistent CooL objects. Objects are automatically retrieved when they are accessed. Persistent objects can be accessed just like transient objects through references, and they can be accessed directly using the FETCH statement or a query. In a FETCH statement you specify the values for a unique clause for a certain object type. The result is the object with that unique value. In a query you can specify a boolean expression. The result of a query is the set of objects of a certain object type for which the boolean expressions evaluate to true.

Accesses to persistent objects are only allowed within a transaction. With regard to persistent objects a transaction is an atomic operation. It either commits or it is rolled back, that is the transaction is executed as a whole or not at all. When a transaction is rolled back, all changes to persistent objects during the transaction are undone. A transaction is also used to sychronize two programs running in parallel and trying to access the same objects. Persistent objects accessed within a transaction are locked until the end of the transaction. CooL supports read and write locks. More than one program can own a read lock for the same object, but when a program owns a write lock for an object no other program can get a read or write lock (multiple readers, single writer). Transactions can be nested. In that case locks are held until the end of the outermost transaction. The following example illustrates the use of persistent objects in CooL.

```
METHOD DisplayOUPresenters();
DO
    printf ("The OU has the following presenters:\n");
    TRANSACTION
        FOR p IN Presenter | p.getCompany() = "Open University"
        LOOP
            printf ("%\n", p.getPresenter());
        END LOOP;
    END TRANSACTION
END DO:
```

4.3.8 Modules and separate compilation

A COOL program consists of one or more modules which may be developed independently and compiled separately from each other. Modules are *compilation units* with a well-defined interface. They are a means to structure large applications and provide separate name scopes and support development by teams. Each module consists of two compilation units, the *implementation module* and the *specification module*. The specification module represents the module's interface. It contains declarations of all entities which can be used by clients of the module. An implementation module contains the hidden implementation of the exported entities of the module. Other modules can (and have to) import whatever other modules export in their specification module.

As an example let us have a look at a module defining a tutorial. The interface consists of an exception, a constant and the interface and state of the object type representing a tutorial. (The state of the object type must be part of the specification module in order to inherit from the object type.) The specification also contains an IMPORT clause which states that all exported entities of the modules participant and presentation may be used in this specification. In this case, the object types Presentation, Presenter and Participant are defined and exported by the modules participant and presentation. The specification module looks as follows.

```
SPECIFICATION tutorial;
    IMPORT participant, presentation;
    EXCEPTION TutorialIsBookedOut;
    CONST MaxParticipants : INT = 50;
    TYPE Tutorial =
            Presentation OBJECT (IN iName: STRING,
                                    ...
                                 IN Presenter: Presenter)
    METHOD addParticipant;
        ...
    METHOD Display;
        ...
    STATE
        particpants: SET [Participant];
    END OBJECT;
END SPECIFICATION tutorial;
```

The corresponding implementation module contains the body of the object type. In general, an implementation module can contain any declaration. But it has to contain implementations at least for all exported declarations unless an exported declaration is a complete definition (as is the case for the constant and the exception declaration in our example). The corresponding implementation module for a tutorial looks as follows:

```
IMPLEMENTATION tutorial;
IMPORT participant, colibri, presentation;
IMPORT print FROM stdio;
TYPE Tutorial = OBJECT
     METHOD Display;
     DO
         printf ("\nT u t o r i a l...\n");
         printf ("name ....: %d\n", name);
         printf ("presenter: %s\n", presenter.getName());
         printf ("location : %s\n", location);
         printf ("time ....: %s\ - %s\n", time.start(), time.end());
     END DO;
     METHOD addParticipant (IN p: Participant);
     DO
         IF participants.Cardinality() < maxParticipants THEN
             participants.Include (p);
         ELSE
             RAISE TutorialIsBookedOut;
         END IF;
     END DO;
  END OBJECT;
END IMPLEMENTATION tutorial;
```

4.3.9 Language binding

CooL is designed to implement application systems. It cannot be expected that low-level system details are programmed in CooL, or that real-time or parallel problems are implemented using CooL. In a multi-language environment different languages should be used for different parts of an application. However, these parts have eventually to be integrated into one system.

CooL supports integration of components written in other languages by offering foreign imports and exports. Foreign imports and exports provide bindings to other languages compatible to C and are used in the same way as normal imports and exports in modules. They represent a type checked interface to imported variables and functions. In combination with the CooL type system, which offers corresponding types for all C types, CooL allows you to read and write external variables and to call external functions. In addition, you can define CooL procedures which can be called from external components like C functions.

4.3.10 Libraries

The CooL environment comes with a variety of predefined classes. The CoLibri library is an encapsulation of the C library. In addition, CooL provides basic types including BCD arithmetic, time-related classes (for time, duration, interval, date, etc.), a string variant, and container classes such as list, ordered list, map and set. Furthermore it provides interface classes for graphical user interfaces, printing jobs, relational databases and test facilities.

4.4 The CooL environment – an overview

In this section[2] we look at the COOL system, which is a complete programming environment specifically designed to support the professional development of large-scale object-oriented application systems. Figure 4.4 depicts a typical COOL development scenario.

The COOL environment comes with a number of tools to support the development of applications with COOL. For debugging purposes the COOL environment provides MaX, a convenient COOL and C source-code debugger. MaX offers the functionality of the Unix *sdb* debugger and is able to process (un)conditional breakpoints, tracepoints, to resolve inheritance, to dereference pointers, *etc.* Additionally, MaX provides command history and re-execution of a history, named command sequences, and an online help facility.

For quality assurance and testing purposes the COOL environment comes with the *test object interface* (TOI). The TOI provides a run-time frame with a command-line interface into which you can integrate any object type. The object type's methods can be executed via the command-line interface providing the arguments interactively. During execution, both intermediate results and the arguments may be recorded and used subsequently as compare targets when running this test battery automatically.

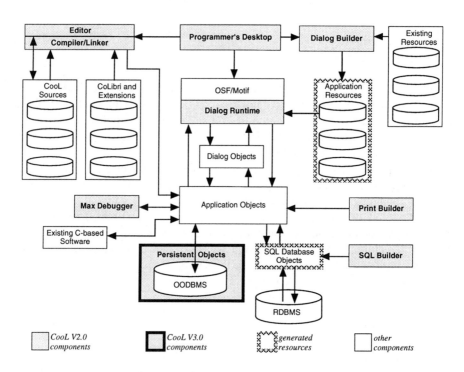

Figure 4.4   The COOL environment.

[2] Parts of this section are excerpts from [Müller, 1993].

CooL supports the development of application systems with graphical user interfaces based on OSF X/Motif. These interfaces may be constructed interactively using the Dialog Builder. A *dialog object interface*, DOI, is available to integrate an application with the run-time system of X/Motif. This interface abstracts from the X/Motif primitives. The DOI is, of course, sufficiently open to allow use of the full functionality of the X/Motif toolkit in addition to the DOI abstraction.

The *SQL object interface* (SOI) is provided to integrate object-oriented applications with a relational database system. This interface offers access to SQL tables via a generated *object type interface*. Access is defined by an explicit description from which a CooL object type for managing the table is generated. This interface is independent of the underlying database systems. This guarantees interoperability of the application in a heterogeneous database system environment. The first product release supports IN-FORMIX as the database system offered by Siemens Nixdorf. Later releases will also support ORACLE.

Last but not least, the *print object interface* (POI) enables an explicit description to be made of forms, lists and reports to be printed on printing devices. The programmatic interface conceals the cumbersome tasks involved, thus relieving the developer of managing print formats (pages, headers, repeating groups), spoolers and devices.

4.4.1 Availability

CooL V2.0 as described in this chapter is available on all Siemens Nixdorf Unix platforms running SINIX 5.41 and higher versions. The current version, V1.0, provides all features of V2.0 except garbage collection, generic object types and modules. Additional software prerequisites for CooL are OSF/Motif V1.13 (if you want to use the dialog builder and the DOI interface) and the INFORMIX V4.x/5.0 database system (if you want to use the SOI interface to access a relational database). We recommend that at least 8MB of core memory be available on your system. A version is also available for SINIX ODT V1.5.

CooL V2.0 will also be available on PCs running Windows NT.

It is possible to port CooL to other Unix platforms, and this can be carried out on request. Experience has shown that porting the CooL compiler, the CoLibri library and the interface classes takes only a few hours (*e.g.* to a Sun Sparc station). The components (MaX, the dialog builder, *etc.*) are not easily portable since they are platform-dependent. However, if your interest is centred on the portability of your applications, this restriction should not bother you. Because CooL produces very portable ANSI C code, an application port is always very easy.

4.5 Conclusion

The previous sections have presented the CooL design criteria, the CooL language and the supporting development environment, which have been built following the design criteria as closely as possible. You should now be in a position to anwer the two main questions on choosing a language. Who should use CooL? Where should CooL be used? If the answers to the who and the where describe an environment where you intend to use a language you should use CooL. If not, you could still use CooL. But in that case you would not get the whole benefit of the language; there should be other languages better suited for your specific environment.

4.6 Postscript

When I wrote this chapter as a paper for the workshop in the summer of 1993 it was planned to develop COOL V3.0 (*i.e.* COOL with persistence) as soon as COOL V2.0 was running. However, by April 1994 SNI had decided not to fund the COOL project any longer. So it seems very unlikely that COOL V3.0 is going to be developed. Instead, the project will develop a 'meagre' version of COOL V2.0 (probably without garbage collection) and put it into the public domain.

So maybe there is another conclusion to draw: even for a big company it is very difficult to develop a new language which can be commercially successful. So everybody should think twice before planning to develop their own language just because no existing one is quite right.

4.7 References

Ader, M., McMahon, S., Müller, G., Nierstrasz, O. and Pröfrock, A. K. (1990), The ITHACA technology: a landscape for object-oriented application development, in *ESPRIT '90, Conference Proceedings*, Netherlands, Kluwer Academic Publishers.

Atkinson, M. P., Bailey, P. J., Chisholm, K. J., Cockshott, P. W. and Morrison, R. (1983), An approach to persistent programming, *Computer Journal*, **26**(4).

CooL (1992), *CooL V1. 0 Language Reference Manual*, Munich.

DeRemer, F. and Kron, H. K. (1976), Programming in the large versus programming in the small, *IEEE Transactions on Software Engineering*, **SE-2**(2), 80–6.

Müller, G. (1993), CooL – An Introduction (ITHACA internal paper).

Object Management Group (1992), *Object Management Architecture Guide*.

5 C++ as an introductory programming language

P. A. Lee and R. J. Stroud

In this chapter we report our experience at the University of Newcastle-upon-Tyne of the familiar problem of choosing an introductory programming language. In an ever-moving subject such as computer science, the problem comes around regularly, although it is perhaps not acted upon as often as it should be. We will discuss some of the factors that led us at Newcastle to decide to change to C++ as our introductory teaching language. Any department that has recently changed its programming language is likely to have spent as much time and effort on this decision process as we did, and will probably sympathize with many of the arguments and points to be considered, if not with our final language choice!

5.1 Introduction

It is not the aim of this chapter to present a detailed technical case for the C++ language. That in itself would require a complete book – indeed, there are as many textbooks on C++ as there are opinions about various aspects of the language! Instead, we concentrate on the reasons for our decision to switch from PASCAL to C++ as our introductory teaching language at Newcastle. First we present the background of the programming course at Newcastle and some of the problems that the previous course was facing, followed in section 5.3 by a description of the new approach that was proposed for the course. There were several candidate programming languages that could have been used to support this new teaching approach. The evaluation criteria for the languages and the candidate languages themselves are given in section 5.4, and a brief summary of the perceived advantages and disadvantages of each language is presented in section 5.5. The reasons for choosing C++ are given next, followed by some of the experiences of using C++ for the first time. Finally, section 5.8 presents some conclusions.

5.2 Background

It is necessary to present some background information about the Newcastle course and the students who take the course since these factors have some bearing on our eventual language choice. Historically, an imperative programming language has been used as the initial teaching language on introductory programming courses at Newcastle, starting with ALGOL-60 and ALGOL-W, changing to PASCAL in 1981 and remaining with that language for the next 11 years.

During their first year at Newcastle, all students in the Faculty of Science are required to take three courses, one of which can be the first-year computing science course, CS1. In its most recent form, CS1 is a two-semester course consisting of two modules: the first module introduces programming and the features of a programming language whilst the second module concentrates on data structures and algorithms, introducing additional programming language features such as pointers as required. Computing science students (and others) take the whole of CS1 which accounts for one third of their workload, whilst a much wider range of students from other degree courses only take the first module from CS1 which is used as an introductory programming course. This latter group of students may not take further computing courses during their time at university although they may continue to write and use programs. Furthermore, within each group of students there is a considerable spread of previous computing experience, from those who have never programmed before to those who (unfortunately) have previous experience of programming (and think they know it all!). Over the years the proportion who have programmed before has increased significantly, although not sufficiently to have prior experience as a prerequisite for the course. Finally, there is a separate intensive programming course for students taking a 1-year MSc conversion course – as these students subsequently take selected courses from the undergraduate degree, it is necessary for the same programming language to be adopted for these MSc students. Note also that mathematics A-level[1] is not a requirement for studying computer science at Newcastle.

In an ideal world, different languages and courses would be used for the different groups of students. However, the usual resource restrictions (equipment, documentation and lecturing) prevent the adoption of this idealized strategy, and consequently a single language is needed for all the students and courses mentioned above in order to make efficient use of our resources. An additional benefit of adopting a single-language approach is that it allows flexibility in switching between degree courses during the first year.

A feature of the old CS1 course was that the nuts-and-bolts of programming were taught in a bottom-up fashion – introducing language features and then showing how to use those features. However, we observed in later years that students who had taken

---

[1] In the U.K. 'A-level' is the highest pre-university examination level.

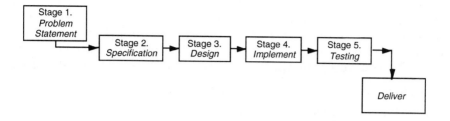

Figure 5.1   Software project stages.

CS1 were not very proficient in three areas: (i) software engineering, (ii) problem solving and (iii) software design. Looking at the approach taken by the old CS1 course towards the five main stages that can be considered to represent the overall process of 'software production' as outlined in Figure 5.1, it is hardly surprising that the students had these deficiencies. The course started by teaching language features to support stage 4, yet the practical sessions started by giving the students problems to solve at stage 1. The students already had difficulties in understanding the problems at stage 1 and the language features required to solve them at stage 4, without the additional complication of appreciating that they had to reach stage 4 via a more structured approach to problem solving (*i.e.* involving stage 3, design, at least!).

Of course, there is something of a 'chicken-and-egg' problem here. It is difficult to instil the importance of the design (problem-solving) stage if the basic programming concepts that are needed to refine the design into the implementation are unknown, especially if students are impatient to start 'real programming'! Thus, you have to cover language features early in an introductory course and neglect the important design stage, which was what happened with the old course. This problem is not helped by languages like PASCAL that only provide language support for functional abstraction and encourage a monolithic (single source-file) problem solution.

We realized, therefore, that it was not just a new programming language that was required. It was also important that a different approach to teaching programming be adopted to try to solve the problems described above. Furthermore, this new teaching approach had to be decided upon first because it would have an impact on the choice of programming language; an important factor in the choice of a programming language for teaching purposes should be how well the language supports the chosen teaching approach. The teaching approach we chose is the subject of the next section.

5.3 Goals and approach to teaching programming

Before deciding how we should approach the teaching of programming, we felt it was necessary to define what we thought the product of the CS1 course should actually be: were we aiming to turn out students with proficiency in one language, proficiency in programming in general, proficiency in software engineering, or all of the above? It is clear that all of these goals are important, yet none of them can be completely achieved in the lecture and practical time available.

We therefore decided that the product of the course should effectively be *apprentice software engineers* – using the term 'apprentice' in the traditional engineering sense of someone who is still learning their craft, understands the basic tools and techniques which form that craft, but requires considerable experience in applying those tools and techniques before the term 'apprentice' can be dropped (to be replaced by 'BSc'!). Thus, we expected that by the end of the full first-year CS1 course students should have:

- an awareness of the overall software engineering process;
- some basic ideas about problem solving;
- some experience of 'designing in the small' (*i.e.* abstraction);
- proficiency in an imperative programming language;
- some experience of using a basic 'tool bag' of computer science ideas, algorithms, tools and techniques.

It is worth commenting on one of our objectives for the CS1 course, namely that students should be proficient in an *imperative* programming language. Early in our debates, we discussed whether to start with a traditional imperative language or to introduce a functional language first. Each approach had its proponents and we were aware that other computing science departments had decided to take the functional language approach. However, we felt that a functional approach was not appropriate for the mix of students taking our course and we were not aware of any convincing evidence for the success of such an approach, so the idea was abandoned quite quickly.

Whilst thinking about the means for achieving our teaching goals, a set of computer science buzzwords and principles naturally came to mind: abstract data types (ADTs), classes, objects, encapsulation, *etc.* Since these terms mean slightly different things to different people, we will state our definitions:

ADT: an ADT describes a type in terms of its behaviour (a set of operations that can be applied to instances of that type) rather than its data representation.

Encapsulation: the enforced separation between the interface to a type (as seen by a programmer using that type) and the representation of the type (as seen by the programmer who implements it).

Class: a mechanism for implementing an ADT in an object-oriented programming language.

Object: an instance of a class.

Object-oriented programming languages extend ADTs with the notions of inheritance and dynamic binding but we felt that the use of ADTs was the key to achieving our goals for the first-year course. ADTs provide a basic mechanism for design-through-abstraction, and for separating issues of use from those of implementation. If ADTs are supported by the programming language used for teaching, then the goals of teaching programming and 'design in the small' can be combined.

Other features of object-oriented programming such as inheritance and dynamic binding are also important and can be tackled in second- and third-year computer science courses (together with other programming paradigms such as functional and logic programming). However, we felt that these language concepts were unnecessary for first-year students, especially for those who do not continue in computer science. Such students would still benefit from an ADT approach though, because the ideas behind ADTs enforce good software practice and can be adopted in programs written in more traditional languages too.

We also felt that using ADTs could help the students to understand the problems they were set in practical classes. In particular, we felt that the initial programming projects used to allow students to experiment with writing their own programs could be expressed in terms of recognizable graphical objects that their programs had to manipulate – for instance, ADTs representing a compact disc player, a car being driven around the screen, a metro ticket machine, a video player, *etc.* We could provide such graphical ADTs and students would hopefully have no difficulty understanding what they represented. Thus, they could concentrate on writing a program to control a CD player (for example) rather than having to write a program to perform some meaningless computation such as finding prime numbers (and getting bogged down with the intricacies of textual I/O).

Defining our new teaching approach was the easy part. The difficult part was in choosing and getting agreement on the best programming language to support this approach, and this is the subject of the next section.

5.4 Choice of programming languages

There are many interrelated issues that can be considered in choosing programming languages for teaching. The main criteria that we considered for language evaluation were the following:

1. vehicle for supporting first-year teaching;

2. availability of suitable textbooks – both reference books and introductory books (ideally) supporting the teaching approach;

3. usefulness for second- and third-year computing courses;

4. usefulness for students who do not continue with computer science but may continue to use computers;

5. usefulness and acceptability to the real world;

6. longevity;

7. availability.

The reasons for the first two criteria are obvious but some of our other criteria are worth discussing further.

As mentioned earlier, the first-year class contains a wide variety of students, and we cannot separate those who will continue with computer science courses from those who will not (especially because of the flexible policy at Newcastle that allows students to transfer between courses during their first year). This in itself raises another issue: should we consider one language for the first-year programming course, and switch to another language for computer science courses in later years? This issue was discussed at length and it was concluded that using one programming language from day one through to the end of the degree course as the main language for practical work was most preferable. This is not to say that computer science students should only ever be exposed to a single language – far from it. But it was felt that there were significant advantages for the students in having three years' exposure to one language, and advantages for the degree course in not having to spend time introducing another language in detail for years 2 and 3.

For second- or third-year students not continuing with computer science, it would be ideal if the initial teaching language was also one that they could use subsequently, that is one with potentially wide availability in the university.

Real-world acceptability is a factor we perhaps used to care little about, witness the earlier use of ALGOL and PASCAL, but that attitude does seem to be changing. For one group of our students, namely the MSc conversion students, it is a particularly important issue. These masters students only have twelve months to gain proficiency in computing, and being able to have an industrially accepted language on their *curriculum vitae* is a significant consideration for them. Similar issues affect the undergraduates, as was perhaps evidenced by the number of students who were doing final-year projects in C++ even though their primary language was PASCAL.

The longevity issue concerns the length of time the chosen language will be useful in its teaching role, a constraint because of the effort needed to change the main teaching language (and also linked to the availability issue).

Availability is the usual practical consideration of equipment and costs. Some languages are only available as commercial offerings, and these offerings rarely encompass the odd-ball set of equipment that students use within our department. Gone are the days when a department produced its own language, compiler and run-time system. In our case, availability was a particular problem because due to historical choices we had an unconventional set of hardware that did not include any of the platforms that commercial language implementations are usually targeted at (*e.g.* PCs, popular models of Unix workstation). This effectively restricted our choice of languages to those for which we could obtain the source code of an implementation that we could port to our own platforms.

The main features we were looking for in the language to be used to support first-year teaching were the following:

- support for abstract data types;
- parameterized types (*e.g.* to support *Stack of T*);
- control abstractions (procedures, loops, exception handling, *etc.*);
- orthogonality;
- minimal 'magic';
- minimal pitfalls;
- ability to teach the full language rather than a subset.

With these features in mind, a list of five candidate languages was drawn up: MODULA-2, MODULA-3, ADA, EIFFEL and CLU. Most of these candidates are obvious, given the factors discussed above. CLU was included primarily to give a benchmark for comparing the other languages' support for ADTs, even though we recognized that CLU was unlikely to be a prime candidate. It is interesting to note, given our eventual choice, that C++ was not on this first list of candidates. Significant consideration of the other languages and identification of their deficiencies against our criteria took place before it was suggested that C++ should at least be considered. If any of the other candidate languages had been a clear front-runner, then C++ would never have been considered. However, we perceived significant deficiencies with the ADT support provided by the other candidate languages and this led us to consider the wider set of related issues described above. As a result, we introduced C++ into the set of candidates, realized it had excellent support for ADTs, and eventually recommended it as the language of choice.

5.5 Evaluation of candidate languages

Even though the desired criteria for the language choice had been identified, evaluating the various languages with respect to those criteria remained a difficult task. Each language was studied and used (if possible), seminars about their relative strengths and weaknesses were given, and an example of a typical ADT, a 'stack of integers', was coded up in each of the languages to show the interface to the ADT, a test program that used the ADT, and the code that implemented the ADT. The purpose of this comparison was to assess how easy it would be for students to use our ADTs and implement their own ADTs in each of the various languages. Once we had completed these evaluations, we then tried to rank the candidate languages in order based on our subjective feelings about each one.

It is impossible within the constraints of this chapter to detail all of the technical discussions that took place (even if we could now remember them all!). Suffice it to say that most of the important issues were the subject of protracted arguments. It is also true to say that there were inevitable differences in opinion as to whether feature x in language Y was better or worse than the same feature in language Z. However, a brief summary of the main advantages and disadvantages we perceived for each language is given in Table 5.1.

Table 5.2 is an attempt to summarize the results of our evaluations. Taking all of the factors into account, it can be seen that C++ has the most ticks against it (although some of the ticks are also crosses – '✗✓' in the table indicates both advantages and disadvantages). However, it is probably worth mentioning that ADA was a close runner-up. The main factors against ADA were our concerns about its suitability for second- and third-year teaching (in particular, its lack of support for object-oriented programming as opposed to simple encapsulated data types) and the fact that ADA compilers were either not available or too expensive for the hardware platforms we use for teaching. We are certainly aware of other computer science departments that use ADA successfully as an introductory teaching language.

5.6 Why C++?

We unsuccessfully tried various ways of coming to a quantitative decision on a language choice based on our evaluation criteria. In attempting this we thus realized that perhaps there was no ideal candidate language, and hence any recommendation would have to be a compromise choice, based on some subjective weighting of all of the factors identified above.

We were not surprised when many people's reaction to the inclusion of C++ was that its disadvantages were such as to make it a non-starter. That was the initial reaction of most of those performing the evaluation, for the following kinds of reasons:

Table 5.1   Main features of languages

MODULA-2
- ✓ small simple language, with few pitfalls
- ✓ fixes PASCAL deficiencies
- ✓ can teach all of the language
- ✗ old, dead language (1979)
- ✗ limited support for ADTs
- ✗ no exceptions or parameterized types
- ✗ limited use for second- and third-year courses

MODULA-3
- ✓ a modern version of MODULA-2
- ✓ exceptions
- ✗ 'hybrid' language – too much mechanism
- ✗ encapsulation of ADTs via modules relies on stylized programming conventions
- ✗ limited and overly complex support for ADTs
- ✗ parameterized types would be cumbersome to use
- ✗ would not teach all of the language

ADA (83)
- ✓ parameterized types
- ✓ exception handling
- ✗ big, middle-aged language; cannot teach it all
- ✗ average support for ADTs
- ✗ exceptions not tied to operations
- ✗ no support for object-oriented programming

CLU
- ✓ best support for ADTs
- ✓ exception handling and parameterized types
- ✗ old language (1977)
- ✗ not a viable candidate

EIFFEL
- ✓ modern object-oriented language with sophisticated environment
- ✓ parameterized types
- ✓ orthogonal
- ✗ average support for ADTs
- ✗ single-paradigm language (just objects)
- ✗ minimalist philosophy
- ✗ peculiar syntax for array indexing
- ✗ unconventional exception handling model
- ✗ would not teach all of the language

C++
- ✓ good support for ADTs
- ✓ exception handling (soon)
- ✓ parameterized types
- ✗ underlying C model must be avoided – many potential pitfalls
- ✗ all mechanism, no policy
- ✗ would not teach all of the language

- too many pitfalls from the underlying C language model;
- lack of compile-time checking;
- ease with which students can 'hang' themselves;
- complexity of C++ mechanism;
- peculiar syntax.

If you believe that C++ is just C with even more bells and whistles, then the above reasons are understandable. This, however, is not the case. It has to be realized that C++ is a very different language from C, and while compatibility with C was a design goal for C++, many things have also changed for the better. Compiler support is vastly different from the days of pre-ANSI C; a modern C++ compiler will apply strong type-checking rules by default, and provide reasonable diagnostic messages. Nevertheless, in the complete C++ language there are many complications and pitfalls for the unwary. We did not propose that the full language be taught in the first year, but that a carefully selected subset be chosen and applied consistently, and we believed that this would help avoid many of the obvious pitfalls.

C++ has very good support for ADTs. Ignoring CLU (which we did not consider to be a feasible choice), C++ came top in our evaluation of support for ADTs. This is perhaps not surprising as Bjarne Stroustrup, the original designer of C++, came from a SIMULA 67 background and carefully designed the language to have all of the right things for ADT support including: encapsulation, value semantics, initialization, operator overloading, control over copying semantics (*e.g.* assignment operator overloading), and extensible I/O.

As a language, C++ is an engineering compromise, and its choice of features reflects its design objective of being used for real software engineering in real-world systems (so it should be of some applicability to computer science students!). However, these features are not necessarily compatible with those required for first-year teaching for a wide group of students.

Teaching a subset of a language provides a partial solution to the problem of avoiding unwanted features, but there are still problems with such approaches. Textbooks are one such problem since books reflect the 'real' language rather than the sanitized bits of it we may wish to teach. Another problem from subsetting is the possibility of strange compilation errors caused by the student accidentally stumbling on a language

Table 5.2   Overall language comparison

Language	1st Year	2nd & 3rd Year	Real World	Other Dept.	Books	Long-evity	Avail-ability
Modula-2	✓	✗	✗	✓	✓	✗	✗✓
Modula-3	✗	✓	✗	✗	✗	✗	✓
Eiffel	✗✓	✓	✗	✗	✗	?	✗
Ada	✓	✗	✓	✓	✓	✓	✗
CLU	✓	✗	✗	✗	✗	✗	✗✓
C++	✗✓	✓	✓	✓	✗✓	✓	✓

feature we have been avoiding. This would have been a problem for all of the candidate languages except MODULA-2. So, unpalatable features cannot be completely hidden from the students – if they look, they can find them.

Availability of compilers was not an issue for C++ which is widely available on both Unix and non-Unix platforms alike. (In contrast, availability of compilers for EIFFEL and ADA on our existing first-year equipment was a serious problem for us.) Although the equipment used in our department is largely Unix-based, some of the best environments for C++ are on PC and Macintosh platforms and this is important for students who have their own machines and want to work at home. Within the department, we expected to use the standard AT & T Cfront Release 3 compiler for which we held a source licence. The GNU implementation of C++ is also widely available but we felt that Cfront's diagnostic error messages were superior and that GNU conformed less to emerging standards.

Note also that there are many books on C++. This is an advantage for students because it gives them different views on language features. Unfortunately, many books are targeted at the C programmer wishing to move to C++ and hence are not suitable for introductory teaching. Introductory books that teach C++ as a first programming language are now becoming available but none of them introduces objects and classes as early as we would wish. Choosing a suitable textbook for the algorithms and data structures part of the course was a particular problem at first since almost all of the texts available were based on PASCAL. Again, this situation has now changed, and there are several possibilities to choose from. ADA and MODULA-2 are the only languages for which textbooks would not have been a problem.

Of course we were aware of several deficiencies with C++. Certain aspects of C++ syntax are notoriously unreadable and error-prone but despite a certain compactness of notation it is perfectly possible to write readable C++ programs by conforming to a good style. (Students can write unreadable programs in any language!) Another problem with C++ syntax and semantics is that it is perfectly possible to write code that is legal but almost certainly not what you intended. A good C++ compiler will warn about questionable constructs and in practice this has proved to be less of a problem than might be imagined. More seriously, most C++ implementations have no run-time checking, for array bounds in particular, and no proper boolean type. These problems were solved by providing our own set of ADTs (for arrays, strings and booleans)[2] which provided the features we felt were vital for novice programmers. However, this does raise the textbook problem mentioned earlier, in that a student cannot use these books to find out about our ADTs (and worse, the student can learn about the less safe equivalents provided directly by C++ or by convention). Finally, although C++ clearly separates the representation of an ADT from its implementation, the visible interface to an ADT (*i.e.* the header file) has to contain details of the representation (the private variables), and this can be confusing to novice users of ADTs. We solved this problem to some extent by providing a simple Unix command for viewing the interface to our ADTs – this also permitted us to hide details of the directory structure in which our ADTs were stored.

C++ does have a lot of mechanism and not much policy (*cf.* EIFFEL), and there are potential pitfalls here. For example, ADTs can be implemented in a number of dif-

---

[2] The committee responsible for standardizing C++ has agreed to the inclusion of a built-in boolean type and is defining array and string classes for the standard C++ library.

ferent ways. Careful choice of features and teaching only those features in a stylized manner can help avoid these problems, but not eliminate them. However, one mechanism that C++ does not provide is garbage collection although it is possible to control the way in which objects are copied and thus implement simple reference-counting data structures. These language features were used in the implementation of the array and string class to manage storage allocation in a way that was transparent to students using these classes. The lack of garbage collection in C++ is not a serious problem for introductory programming (where it can be simply ignored) – but is something that needs to be discussed in the later years of a degree course.

We recognized that there were some risks associated with choosing C++ as our first-year teaching language. However, on balance, we felt that the potential gains outweighed those risks, and that, in any case, there was no obviously better candidate (although we hope one may emerge in the next five years or so!). Thus, C++ was our choice. The potential gains for our computer science students are three years' exposure to one language that can be used throughout their undergraduate career. For both our computer science students and the MSc students there is the advantage for getting employment that they have experience in a language that is becoming widely accepted in many parts of the industry. For non-computer science students, C++ is expected to be acceptable as a teaching language if used properly, but there is perhaps greater risk for these students.

The recommendation for C++ was not made lightly. Indeed, most if not all of those concerned with making the recommendation would have bet money at the start that their recommendation would not have been for C++. A decision to recommend C++ was initially considered only reluctantly, but we came to realize that some of our initial prejudices were false and that, on balance of all of the issues, C++ was the best compromise. It was recognized that this choice was not without risk, and there are criteria against which C++ does not turn out to be the best candidate, but nevertheless our recommendation stood.

5.7 Experiences using C++ as an initial teaching language

The switch to C++ was made for classes starting in October 1992. With hindsight, we do not regret our decision to choose C++ although our initial experiences caused us to rethink parts of the course and we continue to look for ways to improve the material we present.

For the purposes of any evaluation, it is important to realize that we changed four things simultaneously: our programming language, our teaching approach, the format of the examinations, and our equipment infrastructure. It is difficult in any evaluation to separate out the individual effects of these four changes.

From the teaching point of view, the language choice has been satisfactory, and has enabled us to introduce programming language features (*e.g.* statements, control-flow abstractions, basic types, I/O, simple data structures, classes) using ADTs to exemplify these features. However, we severely underestimated the time needed to present the material, especially because of the increased emphasis on software engineering and design in the small. In particular, there has not been time to introduce functions properly in the first term (30 hours of lectures), let alone explain how to write your own class definitions, and consequently this material has had to be fitted into the second half of the course, squeezing the material on algorithms and data structures quite significantly. (We expect that a new modularized course structure with 48 lecture hours per semester will improve matters and allow the material to be spread more evenly between the two halves of the course.)

When class definitions are introduced, students find the conceptual leap from functional abstraction to data abstraction very difficult, even though they have been using data abstractions for some time in the form of the ADTs we provide. In our first year, there was a significant 'drop-out' rate in practicals from this point onwards, perhaps because the projects we set expected too much. By scaling down the projects, we were able to address this problem in our second year of teaching the course. We also experimented by deliberately delaying the definition of classes until students had more experience of defining their own functions, but it is not clear that this made any difference.

The syllabus for the material on algorithms and data structures contained the usual topics and was taught in the following order in our first year: stacks, queues, pointers, lists, recursion, trees, sorting, searching. It was felt that the usual title of this course, 'Algorithms and data structures', reflected an artificial separation of two topics that could be combined using a more ADT-oriented approach, and some attempt was made to unify the material using the abstract notion of a collection. Parameterized data types (templates in C++, generics in ADA and EIFFEL) were used from the start with arrays providing motivation: if students can understand the concept of an 'array of something', they should have no difficulty with the concept of a 'stack, list or queue of something'.

In our first year, the material on pointers stressed the undesirable aspects of C++'s pointer semantics out of necessity but ended up being too negative. We have now reworked it to provide more motivation and put more stress on the idea of using a pointer to refer to something. We are also considering using a 'pointer-to-something' template that will give a better declaration syntax and provide run-time error-checking for C++ pointers (in much the same way that we have cleaned up C++ arrays and strings using substitute classes). Note, however, that many of the pointer manipulations needed for linked lists *etc.* are hidden in a list class that we provide to students. This class includes the ability to iterate along a list and insert and delete list elements selectively. A disadvantage of this approach is that students don't learn how to do these pointer operations for themselves from first principles. One way to address this problem is to show how to implement stacks and queues first using pointers directly and then using a list class.

In our second year, to delay the introduction of classes and give students more experience with functions, we brought forward the material on recursion, sorting and searching to rearrange the topics as follows: recursion, searching, sorting, classes, stacks, queues, lists, pointers. Note that we didn't introduce pointers until after we had explained how to use stacks, queues and lists, thus making a clean separation between use and implementation. However, this ordering of material has the disadvantage that sorting and searching algorithms that rely on data structures that have not yet been introduced (*e.g.* hash tables implemented as arrays of lists) cannot be treated properly.

Because of our need to teach a subset of C++, and because of the lack of directly suitable textbooks, we felt it was necessary to provide the students with detailed lecture notes which covered just those parts of the language that we wished to expose them to. This had the unfortunate side-effect that many students mistakenly decided that it was not worth their while attending lectures. We was also adopted a set of style rules which we expected the students to follow; it was based on accepted good practice in the C++ community and common sense. Official style guides for C++ are now emerging (*e.g.* [Cargill, 1992; Ellemtel, 1992]) but these tend to be too broad in scope for introductory programming.

Implementations of the C++ exception-handling mechanisms are only now beginning to become available (*e.g.* Borland 4.0, HP CC) so as yet we have been unable to use exceptions as we had hoped. We had anticipated that exceptions would be unavailable at first but we believed in the longer term that the specification of interfaces to ADTs would be much simplified when errors could be reported through exceptions rather than through other *ad hoc* mechanisms. However, there continues to be debate about whether exceptions will in fact have this simplifying effect, or whether it is another complication for novice programmers that can be well done without until later in the course. So far a simple error routine which terminates a running program with a message when an error has been detected has proved to be adequate. We had hoped to be able to provide a stack traceback routine for use in conjunction with this error routine, but this has yet to be implemented. We feel that a stack traceback is sufficient debugging information for novice programmers to use. We want to try to encourage them to think about their programs when they have gone wrong in order to deduce the fault, rather than encouraging them simply to 'tinker' with the program by means of an interactive debugger.

Some of the practical aspects of the course were also problematical. The strong type-checking provided by the C++ compiler was, in general, what was required for novice programmers, although sometimes implicit type conversions inserted by the compiler surprised even the 'experts'. However, not all error messages were reported in a form that novices could understand and some errors were reported as warnings. Compiler error reporting and recovery is perhaps the most serious practical problem faced. Another problem is that most C++ systems provide little in the way of run-time checks (not even checks for dereferencing null pointers!). As mentioned earlier, to overcome some of these problems, we provided ADTs for two of the types expected to cause the most trouble, namely strings and arrays, and built into those types the kind of error checking that is desirable (*e.g.* checking of array bounds). These ADTs certainly gave the level of protection that is necessary for novices and in this way we were able largely to avoid the dreaded 'memory fault – core dumped' messages that are so familiar to a novice (or expert!) C programmer.

The programming projects set in the first half of the course made heavy use of an ADT that simulated a compact disc player (CDPlayer). This meant that introductory programs could be expressed in terms of a recognizable real-world object (as discussed earlier in section 5.3). When a program declared an instance of the CDPlayer ADT, a graphical representation appeared on the screen, and operations on this object (*e.g.* open drawer, load disc, play) resulted in visible graphical changes on the screen (we didn't go as far as providing the music, fearing the effect of 40 versions of a Dire Straits album blasting out in the equipment rooms!). Many programming language features were then illustrated using the CDPlayer ADT – for instance, *if* statements were used to check for errors such as 'DISC NOT LOADED', and *for* loops were used to count the number of tracks on a compact disc. Deficiencies in our implementation of the CDPlayer class meant that it was not as much of a debugging help as had been hoped. Students came to view the CDPlayer as a nuisance rather than a convenience and didn't appreciate that the representation on the screen was intended to help them understand what their program was doing. Fixing those deficiencies should enable use of this ADT to achieve our objectives. Interestingly, even after the students had constructed C++ programs that performed a fairly complex set of operations on an instance of a CDPlayer (loading multiple discs, reading each disc to determine the number of tracks, changing the state of the player to show times and calculating average track lengths), and thus demonstrated proficiency in many of the language constructs we were teaching, some of them still wanted to know 'when they would start programming'! This is perhaps encouraging for those students who were initially scared of programming.

The programming projects set for the students in the later part of the course naturally required students to design their own ADTs and use ADTs that were provided and had been discussed in lectures. For example, students were expected to use a List class as the basis for the data structures required for a simulation of a Newsagency, and had to provide their own classes to represent Money, Publications and Customers. Whilst the complexity of these projects was felt to be similar to those set in previous years for PASCAL, the C++ solutions produced by the students were much longer in terms of the amount of code produced, which included the interface/header files, the class implementation files, and the main program. In addition, we required students to follow a more rigorous software-engineering approach, requiring early submission of a preliminary design and a fully tested version of one of the classes they had to write, complete with documentation and test harnesses. Thus, finishing the projects was a heavier demand on the students, and setting the same number of projects as we had expected of PASCAL students was a mistake. However, we would argue that although the students had to do more work to solve a problem, their solutions were 'better' (better design and better abstractions) than a PASCAL equivalent. The C++ solutions also gave more obvious applications of software re-use (re-using ADTs implemented previously), and the projects naturally tried to build up and re-use the work from previous projects. Getting the right balance between large programming projects and small exercises is quite difficult – one approach is to simplify projects by providing students with a class interface and asking them to provide an implementation in terms of a given data representation. However, exercises are still required so that students can practise basic concepts taught in lectures before putting them all together in a larger project.

The idea of submitting a preliminary design about a week into the project was to encourage students to think about the design of their solution before they started implementation and to make sure they understood the problem that had been set. Designs were discussed with students individually during practical sessions although this proved to be very time-consuming and caused a severe back-log to build up by the end of the week. We are now using the BSI structured flowcharting notation [ISO/IEC, 1989] as a design notation for programs, and this has worked very well. However, students find it much harder to grasp the idea of data abstraction for which we do not have a suitable design notation (although we use an informal convention for documenting a class interface). We have tried to teach object-based design by giving the students a chance to think about a problem for themselves, discussing it with them individually in practical classes, and then spending an entire lecture going over the solution we expected with the whole class. Students seemed to find this valuable, but in retrospect an appropriate design notation and more worked examples before the first project involving classes seem to be essential. Perhaps it is also too much to expect students to be able to design a class interface from scratch until they have had more experience with using and implementing classes whose interfaces we have designed.

The examinations at the end of the year are 'open-book' with two papers, one for each half of the course. Each paper consists of a series of short questions and some longer essay questions. The essay questions require the students to design a simple program or class, or illustrate how a particular data structure works. We have also experimented with some program comprehension questions. In contrast, the short questions are intended to test knowledge of C++ syntax and semantics and tend to have simple yes/no answers. A negative marking scheme is employed to penalize guessing, and students find this part of the exam quite tough. We have now modified the marking scheme so that short questions which require more thought and don't have simple yes/no answers are not negatively marked.

The examination and practical marks achieved by the students at the end of our first year were encouraging as far as evaluating the effects of teaching C++ were concerned. There was no obvious increase in the number of students wishing to give up (or being required to!). Indeed, the overall examination marks were no worse than those achieved in past years with PASCAL, although the practical marks were somewhat lower than normal, probably reflecting both the students' lack of prior experience in the language and the heavier demands of the projects as discussed above. This year we believe we have got the balance of practical work about right and the project marks reflect this. There is some evidence to suggest that students find the material in the second half of the course harder than the material in the first half of the course, but this may simply be because both courses are examined in June when the material from the first half has had longer to sink in. Next year, the two halves of the course will be taught as separate modules, examined at the end of each semester, and students will be required to pass both modules individually rather than on average. This may lead to a greater number of students having to resit material in September.

In our first year of teaching C++, the equipment provided for student use was a set of Macintoshes running A/UX which is an implementation of Unix that makes it possible to run Unix, MacOS and X11 applications on the same screen simultaneously! We chose this particular platform because it allowed us to combine the best of the Unix and Macintosh environments, but A/UX proved to be more problematical than we had expected and there were some severe performance problems. Unfortunately, we were unable to provide a nice integrated graphical C++ development environment for the students and had to make do with some simple shell scripts with textual output. This year we have abandoned A/UX and are using Symantec C++ under MacOS. This has provided us with a more homogeneous environment without the performance problems, and practical classes have run much more smoothly. Students tend to have PCs running TURBO C++ with Windows at home rather than Macintoshes but appear to have had little difficulty taking the source code of the classes we provide and getting it to run on a PC.

The critical comments we received from students at the end of the first year were hardly concerned with C++ and mostly focused on the problems with the equipment (primarily just login times) and the projects set. Indeed, the use of C++ was seen as a selling point for the course. While many students had experience of programming in an imperative language (some in C), none had used C++ before.

Did we achieve our 'apprentice software engineers' objective? This is very hard to determine, and until the first group of students have progressed through our computer science degree further we will have no real idea as to whether they are better at problem solving, abstraction, design and engineering than their predecessors. Some subjective reactions from staff at the practical classes are encouraging, as is the feedback from our second-year software-engineering group project, but time will tell.

5.8 Conclusions

Our initial experience with teaching C++ as an introductory language has been encouraging although there is still plenty of room for improvement. Although some students are put off programming and wish to transfer to degrees other than computer science at the end of their first year, the drop-out rate does not appear to be significantly different from when we taught PASCAL. We doubt that we could have accomplished the task of implementing our new teaching approach any better in any of the other candidate languages.

It is clear that any programming language which is intended for real-world software engineering will not be as suitable for teaching as a language designed specifically for that purpose, and the success of PASCAL as an introductory language is difficult to emulate with languages like C++. However, PASCAL is now looking very old-fashioned and does not support a modern object-oriented approach to teaching. There is no obvious replacement for PASCAL as a modern teaching language but there is a case for teaching students to use a 'real-world' language properly as we argued earlier.

Although C++ is widely used, and *de facto* standards exist, the C++ standardization committee is still hard at work. That is the good news, but the bad news seems to be the volume of paper that the standardization effort is producing, indicating the complexities and subtleties involved in many parts of the language. Whether these efforts will lead to significant changes in C++ remains to be seen, and whether these changes will be good or bad for introductory teaching purposes is a further concern. However, as a result of our initial experience of teaching C++, we believe that we have a clear idea of the parts of the language that are difficult for novices, and we intend to address these areas in the way we present the material in the future.

Acknowledgements

Thanks are due to Dan McCue, John Clowes, Martin McLauchlan and Chris Phillips, especially the last two who have suffered with us in the task of teaching C++.

5.9 References and annotated bibliography

Budd, T. A. (1994), *Classic Data Structures in C++*, Addison-Wesley, Reading, MA: goes slightly beyond a first year course and uses inheritance extensively but recommended to 1994 students.

Cargill, T. (1992), *Elements of C++ Programming Style*, Addison-Wesley, Reading, MA: an example of a style guide for C++.

Coplien, J. O. (1992), *Advanced C++ Programming Styles and Idioms*, Addison-Wesley, Reading, MA: good book, but too advanced for first-year students.

Deitel, H. M. and Deitel, P. J. (1994), *C++ How to Program*, Prentice-Hall: one of a number of introductory books on C++ now emerging onto the market.

Ellemtel (1992), *Programming in C++: Rules and Recommendations*, Ellemtel Telecommunications Systems Laboratory: many sensible style rules which University of Newcastle has adopted for their C++ course.

Friedman, F. L. and Koffman, E. B. (1994), *Problem Solving, Abstraction and Design using C++*, Addison-Wesley, Reading, MA: the title is tailor-made for the University of Newcastle course although the contents could be improved; was recommended for 1994 students.

Graham, N. (1991), *Learning C++*, McGraw-Hill, New York: a little known book that was used as the introductory text for 1992 students, but assumes some familiarity with a previous language (*e.g.* C).

ISO/IEC JTC 1 (1989), *ISO/IEC 8631: Information technology – Program constructs and conventions for their representation*, ISO/IEC, Geneva, 2nd edition.

Lippman, S. (1991), *C++ Primer*, Addison-Wesley, Reading, MA, 2nd edition: difficult text; covers many aspects of the language as well as any book, but not a first year text.

Meyers, S. (1992), *Effective C++ : 50 Simple Ways to Improve your Programs and Designs*, Addison-Wesley, Reading, MA: less advanced than Coplien and full of good advice but not a first year text.

Sedgewick, R. (1992), *Algorithms in C++*, Addison-Wesley, Reading, MA: recommended book for the algorithms and data structures part of the course in 1992 and 1993 but perhaps more of a second year book.

Stroustrup, B. (1991), *The C++ Programming Language*, Addison-Wesley, Reading, MA, 2nd edition: includes C++ language reference manual as an appendix; some good descriptions of OO design; covers many subtle and difficult points; not a beginner's book, but an essential reference.

5.10 Appendix – A stack example

The following appendix contains a stack example. In lectures, students are shown several different implementations of a stack, but here we will just show an implementation based on an array class that students are taught to use instead of C++ built-in arrays. Because an array is used instead of a list, each instance of a stack has a fixed capacity that must be specified when it is created. However, we have written the code so that if no size is specified, a default size is used.

In C++, it is usual to put interfaces in header files and keep implementations separate. However, a C++ class definition must include details of its internal data representation, even though this is not accessible to a client of the class. In lectures we emphasize the distinction between a class interface and a class definition, and support this in practical sessions by providing a simple tool that prints out the interface to a class. The output that this tool would produce for the Stack class would look like this:

```
template <class T>
class Stack
{
public:
// constructor
    Stack ( int size = DEFAULT );
// operations
    void      push ( T value ) ;
    T      top () ;
    void      pop () ;
    Boolean   isEmpty () ;
};
```

The full contents of the Stack header file (below) are rather more complex. The first two lines are a convention used to guard against multiple inclusion of the header file. Then the interfaces required for the types used in the Stack type definition are included. Finally, the entire class definition for Stack follows, including both the public and the private part of the class:

```
#ifndef STACK_H
#define STACK_H
#include "Boolean.h"
#include "Array.h"

// Stack class implemented using a dynamic Array class

const int DEFAULT = 10;
template <class T>
class Stack
{

public:
// constructor
    Stack ( int size = DEFAULT );

// operations
    void      push ( T value ) ;
    T      top () ;
    void      pop () ;
    Boolean   isEmpty () ;

private:
// representation
    int      sp ;
    Array<T> stack ;
};

#endif
```

The implementation of the various Stack operations is to be found in a different file. Note the use of a class prefix to define each member function inside class scope. Run-time errors such as stack overflow are reported using a special error routine that we provided.

```
#include "Stack.h"
#include "Error.h"

template <class T>
Stack<T>::Stack ( int size ) : stack(size)
{
    sp = 0;
}

template <class T>
void Stack<T>::push ( T value )
{
    if ( sp < stack.length() )
    {
        stack[sp] = value;
        sp = sp + 1;
    }
    else
    {
        error("Stack overflow");
    }
}

template <class T>
T Stack<T>::top ()
{
    return stack[sp-1];
}

template <class T>
void Stack<T>::pop ()
{
    if ( sp > 0 )
    {
        sp = sp - 1;
    }
    else
    {
        error("Stack underflow");
    }
}

template <class T>
Boolean Stack<T>::isEmpty ()
{
    return (sp == 0);
}
```

As an example of a program making use of the Stack ADT, consider the use of a Stack to reverse a list of name/address pairs supplied as input to a program. A Person ADT is defined to represent the input data using the String ADT, which like Array is taught as a replacement for C++'s native string-handling facilities which are rather low-level and error-prone. As a matter of good style and to simplify the use of templates, the Person ADT is defined in a separate header file although this is not essential:

```
#ifndef PERSON_H
#define PERSON_H
#include "String.h"
```

```
// define a structure to represent a person

struct Person
{
    String    name;
    String    address;
};

#endif
```

Finally, the main program which declares a stack of Person objects and uses a simple input loop to read each Person object and push it onto the stack. When all the data has been read in, the contents of the stack are popped and printed out in turn. The net effect is to reverse the order of the input data. Note the use of user-defined I/O operators to simplify the reading and writing of Person objects. These could have been provided as part of the interface to a more general Person ADT in which case their declaration would have appeared in the Person.h header file.

```
#include <iostream.h>
#include "Stack.h"
#include "Person.h"

// define some I/O operators for Person objects

istream& operator >> ( istream& in, Person& p )
{
    in >> p.name;
    in >> p.address;
    return in;
}

ostream& operator << ( ostream& out, Person p )
{
    out << p.name << " " << p.address;
    return out;
}

// program to read in a list of people and print in reverse order

void main ()
{
    Person       p;
    Stack<Person>  stack;

    // loop to read Person objects from standard input until EOF
    while ( cin >> p )
    {
        stack.push(p);
    }


    // loop to pop contents of stack until empty
    while ( ! stack.isEmpty() )
    {
        p = stack.top();
        stack.pop();
        cout << p << endl;
    }
}
```

6 Using the Turing language across the curriculum

Richard C. Holt, Spiros Mancoridis and David A. Penny

There are a number of programming languages and tools available to educators for teaching programming to undergraduate computer science students. Although efforts have been made to integrate these languages and tools into programming environments, these environments generally do not have all of the ingredients that would make them useful at all levels of a typical undergraduate curriculum.

Current technology used in most undergraduate courses is suitable for teaching students how to code in a particular programming language. Software development tools for activities other than coding such as requirements analysis, design, maintenance, and so on, are not provided. In addition, most programming languages in current use cannot be used in both beginner and advanced courses.

We describe a 'curriculum-cycle' approach to teaching programming, based on the TURING language and its extension to object-oriented TURING (OOT), and elaborate on our related pedagogical experience at all levels of our university's undergraduate curriculum.

6.1 Current practice

We shall refer to the 'curriculum cycle' as three categories of undergraduate computer science courses that require students to write programs. The following itemizes these categories and lists some typical courses found in each.

- *introductory:* basic programming, data structures;
- *intermediate:* programming languages, software engineering;
- *advanced:* operating systems, compilers.

Courses in each of these stages require students to write programs using languages, such as PASCAL and C, and tools, such as editors and compilers. There are three major problems with the current state of technology of programming languages and tools used in undergraduate courses:

1. A *lack of tool integration*, which is the case in the Unix environment but not in PC environments such as Borland's TURBO systems, makes software development tedious and error-prone. A well-known error which is caused by a lack of tool integration occurs when users, unknowingly, edit the same source file under two editor sessions and lose code after saving both files. Integrated program development environments are designed to prevent such inconveniences.

2. The *lack of tools for programming activities other than coding*. Environments like TURBO-PASCAL provide good support for writing code, with integrated tools for editing, compiling, debugging, and so on. Educators, however, now recognize that programming involves more than writing code. Hence, the emphasis on software engineering [Clifton, 1991] and object-orientation [Temte, 1991] in undergraduate curricula. As a result, educators are beginning to use programming environments in conjunction with software development C. A. S. E.[1] tools such as Excelerator [ITC, 1987] in their courses [Granger, 1991].

3. The *proliferation of programming languages and tools* used in the curriculum cycle. The diverse nature of undergraduate curricula in computer science demands a wide range of programming language support. Students are exposed to a variety of programming languages such as PASCAL for introductory programming, MODULA-2 for concurrent programming, C for systems programming, and SMALLTALK or C++ for object-oriented programming. The proliferation of programming languages, environments, and C. A. S. E. tools in undergraduate curricula impose an overload of syntax on both educators and students. Our limited teaching time is wasted introducing new syntax rather than new concepts.

A solution to these problems requires an approach that provides a wide range of language support under a common syntax, combined with an integrated collection of coding and C. A. S. E. tools. Such an approach could be used across the curriculum for teaching programming at all levels in an undergraduate programme in computer science.

6.2 A curriculum-cycle approach

Since 1983 at the University of Toronto, we have successfully taught programming subjects using the TURING programming language. We have used the TURING software on a variety of platforms, including the PC, Macintosh and Unix. The basic TURING software system has been quite successful for the introductory courses in that it provides a convenient integrated system for editing, compiling, executing and debugging programs. For our higher-level courses, we used an extension of TURING, called

---

[1] Computer aided software engineering.

TURING PLUS, whose Unix environment is much like that of C compilers under Unix: namely, the student uses a conventional editor such as 'vi' and standard tools such as the standard Unix linker.

In 1991, we developed the OOT (object-oriented TURING) programming environment. This environment is designed to be used in many courses of our undergraduate curriculum. It is simple enough to be used by students in introductory classes, yet sophisticated enough to be used in courses involving systems and object-oriented programming. The environment combines the efficiency and conceptual simplicity of a TURBO environment, while supporting programming language and tool facilities needed across the curriculum.

We believe that ingredients of an integrated environment for teaching programming should include:

- broad language support;
- integrated tools;
- consistent user interface;
- efficient and portable implementation.

In the following sections we will discuss how OOT satisfies our criteria for a successful teaching environment.

6.2.1 Broad language support

For a programming environment to be versatile enough to be used at all levels of an undergraduate curriculum, it must support a programming language that is easy enough for beginners to use, yet powerful enough to develop sophisticated software using structured methods, systems methods and object-oriented methods.

TURING is the programming language supported by the OOT environment. It is a high-level programming language that is well suited for teaching programming as well as developing industrial-strength software. TURING is versatile enough to be used at all levels of the curriculum cycle while preserving syntactic continuity.

For introductory courses, TURING has all of the features of PASCAL as well as modules, string-handling facilities, type-safe variant records, and dynamic arrays. TURING's unobtrusive syntax and simplicity provide the power and expressiveness of PASCAL and the simplicity of BASIC. This level of language is supported by our already existing implementations of TURING running on the PC and Macintosh.

For intermediate courses, TURING has features for teaching object-oriented programming and concurrency. For object-oriented programming, TURING provides classes, inheritance and polymorphism. For concurrency, students can use monitors which are supported by the language.

Finally, TURING can be used as an alternative to C for systems programming in advanced courses. The language has all of the features of C while encouraging safe and reliable programming style.

In this section we have surveyed the range of applications for using TURING in the undergraduate curriculum. We next cover the features of TURING in more detail.

It is important to note that we are not discouraging educators from teaching students about other programming languages and tools. We believe that this should be done in specialized courses, such as topics in programming languages [King, 1992], found in almost all undergraduate curricula in computer science. These courses will teach students about languages and tools used in industry without interfering with the teaching of concepts.

6.2.2 Integrated tools

The OOT system is an integrated collection of programming tools. This integration eliminates various problems associated with coordinating many stand-alone software development tools.

Figure 6.1 shows the OOT tools as they are used in the operating systems course. The figure is a snapshot of the OOT environment executing the MiniTunis operating system [Holt, 1992] used by our fourth-year undergraduate students. In the top left corner resides the *Control Panel*. Under this is an OOT *File Viewer* containing MiniTunis source code for its MEMORY module. Under the *File Viewer* is the *Interface Viewer* which shows the interfaces and comments associated with the interfaces of the MEMORY module. The OOT *Directory Viewer* is at the top right corner and contains a list of files that make up the MiniTunis operating system. Below the *Directory Viewer* is the *Software Landscape Viewer* which graphically depicts the structure of MiniTunis. The central window, labelled *tty0*, is a run-time window which shows the output generated by running a MiniTunis process. The program being executed is the MiniTunis operating system.

The complete OOT system currently supports ten integrated tools:

1. The *Control Panel* is used to control the overall OOT system activities. This tool has pull-down menus used for specifying global system parameters and for accessing help files, as well as a feedback area used for conveying information to users.

2. The *File Viewers* represent Unix files that may be edited and run.

3. The *Directory Viewer* indicates to users their location in the Unix directory structure and also allows them to navigate through it. It is also an integral part of the on-line help and documentation system. For example, when a user requests help, the *Directory Viewer* changes to the Unix directory containing files that will provide the wanted information.

4. The *Error Viewer* displays error and warning messages generated from attempts to run illegal TURING programs. When the user clicks on a message, OOT brings up the file containing the error with the offending line highlighted.

5. The *Run-time Displays* exhibit both textual and graphical output generated by TURING programs. A single program can create any number of these run-time windows and can concurrently display output on all of them. The TURING language supports convenient graphics routines for drawing lines, boxes, ovals, and so on.

6. The *Execution Viewer* displays a run-time view of the stack of calls and the currently executed line of code. This tool is integrated with the *File Viewer*, allowing users to select a procedure or function call on the stack and show its source code.

7. The *Object-oriented* TURING *compiler* is used to compile programs written in the TURING language. OOT programmers need not specify dependencies between files

containing the sources of the system under development because OOT provides implicit compilation and linking for them. The OOT compiler uses import lists[2] in the source code to resolve these dependencies automatically. The environment records any changes to the source code and recompiles only the files that were modified since the last compilation as well as all of the files that depend on these files. With this *implicit make*, OOT programmers are freed from the complexity of using traditional 'make' tools.

8. The *Software Landscape Viewer* is used as a C. A. S. E. tool. It allows users to create designs consisting of entities and relationships. These designs can be created and explored using a visual direct manipulation metaphor [Shneiderman, 1987]. Analysis documents and source code can be attached to these entities. This facility is used to integrate system design, documentation and code. Hence, the *Software Landscape* tool can be used not only for specifying high-level designs but also to help comprehension during software maintenance.

9. The *Interface Viewer* automatically extracts information from TURING source files that is used to display the interfaces of modules and classes. In Figure 6.1, the interface of the module MEMORY is being displayed on the left-hand side of the screen. The right part of this window contains the comment associated with the Allocate entry point of the MEMORY module.

10. The *Class Browser* allows users to navigate and explore the system's re-usable class library like the SMALLTALK-80 system does [Goldberg, 1983].

OOT's implementation architecture allows for the easy addition of new tools. We have recently added an online reference manual for the language; a student can access a particular section of the manual, for example the section on *if* statements, by placing the cursor at the 'if' keyword in a text file and pressing a function key. We are currently working on a run-time visualization system, called the *Run-time Landscape*. In the future we may add tools for source-code version control and requirements analysis. The OOT system comes with a re-use library that contains common generic data structures such as stacks, queues, mappings and sequences. We are currently working on a class library to support GUIs (graphic user interfaces) for student programs.

6.2.3 Consistent user interface

An important strength of the OOT system is its consistent user interface. To the user, OOT consists of a number of windows easily identifiable by variations in their colour, size, screen position and titles.

Following the Macintosh philosophy of user interface design [Apple, 1987], we made the OOT user interface convenient for both novices and experts. Keeping in mind that OOT will be used throughout the curriculum cycle, the interface design enables expert students to use fast control key sequences for high-frequency operations, as opposed to the slower but conceptually simpler mouse selection interactions typically used by beginner students. It also provides various means of feedback to users via dialogue boxes, windows, and a designated feedback area. The rich set of menus and help facilities supported by OOT reduces the short-term memory load of novice

---

[2] Import lists contain names declared outside the module that are accessed inside the module.

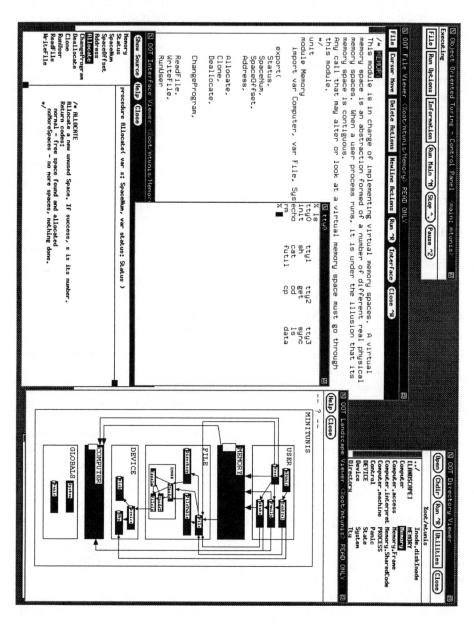

Figure 6.1   A snapshot of the OOT environment.

users and increases their speed of learning. This feature may also aid more experienced users who have not used the system for a while and have forgotten some of its 'short cuts'.

The OOT environment has many online teaching aids such as help, demonstrations, sample programs and a complete language reference manual. It also has a collection of documents and source files for teaching concepts such as concurrency, object-oriented programming, graphics and programming in the large.

6.2.4 Efficient and portable implementation

Our earlier version of the basic TURING software ran on a number of platforms including the PC, Macintosh and Unix. We have designed our new system, OOT, to be as portable as possible. It is common for universities to use different machines for their introductory and advanced courses. For example, introductory courses may use personal computers while intermediate and advanced courses use Unix machines. Also different departments that may want to use the system may have different computers. At our university, for example, the faculty of engineering teaches introductory programming courses running OOT on their Unix MIPS workstations whereas the version of OOT used by the computer science department runs on Unix Sun workstations.

The OOT system features a high-speed pseudo-code compiler. This pseudo-code is stored in the primary memory of the computer and not in the form of an executable file on disk. This allows the compiler to be machine-independent and hence more portable. The compiler is extremely fast; the compilation rate is 24 000 lines compiled per minute.

The OOT system uses the X-windows system to enable our implementation to be ported to any machine running X-windows. We have, for example, run OOT on Sun/4 machines, IBM RS6000's, SGI MIPS and Linux (a public-domain Unix running X Windows). One university (York University in Toronto) is running the OOT system on its NeXT computers. The Microsoft Windows version is now available.

The language processor (compiler and pseudo-code interpreter) for OOT are written in TURING PLUS. We have a compiler that translates this language to C source, thereby allowing us to port easily to any computer that supports the C language. TURING PLUS is a serious systems programming language, in which one can write highly efficient programs. We have written a great deal of systems software, including a multi-CPU version of Unix, in TURING PLUS.

6.3 Pedagogical experience

Since its initial use at the University of Toronto in 1983, the TURING language has spread fairly extensively. By now it is in use in 30 universities and colleges and in roughly 50% of Ontario high schools. In the high schools it has usually replaced BASIC and PASCAL. The high schools use the basic TURING language running on PCs and Macintoshes; the teachers favour TURING over BASIC because it is a structured language and over PASCAL because it is less confusing to the student. The language is also used in distance-learning courses, for example, at the University of Waterloo.

We first began using the OOT system in 1991. A great deal of time and effort is saved by using the same environment throughout the curriculum.

Students in the introductory courses appreciate both the language and the easy-to-use environment[3] in much the same way TURBO-PASCAL users do. Shielded from the complexity of having to use several loosely coupled tools, beginners are able to concentrate on the important task of learning the concepts behind programming. In many introductory courses, TURING's convenient graphics facilities are used extensively. These facilities help make learning enjoyable and are effective for illustrating programming principles.

The OOT environment is used in our undergraduate course on programming languages to teach a unit on object-orientation. Because of OOT's modular separate compilation facility, it is also used in our course on compiler writing.

The OOT environment is used in an advanced course in operating systems. The programming assignments involve modifying and extending the source code of a scaled down version of a Unix-like operating system called MiniTunis.

Under OOT, compilation is an order of magnitude faster than conventional compilers and linkers. Initial compiling and linking of the six-thousand-line MiniTunis system requires only fourteen seconds. Recompilation and linking of modified modules, such as the main driver, is essentially instantaneous, because the OOT system does a dependency analysis to minimize re-compilation. This is essentially an automatic implementation of the 'make' utility for OOT.

From a software engineering perspective, the operating systems course benefits from the *Software Landscape Viewer* and *Interface Viewer*. These tools are used by students to navigate through the design, documentation and source code of a complex software system.

Finally, the OOT environment's multiple run-time windows were used to make powerful visualizations of concurrency by showing the simultaneous execution of several processes under separate windows.

6.4 Language features

The basic TURING language, as designed in 1982, can be thought of as 'PASCAL done right', namely with less verbose syntax and cleaner semantics supported by a learner-oriented implementation. It is edifying to study the list of 'inadequacies' of PASCAL, as recently given by Wirth (PASCAL's creator). Wirth [1993] discusses PASCAL's shortcomings including 'structured statements without closing symbol', function result by assignment to function name, missing exponentiation operator, and missing local scopes. In each case, the design of TURING has corrected the difficulty.

6.4.1 Comparison with Pascal

The simplicity of TURING's syntax, which was inspired by the success of LOGO and BASIC with young children, can be seen in this example TURING program which sums input numbers until encountering a negative number:

```
var n : real
```

---

[3] Similar enthusiasm was found by a group of high-school students using OOT as part of a computer summer camp at our university.

```
var sum : real := 0.0
loop
    get n
    exit when n < 0
    sum += n
end loop
put "Sum=" , sum
```

The corresponding PASCAL program is:

```
program test (output);
    var n, sum : real ;
    begin
        sum := 0.0;
        readln (n);
        while n >= 0.0 do
            begin
                sum := sum + n;
                readln(n)
            end;
        writeln('Sum=', sum)
    end.
```

A token and line count (assuming a conventional pretty-printing scheme for PASCAL) suggests that the TURING program is much less complex than the corresponding PASCAL program: the TURING version has 8 lines and 27 tokens while the corresponding PASCAL version has 12 lines and 48 tokens. This is an indirect measure of the complexity experienced by the student when learning to program. This complexity is measured by the amount of teaching/learning time lost to syntactic trivia such as:

'Is the first PASCAL line really needed?'
'Which of the 12 lines of PASCAL must end with semicolons?'
'What happens if you place a semicolon after 'do'?'
'Why is the begin/end needed in the while loop?'

The near universal opinion of high-school teachers who have used BASIC, TURING and PASCAL is that TURING is as easy to learn as BASIC, and that TURING's syntax eliminates the impediments to teaching and learning found in PASCAL. In the first use of TURING at the University of Toronto, for example, we found that we were able to teach an extra two weeks of material in a 13-week course, largely because we were freed from the syntactic difficulties of PASCAL.

TURING's run-time system is of considerable help to the learner. The most frequent run-time error for learners is the uninitialized variable. TURING implementations detect this error at run-time and isolate it to the offending line, thereby sparing the beginner many confusing and frustrating bug chases. When data structures are taught, uninitialized and dangling pointers are treacherous, because in most PASCAL implementations they result in remote data corruption and system crashes. By contrast, the TURING implementation is 'faithful' in that it checks all possible language violations, including dangling pointers, and isolates the error to the offending line.

6.4.2 Modules and abstract data types

TURING augments the features of PASCAL with *modules*, which are information-hiding units that are ideal for introducing abstract data types (ADTs). For example, here is an

ADT for a stack of `Entry` records, each of which contains a name field and an address field:

```
type Entry :        % This is the record that is to be stacked
    record
        name, address : string (40)
    end record

module stack      % The ADT that holds Entry records
    import Entry
    export push, pop

    const stackSize := 100
    var top : int := 0
    var contents : array 1 .. stackSize of Entry

    procedure push (e : Entry)
        top += 1
        contents (top) := e
    end push

    procedure pop (var e : Entry)
        e := contents (top)
        top -= 1
    end pop
end stack
```

TURING's modules, as illustrated here, are simple enough that they are routinely taught in the introductory programming course. To create and push a record on the stack, one would use statements such as the following.

```
var e : Entry
    e.name := "Nancy Jones"
    e.address := "241 Main Street"
    stack.push (e)        % Push the record onto the first stack
```

Only the exported items (`push` and `pop`) are visible outside the module. The internal data (`stackSize`, `top` and `contents`) are hidden inside the module. Due to this information hiding, we can change the implementation inside the stack module to do storage allocation using linked lists, with no change to its clients.

Section 6.7 lists the features of the basic TURING and section 6.8 lists the additional features in OOT. The many features of OOT will not be discussed in detail; suffice it to say that they have been designed to illustrate and to be useful in many programming situations. The OOT's object-oriented features, discussed next, will be introduced using examples.

6.4.3 Object orientation

A module, for example the stack just shown, would be considered to be an object in object-oriented programming. If more than one stack is needed, one must change the above module so it becomes a class; this is done by simply changing the keyword 'module' to 'class'. (Note that the `Entry` record could be declared as a class instead of a record.) Once this is done, two instances of the class located by p1 and p2 are created in the following way. The pushing of record e onto the the first stack is also shown.

```
var p1, p2 : ^ stack
    new p1
    new p2
    p1 -> push (e)      % Push record e onto first stack
```

With this simple syntax, we can immediately introduce students to the essential idea of classes with instances.

We may want to make our stack 'generic' so it can store various kinds of items. To implement this, in the stack module we remove the import list and we change Entry to a pointer to any class (which we will denote '^anyclass' in the worked example in section 6.9). With this change, the stack now stores pointers to any existing object. The resulting stack is a *dynamically* generic data structure, meaning that the stack can store (pointers to) arbitrary objects. (OOT does not support static genericity, such as is supported by C++'s templates.)

OOT's inheritance feature is used to add items and to override subprograms in an existing class. For example, the following creates a class which is just like the stack class except that it has an additional exported subprogram that gives the stack's depth. The new class also overrides the push subprogram so that it now outputs "Push is called" before executing the original push operation.

```
class stackWithDepth
    inherit stack
    export depth

    function depth : int      % New function in this class
        result top
    end depth

    body procedure push (i : int)    % Override procedure
        put "Push has been called"
        stack.push (i)          % Call original push procedure
    end push
end stackWithDepth
```

OOT's object-oriented features are designed to support convenient re-usability of software. This is supported by providing convenient ways to store re-usable components. In the case of the stack, it is possible to factor the interface (including the signatures of push and pop) from the body (including the internal data and the bodies of the procedures) and to place these in separated compiled files. This approach is used extensively in OOT. For example, there is a re-use library that contains commonly used data structures such as stacks, queues and maps.

6.4.4 Difficulties with C and C++

With the features of OOT, one can teach advanced classes including systems programming and operating systems. The C language and its extension to C++ are often favoured for these courses, because C is used extensively for systems programming in industry. While C must be learned by those who will use it, and while it should be taught somewhere in a university curriculum, it seems to be a mistake to use it when teaching concepts. Consider the following (conjectured) student's attempt to write a simple C program:

```
main () {
    int i, j;
    i = 2;
    j = 4;
    if (i=j)
        printf(i);
    else
        printf(j);
}
```

When this program is run on a Sun/4, it produces this output: Segmentation fault (core dumped). The student's first mistake was to expect that the equality operator '=' in the *if* statement actually means to test for equality (whereas in C it assigns j to i and tests for non-zero). Next, the student thought printf would output the value of j. Sadly, printf expects a formatting string as its first parameter, and, not finding it, provokes a segmentation fault with a subsequent collapse back to the operating system. As this example illustrates, the student spends much time dealing with the unforgiving nature of C, rather than concentrating on deeper issues such as data structuring, information hiding and software architecture.

The fact is, C and C++ remain as 'high-level assemblers' rather than true high-level languages in that they fail to abstract away from low-level details such as memory addresses and segmentation faults. Eventually, the student should learn how to deal with these low-level mechanisms, but this is best done after essential concepts are mastered. It is better to introduce C after concepts have been learned in TURING. In the end, most of our students will not be programming in C or in other languages they learn in university. Universities should concentrate on teaching knowledge which will remain useful in the face of the technological change that will inevitably arise in the years ahead.

6.5 Conclusions

In this chapter we have defined four ingredients that make up a successful curriculum-cycle approach to teaching programming:

- broad language support;
- integrated tools;
- consistent user interface;
- efficient and portable implementation.

Most currently used programming environments in the undergraduate curricula do not fulfil all of these ingredients. In particular, they do not support broad programming language facilities and they lack tools for software development activities other than coding.

Starting with a basic TURING implementation that is targeted to introductory programming classes, we have designed a programming environment that can be used for as many courses in the curriculum as possible. We developed the OOT environment as an integrated set of tools to support coding activities, a good user interface and an efficient implementation. To this we added broad language support, a portable implementation and tools for software development activities other than coding.

A curriculum-cycle programming environment benefits both educators and students. Educators, with the support of integrated tools, are able to focus on teaching concepts rather than syntax and commands. Students learn more by using better methods and tools, and by avoiding syntactic trivia.

Acknowledgements

This chapter is based on [Mancoridis *et al.*, 1993b].

6.6 References and annotated bibliography

Apple (1987), *Human Interface Guidelines: The Apple Desktop Interface*, Addison-Wesley, Reading, MA.

Clifton, J. M. (1991), An Industry Approach to the Software Engineering Course, *SIGCSE Bulletin*, **23**(1), 296–9.

Goldberg, A. (1983), *Smalltalk-80: The Interactive Programming Environment*, Addison-Wesley, Reading, MA.

Granger, M. J. (1991), The Impact of Computer-Aided Software Engineering on Student Performance, *SIGCSE Bulletin*, **23**(1), 62–71.

Holt, R. C. (1990), *Turing Reference Manual*, Holt Software Associates Inc., Toronto, 3rd edition, (361 pages). The third edition contains object-oriented material. This includes an alphabetic listing of every feature supported by the Turing and Object-oriented Turing systems, with examples, explanations and technical details. It also lists all predefined functions, installations instructions, *etc.*

Holt, R. C. and Cordy, J. R. (1988), The Turing Programming Language, *Communications ACM*, **31**(12), 1410–23. This was the feature article of CACM, with a special cover on Turing. This gives the 'academic' presentation of the language and its features.

Holt, R. C. and Hume, J. N. P. (1984), *Introduction to Computer Science Using the Turing Programming Language*, Holt Software Associates Inc., Toronto, 2nd edition, (404 pages). After a concise, but thorough, introduction to the algorithmic and data structuring ideas of PASCAL-like languages, the book concentrates on giving the student a solid understanding of essential computer science concepts, including program design, correctness, graphics, searching and sorting, analysis of algorithms, data structures, modules and abstract data types.

Holt, R. C. and Penny, D. A. (1992), *The MiniTunis Book: Operating Systems and Concurrency Using Object-oriented Turing*, Holt Software Associates Inc., Toronto, (305 pages). This text is used to accompany a standard text on operating systems (Peterson and Silberschatz is used at the University of Toronto). The text includes a complete but simplified operating system called MiniTunis written in Object-oriented Turing in a highly structured fashion. This operating system, which runs as a program under OOT, runs concurrent shells and user programs, and is the basis for student projects.

Holt, R. C. and Perelgut, S. (1991), *Turing Teacher's Manual*, Holt Software Associates Inc., Toronto, This manual contains an extensive set of overhead slide masters that can be used to graphically illustrate fundamental programming ideas, such as looping, selection, variables, records, end-of-file detection, string manipulation, *etc.* The manual also provides you with a set of quizzes and answers to all exercises in the *Turing Tutorial Guide* [Hume, 1989].

Holt, R. C., Matthews, P. A., Rosselet, J. A. and Cordy, J. R. (1987), *Turing Language: Design and Definition*, Prentice-Hall, (323 pages). This book gives the methods and reasons behind the language design. The original Turing Report is included. The complete formal definition of Turing is given. Proof rules (WP formalism) are given; these can be used for correctness proofs.

Holt Software Associates (1993), *Turing Electronic Lessons*, Holt Software Associates Inc., Toronto. These electronic lessons run on a PC and use colour animation to introduce fundamental notions of computing that sometimes mystify novices. Lesson number 1 shows the students how to use the PC Turing editor and how to save and read files. Other lessons animate simple programs containing variables, loops, *if* statements, *case* statements, *etc.*

Hume, J. N. P. (1989), *Turing Tutorial Guide*, Holt Software Associates Inc., Toronto, 3rd edition, (278 pages). This book takes a gentle approach to computer science. It is appropriate for students, possibly non computer science majors, taking a one or two term course concentrating on algorithms, data structuring, files, *etc.*After introductory chapters on repetition, selection and input/output, the book includes chapters on string handling, program structuring, arrays, graphics, subprograms, records and file processing. It is clearly written and contains extensive examples and exercises.

ITC (1987), Excelerator, in *Proceedings Computer-aided Software Engineering Symposium, Andover, MA.*

King, K. N. (1992), The Evolution of the Programming Languages Course, *SIGCSE Bulletin*, **24**(1), 213–9.

Koffman, E. B. and Holt, R. C. (1994), *Turing Problem Solving and Program Design*, Addison-Wesley, Don Mills, Ontario. This is a broad approach to computer science using software engineering concepts including ADTs and data flow diagrams. The book is based on Koffman's widely used Pascal textbook.

Mancoridis, S., Holt, R. C. and Penny, D. A. (1993a), A Conceptual Framework For Software Development, in *21st Annual ACM Computer Science Conference, Indianapolis, February 16–18, 1993*. This article gives the philosophy behind the design of the OOT software development environment.

Mancoridis, S., Holt, R. C. and Penny, D. A. (1993b), A 'Curriculum-Cycle' Environment for Teaching Programming, in *24th ACM SIGCSE Computer Science Education Conference, Indianapolis, Indiana*, 15–9.

Shneiderman, B. (1987), *Designing the User Interface: Strategies for Effective Human–computer Interaction*, Addison-Wesley, Reading, MA.

Temte, M. C. (1991), Let's Begin Introducing the Object-oriented Paradigm, *SIGCSE Bulletin*, **23**(1), 73–7.

Wirth, N. (1993), Recollections about the Development of Pascal, in *History of Programming Languages Conference, Cambridge, MA*, (in *ACM SIGPLAN Notices* **28**(3), March 1993, 333–40).

All materials (except [Holt *et al.*, 1987]) are available from:

```
OOT Distribution Manager
Holt Software Associates Inc.
Suite 305, 203 College Street
Toronto, CANADA.   M5T 1P9
e-mail: ootinfo@turing.utoronto.ca
tel: +1 (416) 978-6476, +1 800-361-8324 (US only)
fax: +1 (416) 978-1509
```

There is an online demonstration version of OOT from the University of Toronto that can be accessed by anonymous 'ftp'. The OOT environment is currently implemented on Unix platforms, such as Sun/4, RS/6000 and SGI, as well as on PC. If you have access to the Internet and Unix, you can get instructions to access the demo by following:

```
ftp 128.100.1.192
ftp> cd pub
ftp> get ootDistrib
ftp> quit
```

The `ootDistrib` file in your directory will now contain details on getting the demo.

6.7 Appendix – Features of the basic Turing language

- DATA TYPES AND OPERATORS

  1. Integers, real numbers, enumerated types, sets, arrays, records.
  2. Pointers with new and free statements.
  3. Unions (secure variant records) with a tag statement.
  4. Varying length strings.
  5. Named types (as in PASCAL).
  6. Operators: +, -, *, /, div, rem, mod, ** (exponentiation), comparisons, *etc.*

- DATA DECLARATIONS

  1. Declarations can appear wherever a statement can appear.
  2. `var` and `const` declarations (constants can be run-time values).
  3. `bind` declarations (analogous to PASCAL's `with`).

- INPUT/OUTPUT

  1. `get`/`put` statements with formatting and end-of-file detection.
  2. `open`/`close` statements including file names.
  3. `read`/`write` statement for binary files.
  4. `seek`/`tell` statements for random-access files.
  5. `getch`, `hasch` (interactive character input/output).

- CONTROL CONSTRUCTS

  1. `if` statements with optional `elsif` clauses and `else` clause.

  2. `case` statements with `otherwise` clause.

  3. `loop` and `for` statements with `exits`.

- SUBPROGRAMS AND MODULES

  1. Procedures with `return` statements.

  2. Functions with `result` statements with scalar and non-scalar results.

  3. Dynamic array and string parameters.

  4. Subprograms as parameters.

  5. Information-hiding units (modules) with import/export lists, which support abstract data types.

- CORRECTNESS

  1. Pre- and post-conditions for subprograms.

  2. Invariants for loops.

  3. Assertions as statements.

- TIMING AND SOUND

  1. `clock, date, sysclock, time, wallclock, delay`.

  2. `play, playdone, sound`.

- SYSTEM

  1. `getenv, getpid, nargs, fetcharg, system`.

- GRAPHICS

  1. `cls, colour, colourback, locate, maxcol, maxrow, maxcolour,` *etc.*

  2. `drawarc, drawbox, drawdot, drawline, drawoval, drawpolygon, drawpic,` *etc.*

- PREDEFINED FUNCTIONS

  1. `abs, max, min, sign, sqrt, sin, cos, arctan, sind, cosd, arctand, ln, exp`.

  2. `ceil, round, intreal, chr, ord, intstr, strint, erealstr, frealstr, realstr, strreal`.

  3. `rand, randint, randomize, randnext, randseed`.

6.8 Appendix – Additional features of Object-oriented Turing

- VARIOUS FEATURES

    1. Natural (unsigned) numbers (the nat type).

    2. Sized numbers, *e.g.* int1 (one-byte integer), nat2 (two-byte natural number) and real8 (eight-byte real number).

    3. Bit manipulation, *e.g.* shifts and bit substrings.

    4. Subprograms as variables.

    5. Characters and fixed-length character strings, *e.g.* the char and char(15) types.

    6. Explicit type coercions (cheats), *e.g.* cheat(c, nat1).

    7. Address arithmetic.

    8. Indirection operator, *e.g.* int@(1636).

    9. Compile-time selection of segments of source.

- OBJECT ORIENTATION

    1. Objects (including modules).

    2. Classes, with instances (objects) created by new statement.

    3. Inheritance: single inheritance, adding fields and overriding subprograms.

    4. Polymorphism: run-time selection of method body.

- CONCURRENCY

    1. Process declarations.

    2. The fork statement, which starts a new thread of execution.

    3. Monitors, for mutual exclusion.

    4. wait and signal statements to block and wake up processes.

    5. Condition queues (immediate, deferred and time-out).

- SEPARATE COMPILATION

    1. Units (modules and classes) can be separately compiled.

    2. Complete checking of separately compiled units.

    3. Separation of body from interface (optional).

- EXCEPTION HANDLING

    1. Handlers in subprograms (optional).

    2. Signalling an exception: quit statements.

6.9 Appendix – Example: Class structure for workshop

This appendix was prepared in response to the request to create a 'suitable type/class structure and operations to process people attending the workshop [on the choice of programming languages]. Presenters, session chairs, exhibitors, delegates from O. U. [Open University], delegates from other institutions/companies are [to be] treated differently and have different state information associated with them (*e.g.* name of paper, slot in timetable, *etc.* are associated with presenters).'

We designed a class structure and prototyped an implementation using the OOT language and its software development environment.

The problem was analysed using an entity/relation (E/R) diagram, which was drawn using OOT's online landscape (diagramming) software. The eventual E/R structure used in the prototype implementation has this structure:

1. listOfAttendees (containing attendees);
2. attendee (with fields for person's name, address, *etc.*);
3. OUDelegate (inheriting from attendee);
4. nonOUDelegate (inheriting from attendee);
5. listOfPapers (containing papers);
6. paper (with fields for name of paper, authors, *etc.*);
7. listOfSessions (containing sessions);
8. session (with field for chair, containing time of day, date, a list of slots, *etc.*);
9. slot (with fields for paper, presenter, *etc.*).

In this structure, a 'presenter' is a field of a slot, a 'session chair' is a field of a session, and the 'timetable' is the listOfSessions.

For the prototype implementation, it was decided to use an object-oriented approach (a more PASCAL-like approach using linked lists would have been possible). In doing this, the three entities that exist as single objects (namely listOfAttendees, listOfPapers, and listOfSessions) were programmed as modules, and the other entities were programmed as classes.

Besides the above units, the prototype included these units:

1. sequenceOfAny and its related classes (these classes, from OOT's library of reusable classes, were used to represent all lists);
2. inputter (a module used to handle all reading of information);
3. main program (directly uses only the three units that are modules).

The prototype was simplified by not implementing the ability to change any information entered into the database, and by not providing the ability to place the data in persistent storage. The prototype allows easy expansion to handle these facilities, without changing the structure.

The prototype was developed using the OOT system and tested by entering sample data, including attendees, papers, sessions and slots. Once the prototype was working, tools were used to create its landscape, which is a diagram showing the modules and classes with their 'use' and 'inherit' relations. This landscape was manually checked to verify that it was homomorphic with the original E/R diagram. Tools were used to created 'unit skeletons' from the prototype, that allow the units (modules and classes) to be browsed by entry point with viewing of parameters and comments and with hyperlinks to the corresponding source code.

As viewed in the OOT environment, the prototype appears as a landscape (a diagram), as a set of file names (seen in OOT directory browser), as a set of interfaces (seen in OOT *Interface Browser*), and as a set of files (one for each module or class). These multiple views are ideal for understanding the structure at increasing levels of detail, from high-level design down to actual code.

Selected parts of the source code are listed below. The units shown in the program code that follows are: `listOfAttendees`, `attendee`, `listOfSessions`, `session` and `slot`.

```
/********************************************************/
/*          List of attendees of the workshop          */
/********************************************************/
unit
module listOfAttendees
    import var sequenceOfAny,
        var attendee, var OUDelegate, var nonOUDelegate
    export handleCommands, numberToName

    var list : ^sequenceOfAny   % List of attendees
    new list
    const stdIO := 0   % File number of standard I/O stream

    procedure addAttendee
        var newAttendee : ^attendee
        put "Is this attendee from OU? (y/n)? " ..
        var answer : string
        get answer : *
        loop   % Repeat until good request is typed
            if answer = "" or answer (1) = "y" then
                new OUDelegate, newAttendee
                exit
            elsif answer = "n" then
                new nonOUDelegate, newAttendee
                exit
            end if
        end loop
        list -> arriveRight (newAttendee)
        newAttendee -> registrationNumber := list -> Length
        put "Attendee registration number is: ",
            newAttendee -> registrationNumber
        newAttendee -> getFields
    end addAttendee

    procedure changeAttendee
        put "Sorry, can't yet change existing attendee"
    end changeAttendee

    procedure putAllAttendee (fileNumber : int)
        for i : 1 .. list -> Length   % For each attendee
            var p : ^anyclass
            list -> fetchItem (i, p)
            const q : ^attendee := p
            if objectclass (q) = OUDelegate then
                put : fileNumber, "OUDelegate"
```

```
                else
                    put : fileNumber, "nonOUDelegate"
                end if
                q -> putFields (fileNumber)
        end for
    end putAllAttendee

    procedure handleCommands
        loop
            var request : string
            put "Attendee: Add, change, list, quit (a/c/l/q): " ..
            get request : *
            case request of
                label "a" :
                    addAttendee
                label "c" :
                    changeAttendee
                label "l" :
                    putAllAttendee (stdIO)
                label "q" :
                    exit
                label :
                    put "Bad command: ", request
            end case
        end loop
    end handleCommands

    /* Convert registration number to attendee name */
    function numberToName (i : int) : string
        if i <= list -> Length then
            var p : ^anyclass
            list -> fetchItem (i, p)
            var q : ^attendee := p
            result q -> name
        else
            result "Bad registration number"
        end if
    end numberToName

end listOfAttendees


/**********************************************************/
/*            An attendee of the workshop               */
/**********************************************************/
unit
class attendee
    import var inputter
    export var registrationNumber,
        getFields, putFields, name

    var registrationNumber : int
    var name : string (50)
    var title : string (15)
    var street : string (40)
    var department : string (50)
    var institute : string (100)
    var city : string (50)
    var province : string (50)
    var postalCode : string (10)
    var country : string (50)
```

```
    procedure getFields
        inputter.getStringField ("Name", name)
        inputter.getStringField ("Title", title)
        inputter.getStringField ("Street address", street)
        inputter.getStringField ("Department", department)
        inputter.getStringField ("Institute", institute)
        inputter.getStringField ("City", city)
        inputter.getStringField ("Province", province)
        inputter.getStringField ("Postal code", postalCode)
        inputter.getStringField ("Country", country)
    end getFields

    procedure putFields (fileNumber : int)
        put : fileNumber,   registrationNumber
        put : fileNumber,   name
        put : fileNumber,   title
        put : fileNumber,   street
        put : fileNumber,   department
        put : fileNumber,   institute
        put : fileNumber,   city
        put : fileNumber,   province
        put : fileNumber,   postalCode
        put : fileNumber,   country
    end putFields

end attendee


/***********************************************************/
/*          List of sessions in the workshop           */
/***********************************************************/
unit
module listOfSessions
    import var sequenceOfAny, var session
    export handleCommands

    var list : ^sequenceOfAny  % List of sessions
    new list

    const stdIO := 0   % File number of standard I/O stream

    procedure addNewSession
        var newSession : ^session
        new newSession
        list -> arriveRight (newSession)
        newSession -> numberOfSession := list -> Length
        newSession -> getFields
    end addNewSession

    procedure changeSession
        put "Sorry, can't yet change existing session"
    end changeSession

    procedure putAllSession (fileNumber : int)
        for i : 1 .. list -> Length   % For each session
            var p : ^anyclass
            list -> fetchItem (i, p)
            const q : ^session := p
            q -> putFields (fileNumber)
        end for
    end putAllSession
```

```
      /* Handle commands for list of sessions */
      procedure handleCommands
          loop
              var request : string
              put "Session: Add, change, list, quit (a/c/l/q): " ..
              get request : *
              case request of
                  label "a" :
                      addNewSession
                  label "c" :
                      changeSession
                  label "l" :
                      putAllSession (stdIO)
                  label "q" :
                      exit
                  label :
                      put "Bad command: ", request
              end case
          end loop
      end handleCommands

end listOfSessions


/**************************************************************/
/* A session in the workshop -- consists of several slots */
/**************************************************************/
unit
class session
    import var slot, var sequenceOfAny, var inputter
    export getFields, putFields, var numberOfSession

    var numberOfSession : int
    var sessionTitle : string (150)
    var timeOfDay : string (5)
    var Date : string (30)
    var isExhibit : string (1)
    var presiders : string (200)

    var list : ^sequenceOfAny    % List of slots in session
    new list

    const stdIO := 0   % File number of standard I/O stream

    procedure addNewSlot
        var newSlot : ^slot
        new newSlot
        list -> arriveRight (newSlot)
        newSlot -> numberOfSlot := list -> Length
        newSlot -> getFields
    end addNewSlot

    procedure changeSlot
        put "Sorry, can't yet change existing slot"
    end changeSlot

    procedure putFields (fileNumber : int)
        put : fileNumber, numberOfSession
        put : fileNumber, sessionTitle
        put : fileNumber, timeOfDay
        put : fileNumber, Date
        put : fileNumber, isExhibit
```

```
            put : fileNumber, presiders
            for i : 1 .. list -> Length    % For each slot
                var p : ^anyclass
                list -> fetchItem (i, p)
                const q : ^slot := p
                q -> putFields (fileNumber)
            end for
        end putFields

        /* Handle commands for this session */
        procedure handleCommands
            loop
                var request : string
                put "Slot: Add, change, list, quit (a/c/l/q): " ..
                get request : *
                case request of
                    label "a" :
                        addNewSlot
                    label "c" :
                        changeSlot
                    label "l" :
                        putFields (stdFile)
                    label "q" :
                        exit
                    label :
                        put "Bad command: ", request
                end case
            end loop
        end handleCommands

        procedure getFields
            inputter.getStringField ("Title of session", sessionTitle)
            inputter.getStringField ("Time of day, eg, 1430", timeOfDay)
            inputter.getStringField ("Date, \eg 93.07.25", Date)
            inputter.getStringField ("Is this a session or exhibit
(s/e)",
                isExhibit)
            inputter.getStringField ("Name(s) of presider(s)",
presiders)
            handleCommands
        end getFields

end session

/****************************************************/
/*      A slot in a session in the workshop         */
/****************************************************/
unit
class slot
    import listOfAttendees, listOfPapers, var inputter
    export getFields, putFields, var numberOfSlot

    var numberOfSlot : int
    var numberOfPaper : int
    var numberOfPresenter : int % Registration number

    procedure getFields
        inputter.getIntField ("Number of Paper", numberOfPaper)
        inputter.getIntField ("Presenter's registration number",
            numberOfPresenter)
    end getFields
```

```
procedure putFields (fileNumber : int)
    put : fileNumber, numberOfPaper, ": ",
        listOfPapers . numberToName (numberOfPaper)
    put : fileNumber, numberOfPresenter, ": ",
        listOfAttendees . numberToName (numberOfPresenter)
end putFields
end slot
```

7 Modula-2 in the first majors' sequence: five years' experience

Steven C. Cater

This chapter reports on five years of experience of a first course, or first sequence, for computer science majors and discusses the related issues involved in the choice of a programming language. MODULA-2 is asserted to be the best choice at present and its advantages in the education of first-year students are illustrated by examples of MODULA-2 code. Finally, the first programming sequence at the University of Georgia is described, as an example of the use of MODULA-2 in a first sequence.

7.1 Introduction

The choice of a first programming language is one of the most important decisions a computer science department can make regarding its undergraduate course of instruction. Although some people doubt the necessity of having a fixed first language [Tucker, 1991] many others have advanced solid arguments for requiring the same [Austing *et al.*, 1978; Koffman, 1988; Koffman *et al.*, 1984; Koffman *et al.*, 1985].

Section 7.2 describes the points one should consider when choosing a first programming language. It is shown that MODULA-2 easily satisfies the requirements for a good first language. Example code is given showing the abstract data typing features available in MODULA-2. In Section 7.3 we describe the use of MODULA-2 in the University of Georgia's first programming sequence. Section 7.4 is a summary of our conclusions.

7.2 Modula-2 as the first programming language

We contend that MODULA-2 is, at present, the best generally available language for teaching a first sequence to prospective computer science majors. Further, we believe that MODULA-2 will remain so for the next few years, possibly as many as ten (by which time the entire curriculum should be updated, including choice of first language).

The following discussion is broken into three parts, comprising major considerations in the choice of programming language, minor reasons for same, and other considerations. We then consider the advantages and disadvantages of MODULA-2 as a first language.

7.2.1 Major considerations in first language choice

The primary consideration is that the first language should be the best available teaching language. This language may or may not be a language widely used in industry. Our purpose is to teach program engineering skills, and not simply to teach syntax. We believe that languages offering economic incentives for acquisition should be taught, but either as service courses or as (non-credit) portions of more advanced courses. Of course, the fact that a language enjoys wide use in industry is no disadvantage, and is probably a minor advantage.

Within the above constraint, the first language should be an imperative language for most students. The vast majority of programs written and maintained today are imperative; we feel it important that a student have the most experience with the type of language to be used after graduation. There are strong arguments in favour of the use of object-oriented and functional languages. In the future, perhaps by the next revision of the Association for Computing Machinery's (ACM) curriculum report, the situation will change; for now, imperative languages are the best first languages.

The first language must be strongly typed. In addition, type checking should be performed before run-time, that is statically. Strong, static typing systems are such tremendous advantages in program engineering that it is difficult to imagine teaching programming to beginning students without them.

Early courses should emphasize program engineering skills, in part as preparation for later software engineering courses. Structured programming techniques must be taught from the beginning, and a language must be chosen which encourages proper use of these techniques. Similarly, proper use of abstract data types (ADTs) must be encouraged from an early point in a student's career. As with structured programming techniques, the language chosen must encourage proper use of ADTs. The chosen language must allow both true, working information hiding, and modular construction. Separate, type-safe compilation goes hand in hand with these two requirements.

Students should be exposed to a well-designed language as a first language. In general, this implies use of a smaller, rather than larger, language. Good language design makes good program design easier. Students should be exposed to the better examples of language design, so they may begin to appreciate the advantages such languages have over poorer designs. In addition, students switching from a poorly designed language to a well-designed one often carry their bad habits with them; students switching from a well-designed language to a poorly designed one quickly learn to program defensively.

The presence of a *de facto* standard for the language, or even a *de jure* standard (possibly even an ISO/IEC standard), is an important criterion. Without some form of standardization, textbooks are hard to find, and, when they exist, are quite likely to describe a language which differs in important ways from the compiler to be used in class.

7.2.2 Minor considerations in first language choice

The following points are of lesser importance in choosing a first language, but should be considered.

The language should be one that can be used in introductory, intermediate and advanced classes. Many students prefer to use their first language in later classes. Since in many advanced classes, students are allowed to choose their programming language, it is an advantage that a language can be used later. Similarly, languages especially designed for beginners are often not good choices. In general, they are too limited for later use (indeed, many are too limited for use in the first sequence), and they tend to be designed solely for first courses, rather than first sequences. Hence, the language must be a general-purpose language. However, if the language has features allowing more specialized applications to be effectively written (*e.g.* real-time systems), it can be considered an advantage, provided the more specialized features do not interfere with teaching the core features of the language.

The availability of textbooks in the appropriate areas makes teaching easier, but is not strictly necessary, as long as a single good introduction to the language is available. It is not too difficult to teach first courses with only a language manual and a language-independent textbook.

A language should not demand too much from the operating system and/or hardware. Many departments must use centralized machines not originally intended for teaching computer science classes; in such situations, minimization of resource usage is imperative. However, with the spread of powerful microcomputers this is becoming less important.

Another consideration is object-oriented programming: many imperative languages are turning into object-oriented languages. If a language has object-oriented features, and if these features do not get in the way of the more important things needed for teaching beginners, then the object-oriented features can be successfully used. Since we advocate use of an imperative language at present, if an object-oriented language is used, we prefer it to be a hybrid imperative–object-oriented language (*e.g.* C++), rather than a pure object-oriented language (SMALLTALK or EIFFEL). (Ten years from now this may no longer be true.) At this level, the main object-oriented features needed are single inheritance (multiple inheritance is not yet well enough understood to teach at this level), and some sort of generic typing facility for teaching container ADTs.

7.2.3 Unimportant considerations in first language choice

The following items are either unimportant or irrelevant in choosing a first language.

Available development environment is not an important issue. The programming that goes on at this level can be supported by the standard development tools available on Unix (`make`, `dbx`, `vi`). If microcomputers are used, equivalent or superior tools

```
DEFINITION MODULE NAStacks;
(* Stacks of name-address records. *)

FROM NAPairs IMPORT (* TYPE *) NAPair;

TYPE NAStack;

PROCEDURE Push (S : NAStack; x : NAPair) : NAStack;
(* Push the value x onto the stack S. *)

PROCEDURE Pop (S : NAStack) : NAStack;
(* Discard the top of the stack.
   PRE-CONDITION: NOT IsEmpty(S). *)

PROCEDURE Peek (S : NAStack) : NAPair;
(* Return the top element of S.  Do not
   change S.  PRE-CONDITION: NOT IsEmpty(S). *)

PROCEDURE IsEmpty (S : NAStack) : BOOLEAN;
(* Is S empty? *)

PROCEDURE Create () : NAStack;
(* Create a new stack. POST-CONDITION: IsEmpty(Create()). *)

PROCEDURE Destroy (VAR S : NAStack);
(* Cleanly destroy S. *)

END NAStacks.
```

Figure 7.1   A definition module for stacks of (name, address) pairs.

are available, either bundled with a compiler or available separately and inexpensively. If a mainframe is used, equivalent tools are readily available.

Local renaming of objects is a plus, but is not supported in many languages at this time. Support for persistence has no place in a language for beginners, but, as with other features, if a language has this support in a non-interfering manner, there is little problem. Support of an assert function is important, but can be easily added to most languages, at least as a procedure.

7.2.4 The choice of Modula-2

We claim that the language which best meets the above requirements is MODULA-2. It is an imperative language of simple and elegant design, having strong support for ADTs, information hiding and modular construction. It has strong, static type-checking. It is a well-known language, having been designed by Niklaus Wirth in 1977 [Wirth, 1988]. Its basic features include the ability to split the definition or public part of a piece of code from its private, implementation part (via separate modules and opaque types). Thus, one can write code for a stack, as shown in Figures 7.1, 7.2, 7.3 and 7.4, and allow access to the data only via the usual stack functions.

As to the other considerations, MODULA-2 has an ISO/IEC standard under construction [ISO/IEC JTC1/SC22/WG13, 1994]. The specialized parts of MODULA-2 (coroutines and low-level features) are independent of the rest of the language, and do not interfere with teaching the remainder of the language. Our experience at the

```
IMPLEMENTATION MODULE NAStacks;
(* A linked implementation of name-address stacks. *)

FROM Storage IMPORT ALLOCATE, DEALLOCATE;
FROM NAPairs IMPORT (* TYPE *) NAPair;

TYPE
    NAStack = POINTER TO Node;
    TPtr = NAStack;
    Node = RECORD
                data: NAPair;
                next: NAStack;
           END;

PROCEDURE Push (S : NAStack; x : NAPair) : NAStack;
(* Push the value x onto the stack S. *)
VAR
    temp : TPtr;
BEGIN (* Push *)
    NEW(temp);
    temp^.data := x;
    temp^.next := S;
    RETURN temp;
END Push;

PROCEDURE Pop (S : NAStack) : NAStack;
(* Discard the top of the stack.
    PRE-CONDITION: NOT IsEmpty(S). *)
VAR
    temp : TPtr;
BEGIN (* Pop *)
    temp := S;
    S := S^.next;
    DISPOSE(temp);
    RETURN S;
END Pop;
```

Figure 7.2   Part of an implementation module for stacks of (name, address) pairs.

University of Georgia (see section 7.3) shows that MODULA-2 is suited for use in any undergraduate course, and that it requires little in the way of hardware or operating system support.

Finally, there are many texts available for a first sequence in MODULA-2. We have used King's text [1988] in our courses, and have had success with Kingston's text [1990] in our advanced data structures course. We have also used the Helman and Veroff text [1988] as a first (intermediate) text. Cooper has written a good book for use in a first class [1990]. Similarly, MODULA-2 compilers are available for most mini- and microcomputer systems.

7.2.5 Weaknesses of Modula-2

The largest single weakness commonly given for MODULA-2 is that no allowance is made for generic typing. While the example code given here allows efficient use of ADTs, together with information hiding, it does not allow for generic typing. This problem can be partially overcome, but all solutions are a bit ugly. Other weaknesses of

```
PROCEDURE Peek (S : NAStack) : NAPair;
(* Return the top element of S.  Do not
   change S.  PRE-CONDITION: NOT IsEmpty(S). *)
BEGIN (* Peek *)
   RETURN S^.data;
END Peek;

PROCEDURE IsEmpty (S : NAStack) : BOOLEAN;
(* Is S empty? *)
BEGIN (* IsEmpty *)
   RETURN S = NIL;
END IsEmpty;

PROCEDURE Create () : NAStack;
(* Create a new stack. POST-CONDITION: IsEmpty(Create()). *)
BEGIN (* Create *)
   RETURN NIL;
END Create;

PROCEDURE Destroy (VAR S : NAStack);
(* Cleanly destroy S. *)
VAR
   temp : TPtr;
BEGIN (* Destroy *)
   WHILE S # NIL DO
      temp := S;
      S := S^.next;
      DISPOSE(temp);
   END; (* while *)
END Destroy;

END NAStacks.
```

Figure 7.3   An implementation module for stacks of (name, address) pairs (cont'd).

```
DEFINITION MODULE NAPairs;
(* Name-address pair definitions. *)

TYPE
   NameString = ARRAY [1..40] OF CHAR;
   StreetString = ARRAY [1..40] OF CHAR;
   CityString = ARRAY [1..20] OF CHAR;
   StateString = ARRAY [1..2] OF CHAR;
   CountryString = ARRAY [1..20] OF CHAR;

   NAPair = RECORD
               name    : NameString;
               street  : StreetString;
               city    : CityString;
               state   : StateString;
               country : CountryString;
            END;
END NAPairs.
```

Figure 7.4   A possible definition module for (name, address) pairs.

MODULA-2 include the lack of automatic destruction of objects defined in modules, and the lack of automatic initialization of multiple objects defined in modules. (The proposed ISO/IEC standard at least partially overcomes these problems, however.)

Two standard solutions to the generic typing problem are commonly encountered:

1. In the code shown earlier, change every occurrence of NAStack to Stack, and every occurrence of NAPair to Element, in both the definition and implementation modules for stacks. Also, rename the imported module to something more generic, say, Elements. The two stack modules will no longer be altered when changing the type of the elements of the stack. All that must be done to instantiate a *single* new stack type is to change the Elements module appropriately and recompile. Of course, having stacks of two different types in the same program requires a bit of copying and minor editing.

2. Import the type ADDRESS and its associated functions from the special (pseudo) module SYSTEM. Create in the stack implementation module a non-typed stack, that is, a stack of ADDRESS. Note that this is not a generic, type-safe stack, but rather an unsafe, untyped stack. The strong typing normally associated with MODULA-2 has been lost.

Of these two methods, only the first should be taught in a first programming sequence. (At the University of Georgia, the SYSTEM module is not used in the first programming sequence. This results in our students knowing only the high-level parts of MODULA-2. We consider this an advantage.) Other approaches can make MODULA-2 look a bit more like an object-oriented language; examples are given by Powell [1993] and Bergin and Greenfield [1989].

We have seen that MODULA-2 meets all the requirements to be used as a first language, and has few real weaknesses. In the next section, we show that it is possible to use MODULA-2 effectively in a first sequence. At this point, however, we should mention that we are not alone in our choice of MODULA-2 as the first programming language. In 1984, Koffman was lead author on what has become the last ACM curriculum report on non-breadth-first first sequences [Koffman *et al.*, 1984; 1985]. These reports discussed language choice, and concluded that PASCAL, PL/I and ADA were suitable languages for ACM 1984 CS 1 and CS 2. MODULA-2 was not mentioned. However, in a later report by Koffman alone [1988], he stated that, in his opinion, MODULA-2 was the (only) proper choice for these two courses, for reasons which included [Koffman, 1988, p. 14]:

- ease of conversion from PASCAL,

- availability of compilers,

- availability of textbooks,

- encouragement of re-use,

- facilitation of data abstraction, and

- enhancement of upper-level courses.

We believe that the situation has not changed significantly since Koffman's report.

7.3 Modula-2 at the University of Georgia

The use of MODULA-2 in the Department of Computer Science at the University of Georgia began in the Spring Quarter, 1988, with the conversion of our second majors' course from PASCAL to MODULA-2. I had argued for a switch since arriving in the department in January 1987, based on early readings in *Byte* [Coar, 1984; Gutknecht, 1984; Paul, 1984] and use of the language on a microcomputer (using the TDI MODULA-2/ST compiler and programming environment [TDI, 1986]). In June 1987, after I became departmental undergraduate coordinator and chair of the departmental curriculum committee, the faculty was persuaded to experiment with a change to MODULA-2.

As time passed, we converted our entire lower division (majors' courses) to MODULA-2. At the University of Georgia, lower-division courses consist of three sequences, one in calculus (taught by the mathematics department), one in theory (discrete mathematics and finite automata/formal languages, all taught by computer science faculty), and one in program engineering principles and techniques. There is also a course, not part of any sequence, in assembler language and machine organization.

All of the program engineering courses are taught using MODULA-2 on Sun workstations running Unix. Each class meets for fifty minutes three times per week, for a total of ten weeks. There are no formal laboratory sessions. Successful completion of each course earns three quarter hours of credit.

Students entering the program engineering sequence are expected to know the basics of a modern imperative programming language, including proper use of control structures, data typing (including enumerated types), and the data constructors *array*, *record*, and *set*.[1] Students are not expected to have any knowledge of MODULA-2. A description of each course in our sequence follows.

7.3.1 CS 202 – intermediate computer programming

CS 202 is our first majors' course. Its name reflects the fact that it was formerly our second course, and will be changed soon.

The first programming project in CS 202 is to construct a program, in MODULA-2, using arrays of records. As such, it serves as a convenient bridge from a student's earlier work to this course. Section 7.6.1 contains a sample first programming assignment for CS 202.

Course work in CS 202 consists of three parts:

- introduction to recursion,
- low-level pointer manipulation (linked lists and binary trees), and
- introduction to ADTs and data structures, including the ADTs for lists, restricted lists, stacks and queues.

Each part has at least one corresponding programming assignment. In addition, at least one programming assignment uses separate modules, and at least one assignment requires that students write non-program modules. A sample programming assignment requiring construction of separate modules is given in section 7.6.2. Upon completion

---

[1] These entrance requirements are derived from the College Entrance Examinations Board's syllabus for a secondary-school advanced placement course in computer science. The required language of the course is PASCAL.

of this course, a student is assumed to know all of the high-level parts of MODULA-2, and be ready to begin writing larger programs.

7.3.2 CS 203 – programming project design

Upon arrival at the University of Georgia, I found that many students were not capable of programming at the level required of them in their senior-year courses. CS 203 was introduced as an attempt to overcome this problem by assigning a program that each individual student knows is too difficult for them to do, and then requiring that they complete it (while giving them enough assistance so that completion is a reasonable request). Successful completion of the assignment illustrates to each student that, if the proper techniques are used, it is possible to write code that is larger than can be easily understood. Since virtually all code written today is considered 'programming in the large' [De Remer and Kron, 1976], the techniques learned in this class solve not only the immediate problem of allowing the senior-level instructors to give realistic assignments, but illustrate to students the necessity of using the programming techniques that they already know, but have not previously needed.

CS 203 was designed by K. J. Kochut and me, based on similar courses given at Louisiana State University, and was taught for the first time during Winter Quarter, 1991, by the author.[2] This aim of this course is to introduce students to the techniques of writing moderate-length programs by having them actually write a program of 1000–2000 lines during a five- or six-week period. In order for this to be possible, an instructor must design the program and be able to clearly explain each design decision. In addition, the instructor must make available working versions of each of the necessary ADTs, implementation modules, as well as the main program, to allow students to more easily debug and test their own programs. MODULA-2 allows the definition modules to be discussed and created in class during the design phase of the classroom discussion, and then allows compiled versions of the corresponding implementation modules and main program to be made available for testing purposes. A sample programming assignment for this half of the course is given in section 7.6.3.

The second half of the course presents the first five weeks of a fifteen-week advanced data structures course. During this time, students are introduced to the list ADT in a formal manner, as an example of the formal definitions needed for accurate description of objects. Basic algorithm design techniques (divide and conquer, dynamic programming, local optimization, *etc.*) and run-time analysis of both recursive and non-recursive algorithms (including an introduction to average-case and amortized analysis) are also taught during this second half of the course. Two programming assignments are given here. The first is an 'ADT within an ADT' assignment (an example is given in section 7.6.4), while the second asks students to build a game tree for a relatively straightforward game (*e.g.* order-four reversi).

---

[2] A more complete description of this course has been given earlier [Cater, 1991]; a similar course, not using MODULA-2, was described by Scott [1991].

7.3.3 CS 303 – data structures

CS 303 is the final course in our first-year programming sequence. In this course, students finish their study of data structures and algorithms. Topics in this last ten-week class include symbol tables (hashing, advanced tree representations, *etc.*), priority queues, more on amortized and average-case complexity, sorting, string algorithms, graph algorithms, and a bit of computational geometry. The programming assignments are typical of most advanced data structures classes, and include assignments on symbol tables, sorting, string algorithms and graph algorithms. The sorting assignment is experimental in nature, asking students to construct programs for quicksort, heapsort, an $O(n^2)$ sort, LSD radix sort, at least one other sort, and then compare and contrast the behaviour of each when run on several sets of data.

7.4 Conclusions

In this chapter, we have described the considerations involved in the choice of a programming language for a computer science major's first programming sequence. It was shown that MODULA-2 satisfied all of the requirements. As an example of the use of MODULA-2 in a first programming sequence, we described our five-year experience in our classes at the University of Georgia. We are quite satisfied with the results, which are given below.[3]

- When the courses were first introduced, a high drop rate (approximately 50%) was experienced. This drop rate, which was not unexpected, was predicted to improve after a year or two. It has now been reduced to approximately 10%, which is in line with our expectations. We find that the drop rate in senior-level classes has been reduced as the student's ability to program has improved, and is now around 5%.

- Students completing the sequence are quite pleased with it. Many describe CS 203 as the best course they have taken. This information is based on the standard course evaluation by students as well as students' personal (anonymous) comments.

- Students can now appreciate the advantages of MODULA-2, having seen for the first time how proper structuring of programs aids development and testing.

- Students are now confident that they can write programs that are larger than anything they have seen before, and that the decomposition techniques taught in class and inherent in MODULA-2 are necessary for such work. This is of course the hoped for result; the student evaluations were quite positive in this respect.

- Students are able to program at expected levels in senior courses.

7.5 References and annotated bibliography

ACM Curriculum Committee on Computer Science (1968), Curriculum 68: Recommendations for the Undergraduate Program in Computer Science, *Communications ACM*, **11**(3), 151–97: the first set of curriculum recommendations from the ACM.

---

[3] The majority of these results are obtained from the project portion of CS 203 and the use of MODULA-2; *cf.* [Cater, 1991].

Austing, R. H., Barnes, B. H., Bonnette, D. T., Engel, G. L. and Stokes, G. (1979), Curriculum '78: Recommendations for the Undergraduate Program in Computer Science, *Communications ACM*, **22**(3), 147–66: recommends a 'widely used' language for CS I, switching if necessary to a language more suited to teaching 'good programming style, expression and documentation' in CS II.

Bergin, J. and Greenfield, S. (1989), What Does Modula-2 Need to Fully Support Object-Oriented Programming?, *Journal of Object-oriented Programming*, 31–8.

Budgen, D. (1989), *Software Development with Modula-2*, International Computer Science Series, Addison-Wesley, New York.

Cater, S. C. (1991), Modula-2 in a Program Design Class, in *Proceedings of the Second International Modula-2 Conference, Loughborough, Leicestershire, England*, 292–301: a detailed description of the use of Modula-2 in the programming design class at the University of Georgia.

Coar, D. (1984), Pascal, Ada and Modula-2: A System Programmer's Comparison, *Byte*, 215–32: an early popular comparison of the languages.

Cooper, D. (1990), *Oh, My! Modula-2!: An Introduction to Programming*, W. W. Norton, New York.

Cooper, D. (1990), *Using QuickMod*, W. W. Norton, New York.

Denning, P. J., Comer, D. E., Gries, D., Mulder, M. C., Tucker, A., Turner, A. J. and Young, P. R. (1989), Computing as a Discipline, *Communications ACM*, **32**(1), 9–23: the earliest report on a breadth-first curriculum.

DeRemer, F. and Kron, H. K. (1976), Programming in the Large Versus Programming in the Small, *IEEE Transactions on Software Engineering*, **SE-2**(2), 80–6.

Gibbs, N. E. and Tucker, A. B. (1986), Curriculum for a Liberal Arts Degree in Computer Science, *Communications ACM*, **29**(3), 202–10.

Gutknecht, J. (1984), Tutorial on Modula-2, *Byte*, 157–76.

Helman, P. and Veroff, R. (1988), *Intermediate Problem Solving and Data Structures*, Benjamin-Cummings Series in Structured Programming, Benjamin-Cummings Publishing Company, Menlo Park, California: the text used at the University of Georgia for CS 202.

ISO/IEC JTC1/SC22/WG13 (1994), *Information Technology – Programming languages – Modula-2 2nd Committee Draft Standard: DIS 10514*, ISO/IEC JTC1 Secretariat, Geneva.

JPI (1988), *TopSpeed Modula-2 User's Manual*, Jensen and Partners International, London: user's guide for an early PC based Modula-2.

King, K. N. (1988), *Modula-2: A Complete Guide*, D. C. Heath and Company, Lexington, MA: one of the best introductions to Modula-2; we have recommended this book to our classes since Spring Quarter, 1988.

Kingston, J. H. (1990), *Algorithms and Data Structures: Design, Correctness, Analysis*, International Computer Science Series, Addison-Wesley, New York: the text now used in Georgia's CS 203 and CS 303; a modern treatment of data structures, using Modula-2.

Koffman, E. B. (1988), The Case for Modula-2 in CS1 and CS2, *SIGSCE Bulletin*, **20**(1), presented at the nineteenth ACM SIGSCE Technical Symposium on Computer Science Education: Professor Koffman was an author of the 1984–1985 CS1 and CS2 ACM curriculum recommendations.

Koffman, E. B., Miller, P. L. and Wardle, C. E. (1984), Recommended Curriculum for CS1, 1984, *Communications ACM*, **27**(10), 998–1001: the most recent detailed ACM curriculum recommendation for a first course in computing.

Koffman, E. B., Stemple, D. and Wardle, C. E. (1984), Recommended Curriculum for CS2, 1984, *Communications ACM*, **28**(8), 815–18: the most recent detailed ACM curriculum recommendation for a second course in computing.

Mulder, M. C. and Dalphin, J. (1984), Computer Science Program Requirements and Accreditation – An Interim Report of the ACM/IEEE Computer Society Joint Task Force, *Communications ACM*, **27**(4), 330–5.

Paul, R. J. (1984), An Introduction to Modula-2, *Byte*, 195–210.

Powell Jr. , J. H. (1993), Modula-2/WOLF: A Safe, Minimal, Object-Oriented Extension to Modula-2, Master's thesis, University of Georgia, Athens, GA, USA.

Scott, T. J. (1991), A Strategy for Teaching Large Programming Projects, in *Proceedings of the 29th Annual Association for Computing Machinery Southeast Regional Conference*, W. B. Day, K. H. Chang and C. McCreary (eds), 238–42, Auburn, AL, Association for Computing Machinery, ACM.

TDI (1986), *TDI Modula-2/ST User Manual*: the user's manual for one of the first microcomputer Modula-2 compilers; this version was for the Atari ST.

Tucker, A. B. (1991), *Computing Curricula 1991: Report of the ACM/IEEE-CS Joint Curriculum Task Force*, ACM Press: the most recent ACM computing curriculum.

Wirth, N. (1988), *Programming with Modula-2*, Texts and Monographs in Computer Science, Springer-Verlag, Berlin, 4th edition: the most recent edition of the original definition of Modula-2.

7.6 Appendix – Programming assignments

In this appendix are listed the programming assignments discussed earlier.

7.6.1 A first assignment in CS 202

For this assignment, you will write a program to present baseball batting statistics.

The input

Input to the program will consist of no more than 100 lines, each containing a player's name, a game number, and the number of at bats and hits for the game for the named player. Data in each line will be tab separated. On each line, the name will begin in column one, and should contain no more than thirty characters. If the name is less than thirty characters, no padding of blanks will occur. The name will be followed by a tab. A game number, in the range 1, ..., 200, will immediately follow the tab. The number of at bats, in the range 1, ..., 10, will follow (after a tab), and will be followed by the number of hits. Each line, including the last, will be terminated by an end-of-line character.

Data validation

Input must be validated. At a minimum, this should include the following.

1. Proper name length. Each over-length name should be flagged with a printed warning, but still be processed. A line having no name (*i.e.* the first character is not alphabetic), should be flagged and not processed.

2. Proper game number range. Lines with improper game numbers should be flagged and not processed.

3. Proper range for number of at bats. Since it is technically possible for there to be more at bats than allowed in the range, lines having more at bats than allowed should be flagged and processed. It is assumed that no input will be given for a player with no at bats in a given game, so that zero is not an allowed number of at bats. Input lines having zero at bats should be flagged and not processed.

4. Proper number of hits. The range for hits is zero to the number of at bats. Lines having hit number outside the proper range should be flagged and not processed.

Flagging information should include the nature of the error, and should be easily distinguished from regular echoes of the input. I suggest beginning such lines with either 'ERROR' or 'WARNING', whichever is appropriate.

The Output

Output from your program must consist of the following, appropriately labelled.

1. The standard identification information (who you are, *etc.*).

2. An echo of the input, with interspersed warning and error messages.

3. A list of (player, batting average) pairs, one pair per line, sorted by player's name. You may assume that the input name will not need to be changed for sorting. Note that batting averages are normally given accurate to three digits.

4. A list of the three players having the highest batting average, presented as three lines of (batting average, player) pairs, sorted by batting average.

5. For each player, a running list of batting averages, by game. This will be in the form of a heading listing the player's name, followed by a line for each game in which the player had at least one at bat. Each of these lines will contain game number, number of at bats, number of hits, and batting average for the games up to and including this one. This data will be sorted by game number.

6. Summary data, which will include:

   (a) the number of distinct players;

   (b) the number of distinct games;

   (c) the player having an at bat in the most number of games (in case of a tie, list all players in the tie);

   (d) the player having an at bat in the least number of games, with a tie handled as before.

Algorithms and data structures

You may use any sorting algorithm that you know, but write your own code. Do not use code from a book; do not use any of the sorts built into Unix. If you do not remember a sort from an earlier class, consider a *bubble sort*: a sort which makes multiple passes through the data, comparing adjacent items and swapping if necessary; stopping after the first pass in which no swaps were made.

You are to use only one array to store the input data. This array should be an array of records of the appropriate type.

A batting average is the number of hits divided by the number of at bats.

7.6.2 A CS 202 assignment requiring use of separate modules

For this assignment, you will construct a sorted list, in several different ways.

The input

Input to the program will consist of an unknown number of cardinal numbers.

The output

The output from your program will consist of several listings of the input data, sorted either ascending or descending. The details are given in the algorithms and data structures section. Be sure to provide the standard identification information.

Algorithms and data structures

This program will give you experience in using pointer variables, and in use and construction of abstract data types. It is not meant to be an approximation to any sort of practical problem, only an exercise in proficiency.

You are to do the following, in the order and manner described below.

1. Read the data an item at a time.

2. As each item is read, store it into a *sorted linked list*, and into an ADT *binary search tree (BST)*. A linked implementation is to be used for the BST.

3. After the data has been read and stored, print out the contents of each data structure, sorted into increasing order. The BST should use an inorder traversal. Each print-out should be labelled.

4. Make a copy of the sorted linked list.

5. Using one copy of the sorted linked list, print the data out in decreasing sorted order by doing an *in-place* reversal of the list, and printing the result.

6. Using the remaining copy of the sorted linked list, and the provided Stack module, print the data in decreasing sorted order.

7. Using a reverse inorder traversal of the BST, print the data in decreasing sorted order.

8. Release all memory.

7.6.3 A CS 203 project

For your first assignment, you will implement a program to assist in solving crypto-quotes. A *cryptoquote* is a quotation, in English, which has had a permutation applied to its letters. Recall that a *permutation* is a finite bijection, so in this case a permutation is a one-to-one, onto function f: 'A', ..., 'Z' $\rightarrow$ 'A', ..., 'Z'.

Hence, the cryptoquote

```
UIF RVJDL CSPXO GPY KVNQFE PWFS UIF MBAZ EPH. - BOPOZNPVT
```

is obtained from the clear text

```
THE QUICK BROWN FOX JUMPED OVER THE LAZY DOG. - ANONYMOUS
```

via the permutation which maps A to B, B to C, ..., Y to Z, and Z to A. Note that blanks and punctuation are not affected by the permutation, and that only capital letters are used in the quotation. In general, there is no pattern to the permutation, unlike in this example. As long as there is a permutation of the letters, a legitimate encryption results.

Program description

This program will be screen-oriented, that is, most of the information will be on the screen at all times, and will be automatically updated as needed. There will be several 'windows' of information, including the main cryptoquote window, the command window, and the guess window. The main body of the program will be a loop which will read a command from standard input, echo it to the command window, execute it, update the appropriate windows, and repeat. There are several commands, each described below.

r *file* Read a new cryptoquote from *file*, and reset the program for a new decryption. On a successful read, no output is performed. Any error messages generated by the read are printed to the command window.

w *file* Write a cryptoquote and its solution (or partial solution) to *file*. Error messages are printed to the command window. See below for output file format.

p Redraw (print) the cryptoquote window.

g x=y Guess that the letter x in the encryption is actually the letter y. If x has previously been guessed, this new guess will replace the old one. Update the guess window.

u x Undo the guess x, and update the guess window.

f1 Based on a comparison of the cryptoquote with a table of single-letter frequencies in English, automatically guess a new letter. The output from this command will be written to a suggestion window, in the same format as the guess window. The guess will be made by choosing the unguessed letter occurring most often in the encrypted text, and matching it with the highest-frequency unchosen letter in clear. Note that the guess will not be made for you; it must still be entered with the 'g' command.

f2 Based on a comparison of the cryptoquote with a table of *digram* (double-letter) frequencies in English, guess one or two letters. The output from this command will be in the suggestion window, in the same format as the guess window. The guess will be made by choosing the unguessed or partially unguessed pair occurring most often in the encrypted text, and matching it with the highest-frequency unchosen or consistent partially chosen pair in clear. Note that the guesses will not be made for you; they must still be entered with the 'g' command.

f3 Based on a comparison of the cryptoquote with a table of *trigram* (triple-letter) frequencies in English, guess up to three letters. The output from this command will be in the suggestion window, in the same format as the guess window. The guess will be made by choosing the unguessed or partially unguessed triple occurring most often in the encrypted text, and matching it with the highest-frequency unchosen or consistent partially chosen triple in clear. As before, guesses will not be made, but only suggested.

m *pattern* Match the given *pattern* with all words meeting the requirements. A pattern is a string consisting of periods, digits and letters. Letters match themselves, periods match any letter, and digits match any letter, but match the same letter each time the same digit appears. Hence,

'.....'	matches any five-letter word
'c...d'	matches any five-letter word beginning with c and ending with d,
'..11..'	matches any six-letter word whose middle letters were the same ('bottle' and 'common', for example), and
'12321'	matches five-letter palindromes (such as 'radar' and 'civic'). The pattern '31213' would also match five-letter palindromes.

Output from the m command (in a match window) will be one word per line, in alphabetical order.

q The quit command causes the program to exit gracefully. A confirmation prompt is printed in the command window. No other output is printed.

I/O, files and calling conventions

The program may be called in two ways: either with just the program name or with the program name followed by a file name. In the first case, the program simply begins to read stdin; in the second, the given file is assumed to be a cryptoquote and is read as if an 'r' command had been given. This program will use Unix standard I/O.

Information about single-letter, digram and trigram frequencies must be read in from separate files. These files must be supplied by the programmer.

Output from the 'w' command will consist of pairs of lines, separated by a single blank line. The first line of each pair is a portion of the cryptoquote, while the second line consists of the current state of the translation of the cryptoquote directly above it. Assuming a forty-character line, a possible printout of the above cryptoquote would be:

```
UIF RVJDL CSPXO GPY KVNQFE PWFS UIF
  E  UI     O   O   U E  OE    E

MBAZ EPH. - BOPOZNPVT
 A    O . - A O   OU
```

Note that the line is broken at the first blank preceding the line length.

Notes

1. Program requirements:

   (a) properly documented program source;

   (b) all programmer-created modules, properly documented;

   (c) all programmer-created accessory files (for the 'f' commands);

   (d) a 'makefile';

   (e) a well-written 'man' page, in standard format;

   (f) a brief programmer's overview of the program; this need be no more than a top-down description of the program, down to the procedure level, with a one- or two-sentence description of each procedure.

2. Any errors in input will be noted in the command window, then ignored.

7.6.4 An 'ADT within an ADT' assignment

In this program you will construct an ADT *Deque* using the ADT *Stack*, with *Stack* implemented as a linked list. The major aim of the program will be to ensure that you maintain proper modularity in your ADTs, while creating a program that is correct and conforms to the accepted means of expression.

The ADTs

The three ADTs to be used in this program are *CharString*, *Deque of CharString* and *Stack of CharString*. Each will be defined.

A *CharString* is a list of one or more ASCII characters, terminated by an end-of-string mark. The end-of-string mark is not a part of the *CharString*. The only two functions that are a part of this ADT are:

$$READ(input) \rightarrow C, \quad \text{and}$$
$$WRITE(C) \rightarrow output,$$

where C is of type *CharString*. The *CharString* will be implemented as a linked list.

A *Stack of CharString* is defined as:

$$PUSH(S, x) \rightarrow S$$
$$PEEK(S) \rightarrow x$$
$$POP(S) \rightarrow S$$
$$ISEMPTY(S) \rightarrow b$$
$$CREATE() \rightarrow S$$
$$DESTROY(S) \rightarrow$$

where S is of type *Stack*, x is of type *CharString*, and b is of type *Boolean*. The definitions of each of these functions, as well as their pre- and post-conditions, will be discussed in class.

A *Deque of CharString* is a restricted list structure that can allow inserts and deletes at either end of the structure, but not in the middle. Its functions are:

$$INSERTF(D, x) \rightarrow D$$
$$INSERTR(D, x) \rightarrow D$$
$$DELF(D) \rightarrow D$$
$$DELR(D) \rightarrow D$$
$$ISEMPTY(D) \rightarrow b$$
$$FRONT(D) \rightarrow x$$
$$REAR(D) \rightarrow x$$

As with the *Stack*, the definitions, pre- and post-conditions of each of these functions will be discussed in class.

The program

You will construct a *Deque of CharString* using the following structure.

```
DEQUE = RECORD
            frontup: STACK;
            rearup: STACK;
            which: (front, rear);
        END;
```

Before the execution of any *Deque of CharString* function, either all the stack elements are in `frontup` or all the elements are in `rearup`; which stack contains the elements is indicated by the variable `which`. This pre-condition is also required to be a post-condition.

You will write a program to implement this *Deque*. The *Stack*s and *CharString*s must be exported as opaque types.

The input

Your program will use standard input and output, and may use any module which allows I/O to be redirected in the normal Unix manner (this includes `InOut`). Each input line will consist of one instruction to the *Deque*. The input instruction set is:

```
insertf S
insertr S
delf
delr
front
rear
printall
```

where S is a variable of type *CharString*. (Note that blanks may occur wherever no ambiguity results.) Each instruction causes its associated ADT operation to be performed, and then causes the front and rear of the deque to be printed to output. The instruction `printall` is a special case; it causes the entire deque to be printed, from front to rear, with one element per line.

The output

Output will be written to standard output. It will consist of an echo of each input line, followed by the values of the front and rear of the deque, each labelled. The `printall` command will cause the entire *Deque* to be printed.

8 Why Ada is for you

Brian Wichmann

The ADA programming language is mature after 10 years of standardized use. The use of ADA in various contexts is explored, including those areas of high and low existing usage. The changes with ADA 95 are analysed. These indicate a broader potential usage over the next ten years.

8.1 Introduction

There is no such thing as an ideal programming language since a language design is a compromise. Nevertheless, it is my contention that ADA is 'better' in almost all respects than the languages in wide use today. Of course, being involved in the original ADA language design means I have a bias!

In choosing a language, the design decisions that have been made must be taken into account. The main ones are:

Static semantic checks: ADA compilers are required to perform many checks so that errors which must be found by program execution in many languages are detected by the compiler. The so-called 'strong typing' is only one part of this.

Dynamic semantic checks: ADA systems are required to undertake dynamic checks so that the majority of programs that execute to completion are well-defined. For example, ADA requires that pointers be checked for `nil` on dereferencing, and array subscripts are checked. *No other ISO-standard language requires that such checks be performed.*

Broad application area: ADA is suitable for many application areas and therefore has all the basic functionality present in FORTRAN, PASCAL and MODULA-2. ADA can be used as a low-level language by using explicit escape mechanisms and controlling the physical representation of data, or as a very high-level language in which all the operations on a data type are provided by the encapsulation.

Large program construction: ADA permits the construction of large programs without loss of security by means of a library mechanism. This means that one can build on top of secure encapsulations and rely upon the ADA system to detect any misuse.

Of course, ADA is an imperative language of the ALGOL school and therefore cannot be compared with PROLOG [Clocksin and Mellish, 1984], VDM-SL [Dawes, 1991] or HASKELL [Hammond *et al.*, 1995], (for example).

Given the above design attributes of ADA, what usage can be expected, what defects does the language have which inhibit take-up? This chapter attempts to throw some light on these matters.

It must be freely admitted that ADA has some defects:

- The language is large and therefore difficult to learn in its entirety. Just like CO-BOL, almost nobody needs to know the entire language. Moreover, in ADA 95, the compilation system can be configured to prohibit the use of some language features, such as tasking, if required.

- Compilers are slow, especially on PC-level machines. This is a consequence of the size of the language and the semantic checks undertaken. Surely it is better to detect errors during compilation rather than execution, or even worse, just produce the wrong results without warning?

- Compilers are sometimes expensive. The initial cost of development was high, but the future looks bright, as we shall see later.

- Some think ADA is verbose, but I see no justification in this claim. One must compare like with like. ADA is designed to aid in producing readable, intelligible code, and I think it succeeds in this respect. However, as always, the key decisions are with the programmer.

- Some also think that ADA is inefficient. This is only true if one compares poor ADA code with the equivalent in languages which provide no run-time checking. Using appropriate range constraints on array subscripts, for instance, produces efficient and secure code. One does pay some cost in compiling times, since an analysis of the program is needed by the compiler to remove the run-time checks.

8.2 Programming paradigms and applications

If a programming language cannot support some basic operations, certain applications will be ruled out. For instance, support of floating-point arithmetic is needed for numerical applications. A contentious issue arose in the ADA language design over fixed-point arithmetic. ADA provides this for signal processing applications on chips without floating-point arithmetic. However, most users would be happy without the facility at all. In ADA 95, the fixed-point facility has been extended to handle financial data as in COBOL.

A language also needs to be able to support various programming paradigms (unless it is just for research purposes). Hence the ADA package mechanism can be used to support abstraction in various styles, some of which are relatively new to most users.

8.2.1 Abstraction

The procedural abstraction of FORTRAN is widely known and understood. The problem with this is the need to combine it with data abstraction, information hiding and other more recent techniques. The ADA *package* provides all of these facilities in a relatively simple mechanism.

In the original language design, the 'Green' proposal (reprinted in [Ichbiah *et al.*, 1991]) went beyond the requirements the US Department of Defense produced to provide default parameters to subprograms. In my view, this choice has been shown to be correct, since the provision of many system facilities rests on defaults, which when expressed in procedural form give rise to default parameters.

As an example of an abstraction in ADA, consider a graphics package in which several forms of line can be drawn. An outline of this might be:

```
package Line_Draw is

   type Point is
      record
         X, Y: Float;
      end record;

   type Dash_Pattern is
      ...

   procedure Draw (From, To: Point; Width : Float := ...;
                   Dashing: Dash_Pattern := ...);

end Line_Draw;
```

The procedure Draw is completely general, but if the default values of the parameters Width and Dashing are used, then the procedure call does not need to specify them. This is much better than providing a mechanism to change the Width and Dashing values separately, since the package itself does not need to preserve state information. Default parameters are widely used in industry, such as in the calls on an operating system.

ADA provides for direct support for data abstraction via private types. Here, some operations on the implemented type are hidden so that the provider of an abstraction can produce an interface matching the logical properties required. Also, even for an ordinary type, ADA provides a mechanism for specifying the actual hardware representation of the type, so that inter-working with the external world can be properly supported.

For instance, the ADA input–output system is specified as an ADA package. Here, the file types are private types which can therefore be chosen to map simply onto the mechanism provided by the operating system.

Unlike MODULA-2, ADA provides support for secure abstraction. This can be achieved by using default initialization of a private type, so that no problems can arise from uninitialized values. Indeed, the default initialization of access values (pointers) to nil makes secure abstraction simple.

8.2.2 Machine orientation

It is important to realize that ADA is a broad-spectrum language. It can be used as a high-level language in which the program design uses several levels of abstraction. There are few restrictions in ADA (unlike non-extended PASCAL) to inhibit the use of a high degree of abstraction.

In contrast, ADA can be used in a mode very close to the actual machine. The pre-defined data types map onto existing architectures in a simple way, so that use of such types results in efficient code. The ability to control the hardware representation of user-defined types also enables a machine-oriented view of program design to be taken. Bitwise conversion of values to avoid the strictures of strong typing is also provided.

For instance, if the input to a program is a complex record with a predefined layout, the layout details are separated from the logical structure (which is given by an ordinary record definition).

8.2.3 Concurrency

Undoubtedly, the most radical part of the ADA 83 design was the concurrency feature built on the rendezvous. It is both secure and powerful, and yet permits several different programming paradigms. However, problems have arisen in obtaining performance comparable with the use of machine-code primitives. For this reason, ADA 95 introduces protected types which allow for a more efficient implementation of concurrent, controlled access to data.

8.3 Ada 95

The project to replace and revise the ADA 83 standard started in 1990 with general requirements [Department of Defense, 1990]. The new standard was published in 1995 [International Standards Organization, 1995]. An overview of the new language, ADA 95,[1] has been written by John Barnes [1993]. ADA 95 is the *first* language standardized by ISO/IEC to support object-oriented programming.

In this section, just a few features of ADA 95 are considered which are thought to be relevant to the choice of a language.

8.3.1 Object-oriented design

The object-oriented view of abstraction is not fully supported in ADA 83, since dynamic binding of operations is not provided. This omission has been covered in ADA 95 by a very comprehensive facility using *tagged types*, in which a type can be extended with both additional fields and operations.

---

[1] Many people still call ADA 95 ADA9X which was the name used between 1990 and 1995.

8.3.2 Cheap compiling technology

One problem with ADA 83 has been the absence of public-domain implementations, especially for academic experimentation. As part of the ADA project, a GNU ADA compiler is being produced by New York University. It is confidently expected that this will be of high quality and will meet the expectations of the academic community. Initial releases will be for Sun SPARC workstations and PC (OS/2), and the source code will be available in due course.

8.3.3 Safety and security applications

Although insecurities have been noted in the language [Wichmann, 1989], ADA 83 is nevertheless a good choice for critical systems, especially using a carefully chosen subset.

A feature of ADA 95 is an annex aimed at addressing issues which arise specifically in the safety and security application areas. This is in addition to a redesign of certain features in ADA 83 to remove some of the insecurities. The annex allows a user to select a subset (that is, a subset in simple syntactic terms) which is enforced by the compiler. Also, and more usefully, an implementation may provide a simplified run-time system for which properties can be deduced to aid the production of critical systems.

8.3.4 External interfacing

In ADA 83, a problem arose in interfacing to such systems as Windows because of the use of 'call back', since the language does not support pointers to subprograms. ADA 95 has resolved this (in a *type-secure* way, of course). In several other ways, ADA 95 acknowledges the outside world by making it easy to produce ADA systems which are not 'embedded'. Some key developments are:

Posix binding: The development of a standard operating system interface is an important advance which allows users to protect their software investment against changes in the underlying hardware. An ADA binding is very well advanced, and should be the second language binding approved for standardization. This implies that ADA is the only type-secure language having such a binding and therefore makes it the most suitable applications-level language for development on top of Posix.

SQL binding: SQL is a very different language from ADA and hence the question of providing a full and effective interface is not straightforward. This issue has been very well addressed and the technical issues resolved, resulting in an ISO standard.

This suggests that, for the first time, serious database applications can be undertaken in ADA without requiring specialized support from an ADA compiler vendor or database-system supplier.

Mathematical routines: One grave embarrassment for me with ADA 83 was the inability to call the square root function in a standard way. In the context of ADA 83, this obvious gap has been filled. For ADA 95 the problem will not exist at all, since implementations will be required to support a number of basic mathematical packages (which are more than those in FORTRAN 90, say).

8.3.5 Outline of the conference example

I shall use the object-oriented features of ADA 95. The basic class is that of a `Person`, so I introduce a package having this as a tagged type:

```
package People_Class is

    type Person is tagged
       record
           Name: ...
           Address: ...
           E_Mail: ...
           Tele: ...
           FAX: ...
       end record;

end People_Class;
```

I have left out details of the actual fields. The `Name` should be further decomposed into `Title`, `First_Name`, `Family_Name`, *etc.*

Obviously, we need to produce a solution to the problem of handling conference information which is general enough to handle most events. To do this, I introduce the package `Conference` which is designed to be generic with respect to the number of sessions and the number of papers. No textual change should be needed to handle a different conference, merely an instantiation of the package.

Within the `Conference` package, we can extend the `Person` record in different ways corresponding to the different types of people involved. Each extension has different information:

```
with People_Class; use People_Class;
generic
    No_Sessions, No_Papers: Positive;
package Conference is

    subtype Session is Positive range 1 .. No_Sessions;
    subtype Paper is Positive range 1 .. No_Papers;

    type Presenter is new Person with
       record
          Session_No: Session;
          Paper_No: Paper;
          Paper_Title: ...
       end record;

    type Chair is new Person with
       record
          Session_No: Session;
       end record;

    type Exhibitor is new Person with
       record
           Company: ...
       end record;

    type Delegate is new Person with
       record
           In_OU, Has_Paid, Hotel_Required: Boolean;
```

```
    end record;

  Chairs: array (Session) of Chair;
  Presenters: array (Paper) of Presenter;

  procedure Print(P: Presenter);
  procedure Print(P: Chair);
  procedure Print(P: Exhibitor);
  procedure Print(P: Delegate);

  procedure Register(D: Person'Class);
  procedure Print_Delegates;
  procedure Print_Conference_Programme;

end Conference;
```

For each of the extensions of Person, we provide a (different) procedure Print which allows the requirements of the (UK) Data Protection Act to be complied with. We allow for an arbitrary number of delegates by handling them within the package – the only interface is to Register and Print_Delegates.

The Register procedure is a class-wide operation so that one can register a Chair, Presenter, *etc.*, as well as an ordinary Delegate. The body would be:

```
  procedure Register(D: Person'Class) is
    begin
    ...
    Print(D);   -- a dispatching operation
    end Register;
```

After the main registration functions, the details of the delegate registered are printed out. However, the particular overloading of the Print procedure called will depend upon the tag associated with D. Hence this is a dispatching operation in which a dynamic choice is made. Note that the alternative of inserting a *case* statement is much less flexible, since all the potential choices would have to be selected in advance – no additions could be made to the Person class.

An alternative design approach is to design our class Person using abstraction and then refine the design by providing actual subprograms to realize the abstraction. The key starting point is the package:

```
package Abstract_Person is

  type Person is abstract tagged null record;

  procedure Print (P: Person) is abstract;

  procedure Register (P: Person) is abstract;

end Abstract_Person;
```

Our root type Person has no components, and since the type is abstract, we cannot declare objects of this type. However, by providing concrete types by adding components and subprograms, we can build up a system to obtain a similar result to the first design. However, the subprograms Print and Register *must* be provided for every type rooted on Person, since this is required by the abstraction. In consequence, the ADA type system enforces the requirement of the aforementioned Data Protection Act to provide a written record of the person's computer data!

The main points from this example are:

- Conventional object-oriented programming is provided by the ADA 95 tagged types.

- Re-use can easily be achieved by appropriate use of generics.

- Package specifications should be easy to follow and understand.

- Package bodies (not given here) are much longer and more detailed, but this is no impediment to the *use* of packages.

- Tagged types means that variant records are only provided in ADA 95 for compatibility reasons. Tagged types are easier to use and more powerful (and safer too).

- Re-use via tagged types *does not even require recompilation* to add significant functionality. The additions can therefore be made with greater confidence.

- The ADA 95 facilities should be viewed as *extension programming*, since designing for extension is important in a rapidly changing world.

8.4 Conclusion – Why choose Ada?

My strong belief is that ADA is a very good choice for a conventional imperative programming language in very many cases. To emphasize this, a number of specific contexts are considered below:

Teaching: ADA provides abstraction (in several forms), concurrency, and exception handling in the context of just one language. This implies that many fundamental concepts can be addressed without being distracted by introducing another language (with trivial issues like syntax and compiler commands, to be addressed yet again). As noted above, a system can be configured to exclude some language features if this simplifies the teaching.

Large projects: The secure separate compilation, in which abstractions can be exported to the entire system, makes ADA an ideal choice. For large projects, it is clear that the compiler should check interfaces at the highest level, not just plug in entry addresses. ADA has 'make' built-in. The high-level features of ADA nevertheless do not require complex support other than ways which are an obvious consequence of the feature being used.

Safety and security: ADA 95 is the only major language to specifically address the complex issues of obtaining very high-assurance software. In contrast, the use of the language C is deprecated in the draft IEC standard [IEC/SC65A/Secretariat 122, 1991] for reasons that are clear: one requires compile-time checking to provide the assurance needed. (This could be increased still further by the use of a specialized language like NEWSPEAK [Currie, 1987].) The advantage of using ADA rather than a special-purpose language for critical systems is the ability to exploit the ADA technology, such as the wide range of compilers, text books [Watt *et al.*, 1987], and knowledge of the language. In Europe, it seems that the majority of the current generation of railway signalling software is written in ADA (such as that in 'The Chunnel').

Portability: The rapidly changing hardware development implies that expensive software must be written to migrate gracefully to numerous platforms. A portable language like ADA is ideal here, especially with the Posix binding which implies that all the software down to a Posix interface can be written in ADA.

Acknowledgements

Useful comments and suggestions were received on earlier drafts of this chapter from Peter Robinson, Kees Pronk and John Barnes.

8.5 References

Barnes, J. G. P. (1993), *Introducing Ada 9X. Ada 9X Project Report*, Technical Report, U. S. Department of Defense.

Clocksin, W. F. and Mellish, C. S. (1984), *Programming in PROLOG*, Springer-Verlag, Berlin, 2nd edition.

Currie, I. F. (1987), New Speak – an unexceptional language, *Software Engineering Journal*, **1**, 170–6.

Dawes, J. (1991), *The VDM-SL Reference Guide*, Pitman, London.

Department of Defense (1990), *Ada 9X Project Report – Ada 9X Requirements*, U. S. Department of Defense.

Hammond, K. (ed.), Augustsson, L., Boutel, B., Burton, W., Fairbairn, J., Fasel, J., Gordon, A., Guzman, M. M., Hughes, J., Hudak, P., Johnsson, T., Jones, M., Kieburtz, D., Nikhil, R., Partain, W., Peterson, J., Peyton Jones, S. and Wadler, P. (1995), Report on the Programming Language Haskell, in *Procs. Functional Programming Languages and Computer Architecture, FPCA '95, La Jolla, California*, also available via the World Wide Web, `http://haskell.systemsz.cs.yale.edu`.

Ichbiah, J. D., Barnes, J. G. P., Firth, R. J. and Woodger, M. (1991), *Rationale for the Design of the Ada Programming Language*, Cambridge University Press, Cambridge, England.

IEC/SC65A/(Secretariat 122), (1991), *Software for computers in the application of industrial safety-related systems*, International Electrotechnical Committee.

International Standards Organization (1995), *Information Technology – Programming Languages – Ada*, ISO/IEC 8652:1995(E), ISO/IEC, Geneva (also available from national standards bodies and via the World-wide Web).

Watt, D. A., Wichmann, B. A. and Findlay, W. (1987), *Ada: Language and Methodology*, Prentice-Hall, Hemel Hempstead, UK.

Wichmann, B. A. (1989), *Insecurities in the Ada Programming Language*, NPL Technical Report DITC 137/89, National Physical Laboratory.

9   About Extended Pascal

David Joslin

This chapter provides a brief history of the development of EXTENDED PASCAL and by means of illustrative examples provides a fairly full picture of the extensions provided by the language. The emergence of compilers and the prospects for revision of the standard are also discussed.

9.1 History

The programming language PASCAL [Jensen and Wirth, 1975] was invented by Niklaus Wirth in the early 1970s, and became very popular, not only as a teaching language but also for systems programming and certain applications. It is a safe, reliable, language, featuring strong data-typing and syntax which encourages top-down design and structured programming. It was standardized by BSI (British Standards Insititution) and ISO (International Standards Organization) in the early 1980s [International Standards Organization, 1990]; this standardized language is very close to Wirth's original design. An important development in popularizing and ensuring adherence to the standard was the production of the PASCAL Validation Suite [Wichmann and Ciechanowicz, 1983]; BSI and other standards bodies have used this to test, and issue validation certificates for, the great majority of PASCAL implementations.

However, it quickly became apparent that various facilities needed to be added to the language to allow its use as a practical tool. Implementations provided these by extensions to the language. When surveys of extensions in PASCAL implementations were carried out by me in 1985 [Joslin, 1985] and by Brian Wichmann and me the following year [Joslin and Wichmann, 1986], some extensions were found to be very common indeed. The ISO PASCAL working group was re-established, and, in conjunction with the US PASCAL committee, produced a new standard, EXTENDED PASCAL [ISO/IEC, 1991]. This standard added many of the widely-found extensions (in a standard way) to the classic PASCAL language, but it also went significantly further, especially in the areas of modularity, data encapsulation, parameterized types, and general binding of internal variables to external entities. Features of the extended language have been described in various papers by Tony Hetherington [Hetherington, 1993a, 1993b] and me [Joslin, 1985a, 1987, 1989].

9.2 Why might one choose Extended Pascal?

The clearest answer to this question is: to gain the features that are desired of a programming language, without losing the immense investment that exists in PASCAL 'legacy' code and expertise. PASCAL has been a *very* popular programming language. There are many implementations of it, much software written in it, many programmers expert in it.

Nicklaus Wirth has produced 'successor' designs for languages – MODULA-2 [Wirth, 1980], OBERON [Wirth, 1988]. Whatever the undoubted merits of these languages, they suffer from a practical viewpoint in not being supersets of PASCAL. They contain sufficient changes and incompatibilities to make them different languages. Existing PASCAL software would have to be converted or rewritten, skills would have to be relearnt.

EXTENDED PASCAL, on the other hand, *is* a true superset of classic PASCAL. For example, when the 'ISO 7185 features only' switch is set in the Prospero EXTENDED PASCAL compiler, it passes the (non-extended) PASCAL Validation Suite [Wichmann and Ciechanowicz, 1983]. There are minimal problems in recompiling existing PASCAL programs with EXTENDED PASCAL compilers – perhaps a few changes to identifiers would be needed, if a program had used any of the new word-symbols (such as MODULE) as identifiers, but that would be all.

9.3 Implementations

One full implementation of the EXTENDED PASCAL standard has been produced: the aforementioned Prospero compiler, which runs on (even quite small) PCs under DOS or OS/2.

DEC PASCAL, for Digital's VAX (VMS) operating system and new ALPHA (Unix or Windows NT) machines, contains most of the features in the EXTENDED PASCAL standard, and looks (to this outside observer) set to develop into full implementation.

Edinburgh Portable Compilers' PASCAL-E (for Unix platforms) also contains many of the features of EXTENDED PASCAL.

Thus, especially for areas such as education which are heavily dominated by PCs and Unix platforms, good implementations are available.

9.4 Future developments

The list of features that were considered for the revision to PASCAL which became EXTENDED PASCAL was huge. Many, many features were *not* incorporated in the standard.[1] Some of these are:

- exception handling,
- concurrent processes,
- alphanumeric labels,
- alternative-precision arithmetic,
- *rem* operator,
- strict-inclusion set operators,
- bitwise logical operators,
- equality tests on arrays and records,
- extended *with* statement,
- *return* statement,
- *loop..exit* statement,
- assert-statement,
- *first* and *last* functions,
- *max* and *min* functions,
- sequential-file *update* procedure,
- *addressof/sizeof* functions.

The next revision of the EXTENDED PASCAL standard is due for the mid-1990s. It may or may not consider some of the above; it may include object-oriented facilities, based on a technical report produced by the US PASCAL committee and ISO PASCAL groups published by ANSI [ANSI, 1993]. Exception handling may also be included, via the new object-oriented facilities. 'Internationalization' – for example the handling of extended character sets in identifiers, strings, *etc.*– is likely to be required of all future programming language standards; the ISO working group is studying this for PASCAL, and is also studying the incorporation of language-independent features, for example the forthcoming language-independent arithmetic standards.

9.5 Features of Extended Pascal

This section provides illustrative examples (rather than full definitions) of what is new in EXTENDED PASCAL, that is, what extensions to classic PASCAL have been introduced. The main features of each extension are shown with brief explanations or commentary given in comments (between braces). Upper-case letters are used for emphasis, that is, to mark the use of new features, new built-in identifiers, keywords or combinations of keywords.

9.5.1 Modules, separate compilation and restricted types

This extension will provide both type-secure separate compilation and, to some extent, data encapsulation. A module's interface will be of the form:

---

[1] This does not, of course, mean that an implementation may not provide types such as SHORTREAL and SHORTINT, or functions such as ADDRESSOF and SIZEOF, but that there will be no standard form of these facilities.

```
MODULE  name  INTERFACE  (parameters, if any);

EXPORT  exported-interfaces        { defines one or more interfaces,
                                     i.e. collections of identifiers
                                     defined in the module, for use
                                     by other modules }

IMPORT  imported-interfaces        { specifies one or more interfaces
                                     to be imported from other
                                     modules into this module heading }

const/type/var  definitions,       { for identifiers in interface    }
procedure/function  headings       { specifications in EXPORT section }

END.  { of Module Heading }
```

Its implementation will be of the form:

```
MODULE  name  IMPLEMENTATION;

IMPORT  imported-interfaces        { specifies one or more interfaces
                                     to be imported from other modules
                                     into this module block }

const/type/var declarations,       {                        }
procedure/function declarations,   { Here's the real stuff! }
initialization and finalization    {                        }

END.  { of Module Block }
```

If separate compilation is not required, the module heading and block may be combined and a slightly simpler notation employed, as in the following example. The example implements a stack of items of the type ItemType; only the identifiers ItemType, push, pop, stackempty and stackfull need to be known outside the stack-manipulation procedures.

Note the syntax for initialization and finalization of modules.

```
MODULE StackModule;

EXPORT StackInterface = (push, pop, stackempty, stackfull);

IMPORT Item;                          { import type for item }

procedure push (val: item);
procedure pop (var val: item);
function stackempty: Boolean;
function stackfull: Boolean;

end;  { of heading }

const  max = ...                      { maximum stack size }

var stack: array [1..max] of Item;    { stack }
    top: 0..max;                      { stack pointer }
```

```
procedure push ;                      { push item onto stack }
   begin
   if  top < max  then
      begin
      top := top+1;
      stack[top] := val
      end
   else  { Error - stack full }
   end;

procedure pop ;                       { pop item from stack }
   begin
   if  top > 0  then
      begin
      val := stack[top];
      top := top-1
      end
   else  { Error - stack empty }
   end;

function stackempty ;                 { stack-empty test }
   begin
   stackempty := (top=0)
   end;

function stackfull ;                  { stack-full test }
   begin
   stackfull := (top=max)
   end;

TO BEGIN DO  top := 0;                { initialization }

TO END DO  if  top > 0  then          { finalization }
   { Error? - stack not emptied };

end.  { of StackModule }
```

The name of a type may be exported without revealing the internal structure, via the RESTRICTED facility. The preceding example can be generalized to permit the module to operate on multiple stacks (of the same item type) which are declared outside the module but which can only be manipulated inside it, because their structure is only known there.

```
MODULE StackModule;
EXPORT
   StackInterface = (StackType, push, pop, stackempty, stackfull);

IMPORT ItemType;                        { import type for item }

const  max = ...                        { maximum stack size }

type  StackRecord =
         record
         top: 0..max  value 0;          { stack pointer }
         stack: array [1..max] of item  { stacked items }
         end;
      StackType = RESTRICTED StackRecord;  { for export }

procedure push (var stk: StackRecord; val: item);
```

```
procedure pop (var stk: StackRecord; var val: item);
function stackempty (stk: StackRecord): Boolean;
function stackfull (stk: StackRecord): Boolean;

end;   { of heading }

procedure push;                                { push item onto stack }
   begin
   with stk do  if  top < max  then
                   begin
                   top := top+1;
                   stack[top] := val
                   end
                else  { Error - stack full }
   end;

procedure pop;                                 { pop item from stack }
   begin
   with stk do  if  top > 0  then
                   begin
                   val := stack[top];
                   top := top-1
                   end
                else  { Error - stack empty }
   end;

function stackempty ;                          { stack-empty test }
   begin
   stackempty := (stk.top=0)
   end;

function stackfull;                            { stack-full test }
   begin
   stackfull := (stk.top=max)
   end;

end.  { of StackModule }
```

Modules also support:

- export of multiple interfaces,
- rename on export and/or import,
- selective import,
- qualified import.

9.5.2 Declaration schemata and type inquiry

These facilities allow arrays to be sized at run time.

Note the example of a type enquiry with TYPE OF.

```
type  range = 1..100;
      VECTOR (N: range) = array [1..N] of real;       { schemata }
      MATRIX (M,N: range) = array [1..M,1..N] of real;

var  k1, k2: integer;
     a: VECTOR (10);                { types selected from schema VECTOR }
     x: VECTOR (50);
```

```
procedure reverse (var v: VECTOR);
    var   m, i: range;
          u: TYPE OF v;         { a variable with the same type as v }
    begin
    m := v.N;                   { schema discriminant }
    for  i:= 1 to m  do
       u[i] := v[m+1-i];
    v := u
    end;

procedure VDA (j,k: integer);
    var   p: MATRIX(j+1,2*k-1); { the Pascal equivalent of }
    ...                         { Algol's 'dynamic arrays' }
    ....
    read(k1,k2);                { k1,k2 not known until run-time }
    ...
    VDA(k1+1,k2-1);             { two uses of procedure VDA, using }
    VDA(k1*k2,35);              { arrays of different sizes/shapes }
    ...
    reverse(a);                 { procedure 'reverse' works for }
    reverse(x);                 { vectors of any size in 1..100 }
```

Schemata also support:

- the use of NEW to dynamically select the type,
- an extended form of WITH statement,
- formal schema discriminants which can be used as variant selectors.

9.5.3 String handling

The term 'string' in classic PASCAL was reserved for constants of packed arrays of character, much to the irritation of programmers used to more dynamic data structures for character sequences, such as string handling in U. C. S. D. PASCAL [Clark and Koehler, 1981]. Instead of adopting that style of data structure, strings are based on the more powerful schema facility. The following code illustrates how both classic packed character arrays and STRING schemata can be used together.

```
var  s: STRING (120);            { predefined schema STRING }
     n: integer;
     p: packed array [1..6] of char; { fixed-length char array }
     ...
     n := s.CAPACITY;            { n:=120 }
     s := 'ABCD';
     p := s;                     { s:='ABCD', p:='ABCD  ' }
     ...
     if  s <> 'AB'  then         { true }
         s := s[1] + 'XYZ' + s[2..4]; { s := 'AXYZBCD' }
     ...
     s[3..5] := 'PQR';          { s := 'AXPQRCD' }
     ...
     n := LENGTH(s) + LENGTH(p); { n := 7+6 }
     ...
     n := INDEX(s,'QR');        { n := 4 }
     s := SUBSTR(s,n,3);        { s := 'QRC' }
```

A variety of built-in procedures are provided: the function TRIM strips trailing spaces; the boolean functions EQ, LT, GT, NE, LE and GE (for 'equal', 'less than', 'greater than', *etc.*) compare strings using true lexicographic ordering. In contrast, the relational operators =, <, >, <>, <= and >= treat the shorter string as padded with spaces to the length of the longer string.

Input and output from and to strings[2] is also supported:

```
var  c: char;  x: real;
     s: string(50);
....
READSTR('3456.789abc',x,c);      { x:=3456.789, c:='a' }
....
WRITESTR(s,c,x:8:2);             { s:='a 3456.79' }
```

9.5.4 Binding of internal variables to external entities

In classic PASCAL, no provision was made for connecting, or binding, 'internal' files (which are really sequence types) to what most programmers think of as files: data sets resident on relatively slow 'external' media. Some implementations extended classic PASCAL's reset and rewrite procedures, while others provided a separate procedure (*e.g.* assign) to bind the internal file to the external entity. EXTENDED PASCAL makes this association explicit by assuming an implementation-defined BINDINGTYPE; notionally this might be defined thus:

```
type  BINDINGTYPE = record
                    NAME: string;
                    BOUND: Boolean;
                    ... { an implementation may
                          define other fields,
                          e.g. STATUS, ACCESS,
                    ...   DISPOSITION, ERR, etc. }
                    end;
```

This allows files to be marked as bindable and bound or unbound as needed:

```
var  f: BINDABLE file of ...;
     extf: BINDINGTYPE;
     ...
     extf := BINDING(f);     { current binding if  file already
                               bound, default binding if not   }
     write('Filename? ');
     readln(extf.NAME);      { get pathname from user }
     UNBIND(f);
     BIND(f,extf);
     extf := BINDING(f);     { current binding }
     if  not extf.BOUND then
         ...;                { error }
     RESET(f);               { or REWRITE  (f) }
```

---

[2] I/O from and to strings is sometimes referred to as 'decode'/'encode' because of the implicit type conversion.

9.5.5 Direct-access I/O and appending to files

Lack of random-access (or direct-access) I/O from classic PASCAL was also often compensated for by implementors providing extensions. EXTENDED PASCAL provides for indexable files in which particular records may be sought and read, sought and written, updated, *etc.* For example:

```
var  f: file [1..100] of string(20);
     n: integer;   s: string(80);
 ....
SEEKREAD(f, 24);                { get record 24 }
n := POSITION(f);               { n := 24 }
s := f^ + '.XYZ';               { use record 24 }
get(f);                         { get record 25 }
 ...
SEEKWRITE(f, n);                { write record n and }
write(f,'ABC');                 { move to record n+1 }
 ...
SEEKUPDATE(f, 10);              { get record 10 }
f^ := f^ + '.XYZ';
UPDATE(f);                      { update record 10 }
 ...
f^ := f^[1..16];
PUT(f);                         { update record 10, get record 11 }
 ....
s := f^ + '.XYZ';               { use record 11 }
 ...
n := LASTPOSITION(f);           { position of last file component
                                  (i.e greatest record number) }
 ...
if  EMPTY(f)  then ...          { test if file empty }
```

A new file-open procedure, EXTEND, has been included to allow the appending of data to files:

```
var  f: file of ...;
 ....
EXTEND(f);                      { used instead of REWRITE,
                                  to open f at end }
f^ := ...;
put(f);                         { write first appended record }
```

9.5.6 Relaxation of rules on declarations

Classic PASCAL is strict in the ordering of declarations and does not provide for initial or default values. EXTENDED PASCAL provides for:

- initial-value specifiers (*cf.* use of VALUE below);
- constant expressions (*cf.* constant Q below);
- structured value constructors (*cf.* constant v below);
- functions of any type (except file types) (*cf.* function CADD below);
- function result variable (*cf.* use of RSLT below).

```
const   N = 10;
        Q = 2*N-1;

var   A: array [1..Q] of 0..N;

type   compxy = record x,y:real end;
       vector = array [1..10] of integer;
const   i = compxy[x: 0.0; y: 1.0];
        v = vector[1: 5; 3..6: 0; otherwise -1];

var   X: real VALUE 2.5;   BEL: char VALUE CHR(7);
      S: string(100) VALUE 'ABC';
      B: set of Boolean VALUE [true];

type   E = (red, green, blue) VALUE red;
var   E1: E;                          { initial value: red   }
      E2: E VALUE green;              { initial value: green }

function CADD (c1,c2: compxy): compxy;
   begin
   CADD := compxy[x: c1.x+c2.x; y: c1.y+c2.y]
   end;

function innerproduct (a,b: vector) = RSLT: integer;
   var   i: 1..10;
   begin
   RSLT := 0;
   for   i:= 1 to 10   do
      RSLT := RSLT + a[i]*b[i]
   end;
```

9.5.7 Binary/octal/hex constants

The radix may be specified by preceding a number token with the base and a # symbol. All the following constants specify the decimal number 163.

```
const   bin = 2#10100011;
        oct = 8#243;
        hex = 16#A3;
        dec = 163;
```

9.5.8 Environmental enquiries

Additional predefined constants (analagous to MAXINT) are provided to obtain implementation-defined values:

MAXCHAR :   largest value of type CHAR;

MINREAL :   smallest positive value of type REAL;

MAXREAL :   largest positive value of type REAL;

EPSREAL :   smallest value of type REAL such that $1.0 + EPSREAL >$
            1.0 (a measure of the precision of real arithmetic).

9.5.9 Extensions to CASE statements

EXTENDED PASCAL standardizes the extensions many implementors provided that allowed label ranges and an *otherwise* clause in *case* statements:

```
var   ch: char;
....
CASE   ch  OF
    'A'..'Z','a'..'z':  ...;          { process letter }
    '0'..'9':  ...;                   { process digit }
    '-':  ...                         { process hyphen }
OTHERWISE
    ...                               { process other characters }
END;
```

9.5.10 Extensions to record variant parts

Similarly, label ranges and an *otherwise* clause are now provided for record variant parts:

```
RECORD
....
CASE   tag: integer   OF
    1,3,5,7,9:      { ... variant for tags 1,3,5,7,9 ... } ;
    -maxint..-1:    { ... variant for negative tags ...   } ;
    256:            { ... variant for tag 256 ... }
OTHERWISE
    { ... variant for all other tag values ... }
END;
```

Another addition allows a chosen variant to be initialized.

9.5.11 Short-circuit logical operators

Short-circuit evaluation provides for boolean expressions in which the order of evaluation is specified: the first operand is evaluated and then only if necessary is the second operand evaluated.

x AND_THEN y :   false if x is false, otherwise the value of y

x OR_ELSE y :   true if x is true, otherwise the value of y

These operators allow safe use of mutually dependent conditions such as:

```
if (i <= n) AND_THEN (a[i] = x) then ...

if (x = 0) OR_ELSE (z = y/x) then ...
```

9.5.12 Date and time procedures

A TIMESTAMP data type is provided that is notionally defined by:

```
type TIMESTAMP = record
                DATEVALID, TIMEVALID: Boolean;
```

```
YEAR: 1..maxint;
MONTH: 1..12;
DAY: 1..31;
HOUR: 0..23;
MINUTE: 0..59;
SECOND: 0..59;
... { other info if available)
end
```

An example of programming with TIMESTAMP follows.

```
var   stamp: TIMESTAMP;
   ...
   GETTIMESTAMP(stamp);         { get numeric date/time }
   if stamp.DATEVALID  then     { if valid date then     }
      d := DATE(stamp);            { convert to alphanumeric form }
   if stamp.TIMEVALID  then     { if valid time then     }
      t := TIME(stamp);            { convert to alphanumeric form }

function LeapYear (ts: TIMESTAMP): Boolean;
   begin
   LeapYear :=
      (ts.YEAR mod 4 = 0) and_then
      ((ts.YEAR mod 100 <> 0) or_else (ts.YEAR mod 400 = 0))
   end;
```

9.5.13 Underscore in identifiers and generalized SUCC/PRED

```
type  suit = (club, diamond, heart, spade, NT);

var   Suit_to_Bid: suit;
....
Suit_to_Bid := SUCC(club,3);    { equivalent to Suit_to_Bid := spade }
```

9.5.14 Zero field width output

```
write (e:N);    { N = 0 :  NOTHING printed if e is a string or is
                           of type char or Boolean;  same effect
                           as  N = 1  if e is real or integer     }

write (e:N:M);  { M = 0 :  NO fraction digits printed after the
                           decimal point, if e is real            }
```

9.5.15 Set extensions and FOR...IN statement

The new set symmetric difference operator '><' has been introduced; it is analogous to a boolean exclusive OR:

```
s1 >< s2  =  (s1 - s2) + (s2 - s1)
          =  (s1 + s2) - (s1 * s2)
```

The function CARD has been introduced which returns the cardinality of a set, that is, the number of members present in the set.

A new form of *for* loop has been provided – FOR...IN – which allows iteration over discrete values in a set in any order:

```
FOR  i IN [0,3..16,126]  DO    { loop performed for i = 0, 3,     }
    ...                        { 4, ... 15, 16, 126,  in some     }
                               { implementation-dependent order   }
```

9.5.16 HALT procedure

The procedure HALT terminates execution of the program.

9.5.17 COMPLEX numbers

Complex numbers have been introduced with the new type COMPLEX supported by operations CMPLX (for forming a value of type COMPLEX), POLAR (for forming a value of type COMPLEX from polar coordinates) and RE, IM, ABS and ARG functions (for returning the real part, imaginary part, modulus and argument, respectively). The operators = and <> are allowed in COMPLEX comparisons and the functions SQR, SQRT, EXP, LN, SIN, COS and ARCTAN have been extended to work with COMPLEX values.

```
var   z, z1, z2: COMPLEX;              { new 'simple' data type }
      x, y, r, theta: real;
      ...
      z1 := CMPLX(1,2);                { z1:=1+2i }
      z2 := POLAR(r,theta);            { z2:=r*exp(i*theta) }
      z := (z1-1.5)/(z1*z1+z2*z2);     { complex arithmetic }
      ...
      x := RE(z2);  y     := IM(z2);   { real & imaginary parts }
      r := ABS(z);  theta := ARG(z);   { modulus & argument }
      ...
      if  sqrt(z1+x-2) = -z  ...
```

9.5.18 Exponentiation operators

Two new convenient pieces of notation for exponentiation are now provided – POW, whose second argument must be an integer, and **, whose second argument can be real.

```
p POW n : p * p * ... * p  { p integer/real/complex, n integer }

p ** q  : exp( q * ln(p) ) { p integer/real/complex, q real/integer }
```

9.5.19 Protected parameters and exported variables

To prevent the changing of formal parameters in a procedure or function the new keyword PROTECTED can be employed, as in the following two examples.

```
module  RealTimeClock  interface;
export  ClockInterface = (PROTECTED clock);
var  clock: bindable integer;
end.
```

The first example causes the module implementation to bind the variable clock to the real-time clock; the variable can be used by an importer but not altered.

```
procedure p (PROTECTED x: real;  PROTECTED var y: integer; ... );
```

Within an activation of the procedure p in the second example, the formal parameter x cannot be altered; and the formal parameter y cannot be altered directly (although its value may change if the actual parameter's does, via aliasing).

9.6 References

ANSI-X3 (1993), *Object-oriented Extensions to Pascal*, Technical Report X3J9/93-033, ANSI, New York.

Clark, R. and Koehler, S. (1981), *The U. C. S. D. Pascal Handbook: A Reference and Guidebook for Programmers*, Prentice-Hall, Englewood Cliffs, NJ.

Hetherington, G. A. (1993a), An introduction to the Extended Pascal language, *SIG-PLAN Notices*, **28**(11), 42–51.

Hetherington, G. A. (1993b), *Extended Pascal A New Standard in Computer Languages*, Prospero Software, London.

International Standards Organization (1990), *Information technology – Programming languages – Pascal*, ISO/IEC, Geneva, replacing ISO/IEC, *Programming languages – PASCAL*, ISO 7185:1983, which incorporated by reference British Standards Institution, *Specification for Computer Programming Language Pascal*, BS6192, BSI, London.

International Standards Organization (1991), *Information Technology – Programming languages – Extended Pascal*, ISO/IEC (and BSI), Geneva (and London).

Jensen, K. and Wirth, N. (1975), *Pascal User Manual and Report*, Springer-Verlag, New York, 2nd edition.

Joslin, D. A. (1985a), Extended Pascal – Illustrative Features, *SIGPLAN Notices*, **21**(12), 131–8.

Joslin, D. A. (1985b), Extensions in Pascal Implementations, *SIGPLAN Notices*, **20**(11), 39–46.

Joslin, D. A. (1987), Extended Pascal – Illustrative Features – Update, *SIGPLAN Notices*, **22**(6), 7–8.

Joslin, D. A. (1989), Extended Pascal – Numerical Features, *SIGPLAN Notices*, **24**(6), 77–80.

Joslin, D. A. and Wichmann, B. A. (1986), *A Survey of Extensions in Pascal Implementations*, Technical Report DITC 69/86, National Physical Laboratory, Teddington, Middlesex.

Wichmann, B. and Ciechanowicz, Z. J. (eds) (1983), *Pascal Compiler Validation*, John Wiley and Sons, Chichester.

Wirth, N. (1980), *Modula-2*, Technical Report Report No. 36, ETH Zürich.

Wirth, N. (1988), The Programming Language Oberon, *Software – Practice and Experience*, **18**(7), 671–90.

10 From ML to C via Modula-3: an approach to teaching programming

Peter Robinson

The computer science course at the University of Cambridge teaches ML as an introductory language at the beginning of the freshman year, and then uses MODULA-3 to introduce imperative programming at the end of that year. Further lectures on advanced features of MODULA-3 are given early in the second year, together with separate lectures on C. Other specialized languages are introduced subsequently as the course progresses.

This chapter explains why this strategy for teaching was adopted and evaluates its operation in practice. The key features of ML and MODULA-3 are presented and illustrated through a collection of example programs. Finally, a general assessment of the two languages is also presented.

10.1 Introduction

Choosing the right programming language for a commercial computing project involves balancing a number of conflicting requirements, but is usually resolved by commercial considerations rather than technical ones. Choosing the right language for introducing newcomers to computer science is free from such external constraints, and is therefore much harder. Indeed, students in scientific disciplines are often taught to program when it is no longer clear that this is relevant as part of their professional development; teaching them to use standard software packages may be more appropriate.

The main computer science course at the University of Cambridge is the three-year computer science tripos.[1] Half of the first year is devoted to computer science topics (including discrete mathematics), and the other half to lectures given to students of the natural sciences, including continuous mathematics and a particular science subject.

Until recently, all students of the natural sciences were taught elementary programming in FORTRAN as part of the mathematics component of their first year course. This has now been changed so that they receive instead lectures on utility computing, using a word processor (Microsoft Word), a spreadsheet (Microsoft Excel) and a symbolic mathematics system (MathCad). These are used to convey the principles of data handling and algorithm design (even going so far as to illustrate the numerical solution of differential equations in a spreadsheet), which seems sufficient for students who will be computer users rather than developers of new computer systems.

10.1.1 The first language

Students of computer science are, of course, rather different. They need to start with a sound foundation for programming that can establish the principles which will subsequently be applied in many different languages. Three main objectives can be established:

Mathematical basis: Formal manipulation of computer programs and proof of their correctness is becoming increasingly important. Students need to see programs as formal descriptions of abstract algorithms. A mathematical language also relates directly to parallel first-year courses in digital logic and discrete mathematics.

Strong typing: The value of strong typing in writing correct and maintainable programs is now well established. This is particularly important in evolution of large systems where a team of programmers may have to work together over a number of years. A rich type system also allows data structures to be introduced clearly.

Functional emphasis: A functional style of programming is conducive to correct programming, and also lends itself to mathematical analysis of algorithms.

It should also be said that a friendly environment for experimenting is a great virtue; this probably implies the use of an interpreted language.

However, it is important to emphasize that commercial relevance is not in this list. A university computer science course is not an industrial training course. The graduates' value comes not from their skill with a particular language that happens to be popular at the moment, but from understanding the principles of programming languages in such a way that they can learn and evaluate new languages as they encounter them in their professional careers.

These objectives led us to the choice of ML as the initial teaching language for computer science students. This choice also has an interesting side-effect. Students entering the course vary widely in their previous experience of computers and programming, from those who have hardly touched a keyboard to those who may have spent a year programming in industry before coming to university. It is important not to make the beginners feel themselves to be at a disadvantage, and also not to bore the experts. ML meets these requirements nicely – the experts tend to have used imperative languages

---

[1] The honours degree at the University of Cambridge.

such as BASIC, C or PASCAL and find themselves with no great advantage over the beginners. Indeed, their preconceptions and self-taught programming habits often put them at a disadvantage.

10.1.2 The second language

After starting with ML, it is useful to move on to a more conventional imperative programming language with a new set of objectives:

Completeness: The language should exhibit all the facilities of a modern language – objects and inheritance, exception handling, garbage collection and concurrency.

Large-scale programming: Strong typing should extend across separately compiled modules, but there should be a controlled way of circumventing its protection for low-level code. This suggests the use of a separate interface description language.

Libraries and environment: Extensive libraries serve two purposes. First they serve as illustrations of programming style and the construction of re-usable code. Secondly, they provide a rich environment of facilties which students can draw on when they undertake substantial projects of their own later in the course.

At the same time, the language should not lose sight of the objectives for an initial programming language listed above.

Again, there is no requirement for the language to be popular with industry; it is the principles that matter.

MODULA-3 meets these requirements and is introduced towards the end of the first year of the computer science course. The languages thread of the course continues with lectures on C/C++ and PROLOG, together with brief historical excursions into LISP and COBOL. C is included as a concession to its widespread use as a sort of machine-independent low-level language, and PROLOG introduces a rather different style of programming. This exposure to a variety of programming idioms equips the students to understand, assess and use a very wide variety of languages in practice. For example, many use embedded scripting languages such as TCL, PYTHON or OBLIQ in their final-year projects with no further formal training.

ML and MODULA-3 will now be discussed in more detail, and the chapter concludes with an evaluation of their strengths and weaknesses. This is not intended as a complete description of either language, but rather as a summary of their distinguishing characteristics, illustrated by examples.

10.2 ML

Standard ML is descended from the meta-language (hence 'ML') for the LCF proof system developed at Edinburgh in the 1970s [Gordon *et al.*, 1978]. It is defined in a report from the University of Edinburgh [Harper *et al.*, 1988] which is accompanied by a gentler introduction [Harper, 1988]. The language has become popular for teaching programming, and a number of introductory texts have now been published [Myers *et al.*, 1993; Ullman, 1993; Wikström, 1987], together with a more advanced book illustrating the language's use for a wide variety of problems [Paulson, 1991].

The key features of ML are [Harper, 1988]:

Functional: Functions are first-class data objects which may be passed as arguments, returned as results and stored in data structures. Assignment and other side-effects are discouraged.

Interactive: Phrases are typed in, analysed, compiled and executed interactively with any results being printed out directly. There are also more conventional compilers.

Strong typing: Every legal expression has a type which constrains its use. However, most types are inferred by the compiler rather than having to be specified by the programmer.

Polymorphism: The compiler infers the most general type of an expression, and this is specialized in actual use. This supports generic programming with no additional effort by the programmer.

Abstract types: Types can be defined in terms of permitted operations while keeping implementation details private.

Static scoping: All identifiers are resolved at compile time. However, procedure execution can be controlled by pattern matching of arguments at run-time.

Type-safe exceptions: Exceptions allow procedures to return out-of-band results (often arising from abnormal conditions) to be communicated in a type-safe way.

Modules: Type safety is maintained when large programs can be constructed out of separately compiled components.

The language will now be illustrated by a number of examples and then evaluated.

10.2.1 Big numbers

Consider, as an example,[2] the manipulation of arbitrarily large natural numbers, stored as a list of digits to the base 10. It is convenient to use a 'little-endian' convention, storing the least significant digit at the head of the list. We can start with a couple of utility routines to convert between big numbers and ordinary integers. These can be typed directly into the ML interpreter: the – is its normal prompt and = its prompt for a continuation line of a phrase. Each complete unit of input concludes with a semicolon. The interpreter responds by printing out the value and type of the input which is also stored as the current value, it, initially empty.

```
val it = () : unit
- fun big2int nil = 0
=     | big2int (b :: bb) = b + 10 * big2int bb;
val big2int = fn : int list -> int
- big2int [1, 2, 3];
val it = 321 : int
-   big2int [1, 2, 3, 4, 5, 6, 7, 1, 2, 3, 4, 5, 6, 7];
uncaught exception Overflow
```

[2] More recent ML systems use arbitrary-length integers by default, so this would still work. Of course, it would also render this example somewhat pointless.

In this we see the function big2int defined and then tested on a couple of input values. The function is defined using *pattern matching*; if the input value is an empty list, nil, the literal value 0 is returned, otherwise the input is a list with first element b and tail bb which represents the integer value of b plus 10 times the value of the tail. These patterns appear after the fun keyword as repeated definitions of the function separated by vertical bars, |. The ML type system infers that the input must be a list of integers and that the result is a single integer, and consequently the interpreter prints the signature of big2int as   fn : int list -> int.

This is then tested by trying it out on a couple of lists of integers. The first duly prints out the value 321 as the value of the expression stored in it but the second raises a run-time exception when there is arithmetic overflow because the input list represents a number that is too big to fit into an integer.

The converse function int2big is defined and tested similarly:

```
- fun int2big 0 = nil
=   | int2big i = (i mod 10) :: int2big (i div 10);
val int2big = fn : int -> int list
- int2big 123;
val it = [3,2,1] : int list
```

In this case the : : operator is used to construct a list. Notice how recursion is used to manipulate recursive data structures.

Finally, a procedure to add big numbers and so to compute powers of two can be written:

```
- fun add aa bb =
=    let fun doadd (nil, nil, c) = if c = 0 then nil else [c]
=            | doadd ((a::aa), nil, c) =
=                ((a+c) mod 10) :: doadd (aa, nil, (a+c) div 10)
=            | doadd (nil, (b::bb), c) = doadd ((b::bb), nil, c)
=            | doadd (a::aa, b::bb, c) =
=                ((a+b+c) mod 10) :: doadd (aa, bb, (a+b+c) div 10)
=    in
=        doadd (aa, bb, 0)
=    end;
val add = fn : int list -> int list -> int list
- fun twoto n = if n < 1 then [1] else
=    let val h = twoto (n-1)
=    in add h h
=    end;
val twoto = fn : int -> int list
- twoto 7;
val it = [8,2,1] : int list
- big2int it;
val it = 128 : int
```

An auxiliary function doadd is defined locally with an extra argument (the carry between the addition of successive digits). In fact there is a further subtle difference between the signatures of add and doadd relating to the fact that all ML functions take a single argument. add is *curried*, so this argument is just the first big number, aa, and it returns an anonymous function that takes the argument bb, returning the sum of the lists. This is reflected in the signature printed by the interpreter. doadd on the other hand takes a triple consisitng of two lists and an integer as its single argument. Its signature is not printed, but would be `fn : int list * int list * int -> int list.`

Finally, this is tested by working out 2^7 and converting the result back to an integer.

10.2.2 A stack of records

The triple in doadd is an example of a record, but its fields are identified by their order. It is also possible to name fields, for example:

```
- val pr = {name = "Peter Robinson", address = "Cambridge"};
val pr = {address="Cambridge",name="Peter Robinson"}
  : {address:string, name:string}
- val mw = {address = "Milton Keynes", name = "Mark Woodman"};
val mw = {address="Milton Keynes",name="Mark Woodman"}
  : {address:string, name:string}
```

This defines values pr and mw, both of whose types are records with two named fields, both of type string. The order of the fields in the definition is irrelevant; they are automatically arranged in a canonical order. Individual fields can be extracted with a selection operator:

```
- #name pr;
val it = "Peter Robinson" : string
```

The simplest way to make a stack of such records would be to write a couple of functions manipulating lists:

```
- fun push (s, r) = r :: s;
val push = fn : 'a list * 'a -> 'a list
- fun pop (r :: s) = (s, r);
std_in:0.0-0.0 Warning: match nonexhaustive
          r :: s => ...
val pop = fn : 'a list -> 'a list * 'a
```

The type inference system works out that the push function is generic, that is it can operate on stacks of any base type. This is represented by the use of 'a (read as α) for a type variable. pop takes a stack and returns a pair consisting of the popped stack and its former first item. However, there are a couple of deficiencies in this approach: the empty stack is represented by the empty list, nil, which is untidy, and the action of pop on an empty stack is undefined. This is identified by the ML interpreter as an incomplete set of patterns for the arguments to pop; an empty list does not match the single pattern and so would give rise to a run-time exception.

A better approach would be to define a stack by the operations permitted on it, more in the object-oriented style. We can define a stack to be either empty or constructed by pushing an item of an arbitrary type α onto an existing stack of αs:

```
- datatype 'a stack = empty | push of ('a stack) * 'a ;
datatype  'a stack
  con empty : 'a stack
```

```
    con push : 'a stack * 'a -> 'a stack
- empty;
val it = empty : 'a stack
- push (it, pr);
val it = push (empty,{address="Cambridge",name="Peter Robinson"})
    : {address:string, name:string} stack
- push (it, 42);
std_in:7.1-7.13 Error: operator and operand don't agree (tycon
mismatch)
    operator domain: {address:string, name:string} stack
                    * {address:string, name:string}
    operand:        {address:string, name:string} stack * int
    in expression:
      push (it,42)
```

Here, an abstract generic type, an α stack, is defined by its two possible constructors: empty which gives an empty stack and push which puts an extra item onto the stack. empty is then used to produce an empty stack which appears as the current expression, it. Note that it has a generic type at this point. A name and address record is then pushed onto the stack, whose type now becomes specifically that of a stack of name and address records. It would now be possible to push other such records (such as mw defined above) onto the stack, but instead an attempt is made to push an integer onto the stack; this is an incompatible type, and a diagnostic message is printed.

A function to pop items off the stack matches against the two possible patterns, but first an exception is defined to deal with the special case of an empty stack:

```
- exception nocando;
exception nocando
- fun pop empty = raise nocando
=   | pop (push (s, r)) = (s, r);
val pop = fn : 'a stack -> 'a stack * 'a
- pop it;
val it = (empty,{address="Cambridge",name="Peter Robinson"})
    : {address:string,name:string} stack * {address:string,name:string}
- #1 it;
val it = empty : {address:string, name:string} stack
- pop it;
uncaught exception nocando
```

The #1 operator picks the first element of a tuple rather like selecting a field from a record.

A client using these routines could catch the exception simply by following the invocation of pop by a clause handle nocando => ... where the ellipses denote an appropriate expression to be returned in this case, which would have to have the same type as the normal return from pop. An example of this will be given later.

10.2.3 A workshop database

Finally, consider a type structure for a database to process people attending a workshop. The main record structure could be roughly as for the names and addresses above, but additional information is needed for particular classes of person. This is most easily handled by defining a new type, property, together with a function to yield a text string explaining the property:

```
- datatype property = presenter of (string * string) | chair of string
| ou;
datatype  property
  con chair : string -> property
  con ou : property
  con presenter : string * string -> property
- fun text (presenter (s, t)) = "Presenting " ^ s ^ " at " ^ t
=    | text (chair (s)) = "Chairing " ^ s
=    | text ou = "from Open University";
val text = fn : property -> string
```

Pattern matching is used in the `text` function to distinguish the different variants of the `property` type, and `^` is the string concatenation operator.

A stack of properties could then be attached to each person attending the workshop:

```
- empty;
val it = empty : 'a stack
- push (it, presenter ("From ML to M3", "15:50"));
val it = push (empty,presenter ("From ML to M3","15:50")) : property
 stack
- push (it, ou);
val it = push (push (empty,presenter #),ou) : property stack
- fun props ps =
=    let val (s, p) = pop ps
=    in (text p) ^ "\n" ^ props s end
=    handle nocando => "";
val props = fn : property stack -> string
- props it;
val it = "from Open University\nPresenting From ML to M3 at 15:50\n" :
string
- print it;
from Open University
Presenting From ML to M3 at 15:50
val it = () : unit
```

Here an empty stack is created and then two properties (the `presenter` property with two field values and the unparameterized `ou` property) pushed onto it. The `props` function concatenates all the properties on the stack into a single string. Note how the exception for an empty stack is caught and used to return an empty string and how the result from `pop` is split into its components with a nested `let` clause. `"\n"` indicates the new-line character, as is shown when the final string is printed.

10.2.4 Evaluation

These examples should have given the general flavour of ML, but what is its real role? It certainly meets all the criteria for an initial teaching language, but it has much broader uses than that. ML has been widely used for research work on theorem proving and, in particular, for work on formal verification of hardware and software. This is now moving into industrial projects, and full commercially supported implementations are available on small PCs as well as professional workstations, although development environments are still rather limited.

The core of the language is very simple and can be defined in just a few pages; however, it is also quite appropriate to use it for large projects. Its mathematical basis gives it great coherence and uniformity. The strong type-checking and abstract data types shown in the examples are obviously of value in large systems and ML also supports a mechanism for hiding internal information in packages, revealing only a chosen set of definitions through a signature. This facilitates the orderly construction and maintenance of large systems consisting of many separately compiled files of code.

The language lends itself to formal specification and analysis, but is not so well suited to some applications. For example, commercial data processing does not fit well with a functional style of programming (although spreadsheets have been written in ML).

Although this was deliberately omitted from the examples above, it is possible to define mutable variables and for functions to have side-effects, but these are not comfortable within the language. Garbage collection and an interpreted implementation are not obviously suitable for real-time systems either, although there are now compilers generating efficient code and modern garbage collectors are not as disruptive as their predecessors.

10.3 Modula-3

MODULA-3 is descended from PASCAL [Wirth, 1971; Jensen and Wirth, 1975] via MESA [Mitchell *et al.*, 1979], CEDAR [Lampson, 1983], MODULA-2 [Wirth, 1980; 1988] and MODULA-2+ [Rovner *et al.*, 1985]. MODULA-3 is defined in Greg Nelson's book [1992], which also gives a rationale for the language design and gives examples of its novel features in use. There is an introductory textbook [Harbison, 1992] and a version of Robert Sedgewick's book on algorithms using MODULA-3 [1993].

The language's design goals are encapsulated in the preface to the MODULA-3 report [Cardelli *et al.*, 1989]:

> The goal of MODULA-3 is to be as simple and safe as it can be while meeting the needs of modern systems programmers. Instead of exploring new features, we studied the features of the MODULA family of languages that have proven themselves in practice and tried to simplify them into a harmonious language. We found that most of the successful features were aimed at one of two main goals: greater robustness, and a simpler, more systematic type system.

> MODULA-3 descends from MESA, MODULA-2, CEDAR, and MODULA-2+. It also resembles its cousins OBJECT PASCAL, OBERON [Wirth and Reiser, 1992], and EUCLID [Lampson *et al.*, 1977].

> MODULA-3 retains one of MODULA-2's most successful features, the provision for explicit interfaces between modules. It adds objects and classes, exception handling, garbage collection, lightweight processes (or threads), and the isolation of unsafe features.

The key features of MODULA-3 are [Nelson, 1992]:

Interfaces: An explicit interface reveals only the public declarations in a module, while allowing other parts of it to be kept private. Each module *imports* the interfaces which it requires and *exports* the interfaces that it implements. The interface can be thought of as a contract between the supplier and client of a library module, specifying (amongst other things) the signatures of its procedures, while deferring until later the exact nature of their implementation. Interfaces form a natural part of the design documentation of a large program.

Objects: An object is an abstract data type defined in terms of the operations or *methods* permitted on it. A new object type can be defined as a subtype of an existing type, in which case it *inherits* all the methods of the parent type while possibly adding new methods. It can also *override* the existing methods with alternative implementations having the same signature. (It is also possible to mask an inherited method by a new method with the same name but a different signature, but the obscured method can still be invoked.) Objects and interfaces are combined in MODULA-3 to provide *partially opaque types*, where some of an object's fields are visible in a scope while others are hidden.

Generics: MODULA-3 does not provide the full polymorphism of ML, but does allow a module (both interface and implementation) to be parameterized by another module. The generic module acts as a template in which some of the imported interfaces are regarded as formal parameters, bound to actual interfaces when the generic is instantiated. This is effectively a textual operation, undertaken at compilation time.

Threads: Dividing a computation into concurrent processes (or threads of control) is a fundamental technique for separating concerns. In particular, any program dealing with external activities – filing system, communications network, human users and so on – should not suspend its dealing with all of them while waiting for just one to respond. Separating the program's activities into separate threads which can block individually without affecting the others' execution makes this simpler to deal with.

Safety: Many of the problems with low-level languages such as C arise through accidental corruption of a program's code or data after using an invalid array index or performing incorrect address arithmetic. Such programs can be protected (at least from each other) by placing them in separate address spaces, but this may limit performance. It is better to check for incorrect behaviour and handle it gracefully, rather than allow the program to continue unpredictably.

Garbage collection: A particular unsafe run-time error is to free a data structure still referred to by dangling pointers. Alternatively, storage *leaks* caused by failure to free unreachable structures cause an executing program's data to grow without bound. Both of these problems can be resolved by tracing references and recovering redundant space by automatic garbage collection.

Exceptions: Another class of unsafe error arises when procedures report errors by returning special values, which are too easily left unchecked by the programmer. Exceptions allow such out-of-band results to be returned and checked with very low overhead in the normal, error-free case, while making the behaviour clear in the abnormal case.

Type system: MODULA-3 is strongly typed and particular attention has been paid to making the type system uniform. In particular, a subtype relation is defined and used to specify assignment compatibility and inheritance rules; the type of every expression can be determined from its constituents independently of its use and there are no automatic type conversions.

Simplicity: C. A. R. Hoare has suggested that as a rule of thumb a language is too complicated if it can't be described precisely and readably in 50 pages. The designers of MODULA-3 elevated this to a design principle, which they only narrowly failed to achieve.

As with ML, the language will be illustrated by a number of examples and then discussed.

10.3.1 Big numbers

Again consider the example of arbitrarily large natural numbers to be stored as a list of digits to the base 10. However, in MODULA-3 the list is constructed explicitly with pointers rather than being manipulated directly within the language as in ML.

The MODULA-3 compiler operates on complete modules, so it is useful to see the entire program at once:

```
MODULE Main;

IMPORT Char, Stdio, Text, Wr;

CONST Base = 10;

TYPE
  BigNum = REF RECORD
                 digit: INTEGER;
                 rest : BigNum    := NIL;
              END;

PROCEDURE Create (i: INTEGER): BigNum =
  BEGIN
    IF i = 0 THEN
      RETURN NIL
    ELSE
      RETURN
        NEW(BigNum, digit := i MOD Base, rest := Create(i DIV Base));
    END;
  END Create;

PROCEDURE Add (a, b: BigNum; carryIn := 0): BigNum =
  BEGIN
    IF a = NIL THEN
      IF carryIn > 0 THEN
        RETURN Add (b, Create (carryIn))
      ELSE
        RETURN b
      END;
    ELSIF b = NIL THEN
      IF carryIn > 0 THEN
        RETURN Add (a, Create (carryIn))
      ELSE
        RETURN a
      END;
    ELSE
      WITH d = a.digit + b.digit + carryIn DO
        RETURN NEW (BigNum, digit := d MOD Base,
                    rest := Add (a.rest, b.rest, d DIV Base));
      END;
    END;
  END Add;

PROCEDURE ToText (b: BigNum; first := TRUE): TEXT =
  BEGIN
    IF b = NIL THEN
      IF first THEN RETURN "0" ELSE RETURN "" END
```

```
      ELSE
        RETURN ToText (b.rest, FALSE)
                  & Text.FromChar (VAL (ORD('0') + b.digit, CHAR))
      END;
    END ToText;
  PROCEDURE FromText (t: TEXT): BigNum =
    VAR b: BigNum := NIL;
    BEGIN
      FOR i := 0 TO Text.Length (t) - 1 DO
        WITH ch = Text.GetChar (t, i) DO
          IF ch IN Char.Digits THEN
            b := NEW(BigNum, digit := ORD(ch) - ORD('0'), rest := b);
          END;
        END;
      END;
      RETURN b;
    END FromText;

  VAR bi := Create (1);

  BEGIN
    FOR i := 1 TO 100 DO
      bi := Add (bi, bi);
      Wr.PutText (Stdio.stdout, ToText (bi) & "\n");
    END;
    Wr.Close (Stdio.stdout);

  END Main.
```

The first observation is that there is a lot more *boiler-plate* text wrapped round this program than is needed for its equivalent in ML. First, there is a heading identifying the module; in fact this has the special name Main identifying it as the main program. Secondly, there are explicit IMPORT requests for separately compiled modules used by this program. The definitions in the corresponding interfaces are made available in the ensuing scope. Thirdly, all the type information is explicit; every detail of the BigNum is specified as a pointer to a record with two fields. A small detail worth noting is that the fields can have default values, initialized whenever a record is allocated. In this case the tail pointer is set to default to NIL.

As noted above, the type of an expression is computed from its constituents. In this example, the type of the constant Base will be inferred to be an integer, and this tested for compatibility wherever it is used. This can often be done by the compiler, but may require a run-time check.

The bulk of the program is taken up with the definition of four procedures which should be fairly self-explanatory. The NEW procedure allocates space on the heap, returning a pointer. Its first argument is a reference type and any further arguments specify initial values for fields in the record referred to. The third argument to the Add procedure has a default value of 0; this avoids the need for the auxiliary doadd function used in the ML equivalent above. Otherwise, the procedure is roughly equivalent to the ML, except that the pattern matching of arguments is replaced by explicit testing. Conversions between big numbers and MODULA-3's built-in TEXT type make use of utility routines in the standard Char and Text interfaces.

Finally, the body of the module creates a big number with value 1 and adds it to itself repeatedly, printing out values from 2^1 to 2^{100}. Incidentally, the repeated assignment to the variable bi and the various manipulations of the TEXT type will result in the generation of large amounts of unreachable heap storage which will be recovered by the garbage collector.

10.3.2 A stack of records

A name and address record could be defined as a type in MODULA-3 as follows.

```
TYPE Record = RECORD
                name,
                address: TEXT := "";
              END;
```

Both fields are of the built-in TEXT type and have default values of empty strings. The language is case-sensitive, so there is no confusion between the user-defined Record type and the built-in type constructor RECORD.

It is common practice to have a separate interface for each abstract data type, so a better definition might be to create a separate file:

```
INTERFACE Record;
  TYPE T = RECORD
             name,
             address: TEXT := "";
           END;
END Record.
```

It is conventional to call the main type in an interface T and it is then referred to in other modules in qualified form as Record.T.

A stack of these records could then be constructed using a linked list as follows:

```
MODULE Main;

IMPORT Record, Stdio, Wr;

TYPE Stack = REF RECORD
                   item: Record.T;
                   next: Stack := NIL;
                 END;

EXCEPTION NoCanDo;

PROCEDURE Push (VAR s: Stack; r: Record.T) =
  BEGIN
    s := NEW (Stack, item := r, next := s);
  END Push;

PROCEDURE Pop (VAR s: Stack): Record.T RAISES {NoCanDo} =
  BEGIN
    IF s = NIL THEN RAISE NoCanDo
    ELSE
      VAR r := s.item;
      BEGIN
        s := s.next;
        RETURN r;
      END;
```

```
      END;
    END Pop;

VAR stack: Stack := NIL;

BEGIN
   Push (stack, Record.T {name := "Peter Robinson",
                          address := "Cambridge"});
   Push (stack, Record.T {name := "Mark Woodman",
                          address := "Milton Keynes"});
   TRY
      LOOP Wr.PutText (Stdio.stdout, Pop (stack) .name & "\n") END;   ^
   EXCEPT
      NoCanDo => Wr.PutText (Stdio.stdout, "That's all folks!\n");
   END;
   Wr.Close (Stdio.stdout);
END Main.
```

This is fairly standard imperative programming. Both the Push and Pop procedures take the stack as a variable argument, implying call-by-reference, and allowing them to have side-effects, modifying the contents of the stack. A more functional approach would be to return the modified stack, as in the ML example above. The initial stack is empty, indicated by a NIL value. Push is then invoked on it with a couple of literal record constructors to insert some data. The Pop procedure raises an exception when passed an empty stack as its argument and this is used in the main body of the program to terminate an otherwise infinite loop. When run, this program would print out the two names on the stack, together with the message That's all folks!

This program can be refined in three ways: the stack can be made generic, capable of stacking elements of any type, it can be made into an abstract data type as an object with *push* and *pop* methods, and the implementations of these methods can be hidden. The finished result would consist of several further files. In addition to the Record interface above, there is a generic stack interface:

```
GENERIC INTERFACE Stack (Value);

EXCEPTION Empty;

TYPE
   Public = OBJECT METHODS
               push (v: Value.T);
               pop (): Value.T RAISES {Empty};
            END;

   T <: Public;
END Stack.
```

This has the formal parameter Value which will be instantiated to an actual interface name later; it can be thought of as a further imported interface. The actual interface will have to provide a definition for a type T since this interface refers to Value.T. For this application the Record interface defined above will be suitable, but so would many others including, for example, the standard Text interface.

The type declarations achieve the second and third refinements. Public is an object type with two methods whose signatures are given. The actual procedures supplied later to implement these methods all have an additional first argument which identifies the instance on which they are being invoked.

T is simply defined to be a ixspecialization of `Public`; it will provide the same methods but their implementations are hidden and extra data fields may be added to the object. This is an example of an *opaque type* in MODULA-3 – there is only a *partial revelation* of T.

This would be accompanied by a generic implementation:

```
GENERIC MODULE Stack (Value);

TYPE
  List = REF RECORD
                item: Value.T;
                next: List := NIL;
             END;

REVEAL
  T = Public BRANDED OBJECT
                        list: List := NIL;
                     OVERRIDES
                        push := Push;
                        pop := Pop;
                     END;
PROCEDURE Push (self: T; value: Value.T) =
  BEGIN
    self.list := NEW (List, item := value, next := self.list);
  END Push;

PROCEDURE Pop (self: T): Value.T RAISES {Empty} =
  BEGIN
    IF self.list = NIL THEN RAISE Empty
    ELSE
      VAR v := self.list.item;
      BEGIN
        self.list := self.list.next;
        RETURN v;
      END;
    END;
  END Pop;

BEGIN
END Stack.
```

This more-or-less follows the earlier, direct program with the important addition of a revelation of the implementation of T within the scope of this module. In fact, T is declared to be a specialization of `Public`, it is BRANDED to make its type unique, it has a private data field to hold the linked list storing the contents of the stack, and it overrides the (null) methods of the `Public` type with new implementations.

`Push` and `Pop` have signatures that match the method declarations in `Public`, with the addition of an additional first argument identifying the particular instance of the `Stack.T` object for which they are being invoked. The code is much as before.

The generic interface and implementation are instantiated for the `Record` interface to give specific `RecordStacks`:

```
INTERFACE RecordStack = Stack (Record) END RecordStack.
MODULE RecordStack = Stack (Record) END RecordStack.
```

Finally, these can be tested by a new main program:

```
MODULE Main;
IMPORT Record, RecordStack, Stdio, Wr;
VAR
  stack := NEW (RecordStack.T);
BEGIN
  stack.push (Record.T {name := "Peter Robinson",
                        address := "Cambridge"});
  stack.push (Record.T {name := "Mark Woodman",
                        address := "Milton Keynes"});
  TRY
    LOOP Wr.PutText (Stdio.stdout, stack.pop () .name & "\n") END;
  EXCEPT
    RecordStack.Empty =>
      Wr.PutText (Stdio.stdout, "That's all folks!\n");
  END;
  Wr.Close (Stdio.stdout);
END Main.
```

which works in exactly the same way as its predecessor.

10.3.3 A workshop database

As with the ML example, the main record structure is fairly straightforward, but a new
type is needed to handle the properties of delegates. A stack of these properties could
then be included in the main record.

The interface looks like this:

```
INTERFACE Properties;
TYPE
  T = OBJECT METHODS
        text (): TEXT;
      END;

  PresenterP = T OBJECT METHODS
                  init (subject, slot: TEXT): Presenter;
                END;
  Presenter <: PresenterP;

  ChairP = T OBJECT METHODS
             init (session: TEXT): Chair;
           END;
  Chair <: ChairP;

  OU <: T;

END Properties.
```

A base type, Properties.T is defined which has a single method that yields a text
string describing the property. Separate public subtypes PresenterP and ChairP
are derived from this for each property to be stored. These have distinct init methods
that allow their private data fields to be given appropriate initial values. Finally,
Presenter and Chair are partially revealed to be subtypes of these.

The implementation supplies revelations for the opaque types together with implementations of all their methods:

```
MODULE Properties;

REVEAL
  Presenter = PresenterP BRANDED OBJECT
                             subject,
                             slot: TEXT;
                         OVERRIDES
                           init := PresenterInit;
                           text := PresenterText;
                         END;

  Chair = ChairP BRANDED OBJECT
                         session: TEXT;
                     OVERRIDES
                       init := ChairInit;
                       text := ChairText;
                     END;

  OU = T BRANDED OBJECT OVERRIDES
                   text := OUText;
                 END;

PROCEDURE PresenterInit (self: Presenter;
                         subject, slot: TEXT): Presenter =
  BEGIN
    self.subject := subject;
    self.slot := slot;
    RETURN self;
  END PresenterInit;

PROCEDURE PresenterText (self: Presenter): TEXT =
  BEGIN
    RETURN "Presenting " & self.subject & " at " & self.slot;
  END PresenterText;

PROCEDURE ChairInit (self: Chair; session: TEXT): Chair =
  BEGIN
    self.session := session;
    RETURN self;
  END ChairInit;

PROCEDURE ChairText (self: Chair): TEXT =
  BEGIN
    RETURN "Chairing " & self.session;
  END ChairText;

PROCEDURE OUText (self: OU): TEXT =
  BEGIN
    RETURN "from Open University";
  END OUText;

BEGIN
END Properties.
```

This is somewhat verbose, but most of the code is mechanical in nature. Note how the different overriding implementations of the text method for the specializations of Properties.T compose the appropriate text strings for the respective properties.

The interface and implementation for a property stack can now be instantiated from the generic stack:

```
INTERFACE PropStack = Stack (Properties) END PropStack.
MODULE PropStack = Stack (Properties) END PropStack.
```

Finally, a test program can use all this:

```
MODULE Workshop EXPORTS Main;
IMPORT Properties, PropStack, Stdio, Wr;
TYPE
   Person = OBJECT
               name: TEXT := "";
               props: PropStack.T;
            METHODS
               init (name: TEXT): Person := Init;
               text (): TEXT := Text;
            END;

PROCEDURE Init (self: Person; name: TEXT): Person =
   BEGIN
      self.name := name;
      self.props := NEW (PropStack.T);
      RETURN self;
   END Init;

PROCEDURE Text (self: Person): TEXT =
   VAR t := self.name & ":\n";
   BEGIN
      TRY
         LOOP t := t & self.props.pop () .text () & "\n" END;
      EXCEPT
         PropStack.Empty => RETURN t;
      END;
   END Text;

VAR p := NEW (Person) .init ("Robinson");

BEGIN
   p.props.push
      (NEW (Properties.Presenter).init ("From ML to M3", "15:50"));
   p.props.push (NEW (Properties.OU));
   Wr.PutText (Stdio.stdout, p.text ());
   Wr.Close (Stdio.stdout);
END Workshop.
```

The same general approach is taken here. A Person type is defined whose initialization method stores a name in the record and sets up an empty stack of properties. Various properties are then pushed onto the stack. These have different types, but
they are all subtypes of properties.T and so are compatible for pushing onto a
PropStack.T, and this can be checked by the compiler with no run-time overhead.
A text method pops all the properties off the stack and concatenates them into a text
string. (A purist might argue that the definition of the Person type and its methods
should be removed to a separate module, and would probably be right.)
    When run, the program would print out:

```
Robinson:
from Open University
Presenting From ML to M3 at 15:50
```

The observant reader will have noticed that calling the `text` method on a `person` removes all their properties; such are the perils of programming with side-effects. In practice, a new method would be added to the generic stack to allow iteration over its elements without actually popping them.

10.3.4 Evaluation

MODULA-3 is still a relatively young language and its use is mainly concentrated in universities and commercial research laboratories. The most widely used implementation comes from DEC's Systems Research Center in Palo Alto and runs on many Unix platforms. An experimental PC implementation is available and further developments, including a GNU implementation, should be available later. Several hundred library modules are freely distributed. These include a general toolkit for the X window system [Manasse and Nelson, 1991a; 1991b], a more specialized interface toolkit [Brown and Meehan, 1993a], and a system for building graphical user interfaces [Brown and Meehan, 1993b]. There are also three different implementations of *network object* systems for writing distributed programs.

The latest DEC SRC implementation uses the GNU back-ends which makes it reasonably efficient and highly portable. However, programs tend to be rather large, not least because of the run-time library needed to manage threads, garbage collection and so on, although shared libraries alleviate this where the operating system permits it.

The language is not suitable for teaching as a first language: it is too big, too much knowledge about the environment is needed, the turnround for compiling and linking is too slow, debugging facilities are primitive. However, it serves very well as a vehicle for exploring programming techniques in a conventional data structures and algorithms course, for teaching concurrency and programming language design, for looking at compilation issues, and for practical software engineering. It is excellent for students' final-year projects where the modules facilitate the management of a large system and the extensive libraries can be exploited. The easy construction of graphical user interfaces for MODULA-3 programs is particularly attractive.

The same considerations mean that MODULA-3 is an excellent vehicle for large commercial projects, and it has been used for a number of substantial systems running to hundreds of thousands of lines of code at DEC and Xerox. These include operating system work, real-time communications and straightforward applications. At the moment, the programming environment and project management tools tend to be constructed from standard Unix tools, which is a disadvantage, although work on more conventional development systems is being undertaken.

The goal of MODULA-3 was to be as simple and safe as it could be while meeting the needs of modern systems programmers. This goal has substantially been met. Exceptions, threads and garbage collection all help to avoid common errors in programs, particularly those that will have to run continuously for long periods. Strong typing extended through interfaces across separately compiled modules is a proven technique for building large systems and assists the re-use of existing code, especially in conjunction with generics. The use of objects and partial revelations gives control over levels of abstraction in libraries, allowing compromises to be made between modularity and efficiency as the need dictates.

Some might question MODULA-3's restriction to single inheritance where each object type is derived from a single parent type. This restriction gives much cleaner semantics to the language, which is important for formal verification, and also admits more efficient implementations. Moreover, there seem to be very few practical cases where multiple inheritance is actually of significant value.

The type system for MODULA-3 was to some extent dictated by considerations of type safety in distributed systems. In particular, it was designed to allow structured values to be passed between programs safely. As a consequence it is also possible to save data structures in a filing system and recover them in a type-safe way through a system which provides the basis for programming persistent systems.

10.4 Conclusion

This chapter has presented a set of guidelines for selecting initial languages for teaching programming and has suggested that two languages – ML and MODULA-3 – are particularly well suited to the task. The main features of these two languages were then presented and illustrated through extended examples, and the languages evaluated.

ML has been used as the initial teaching language for the computer science tripos at Cambridge since 1987 and this has been followed by MODULA-3 since 1990. Sixteen hours of lectures are budgeted for ML, but some of the more advanced features of the language (exceptions and modules) are omitted. These are accompanied by a series of graduated practical classes and exercises. The whole of MODULA-3 is taught in two series of 12 lectures each, again accompanied by practical work [Robinson, 1991].

The use of practical classes is important. Programming is a practical skill and cannot be taught purely through lectures; carefully supervised classes are vital if the students are to develop reasonable programming style as well as technical familiarity with the language. Each language has its own idiomatic usage which can be illustrated through examples in lectures (and, indeed, in this chapter), but this can only be fully appreciated when it is being applied to a new problem. Lectures on dynamics cannot teach you how to ride a bicycle!

Moreover the approach appears to be popular with the students. ML and, particularly, MODULA-3 are the languages of choice for final-year projects. There also appears to be a correlation between the use of these languages and higher marks for the project. It would appear that all desiderata for systems programming are genuinely valuable and a language like MODULA-3 is conducive to higher productivity.

The same considerations suggest that ML and MODULA-3 would be of value in commercial projects. ML has already found favour where mathematical analysis is deemed to be important and its interpreted implementation lends itself to rapid prototyping of systems. However, MODULA-3 is still mainly used in academic and research environments. This seems odd: MODULA-3 meets the requirements of a language like ADA but avoids unnecessary complexity and achieves greater coherence. Further competition comes from C++, which is widely used but shares the worst aspects of C's syntax and unsafe features. Indeed, a common complaint amongst systems programmers is that company policy dictates the use of C++ when their professional judgement would be to use a safer language such as MODULA-3. Of course, it is possible to write correct and maintainable programs in any language, but a language like MODULA-3 makes it more natural. Fortunately, students who have learned the idiom of MODULA-3 are then able to approach other languages, learn them, and use them in a disciplined way. Perhaps the availability of better-supported implementations will allow more rational policies to be adopted and such contortions avoided.

10.5 References

Brown, M. and Meehan, J. (1993a), *The FormsVBT Reference Manual*, Technical Report, DEC Systems Research Center, Palo Alto, CA.

Brown, M. and Meehan, J. (1993b), *VBTkit Reference Manual*, Technical Report, DEC Systems Research Center, Palo Alto, CA.

Cardelli, L., Donahue, J., Glassman, L., Jordan, M., Kalsow, B. and Nelson, G. (1989), *The Modula-3 Report (revised)*, Technical Report, DEC Systems Research Center and Olivetti Research Center.

Gordon, M., Milner, R. and Wadsworth, C. (1978), *Edinburgh LCF*, Springer-Verlag, London.

Harbison, S. (1992), *Modula-3*, Prentice-Hall, Englewood Cliffs, NJ.

Harper, R. (1986), *Introduction to Standard ML*, Technical Report ECS-LFCS-86-14, University of Edinburgh, Laboratory for Foundations of Computer Science.

Harper, R., MacQueen, D. and Milner, R. (1986), *Standard ML*, Technical Report ECS-LFCS-86-2, University of Edinburgh.

Jensen, K. and Wirth, N. (1975), *Pascal User Manual and Report*, Springer-Verlag, New York, 2nd edition.

Lampson, B. (1983), *A Description of the Cedar Language*, Technical Report CSL-83-15, Xerox PARC, Palo Alto, CA.

Lampson, B. W., Horning, J. J., London, R. L., Mitchell, J. G. and Popek, G. J. (1977), Report on the Programming Language Euclid, *SIGPLAN Notices*, **12**(2).

Manasse, M. and Nelson, G. (1991a), *Trestle Tutorial*, Technical Report 69, DEC Systems Research Center, Palo Alto, CA.

Manasse, M. and Nelson, G. (1991b), *Trestle Reference Manual*, Technical Report 68, DEC Systems Research Center, Palo Alto, CA.

Mitchell, J., Maybury, W. and Sweet, R. (1979), *Mesa Language Manual*, Technical Report CSL-79-3, Xerox PARC, Palo Alto, CA.

Myers, C., Clack, C. and Poon, E. (1993), *Programming with Standard ML*, Prentice-Hall, Hemel Hempstead.

Nelson, G. (1992), *Systems Programming with Modula-3*, Prentice-Hall.

Paulson, L. (1991), *ML for the Working Programmer*, Cambridge University Press.

Robinson, P. (1991), Modula-3 in an undergraduate Computer Science course, *Proc. 2nd International Modula-2 Conference*.

Rovner, P., Levin, R. and Wick, J. (1985), *On Extending Modula-2 for Building Large Integrated Systems*, Technical Report 3, DEC Systems Research Center.

Sedgewick, R. (1992), *Algorithms in Modula-3*, Addison-Wesley, Reading, MA.

Ullman, J. D. (1993), *Elements of ML Programming*, Prentice-Hall, Englewood Cliffs, NJ.

Wikström, Å. (1987), *Functional Programming Using Standard ML*, Prentice-Hall, Hemel Hempstead.

Wirth, N. (1971), The programming language Pascal, *Acta Informatica*, **1**(1), 35–63.

Wirth, N. (1980), *Modula-2*, Technical Report No. 36, ETH Zürich.

Wirth, N. (1988), *Programming with Modula-2*, Texts and Monographs in Computer Science, Springer-Verlag, Berlin, 4th edition.

Wirth, N. and Reiser, M. (1992), *Programming in Oberon: Steps beyond Pascal and Modula-2*, Addison-Wesley, Reading, MA.

11 Rationale behind choosing Oberon for programming education at ETH Zürich

Josef Templ

This chapter describes the rationale behind the development of the OBERON programming language and system and choice of OBERON for mainstream programming education at ETH Zürich. It roughly describes the reasons why it has been necessary to replace MODULA-2 by a new language, although the former served very well as a tool for programming education and also met with some acceptance in industry. We consider individual criteria which are important for choosing a programming language for education and describe how OBERON satisfies them. Most of the properties apply to programming language selection in general as well. Finally, we have some examples to show what OBERON programs look like.

11.1 Introduction

OBERON is the name both of a programming language and of a supporting operating environment. It has been developed by N. Wirth and J. Gutknecht at the Institute for Computer Systems, ETH Zürich as a successor to PASCAL and MODULA-2, which were also developed there. The first OBERON papers were published in 1987 and after two years of daily use in a research environment, OBERON has been introduced for mainstream programming education in the Department of Computer Science. It is now used at all levels of education, ranging from introductory programming courses to PhD research. It is also used as a tool for the daily work of the teaching staff and secretary and serves to prepare documents (such as the first draft of this one) to send e-mail and much more. Other departments at ETH are also now switching to OBERON, but this is a rather slow process. Probably the most important reason for the slow movement to OBERON is that the programming language MODULA-2 was established for programming education only a decade ago. With good experiences in using MODULA-2 and with all the programming courses and teaching material adapted to it, it seems to be a waste of time to switch to a new language if there are not very good reasons to do so.

The reasons that Wirth and Gutknecht started the enterprise of introducing a new language were the shortcomings of MODULA-2 with respect to extensibility, which became obvious when we tried to build an extensible operating system with MODULA-2. The lack of type extension was an obstacle for programming extensible components (such as the viewer or tasking system) without having to use unsafe machine-level features. Therefore, some language extensions were necessary that finally led to the OBERON programming language. OBERON may be best thought of as MODULA-2 with some extensions and some simplifications. The simplifications make OBERON not fully source-code-compatible with MODULA-2 and are the reason for its new name. Without going into details, the most important simplifications are the dropping of nested modules, variant records, enumeration types, subranges and type CARDINAL. The most important extensions are the concept of record type extension (replacing variant records), automatic storage management, hierarchy of numeric types, basic string operations, and selective export. More extensions have been added later on and are known as the OBERON-2 extensions. They include type-bound procedures (methods), pointer to open arrays, and read-only export.

The outcome of the above-mentioned operating system project is also known under the name OBERON, which continues the tradition of identifying a language and a supporting environment by the same name (*cf.* SMALLTALK, CEDAR, TURBO-PASCAL). When considering OBERON, one has to keep this ambiguity in mind to avoid confusion.

11.2 Criteria for programming language selection

Let us start the discussion about criteria for programming language selection with a quotation from *Programming in Oberon* [Wirth and Reiser, 1992]. In the introduction, the authors raise the question: 'Why should the reader be interested in learning to program in OBERON instead of one of the widely known languages?' The answer presented by Wirth and Reiser points out that Hoare's hints on programming language design [Hoare, 1973] have been taken seriously for the design of OBERON:

> The answer is because it is a language that is defined in terms of relatively few, fundamental programming concepts, because it is rigorously structured, and because it is efficiently implemented on modern computers. These are essentially the same reasons that 20 years ago spoke for the language PASCAL. These properties encourage a systematic approach to the design of programs, and are the prerequisites for using the essential technique of modular design based on abstraction. OBERON is a 'small' language, which makes it particularly suited as notation for introduction to programming. Yet its concepts are general and powerful, making it equally appropriate for the construction of large software sys-

tems. These claims have been substantiated by use of OBERON both in teaching and in the design of the OBERON system itself.

The following sections discuss the above criteria in more detail and pay special attention to programming education. The criteria are divided into two groups, where the first group covers language properties, and the second group deals with properties of the supporting operating environment. For each point, we see how OBERON relates to it. We shall measure the quality of the language as the minimum grading on individual properties, not as their sum or average. A zero or very low grading on one of the properties renders a language useless and cannot be compensated by a high grading on another property.

11.3 Language criteria

11.3.1 Size of a language

A language should be small in order to be comprehensible in all details. OBERON may be described in 20 to 30 pages. An OBERON compiler can be written with about 5000 lines of OBERON code. Committee languages tend to be at least a decimal order of magnitude larger without being a decimal order of magnitude more powerful.

11.3.2 Textbooks

To be useful for education, there must be some documentation available, preferably in the form of textbooks. Currently, there are three OBERON books in English (from Addison-Wesley) [Reiser,1991; Wirth and Reiser,1992; Wirth and Gutknecht, 1992] and one in German and English (from Springer) [Mössenböck, 1993].

11.3.3 Stability

The definition of a programming language should be stable. This requirement seems to be in contradiction to technical improvement, but it is important for educational purposes as well as for industrial usage to protect the investments made in a language. In the case of education this means the investments in textbooks, programming systems, manuscripts, programming course design, and the like. Care has to be taken with experimental language extensions, as the students often cannot distinguish between experimental and settled subjects. The operating environment should also show some stability, but as this is a collection of many tools, with the compiler being just a small part, one has to expect more changes and enhancements over time. The OBERON language was defined in 1987 and slightly revised in 1990. Since the introduction of the OBERON-2 extensions in 1991, there have not been any changes except for some clarifications. The OBERON system has been under continuous development since its introduction in 1987, with the change rate dropping to almost zero in the last two years. However, a slight modification of the system may be in order to provide for the seamless integration of an alternative user interface aiming at the specific needs of end-users rather than at the needs of programming education.

11.3.4 Expressivity

A language used for mainstream programming education should be a general-purpose language that allows us to express various programming styles. It should allow education in different areas such as introductory courses, data structures, modular design, system software, object-oriented programming, parallel programming and compiler writing without changing the programming language or system. By staying with a familiar environment, productivity is greatly boosted simply by avoiding any educational overhead. At ETH, introductory programming courses actually start with predicate calculus and program construction in the small without any implemented language at all. After this phase, only a small, provable subset of the OBERON language is used for exercises. Programming courses are intended not to start with object-oriented programming as this is considered more appropriate for programming in the large. OBERON also allows machine-level programming very much like MODULA-2 does. We are especially pleased with the seamless integration of imperative and object-oriented programming in OBERON.

11.3.5 Industrial relevance

Programming education at a university should not be considered as education for a future employer but should focus on important concepts with as little overhead as possible. It should not pay too much attention to what is currently used in industry. Quite to the contrary, universities should set the standard for future industrial programming practice. By industrial relevance we mean the potential impact of a system or language on future progress in industrial programming practice. The potential impact of OBERON, besides the well-known advantages of statically typed high-level languages, lies in the term 'extensibility'. We expect future applications to be extensible rather than fixed by a program linker. Typical OBERON applications consist of a small core and a potentially unlimited number of extensions. This approach naturally structures big applications into manageable parts and thereby improves software quality and programmer productivity. Initial interest in this approach has already been expressed by representatives of the software industry. This can be seen from the fact that the foundation of the Swiss OBERON User Group was suggested by industry. There has also been some work to bring OBERON closer to the end-user by better integration of OBERON programs into a specific target environment and by including an end-user interface into the OBERON system. Several companies are currently working on commercial OBERON implementations.

11.4 Operating environment criteria

11.4.1 Environment

A language must be embedded in a programming environment which is flexible and powerful yet simple to use. Current OBERON implementations provided by ETH are integrated into the OBERON operating environment. The power of the OBERON environment can be seen from the fact that it is used as the native operating system on the Ceres computers (where it was developed). Ease of use comes from a radically new approach to user interfaces which avoids modal dialogues. Instead, OBERON relies on a kind of postfix logic which requires specifying the operands first and then issuing a command. Much of OBERON's flexibility comes from an integrated text data structure that serves as a base for editing and compiling programs, formatting text documents, handling electronic mail, and also for executing commands. An OBERON command is an exported parameterless procedure that may be represented in textual form as M.P, where M denotes the module and P the procedure. In OBERON, commands are the units of executable code that may be directly invoked by the user. Referenced modules are loaded on demand and stay in memory until explicitly unloaded. Commands provide executable code units of finer granularity than the more traditional notion of executable (main) programs.

11.4.2 Availability

The system and language need to be available on a wide range of machines. This avoids dependence on a special vendor and supports the use of personal computers which many students own. Currently, there are OBERON implementations available for MS-DOS, Windows, Windows-NT, Macintosh II, SUN Sparc (SunOS 4.x and SunOS 5.x), IBM RS/6000, DECstation, Silicon Graphics and HP-PA, DEC Alpha, PowerPC Macintosh and Amiga. All implementations support the same document formats and allow the porting of programs from one platform to another by simply recompiling them even if they contain window or graphics operations.

11.4.3 Efficiency

By 'efficiency' we mean both the efficiency of the programming system and the efficiency of program execution. For educational purposes, compilation times are actually more important than execution times, because programs are far more often compiled than executed. Because of the small language, OBERON compilers are fast (more that 1000 lines per second) and produce fast code, which is usually much better than unoptimized C code and only slightly slower than optimized C. Since OBERON also avoids an extra linking step and compilation can be done without leaving the program editor, users feel as though they are working with an interpreted system. They also have the advantage of static type-checking and efficient execution.

11.4.4 Costs

The system should be as cheap as possible in terms of money and system resources. This property is particularly important in an educational environment, where hundreds of licences have to be bought to equip student labs with software or software upgrades. OBERON versions provided by ETH can be obtained free of charge and run well with 2 Mb of main memory and with three or 4 Mb of external storage.

11.4.5 Robustness

A system used for education should be as robust as possible. There should not be such things as dangling pointers crashing the system in unexpected ways. Run-time checks related to memory consistency such as NIL-checks, index checks and type guards should be a matter of course. OBERON implementations from ETH use garbage collection to guarantee memory consistency. It is neither necessary nor possible to explicitly deallocate data structures.

11.4.6 Tools

A programming system should provide some basic programming tools besides the compiler and linker/loader. One of the most important tools is a text editor to allow the convenient editing of program texts. The OBERON system features a text editor that is tightly integrated with the compiler, although both are separate tools. This integration comes from the general OBERON system philosophy of having a single address space shared by all programs. Therefore, the compiler can access the text data structure being edited in a certain window and compile it without even storing the text to a file. There is actually more than one text editor available, but all operate on the same text data structure. Another important programming tool in OBERON is the interface browser, which takes a module name or a qualified name as input and displays in textual form the interface of the module or object. This tool essentially replaces the separate definition module found in MODULA-2. Other available tools include instrumenting or statistical profilers, a static program analyser, and electronic mail. The OBERON systems provided by ETH also have debugging facilities based on post mortem dumps, and the ability to inspect the values of global variables. There is no fully fledged dynamic debugger provided by ETH, because our education is oriented towards systematic programming, assertions and invariants. It should also be noted that debugging effort is considerably reduced in OBERON, because many errors, most notably memory inconsistencies, cannot occur.

11.4.7 Extensibility

A programming system should be extensible and customizable. It should be possible to add one's own tools and to integrate them well into the existing environment. It should not be necessary to learn a new special-purpose programming language to extend or customize the system. Many commercial programming systems are linked into one big program that cannot be extended. It is our experience that there is no such thing as a perfect tool that includes all the necessary features from the very beginning. Therefore, the OBERON system has been designed as an extensible system that does not distinguish between system and user programs. The OBERON system can be extended by simply writing OBERON programs. Through the integration of text editing and command interpretation, customization of the user interface can be done by editing texts.

11.4.8 Fun

A programming system used for education should provide some fun in order to motivate students and teaching staff rather than frustrate them. Although fun is not a technical term, there are obvious examples of programming systems that are not fun to use because they are too complex, too inconvenient, or too slow. Much of the fun comes from a deep understanding of a system's functionality; this was one of OBERON's main design goals, namely to have a system that can be taught and understood in all details. At ETH, students can reimplement parts of the system such as the file system or the automatic memory management system and gain a deep understanding of OBERON's internal behaviour.

11.5 Examples

This section contains simple examples to give the reader the 'look and feel' of the language.

11.5.1 A stack ADT

We present only the interface not the implementation:

```
MODULE Stacks;
  TYPE
    Stack* = RECORD ... END;

  PROCEDURE Init*(VAR s: Stack); ...
  PROCEDURE Push*(VAR s: Stack; name, address: ARRAY OF CHAR); ...
  PROCEDURE Pop*(VAR s: Stack; VAR name, address: ARRAY OF CHAR); ...
END Stacks.
```

Selective export (expressed by a '*' mark after a name) allows us to export type Stack without exporting its components. Thus the implementation is completely hidden in module Stacks. By using statically bound procedures we have actually defined a 'sealed' type Stack, which cannot be extended later on. If we use type-bound procedures for Push and Pop:

```
PROCEDURE (VAR s: Stack) Push*(name, address: ARRAY OF CHAR); ...
PROCEDURE (VAR s: Stack) Pop*(VAR name, address: ARRAY OF CHAR); ...
```

it is possible to subclass the type Stack later to implement, for example, a class called FiniteStack (i.e. a stack that introduces a stack limit).

11.5.2 A generic stack

There are no parameterized types or templates in OBERON. We can, however, use record extension to simulate the effect. The main difference to a parameterized stack type is that our stacks are heterogeneous and that fewer compile-time checks are possible.

```
MODULE GenericStacks;
  TYPE
    Stack* = RECORD ... END;
    Elem* = POINTER TO ElemDesc;
    ElemDesc* = RECORD END ;
```

```
      PROCEDURE Init*(VAR s: Stack); ...
      PROCEDURE Push*(VAR s: Stack; x: Elem); ...
      PROCEDURE Pop*(VAR s: Stack; VAR x: Elem); ...
   END GenericStacks.
```

This solution allows us to push and pop data of any type that is an extension of type Elem and thus compatible with the stack element type.

11.5.3 Conference organization

The following gives only the outline of a possible solution that does not make too many assumptions about a real conference. We also refrain from introducing a proper modularization. The solution is built around a simple type hierarchy which is rooted in the type Delegate, which defines the common properties of all kinds of delegates.

```
TYPE
  Delegate = POINTER TO DelegateDesc;
  DelegateDesc = RECORD
    name, address: String;
    arrival, departure: Time;
    toPay: Money
  END;

  Presenter = POINTER TO PresenterDesc;
  PresenterDesc = RECORD (DelegateDesc)
    paper: String;
    from, to: Time
  END;

  SessionChair = POINTER TO SessionChairDesc;
  SessionChairDesc = RECORD (DelegateDesc)
    toDo: Text;
  END;

  Exhibitor = POINTER TO ExhibitorDesc;
  ExhibitorDesc = RECORD (DelegateDesc)
    exhibition: String
  END;

  DelegateOpenUniv = POINTER TO DelegateOUDesc;
  DelegateOUDesc = RECORD (DelegateDesc)
    faculty, institute: String;
  END;

  DelegateOther = POINTER TO DelegateOtherDesc;
  DelegateOtherDesc = RECORD (DelegateDesc)
    organization: String;
  END;

PROCEDURE (a: Delegate) Arrive (at: Time); ...
PROCEDURE (a: Delegate) Pay (amount: Money); ...
PROCEDURE (a: Delegate) Leave (at: Time); ...

PROCEDURE (c: SessionChair) Arrive (at: Time); ...
```

A natural way to express the hierarchy of conference delegates in OBERON is to define a hierarchy of record types. We can employ type-bound procedures to process delegates in a type-specific way. Without going into details, it should be noted that type-bound procedures are bound to the dynamic type of the leftmost parameter, which is also called the *receiver*. By using type-bound procedures, it is for instance possible to override the `Arrive` procedure in honour of the session chair and (given a multimedia workstation) to play a fanfare on their arrival.

11.6 Conclusions

Our experience of education with OBERON has been very encouraging. In particular, novices with no previous experience in computer usage soon get used to the system. Experienced students sometimes have the problem that they must relearn computer usage, and some of them therefore dislike the system at first. In either case, students are productive with the system right from the first session. The advantage of OBERON over other educational systems is that it is not restricted to introductory programming but is actually a tool that grows with the user.

11.7 References and annotated bibliography

Hoare, C. A. R. (1973), *Hints on Programming Language Design*, Technical Report AI-Memo, AIM-224, STAN-CS-73-403, Stanford University: keynote address at the ACM SIGPLAN conference, October 1973; this is still the up-to-date guide for anyone who designs a new language or language extension.

Mössenböck, H. (1993), *Object-oriented Programming in Oberon-2*, Springer-Verlag, Berlin, (also available in German): an introduction to object-oriented programming using OBERON-2 as a teaching vehicle.

Reiser, M. (1991), *The Oberon System. User Guide and Programmer's Manual*, Addison-Wesley, Reading, MA: user manual for the programming environment and reference for the standard module library.

Wirth, N. and Gutknecht, J. (1992), *Project Oberon. The Design of an Operating System and Compiler*. Addison-Wesley, Reading, MA: program listings with explanations for the whole OBERON system, including the compiler for NS32000.

Wirth, N. and Reiser, M. (1992), *Programming in Oberon: Steps beyond Pascal and Modula-2*. Addison-Wesley, Reading, MA: tutorial for the OBERON programming language and concise language reference.

Contact addresses

```
internet:
  e-mail - Institut fuer Computersysteme: oberon@inf.ethz.ch
           Swiss Oberon User Group: oberon-user@inf.ethz.ch
  ftp    - ETHZ-Oberon implementations are provided by
           anonymous ftp on: ftp.inf.ethz.ch:/Oberon
usenet:
  comp.lang.oberon
world-wide-web:
  ftp://ftp.inf.ethz.ch/pub/software/Oberon
```

12 The suitability of Eiffel for teaching object-oriented software development

Ray Weedon

This chapter assumes that the case for object-oriented languages has been accepted and argues that EIFFEL is a highly suitable language for teaching software engineering as part of an object-oriented approach to software development.

12.1 Introduction

It is not the intention of this chapter to argue the case for teaching an object-oriented language in place of traditional languages like PASCAL or C. Rather, it is assumed that the case has been accepted that object-oriented languages have advantages in the following ways.

1. They extend the capabilities of traditional (imperative) languages by making it possible to analyse, design and implement software within a uniform framework of classes based on abstract data types.

2. They provide a more powerful modular construct for software development (the class as a collection of data, procedures or functions) than that used in the traditional approach (the procedure or function).

3. They embody to a higher degree than older languages the important principles of software development which any course on the topic should be seeking to instil, such as:

- modularization;
- re-use;
- information hiding;
- extensibility.

Neither does the chapter argue the case for which language paradigm – functional, logical, or imperative (*i.e.* object-oriented) – should be taught as a first programming language. In my opinion all three should be taught since, as Goguen and Mesegeur argue [1987], the ultimate objective should be to synthesize the three paradigms.

What the chapter does argue is that EIFFEL is a highly suitable language for teaching as part of an object-oriented approach to software development. It is a so-called 'pure' object-oriented language (not a hybrid), and can be used to illustrate extremely well the major principles of program development. It incorporates mechanisms that make it suitable to teach at all levels, from introductory to advanced, and has a notation which has been integrated into an analysis and design method called BON [Nerson and Walden, 1994].

EIFFEL was designed by Bertrand Meyer in the mid-1980s as a production-level language addressing the major software engineering concerns of:

- reliability;
- re-use;
- extensibility;
- robustness;
- openness;
- portability;
- efficiency.

The language was designed to support a style of software development based on abstract data types (ADTs) and its proponents claim that it provides a notation which supports the analysis, design and implementation phases of the software development cycle. Therefore we begin our consideration of EIFFEL with ADTs.

Then, in section 12.3, we consider how EIFFEL provides features that can be used for teaching at all levels of an undergraduate curriculum and beyond. Section 12.4 looks briefly at EIFFEL's use in industry and its suitability for developing different types of application. Prior to presenting my conclusions, in section 12.5 I consider the different implementations of the language which are presently available and the support they give for teaching the language and for developing software according to sound engineering principles.

12.2 Abstract data types and Eiffel

As mentioned above, EIFFEL is designed on the basis of ADTs. In order to see what this implies, we look briefly at an example of an ADT and suggest the mechanisms needed in a language to support its implementation.

12.2.1 Specifying an ADT

The ADT approach to developing software is based on the idea that real-world applications can be modelled as interrelated sets of objects, each set of which exhibits similar behaviour. This economizes on the effort of having to treat every object in the application as a unique separate case. It also implies that the way the behaviour of an object is implemented should be transparent to the user of the object.

The following specification of an ADT called Stack is based on the notation used in [Thomas *et al.*, 1988].

NAME OF TYPE
>   Stack[X]

SYNTAX OF OPERATIONS
>   **Createstack** : $\rightarrow$ Stack[X]
>   **Top** : Stack[X]: $\rightarrow$ X
>   **Pop** : Stack[X] $\rightarrow$ Stack[X]
>   **Push** : X, Stack[X]: $\rightarrow$ Stack[X]
>   **Isemptystack** : Stack[X] $\rightarrow$ Boolean
>   **Isfullstack** : Stack[X] $\rightarrow$ Boolean

SEMANTICS OF OPERATIONS
>   Forall x, y: X;
>   b : Boolean; *max_size* a constant of type Integer;
>   s, t : Stack[X] (where the underlying model is a list):
>
>   **pre-Createstack**() ::= **true**
>   **post-Createstack**(s) ::= **Isemptylist**(s)
>
>   **pre-Top**(s) ::= **not Isemptystack**(s)
>   **post-Top**(s; x) ::= x = **head**(s)
>
>   **pre-Pop**(s) ::= **not Isemptystack** (s)
>   **post-Pop**(s; t) ::= t = **tail**(s)
>
>   **pre-Push**(x, s) ::= **true**
>   **post-Push**(x,s; t) ::= r = **append**(x, s)
>
>   **pre-Isemptystack**(s) ::= **true**
>   **post-Isemptystack**(s; b) ::= b = **Isemptylist**(s)
>
>   **pre-Isfullstack**(s) ::= **true**
>   **post-Isfullstack**(s, b) ::= b = (**length**(s) = *max_size*)

Basically, an ADT denotes a set of instances whose behaviour is defined by a collection of operations. The word 'abstract' in the term 'abstract data type' is used to convey two related concepts:

- the instances of the ADT are defined by their behaviour (*i.e.* the collection of operations specified by the ADT) and not by the way they are represented or structured;

- the operations themselves are specified in a way which is independent of any programming language.

In the above ADT specification the behaviour of instances of Stack is defined by the operations (or functions): **Push, Pop, Top, Isemptystack** and **Isfullstack**. The operation **Createstack** is not considered to be part of the behaviour of **Stack** because creation operations are special; they are considered as representing all the valid instances of the ADT that can be called into existence using such an operation. Getting hold of an object in this way clearly has nothing to do with the way it might then be made to behave.

The **NAME** part of the ADT specifies its name and also shows whether or not it is to be a parameterized ADT. As indicated in the specification of **Stack**, it has a single formal generic parameter **X**. This indicates that instances of stacks can be parameterized to hold instances of any other ADT. For example, we could create a stack of integers using the actual generic parameter **Integer** in place of **X**.

The **SYNTAX** part of the ADT shows which ADT instances are to be considered valid source and results data for each function. For example, **Isemptystack** takes an instance of **Stack** and returns an instance of **Boolean**.

The **SEMANTICS** part of the ADT specification defines the meaning of each function. We have used a constructive approach to specifying these semantics[1] rather than an axiomatic approach[2] because this accords with the manner of representing these semantics in EIFFEL implementations of ADTs. One implication of the constructive approach is that an underlying model (one or more instances of other ADTs) is required to specify the pre-conditions and post-conditions. In the case of the **Stack** ADT, the underlying model includes an instance of an ADT **List** (which is assumed to have behaviour defined by the operations: **Head, Tail, Addtofront, Length,** *etc.*). The specification also uses the constant **max_size** (of the abstract type **Integer** and the variable b (of type **Boolean**).

An important concept embedded in an ADT is that of the client–supplier contract. This specifies the rights and obligations of the parties involved in using the ADT. For example, the user of the **Top** operation (*i.e.* a *client* of **Stack**) is *contracted* by the SYNTAX and pre-condition of **Top** to call the function with a stack which is not empty. Given that this obligation has been met, then **Top** (as part of the *supplier* **Stack** ADT in this case) is contracted to meet its post-condition. For all other inputs the function is undefined. The client–supplier contract is an important means of distinguishing between those cases an application is designed to deal with and those for which it is undefined.

In summary, it is clear how a **Stack** ADT can be defined in terms of other ADTs, in this case **Boolean, List** and **X** (an as-yet-unspecified ADT) in a way that can be supported by EIFFEL (more of this next). We have also seen that the **SYNTAX** and **SEMANTICS** part spells out the contract between the ADT and those who will use it (*i.e.* its clients).

12.2.2 Specifying an ADT as a subtype of other ADTs

Let us assume that we wish to specify a stack containing items of type **Frame** and which has the additional behaviour of being able to return the number of frames in a

---

[1] The constructive approach uses pre- and post-conditions expressed in terms of predicate calculus expressions.

[2] The axiomatic approach defines the functions of the ADT in terms of each other.

stack. This can be easily achieved, without having to repeat the specification above, by using the subtyping mechanism shown below.

NAME OF TYPE
    Frame_Stack
SUBTYPE OF
    Stack[Frame]
SYNTAX OF OPERATIONS
    Count : Stack[Frame] $\rightarrow$ Integer
SEMANTICS OF OPERATIONS
    Forall s of type Stack[Frame] and i of Integer:

    pre-Count (s) ::= true
    post-Count(s: i) ::= if **Isemptylist**(s) then
                    i = 0
              else
                    i = 1 + **Count**(**tail**(s))

From the above specification it should be clear that this approach to specifying ADTs is useful in the object-oriented context; we could go on to explore how this notation can be extended to specify an ADT having multiple (abstract) supertypes or which allows functions which are inherited from the supertype to be renamed and redefined to fit the requirements of the subtype. Subtyping and redefinition open up the possibility of polymorphism without compromising the benefits of strong typing.

12.2.3 Support needed for implementing ADTs

The brief analysis of ADTs above suggests the following important mechanisms to support their implementation in a programming language:

- parameterized routines to implement the operations of the ADT;
- subtyping;
- generic parameters;
- the facility to hide the way the instances of the ADT are represented (*i.e.* provide the equivalent of an underlying model);
- a mechanism to add new ADT implementations to a library of such types and re-use them;
- representing the client–supplier contract;
- a mechanism to deal with breaches of contract;
- support for polymorphism.

12.2.4 Implementing ADTs in Eiffel

Table 12.1 contains program code which shows how the Stack ADT might be implemented as an EIFFEL class using an underlying model of a linked list – one of the classes contained in the EIFFEL library.

The class shown has been 'stretched' apart into three columns to illustrate how the

Table 12.1   The Stack ADT implemented as the EIFFEL class STACK

NAME and SYNTAX	SEMANTICS	
	Pre- and post-conditions and underlying model	Instructions
`class STACK[X]` `creation` `  createstack`	`feature {NONE}` `   max_size:  INTEGER` `   s:  LINKED_LIST[X]`	
`feature ANY` `  createstack is`	`--Creates stack object` `require` `  isemptystack`	`do` `  !!s.createlist` `end--createstack`
`  push(x:  X) is`	`--Adds x to the stack` `ensure not full` `require` `  s.count=old s.count+1`	`do` `  s.first` `  s.put(x)` `end--push`
`  pop is`	`--Removes x from stack` `require` `  s.count=old s.count-1`	`do` `  s.first` `  s.remove` `end--pop`
`  isemptystack is`	`--Is stack empty?` `require` `  Result=s.empty`	`do` `  Result:=s.empty` `end--isemptystack`
`  isfullstack is`	`--Is stack full?` `require` `  Result=` `   (s.count=max_size)`	`do` `  Result:=` `   (s.count=max_size)` `end--isfullstack`
`end--class STACK[X]`	`invariant` `  s /= Void;` `end--class STACK[X]`	`end--class STACK[X]`

STACK class in EIFFEL corresponds to the Stack ADT. The first column corresponds to the **NAME** and **SYNTAX** parts of the ADT and shows the class name and the headings of the features which are to represent the behaviour of the class. The name of the class STACK[X] indicates that it is parameterized with the formal generic parameter indicating that a stack object may contain items of any type. It is also possible in EIFFEL for classes to have more than one formal generic parameter. In addition these parameters can be constrained. For example, the class defined as

```
class MATRIX[X] -> NUMERIC
```

specifies that the class MATRIX can be associated with any type of element provided the element has the property of being numeric (*i.e.* it can be added, subtracted, *etc.*).

EIFFEL provides three types of *feature*: *procedures* (like pop and push), *functions* (like top and isemptystack), and *attributes* (like s). Attributes perform two roles. To the client of a class, they look no different from a function, since, given an instance of the class, they return a value, and like functions cannot be changed by the client. However, from inside the class, attributes have the status of variables referencing storage which can be modified by the routines (procedures and functions) of the class. In other words, attributes can be thought of as functions which store their return value, and this value can only be modified from within the class.

As shown in the first column of the table, the creation procedure in EIFFEL is considered special and requires a special clause to indicate that the procedures named in the clause can be used when creating a stack object. (See below for more details on creating objects in EIFFEL.)

The second column shows how the semantics, that is, pre-conditions and post-conditions, of the ADT operations are represented by EIFFEL *require* and *ensure* clauses respectively. These clauses contain assertions (equivalent to boolean expressions) stating what should be true before and after a routine executes.[3] (If no explicit relational operator is used between assertions they are implicitly *anded* together.)

EIFFEL assertions do have limitations. They lack the full semantic power of the predicate calculus in that they do not allow existential and universal quantification. Also, whether or not they can fully capture the semantics expressed at the ADT level depends on the behaviour of the classes used as the 'underlying model' or representation of the new class. For example, the class LINKED_LIST, used as an underlying model is not as comprehensive as the list used to define the Stack ADT and consequently it has not been possible to capture the full semantics of the STACK class without developing or using a more powerful representation.

It seems at first sight as if *require* and *ensure* clauses are little different to clauses containing *check* statements – a common mechanism in other programming languages. This is not the case. In EIFFEL they perform an important role in specifying the contract between client and supplier and, as we shall see in section 12.3.6, allocating responsibility when this contract is broken. It is, however, possible, in EIFFEL, to use assertions in ordinary check statements. EIFFEL also provides for their use in loop variants and loop invariants which enable the semantics of an iteration to be enforced.

Included in the semantics of the class shown in Table 12.1 is an *invariant clause*. Essentially the role of the invariant is to constrain the values of the representation to those which constitute valid instances of the ADT.[4] The invariant must be valid at all times when routines of the class are not executing.

Finally, the third column of Table 12.1 shows how the semantics expressed in the require and ensure clauses are effected by EIFFEL instructions.

12.3 Programming principles embodied in Eiffel

In this section we look at the features which make EIFFEL an excellent language for teaching the principles of programming from introductory to advanced level. Follow-

---

[3] Note the use of the reserved word old in the second column. It can only be used in assertions and enables one to refer to the value of an attribute as it was before the routine was called.

[4] Technically this is expressed by saying that the invariant defines the domain of the abstraction function.

ing the earlier discussion of ADTs, we look first at object-oriented programming in EIFFEL.

12.3.1 Creating, sharing and manipulating objects in Eiffel

In general there are three steps involved in creating an object in a programming language:

1. provide a name for the object;
2. allocate storage for it;
3. initialize it.

In EIFFEL, Step 1 is achieved using a declaration as in:

```
astack: STACK[INTEGER]
```

This brings into existence a name, in this case astack, which is called an *entity* in EIFFEL. Henceforth astack refers to an object of type STACK. Apart from the basic types, INTEGER, REAL, DOUBLE, BOOLEAN, CHARACTER and BIT, an entity like astack is the symbolic name of an address where a pointer to a stack is stored. At the time of declaration this pointer is set to the value void.

To effect Step 2 of the creation process and to allocate storage for the stack object, it is necessary to apply the creation procedure, !!, to astack as follows:

```
!!astack.createstack
```

where createstack is an (optional) specialized creation procedure for objects of the STACK class. In fact, the above creation statement not only allocates storage for each attribute of the object referred to by astack (in this case s of type LINKED_LIST) but also effects Step 3 of the creation process and initializes the attribute as well – by creating a linked list object for s. If there had been no creation procedure defined for STACK, then the default creation would have been:

```
!!astack
```

and the attribute s of the resulting object would have been given the default initialization of void. However, such an object would not be a valid instance of a stack (see invariant for STACK) which is why a user-defined creation procedure is necessary.

Although astack is a pointer to a stack, there is no need in EIFFEL to dereference the pointer when applying stack operations to it and calls like astack.top and astack.push(7) are unambiguously 'object' operations.

Using pointers to refer to objects means that objects can be shared. For example, assuming astack2 has also been declared of type STACK, the assignment

```
astack2 := astack
```

is a pointer operation and would cause `astack2` to reference the same object as that referenced by `astack`.[5] This is also referred to as *aliasing*.

Pointers are also necessary for dynamic binding. However, they do have a cost in that there is a need for two types of semantics regarding equality, assignment and copying: reference semantics for dealing with pointers and object semantics for dealing with the objects being pointed to. For example, we have seen that assignments involving pointer entities bring about object sharing. However, assignments like

```
i := j
```

where `i` and `j` are integers (*i.e.* objects of basic type), result in copying. To obtain copying for objects of pointer type requires the use of the `copy` operation which is inherited by all classes.

12.3.2 Building a class using inheritance

Earlier (on page 185), the ADT **Frame_Stack** was specified as a subtype of **Stack**. The following code shows how it can be implemented in EIFFEL using inheritance.

```
class FRAME_STACK
inherit
    STACK
creation
    createstack
feature
    count; integer is
        -- the number of frames in the stack
        local
            temp: FRAME_STACK
        do
            temp := Current
            if temp.isemptystack then
                Result := 0
            else
                Result := 1 + temp.pop.count
            end
        ensure
            (isemptystack implies Result = 0 or
            (Result = 1 + pop.count)
        end -- count
end -- class FRAME_STACK
```

The main point to note about this class is the creation clause. Although the operation `createstack` is inherited by FRAME_STACK it is not inherited as a creation operation which can be used with ! !. To make it into a creation operation it is necessary for it to be named in a creation clause. This highlights the point that the creation operation is special and that when defining a class careful thought needs to be given to it to ensure that only valid instances of an object are brought into existence.

Note that the call `temp.pop.count` is only valid if the feature `pop` in STACK has been defined as a function. We have assumed it is for this example; otherwise it would

---

[5] Operations like pointer arithmetic are not permitted in EIFFEL.

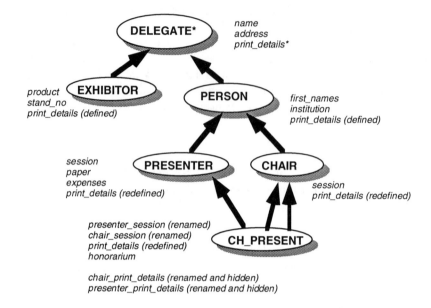

Figure 12.1   Class hierarchy showing different types of delegate to a workshop.

not be possible to express completely the assertion in the `ensure` clause. Also this assertion is only valid if the feature `pop` has been defined as a function that returns a stack with the top element removed as follows

```
pop : STACK is
   --  pop defined to remove top element
   do
       Result := clone(Current).s.first
       Result.s.remove
end -- pop
```

12.3.3 Multiple and repeated inheritance

EIFFEL supports multiple and indeed repeated inheritance. Consistent with the idea of subtyping, all features of parent classes are inherited including those that are hidden. However, EIFFEL provides extensive facilities to adapt features which are inherited including:

- renaming;
- redefinition;
- changing export status;
- making deferred features effective.

These features are illustrated using a simple example of the classes that might be defined to represent the different types of delegate to a workshop, shown in Figure 12.1 as a hierarchy of classes related by inheritance.

At the top of the tree is a deferred (or abstract) class, DELEGATE. (Deferred classes and features are denoted in EIFFEL by an asterisk.) No objects of such a deferred class can be created. Its role in this case is to capture the most general features of a delegate such as name, address and print_details. By doing this a deferred class supports the use of polymorphism and dynamic binding. For example, as we shall see below, we could provide a polymorphic data structure such as a list of delegates which, with the use of redefinition and dynamic binding, could be used to apply specialized features to objects of each class in the list.

Notice that the print_details feature in DELEGATE has also been deferred, indicating that each of the effective classes lower in the tree must provide a definition of this feature. Both PERSON and EXHIBITOR provide their own definitions, while the classes lower down the tree provide their own redefinitions.

The class CHAIR_PRESENTER illustrates both multiple and *repeated inheritance* because CHAIR_PRESENTER repeatedly inherits from PERSON as well as CHAIR. (The reason for this will be discussed below.) The definition of the class given next shows how the potential problems arising from these types of inheritance are resolved.

```
class CHAIR_PRESENTER
inherit
    PRESENTER
        rename
            session as presenter_session,
            print_details as presenter_print\_details
        export
            {NONE}    presenter_print_details
        end
    CHAIR
        rename
            print_details as chair_print_details,
            session as chair_session
        export
            {NONE}    chair_print_details
        end
    CHAIR
        rename
            session as chair_session
        redefine
            print_details
        select
            print_details
        end

creation
    ...
feature
    honorarium: MONEY
        -- ex-gratia payment for chairing and presenting
    print_details
            -- redefined procedure for objects of this class: re-uses
            -- print routines which are inherited under different
            -- names from PRESENTER and CHAIR
        do
            chair_print_details
            presenter_print_details
            io.putstring("Honorarium = ")
            honorarium.printmoney
        end -- print_details
end -- class CHAIR_PRESENTER
```

This code shows how the name clash resulting from inheriting two different `print_details` from different parents is resolved. That version inherited from PRESENTER is renamed `presenter_print_details` while that from CHAIR is renamed `chair_print_details`.

Repeatedly inheriting a feature via different branches of the inheritance tree does not cause a problem in EIFFEL. Provided both features are not renamed differently or redefined along their different paths there is no clash, and only one feature is assumed to be inherited. So, for example, `first_names` and `institution` are inherited by CHAIR_PRESENTER from PERSON as single features even though they 'arrive' by two different paths. However, if repeatedly inherited features have been renamed as in the case of `session` (renamed `presenter_session` when inherited from PRESENTER and `chair_session` when inherited from CHAIR) then two features are inherited. This clearly accords with the needs of CHAIR_PRESENTER, the objects of which must have a presentation session and a chairing session.

The repeated inheritance of CHAIR by CHAIR_PRESENTER needs some explanation. The latter class, like all its parents, requires a specialized `print_details` routine. In our example, it is assumed that the parent's `print_details` fulfils part of the task and can be re-used. The way to accomplish redefinition with re-use in EIFFEL requires the use of repeated inheritance – down one path from CHAIR, feature print_details is renamed, and down the other path it is redefined. (The redefined version can now use the parent's version in its renamed form.)

Two final points should be noted regarding the code for the CHAIR_PRESENTER class. One is the use of the export clause which allows the implementor of this class to change the export policy of features inherited from its parents. For example, the `print_details` features of CHAIR and PRESENTER are turned into hidden features in CHAIR_PRESENTER (using the key phrase {NONE}) because it will be exporting its own redefined version of this feature.

The other point to note is the use of the select clause. This is necessary for the purposes of dynamic binding. Our example shows that, via repeated inheritance, three versions of `print_details` are inherited by CHAIR_PRESENTER. The system needs to be told which of these is to be chosen when dynamic binding takes place. The select clause associated with the path in which `print_details` is redefined indicates to the system that it is this redefined version which is to be used.

12.3.4 Redefining features and the client–supplier contract

Redefining a feature which is inherited opens up the risk that the new feature radically departs from the spirit of the original. Taking an extreme example, what is to stop the implementor of a RECTANGLE class, which inherits a perimeter feature from POLYGON, from redefining it so that it returns the area of the rectangle rather than the perimeter? Clearly, in a situation where polymorphism and dynamic binding are being used, this could violate the client–supplier contract, as the following simple example illustrates.

```
p: POLYGON
r: RECTANGLE
i: REAL
```

```
!!.r.make              -- create an object for r
p := r                 -- assign r to p
i := p.perimeter
```

The client of POLYGON has here sent the perimeter message to p and assumes that the result returned would meet the post-condition of POLYGON's perimeter – which we assume is defined in the conventional way. However, at the time of the call, the actual object referenced by p is an object of type RECTANGLE and dynamic binding would cause the use of the perimeter feature to be redefined for rectangles to return the area – a clear breach of contract as far as the client of p is concerned.

In EIFFEL, the assertion mechanism using require and ensure clauses can be used to prevent such a breach of contract. No redefined feature is allowed to strengthen the pre-condition of the original or weaken the post-condition. EIFFEL views a redefined feature as subcontracting the task of the feature it redefines and as such it must not violate the contract which binds that original feature.

12.3.5 Once functions

EIFFEL does not have class variables. However, it does provide a similar facility via the use of *once functions*. Essentially a once function provides a constant reference to an object which is accessible to all the objects in its hierarchy. For example, the once function delegate_list in the class DELEGATE provides a structure which can be used to hold every delegate created (including subtypes).[6] This list can then be accessed through every object in the hierarchy.

12.3.6 Eiffel's exception mechanism

Programming in EIFFEL is based, as we have seen, on the notion of ADTs and the client–supplier contract. This encourages a style of programming referred to as *programming by contract*. What this means is that implementors are encouraged to write classes which deal only with the valid source and result data as set out by this contract. For example, the top routine in STACK is not contracted to deal with any source data other than non-empty stacks and therefore can ignore the possibility of being called with an empty stack (it being the client's responsibility to prevent this possibility and the pre-condition's responsibility to check on the client).

Programming by contract does not mean that a program ignores the possibility of invalid data being used, but simply that a clear separation is made between those parts of a program which deal with valid and invalid data. EIFFEL's exception mechanism, which is based on the assertion mechanism, supports such a separation. What this means is that when a contract is broken through the violation of a pre- or post-condition, normal processing is interrupted: an *exception* is *raised* and control passes to an exception *handler* located in the routine which has been responsible for breaking the contract. So, for example, if the top routine in STACK had been called with an empty stack, it would be the client's exception handler which would be invoked. On the other hand if

---

[6] The creation procedure of every class in the hierarchy would need to add each new object to the list.

the exception had been raised because t op had failed to fulfil its post-condition then control would pass to its own exception handler.

An important part of the philosophy of programming by contract is that it is not the exception handler's responsibility to remedy a broken contract; this is the responsibility of the main part of the code. (If the exception handler knew how to complete the contract, this knowledge should have been coded into the part of the program responsible for valid data!) Rather, it is the exception handler's responsibility to

1. raise an alarm;

2. ensure the object being manipulated is left in a valid state;

3. retry its routine if, for example, the cause of the exception is external to the program and might remedy itself (as in a transmission failure) or if, as another example, one is using *N*-version programming.[7]

Note that, if the post-condition of a routine still cannot be satisfied after a retry, then the exception 'passes' to the caller, that is, control is passed to the caller's exception handler (if there is one) and so on up the call chain. If during this process the exception cannot be remedied, the whole program will fail and control will be returned to the run-time environment.

12.3.7 Persistence

EIFFEL has two persistence mechanisms. One allows single objects (including all its associated objects) to be stored, while the other enables the programmer to declare an environment in which a number of objects can be made persistent together.

12.3.8 Compilation and access to other languages

EIFFEL uses C as its intermediate language. Some compilers have the facility for developing a C package from EIFFEL source code, which can then be compiled on any machine running a C compiler.

All classes in EIFFEL are separately compilable but the system holds the knowledge of all the interrelationships which may exist between classes. In other words there is no need for the C equivalent of 'make' files.

EIFFEL supports the use of C library routines and is in principle open to the use of routines from any other language.

Libraries in EIFFEL are clustered into classes which have something in common. For example, the container *cluster* consists of classes like LIST, STACK and TREE. In developing new classes, one is encouraged to add them to appropriate clusters. Applications are then built by producing a system description which specifies which clusters are being used, which is to be the root class of the system, and what compiler options are required. Although not part of the EIFFEL language definition, various notations for building Eiffel systems are used by different implementations.

---

[7] *N*-version programming involves trying out different implementations of an algorithm if one version fails to meet the post-condition of the routine.

12.3.9 Concurrency

The major omission in EIFFEL at the present time is a mechanism to support concurrency. This issue is presently being addressed and it is planned to introduce such a mechanism into future releases of the language.

12.4 Eiffel's role in industry

EIFFEL claims to be an all-purpose programming language and has been used to develop applications in the fields of telecommunications, CAD/CAM, graphics, AI, robotic real-time systems, time and data management and databases [Nerson and Meyer, 1993].

12.5 Support for teaching Eiffel

12.5.1 Implementations

Until a few years ago, the main vendor of EIFFEL was Bertrand Meyer's company, ISE. Since then the trade mark for the language has been vested in a non-profit organization called NICE which now has the responsibility for overseeing the development of the language and its standardization.

Version 3 of of the language has been defined but at the time of writing only one implementation (called EIFFEL/S from Sig Computers in Germany) has been marketed. Others, including one from ISE and one from Tower Technology, are expected.

Applied Logic Developments in the UK is presently marketing a product called LogicAL which, using EIFFEL/S, provides a programming environment which offers strong support for developing user-interface and relational-database applications.

At the present time there are two products available for teaching EIFFEL. One is EIFFEL/S which runs on PCs running DOS, and on a range of other platforms including Unix workstations. This has a fairly extensive set of libraries but little support, in terms of browsers or editors, for developing EIFFEL applications.

Another is the LogicAL product from Applied Logic Developments which has also been developed to run on a wide range of platforms and which has a very good environment (based on X-Windows) for developing applications, including a windows-based browser and editor, and classes which support the development of sophisticated user interfaces and relational database applications. As yet there are no tools for supporting project management or analysis and design.

ISE EIFFEL is expected, like LogicAL, to have a comprehensive development environment (including a structured editor) and support for developing user interfaces and accessing databases. It too will run on all major platforms.

12.5.2 Debugging tools

Existing implementations of EIFFEL rely heavily on assertion checking to debug programs. Compiler options allow one to switch pre- and post-conditions and invariants on and off on a class basis. The same goes for loop variants and invariants and check clauses. Assertion violations detected in this way will generate a file containing a failure history.

It is also possible to trace the execution of a program through the routines of specified classes. This will show the trace of every routine call, including the values of actual arguments and result (for functions).

Debug statements can be used and switched on and off as required.

12.5.3 Analysis and design methodologies

One of the design aims of EIFFEL was to provide a uniform notation that could be used throughout the software development cycle. A recent book [Nerson and Walden, 1995] describes BON, business object notation (or a better object notation?), which is an analysis and design method based on EIFFEL.

12.5.4 Documentation

All classes in EIFFEL are meant to be self-documenting in that they should incorporate header comments and pre- and post-conditions. EIFFEL notation also permits the inclusion of an *index clause* which can hold information at a higher level of abstraction than that contained within the class, such as indexing categories, design and implementation decisions and references to published algorithms. Various tools which come with the language use this information to produce browsers and shortened versions of the classes which show the interface features together with their semantics (*i.e. require* and *ensure* clauses plus header comments).

12.5.5 Language definition and textbooks

The range of textbooks on EIFFEL is still small. Bertrand Meyer's *Eiffel the Language* [Meyer, 1992b] is the main reference for a detailed definition of the language, while his *Object Oriented Software Construction* (using EIFFEL) [Meyer, 1988] is still a classic text on the subject. Meyer's article [1992a] describes design by contract.

Meyer has produced a BNF-style definition of the language in [Meyer, 1992b]; this book also includes all the validity constraints which govern the correct use of the language. He has also published works on ISE's environment [Meyer 1994a; 1994b].

A comprehensive collection of papers which discuss many of the issues underlying the design of EIFFEL is *The Eiffel Collection*, published by ISE [Meyer *et al.*, 1990]. Meyer has also written a booklet comparing EIFFEL and C++ [Meyer, 1990]. Al-Hadda has written about reusability in C++ and EIFFEL [Al-Hadda, 1991].

An introductory text by Robert Switzer has been published by Prentice-Hall [1993]. Another book from the same publisher, called *Object-oriented Applications* [Nerson and Meyer, 1993], describes seven major industrial applications using EIFFEL.

In 1995 Addison-Wesley published another introduction to EIFFEL by Thomas and Weedon [1995] which takes a strongly ADT approach in presenting the language.

12.6 Summary and conclusions

At the technical level, EIFFEL has all the mechanisms, apart from concurrency, which support the development of software based on ADTs, and includes a sophisticated inheritance mechanism which allows inherited features to be adapted in various ways. This range of mechanisms makes it a suitable language for teaching introductory to advanced programming.

The language incorporates all the sound principles of program development such as modularization, information hiding, re-use and extensibility. In addition, it supports programming by contract which is based on the client–supplier relationship embodied in the specification of ADTs. In EIFFEL, this contract also incorporates the concept of a subcontract which constrains the redefinition of inherited features.

As well as a mechanism to support programming by contract, EIFFEL also has a complementary mechanism, the exception mechanism, for dealing with breaches of contract. This enables EIFFEL programs to separate the code for dealing with valid and invalid cases.

The EIFFEL notation has also been integrated into an analysis and design method called BON which makes it possible to develop applications in a consistent way from analysis through to implementation.

Although there are as yet few implementations of EIFFEL, the version from Applied Logic Developments, called LogicAL, provides an environment which is suitable for teaching the language and developing applications ranging from the very simple to those which interface with relational databases and have sophisticated user interfaces. ISE EIFFEL also promises to be a system having similar capabilities to LogicAL.

In conclusion, EIFFEL, technically, is an excellent language for teaching sound principles of programming. Its drawback is that it is not yet a major industrial language.

12.7 References

Al-Hadda, H. (1991), Approaches to reusability in C++ and Eiffel, *Journal of Object-oriented Programming*.

Goguen, J. and Mesegeur, J. (1987), Unifying Functional, Relational and Object-oriented Programming, in *Research Directions in Object-oriented Programming*, B. Shriver and P. Wegner (eds), MIT Press, Cambridge, MA, 417–77.

Meyer, Bertrand (1988), *Object-oriented Software Construction*, Prentice Hall, (translations available in Italian, Japanese, French, German, Dutch, Spanish, Chinese).

Meyer, B., (1990), *Eiffel and C++: A Comparison* (booklet). Unpublished but obtainable Interactive Software Engineering Inc., 270 Storke Road, Suite 7, Goleta CA 93117.

Meyer, B. (1992a), Applying 'Design by Contract', *IEEE Computer*.

Meyer, B. (1992b), *Eiffel – The Language*, Prentice-Hall, Englewood Cliffs, NJ: complete language description.

Meyer, B. (1994a), *An Object-oriented Environment: Principles and Applications*, Prentice-Hall, Englewood Cliffs, NJ.

Meyer, B. (1994b), *Reusable Software: The Base Object-oriented Libraries*, Prentice-Hall, Englewood Cliffs, NJ.

Meyer *et al.* (1990), B., *An Eiffel Collection* (booklet), obtainable Interactive Software Engineering Inc., 270 Storke Road, Suite 7, Goleta CA 93117.

Nerson J.-M. and Meyer, B. (eds) (1993), *Object-oriented Applications*, Prentice-Hall, Englewood Cliffs, NJ.

Nerson, J.-M. and Walden, K. (1994), *Seamless Object-Oriented Software Architecture: Analysis and Design of Reliable Systems*, Prentice-Hall, Englewood Cliffs, NJ.

Rist , R. and Terwilliger, R. (1995), *Object-oriented Programming in Eiffel*, Prentice-Hall, Syndey.

Switzer, R. (1993), *Eiffel – An introduction*, Prentice-Hall, Englewood Cliffs, NJ.

Thomas, P., Robinson, H. and Emms, J. (1988), *Abstract Data Types*, Oxford University Press, Oxford.

Thomas, P. and Weedon, R. (1995), *Object-oriented Programming in Eiffel*, Addison-Wesley, Wokingham.

13 Choosing Smalltalk – a consultant's view

Brian Shearing

This chapter presents a consultant's view of language choice: of choosing SMALL-
TALK. I consider that SMALLTALK is a suitable basis for education in computer programming and present arguments to support the case. However, these are drawn from
many years' commercial experience and will be of interest to non-academic readers.
The chapter reviews managerial, practical and technical aspects of the language. It includes an example of a generic stack and a more complex example that models a conference, its participants and its sessions.

13.1 Introduction: practical and managerial matters

In this section we consider practical and managerial matters such as the availability of
development environments for SMALLTALK, its support for databases, and its performance.

13.1.1 History

SMALLTALK is a mature language. It evolved from SMALLTALK-72 through SMALL-
TALK-76 to SMALLTALK-80. During this period it was under the control of its creators
at the Xerox Palo Alto Research Center. By 1980 the Xerox Corporation had decided to
permit dissemination of SMALLTALK to the world outside the corporation. In Septem-

ber 1981 the 'First Ever SMALLTALK-80 Implementors' Conference' was held in Palo
Alto. By that time implementations were in hand on various kinds of computer.

See [Kranser, 1984] for a history of early implementations which were based on
beautifully documented designs from Xerox, subsequently published in [Goldberg and
Robson, 1983] and [Goldberg, 1984]. Alan Kay has also written of the history of
SMALLTALK in [Kay, 1993]. The following is my view of the main developments
in the evolution of SMALLTALK as a practical and serious programming language.

SMALLTALK/V: Digitalk, Inc. produced its first version of SMALLTALK in 1985. It
was a text-based system entitled METHODS that ran on personal computers. In 1986
the company introduced a graphics-based version, SMALLTALK/V, and that has now
evolved into a product that runs under 16-bit Windows, 32-bit Windows, OS/2 and
the Macintosh.[1]

OBJECTWORKS\SMALLTALK: Whilst Digitalk was creating SMALLTALK/V some
of the team that designed SMALLTALK inside the Xerox Corporation formed
a company to create a version of SMALLTALK for PCs, Macintoshes and Unix workstations. The company was ParcPlace Systems. Its first product was
OBJECTWORKS\SMALLTALK.

It is interesting to compare the approaches of Digitalk and ParcPlace, particularly
regarding the design of classes providing the graphical interface. Both products execute on a variety of systems, each with different underlying interfaces. Digitalk
products provide relatively direct access to the underlying interface. It is possible
to program in a portable way, but also quite easy to write code that does not travel.
For example, you need to take care when drawing pictures to avoid depending on the
fact that the direction of increasing value along the y-axis under OS/2 is upwards but
under Windows is downwards. In contrast, ParcPlace provides a class library that is
unchanged – from the programmer's perspective – from one computer or operating
system to another.

ParcPlace–Digitalk: During the preparation of this chapter, ParcPlace and Digitalk announced their intention to merge into a single company to be known as
ParcPlace–Digitalk, Inc.

VISUALAGE: IBM is a recent arrival on the SMALLTALK scene. The company has
released a product entitled VISUALAGE that it promotes as particularly suitable for
developing client–server systems. For some years IBM worked in partnership with
Digitalk and the products from the two companies exhibit their shared heritage.

Free SMALLTALKs: Several versions of SMALLTALK are available at no cost except
that of their downloading. Some free SMALLTALKs have a textual rather than a
graphical interface. SMALLTALK/X, which is graphical, is available not only commercially but also in a free unsupported version.

---

[1] The 'V' in SMALLTALK/V is the letter V and not the Roman digit five. The letter denotes 'virtual' and
records the singular fact that the first release of the product provided virtual memory, for all objects, automatically. It was the first product that I used on a PC that 'broke the 640k barrier' without programming
effort.

Table 13.1   Some sources of SMALLTALK

Product	Source	Level	Platforms†	Free?
GNU-SMALLTALK	FSF	Textual	D, U	⋆
IBM SMALLTALK	IBM	Graphical	32, O	
LITTLE SMALLTALK	Timothy Budd	Textual	16, D, M, U	⋆
OBJECTWORKS	ParcPlace–Digitalk	Graphical	M, U	
SMALLTALK AGENTS	QKS	Graphical	M, P	
SMALLTALK/V	ParcPlace–Digitalk	Graphical	16, M	
SMALLTALK/X	Claus Gittinger	Graphical	U	⋆
VISUALAGE	IBM	Enterprise	32, A, M	
VISUAL SMALLTALK	ParcPlace–Digitalk	Enterprise	32, O	
VISUALWORKS	ParcPlace–Digitalk	Enterprise	32, M, O, P, U	

†**16**-bit, **32**-bit Windows; **A**S/400; **M**S-DOS; **M**acintosh; **O**S/2; **P**owerPC; **U**nix.

13.1.2 Commercial availability

Table 13.1 shows some sources of SMALLTALK systems. Systems marked with a star are available at no cost.[2]

13.1.3 Performance

It has been a common view that SMALLTALK was excellent for prototyping but not so satisfactory for building delivered products. Some of this perception was based on considerations of performance. In the past, SMALLTALK programs were executed by an interpreter. Recent realizations employ a mixture of interpretation and compilation. This retains the advantages of rapid development whilst providing levels of performance that, the vendors claim, match and sometimes exceed equivalent programs written in traditional fully compiled languages.

One technique that enables modern SMALLTALKs to achieve high speeds of execution is to maintain a buffer in memory containing the machine-code versions of methods executed recently. When a method is first invoked the system converts it into machine code and retains it in the buffer in case it is needed again. Space is recovered from the buffer on a least-recently-used basis.

13.1.4 Development, databases, and screen painters

A distinctive aspect of SMALLTALK is the way that a developer saves the state of the computer at the end of final testing and delivers this frozen *image* to the customer as the developed product, somewhat in the manner of the programming language BASIC. Whilst having little effect on teaching – except for making it rather easy to deliver partial solutions for students to complete – this rather cumbersome delivery mechanism has sometimes been a deterrent to commercial use of SMALLTALK.

---

[2] I am pleased to acknowledge the help of Douglas Shaker of The SMALLTALK Store in filling gaps in my knowledge of available SMALLTALK realizations. Contact the Store on 75046.31600@compuserve.com for details of these and other SMALLTALK products. All of the freely available products can be downloaded from a SMALLTALK BBS on +1 415-854-5581 or through telnet as bbs.smaltalk.com.

This same mechanism reinforced the view of SMALLTALK as splendid for a development team as long as the number of its members did not exceed one! It was perceived as difficult to manage the programming of members working independently, and awkward to merge the disparate images developed by each member.

The commercial world demands of a development environment that it address a database at its back and that it can be used to 'paint' screens at the front. Recent versions of SMALLTALK from all of the major vendors provide such facilities. These are the systems marked as 'Enterprise' in Table 13.1.

13.1.5 Appropriateness

SMALLTALK is an appropriate language to employ for teaching at all levels. At the introductory level there is no better medium to teach the essentials of the object approach. Its simplicity allows the student to concentrate on the principles without getting involved in extraneous detail. See, for example, Figures 13.1 and 13.2 which specify the lexis and concrete syntax for the whole of the language.

string =	' ' ' { *character* | '''' | ' ' ' ' ' ' } ' ' '.
char =	'\$' *character* | '\$' ' ' ' | '\$' ''''.
character =	*letter* | *D* | *selector* | '[' | ']' | '(' | ')' | '-' | '-' | '~' | ';' | '\$' | '#' | ':' | '.' | '{' | '}' | ' '.
selector =	',' | '+' | '/' | '\' | '*' | '~' | '¿' | '¡' | '=' | ' ' | '%' | '|' | '&' | '?' | '!'.
symbol =	*unarySelector* | *binarySelector* | < *key* >.
unarySelector =	*identifier*.
binarySelector =	*selector* [*selector*] | '-'.
key =	*identifier* ':'.
identifier =	*letter* { *letter* | *D* }.
number =	[< *D* > 'r'] ['-'] < *H* > ['.' < *H* >]
	['e' ['-'] < *D* >].
H =	*D* | *capital*.
letter =	'a'...'z' | *capital*.
capital =	'A'...'Z'.
D =	'0'...'9'.

Key:
$A \mid B \Longrightarrow A$ or B; $[A] \Longrightarrow \phi \mid A$; $\{A\} \Longrightarrow [<A>]$; $<A> \Longrightarrow A\{A\}$

Figure 13.1　Lexis of SMALLTALK.

Aspects of SMALLTALK and its environment are appropriate at the intermediate level. Examples include the concepts and design of a class library, the process model, the model–view–controller architecture (MVC) [Krasner and Pope, 1988], the GUI interface, and the 'update-me-when-you-change' mechanism.

In spite of the essential simplicity of the SMALLTALK model there is much to be explored at the advanced level. One example is the setting and catching of exceptions using *blocks*. This could be combined with a compiler-writing project for which the

comment =	*""* { *character* | *" ' "* } *""*.
method =	*pattern* [*primitive*] [*' | '* { *var* } *' | '*] *sequence*.
pattern =	*unarySelector* |
	binarySelector var |
	< *key var* >.
primitive =	*'<'* 'Primitive:' *number* *'>'*.
sequence =	{ *expression* *'.'* } [[*'^'*] *expression*].
expression =	{ *var* *': ='* } *factor*.
factor =	*primary* | *message* { *';' cascade* }.
primary =	*var* | *literal* | *block* | *'(' expression ')'*.
block =	*'['* [{ *':' var* } *' | '*] *sequence* *']'*.
message =	*unaryExpression* |
	binaryExpression |
	keyExpression.
cascade =	*unarySelector* | *binaryMessage* | *keyMessage*.
unaryExpression =	*primary* < *unarySelector* >.
binaryExpression =	*unaryValue* < *binaryMessage* >.
keyExpression =	*binaryValue keyMessage*.
binaryMessage =	*binarySelector unaryValue*.
keyMessage =	< *key binaryValue* >.
unaryValue =	*unaryExpression* | *primary*.
binaryValue =	*binaryExpression* | *primary*.
literal =	*constant* | *'#' symbol* | *'#' array*.
array =	*'(' { constant | symbol | array } ')'*.
constant =	*number* | *string* | *char*.
var =	*identifier*.

Figure 13.2   Concrete syntax of SMALLTALK.

technique is an elegant solution to the problem of recovering from failures when deep inside a recursive-descent compiler.

Exploration of the concept that classes are also objects, and of the rationale for the class *Metaclass*, are natural candidates for advanced work.

13.1.6 Relevance

The growth of SMALLTALK as a tool for prototyping has been steady if unremarkable, but its use for developing production systems is its fastest area of growth. Several co-incidences have led to this increasing take-up by industry. Economic pressures have increased the importance of techniques for rapid development. C. A. S. E. tools promised much in this area but, on the whole, failed to justify hopes – partly because of their innate inflexibilities. In many ways SMALLTALK has much in common with a rather simple third-generation programming language, and yet it seems to make possible development as rapid as almost any with a C. A. S. E. tool or 4GL.

Another reason for SMALLTALK's increasing use in industry is the quality and capabilities of the latest generation of products from the primary vendors. These combine project management and version control with class libraries that support databases, networks, user interfaces to legacy systems, and group-working. Furthermore, the performance of the resulting systems is more than sufficient for most commercial requirements.

The acceptance of the graphical user interface has accelerated the take-up of SMALLTALK as a programming language. It should be no surprise that SMALLTALK and GUIs fit together comfortably, as they evolved hand-in-hand.

Further evidence of the growing importance of SMALLTALK is given by the fact that large software companies and major commercial institutions have dropped C++ as their primary programming language in favour of SMALLTALK.

13.1.7 Summary of practical and managerial matters

The following summary includes not only those practical and managerial matters discussed above but others also.

- The **availability** of SMALLTALK is high and increasing.

- All vendors of SMALLTALK support essentially the same language. ANSI Committee X3J20 is deriving a **standard** dialect.

- The typical modern **development environment** has its roots in the browsers devised as part of the SMALLTALK project.

- Not only do SMALLTALK development environments include **editors** but the software that provides a scrolling editable window is in the class library and can be invoked from any program.

- All SMALLTALK development environments include impressive debuggers that do not need special priming to fire-up.

- The **resource requirements** for most SMALLTALKs are modest compared with many of today's products, but not ignorable. For example, SMALLTALK/V for Windows needs four megabytes of main memory for teaching, eight megabytes for real applications, or sixteen megabytes if connected to a database. Disk demands are modest at a few megabytes.

- Help facilities are built into the typical SMALLTALK development environment.

- At least one of the commercially available SMALLTALK systems provides an on-line **tutorial** of high quality. That one product has arguably taught more programmers the principles of object-oriented programming and design than any other single textbook, method, or course. Books on SMALLTALK include [Budd, 1987], [Pinson and Wiener, 1988], [Savic, 1990], [LaLonde and Pugh, 1990; 1991; 1994], [Smith, 1991], [LaLonde, 1993], [Lewis, 1995] and [Skublics et al., 1996].

- SMALLTALK is excellent for **transaction processing work**. It can also be used for **real-time projects**, but care must be taken to ensure that garbage collection does not interfere with response times. Commercial SMALLTALKs provide support for handling interrupts properly.

- The issue of **performance** always worried people outside the SMALLTALK community more than it did those who knew the facts. Recent developments in hybrid compilation and interpretation have finally laid the matter to rest.[3]

- SMALLTALK has **appropriate** features to explore at introductory, intermediate and advanced levels.

- The **commercial take-up** of SMALLTALK has always been high for prototyping. Now it is growing for delivery of production systems.

13.2 Technical matters

In this section we present a brief overview of some technical aspects of SMALLTALK.

13.2.1 Example

We illustrate SMALLTALK with an example that models a conference. The example does not teach the reader the whole of SMALLTALK, but illustrates the nature of the language. One aspect of SMALLTALK that is difficult to convey in a written piece is what it feels like to develop SMALLTALK software. The process makes much use of the graphical user interface – an idiom of interaction with computers that the designers of SMALLTALK invented.

Conference model

Our model of the conference must be able to produce a list of members and a conference timetable. It should also respond to particular queries requesting, for example, a list of lectures presented or sessions chaired by a given individual. Means for building and editing the model must also exist.

```
WorkshopElement(conference: Conference)
    Conference(members: list of Member; sessions: list of Session)
    Member(name: String; base: Base)
        Speaker
        Delegate
        Exhibitor(product: String)
    Base(name: String)
        OU
        Home(address, hotel: String)
    Session(date: Date; topic: String; events: list of Event)
        Meeting(serial: Integer; chair: Speaker)
    Event(time: Time; topic: String)
        Presentation(presenter: Speaker)
```

Figure 13.3   Class structure of workshop (attributes in parentheses).

Figure 13.3 shows a class structure and Figure 13.4 an object model that we have

---

[3] It is interesting that Bertrand Meyer's system for EIFFEL (named *melting ice*) has arrived at a similar technological solution as those of the vendors of SMALLTALK, but from different directions. Meyer added interpretation to a system previously based on compilation. The SMALLTALK vendors introduced compiling technology into interpreted systems.

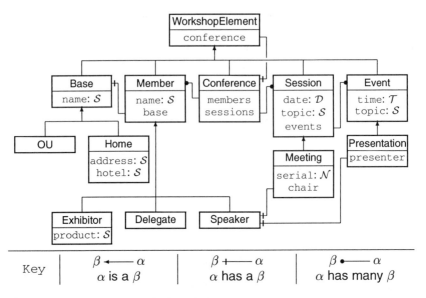

Figure 13.4   Object model of workshop.

devised for the example. Figure 13.5 illustrates a collection of objects satisfying the model. From Figure 13.4 we see that a *Conference* has *Members* and *Sessions*. A member is an *Exhibitor*, *Delegate*, or *Speaker*. All members have a name which is a *String*, and a *Base*. An exhibitor has a product also. A base is the *OU* or *Home*, where a home has an *address* and a *hotel*. All bases have a name such as 'Computing Department' for the OU ('Comp' in Figure 13.5) or 'The Software Factory' ('TSF' in Figure 13.5) for a home base.

A session has a *date*, *topic* and list of *events*. A *Session* is either a collection of events such as registration, or a *Meeting* of presentations with a *serial* number and chairperson who is a speaker. All events have a *time* and *topic*. A *Presentation* is an *Event* with a *Speaker*.

Each component of the model is a *WorkshopElement*, and includes the conference itself. This arrangement ensures that the humblest subobject has access to the model that it is part of, if needed.

Conference model in Smalltalk

The following snippet of SMALLTALK declares class Session as a subclass of WorkshopElement, with 'instance' variables date, topic and events.

```
WorkshopElement subclass: #Session
   instanceVariableNames: 'date topic events'
   classVariableNames: ' '
   poolDictionaries: ' '
```

SMALLTALK has several kinds of variable. An *instance variable* is accessible only to its own object. A *class variable* is a single item that is accessible by all objects of its class. A *pool dictionary* is a global dictionary that is accessible to all classes that nominate it. The only other kinds of variable are temporary variables, which are most

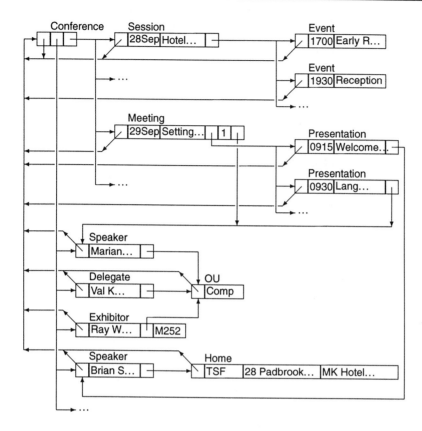

Figure 13.5   Example of data-structure of workshop.

often used as local variables within the code of a method, and global variables, which are available to all. It is a rule of the language that the names of an instance or temporary variable starts with a lower-case letter. The names of classes, class variables, pool dictionaries and global variables are capitalized. The conference model does not use class variables, pool dictionaries, or global variables.

In practice, the programmer does not type such code as in the example. Instead he or she selects the superclass, WorkshopElement, from a pick-list in the *Class Hierarchy Browser*, chooses *add subclass* from a menu, and enters the names of the new subclass and its variables.

The example demonstrates that ruthless application of simple principles reduces complexity. In SMALLTALK there are only objects. There is no distinction between a thing and a reference to that thing. Integers, dates, conferences and strings are objects of equal standing. (One consequence of this unified approach is that SMALLTALK has no pointer variables.) Not only are many possible errors avoided but the program as written corresponds directly to the logical model. This is particularly helpful when trying to applying formal methods to bridge the gap between logical design and physical realization.

13.2.2 Arity of inheritance

Unlike, for example, EIFFEL, SMALLTALK provides only single inheritance. Every class is a subclass of exactly one other, except for the built-in class named `Object`. In the example, the class `WorkshopElement` is a subclass of class `Object`.

13.2.3 Types

The declaration of class `Session` illustrates that a variable such as `topic` has a name but no type. In SMALLTALK an assignment transfers not only a value but also a type. After the following example the variable `topic` has the value shown and is of type `String`. Any previous value and any previous type are lost.

```
topic := 'Setting the scene'
```

Regarding types, we can classify programming languages into four kinds:

1. languages such as C that pretend to no type checking;
2. languages such as C++ that proffer type checking but still permit unchecked mistakes of type;
3. languages that permit no errors of type but which check for errors at run time;
4. languages that permit no errors of type and which detect errors at time of compilation.

We denote the typing of these categories of language as *absent, illusory, weak* and *strong*, respectively. In these terms SMALLTALK is weakly typed.

13.2.4 Built-in types

In SMALLTALK the words 'type' and 'class' mean the same thing. Because classes cannot be parameterized in the EIFFEL sense there is no need to distinguish between the notions of type and class. (But see section 13.2.5 below.)

SMALLTALK has no type built into the language itself – not even types `Integer` or `Character`. Every realization of SMALLTALK is accompanied by a *class library* that includes not only `Integer`, `Character` and other scalar types but also a comprehensive range of structured types. Figure 13.6 is an extract from the inheritance hierarchy of a typical SMALLTALK system.[4]

One reason that SMALLTALK is an attractive vehicle for learning about software is that the text of the class library is readable all the time. The process of building a SMALLTALK program is by extending the system as delivered. The text of supplied classes is as accessible as code written by the programmer. A class library constructed by the inventors of the class library, and honed by many years of real use, is a joy to explore. The author has learned much whilst browsing the source of standard SMALLTALK class libraries. There can be few more efficient ways of learning object-oriented principles and of extending one's programming skills than spending time with a SMALLTALK browser.

---

[4] In practice, SMALLTALK compilers do presume a knowledge of low-level types such as `Integer`, `Boolean` and `Character` so that they can generate efficient code.

```
Object (
      Behaviour ( Class )
      Boolean ( False True )
      Collection (
            Bag
            FixedSizeCollection ( Array String )
            OrderedCollection
            Set ( Dictionary SystemDictionary ))
      Compiler
      File
      Font
      GraphicsMedium ( Bitmap Printer Screen StoredPicture )
      InputEvent
      Magnitude (
            Character
            Number ( Float Fraction Integer ))
      Semaphore
      Stream ( ReadStream WriteStream )
      ViewManager ( ClassBrowser Inspector Prompter )
      Window (
            ApplicationWindow ( TopPane )
            Subpane (
                  Button ( Toggle ( CheckBox RadioButton ))
                  EntryField ( TextEdit )
                  ListBox ( ComboBox ListPane MultipleSelectBox )
                  GraphPane ( AnimationPane ))))

Key:      𝒜 ( ℬ 𝒞 ) ⟹ ℬ and 𝒞 inherit from 𝒜
```

Figure 13.6   Part of typical SMALLTALK class library.

Returning to our example, the following assignment employs the SMALLTALK library class `OrderedCollection` to create an empty list and assign it to variable `events`.

```
events := OrderedCollection new
```

In the following two sections we pause in our developemnt of the conference model and turn to the example of a stack of elements of varying type.

13.2.5 Genericity

Class `OrderedCollection` is one of the most commonly used types of the class library. For example, the following snippet creates a stack, pushes two integers onto it, and pops one of them into variable `poppedResult`. The example illustrates the declaration of local, temporary variables by writing their names between a pair of vertical bars.

```
| stack poppedResult |
    stack := OrderedCollection new.
    stack add: 25.
    stack add: 173.
    poppedResult := stack removeLast
```

Although SMALLTALK does not support the defining of generic classes, its run-time type-checking permits general-purpose 'collection' classes such as OrderedCollection, Set, Array and Dictionary to be employed for any type of object. This freedom provides genericity without special syntax or rules.

13.2.6 Methods

A SMALLTALK class has *methods* that define its behaviour. A method is a named body of code with optional input parameters and an optional result. A method is the only place where code appears. Declaring classes and variables, and defining the methods of classes, constitute the whole of the process of programming in SMALLTALK.

A method is either a *class method* or an *instance method*. A class method can address only class variables, pool dictionaries and global variables. An instance method (or *method*, for short) relates to a specific object and can address its instance variables in addition to its class variables and any pool dictionaries and global variables.

To provide a tidier realization of a stack, with operations named push and pop rather than add and removeLast, we could declare type Stack as a subclass of OrderedCollection:

```
OrderedCollection subclass: #Stack
```

We declare and define two instance methods, push and pop:

```
push: anObject
    "Push anObject onto the stack."
    self add: anObject
```

```
pop
    "Pop an object from the stack, and answer the popped object."
    ^ self removeLast
```

These methods illustrate several SMALLTALK idioms. The first line of a method declares its name and any parameters. The second line, or as many lines as necessary, provide commentary written between a pair of double quotation marks. The term 'answer' in pop's comment is SMALLTALK-speak for returning an object as the result of a method. The operator that exits from a method with a value – the answer operator – is the caret (^).

The word self is a reserved variable name that represents the object itself. The only way to do something in SMALLTALK is to call a method, say m, of an object o or a class c using the syntax o m or c m respectively. To call a method of one's own – or to call a method inherited from one's ancestors – the word self is written as the target object or class. In SMALLTALK-speak, we 'send a message to ourselves'.

The following is an example of the use of type Stack.

```
| stack poppedResult |
    stack := Stack new.
    stack push: 25.
    stack push: 173.
    poppedResult := stack pop
```

In addition to the implemented methods push and pop, methods such as size, isEmpty and copy are inherited from the class OrderedCollection and can be applied to objects of type Stack. Other inherited methods that are available with no additional programming include: `printOn:`[5] for writing the contents of the stack to a nominated *stream*; `do:` for iterating over all elements of the stack; and `detect:` for searching the stack for a particular value.

13.2.7 Information hiding

The class is the unit of information-hiding in SMALLTALK. The language avoids explicit declarations of export and import by three rules: (1) an instance variable or class variable declared in a class can be accessed by a method of the class or its descendants; (2) no variable, whether an instance variable or a class variable, can be seen by a method of any class other than the class in which the variable was declared or its descendants; and (3) all methods of a class can be invoked by other classes. In the jargon of C++, variables are 'protected' and methods are 'public'.

Returning to our model of the conference, we populate its classes with methods that provide the required functionality. The following example defines method `sortedMembers` that returns a list of members sorted by name.

```
sortedMembers
    "Answer a sorted collection of members."
    ^ members asSortedCollection: [ :p :q | p name < q name ]
```

Read the body of the method in the following way: 'Return the members as a sorted collection in which, for all p and q, member p precedes member q if p's name is earlier than q's name.' The example illustrates that SMALLTALK is an *expression language*. This encourages a functional style of programming which, in turn, makes it natural to write SMALLTALK code that reflects formal specifications in a direct way.

13.2.8 Dynamic binding

Not only is sending a message to an object the only way to do something in SMALLTALK, but every such invocation is bound to a particular method dynamically, according to the current type of the object.

Let us implement a method of the class `Conference` that appends a schedule of names and addresses of all members to a given stream. The heading of the method is as follows. (We shall supply its implementation later.)

```
sortedNamesAndAddressesOn: aStream
    "Append sorted names of all members, together
    with their addresses, to aStream."
```

Addresses come from the class `Base`. We define a method of Class `OU` that appends the address of an Open University member to a stream:

```
addressOn: aStream
    "Append the address of an OU member to aStream."
    aStream nextPutAll: 'OU department ', name; cr
```

Streams provide the method `nextPutAll:` to append a collection of, in this case, characters, and the method `cr` to append an end-of-line. The comma is the concatenation operator.

---

[5] Note that in SMALLTALK a colon can be part of a method name to indicate that an argument follows.

We provide a similar method in the class Home for members with a home base:

```
addressOn: aStream
    "Append the address of a home-based member to aStream."
    aStream nextPutAll: name, address; cr
```

The names and addresses of members do not depend on whether they are exhibitors, delegates, or speakers. So we define a method of the class Member to append the name and address. The method first appends the name of the member, and then sends the message addressOn: to the base to cause the address to be appended. This might cause either of the two methods of that name to be invoked, depending on the kind of base.

```
nameAndAddressOn: aStream
    "Append the name and address of member to aStream."
    aStream nextPutAll: name; tab.
    base addressOn: aStream
```

It remains to complete the required method of class Conference which loops through the sorted members appending the name and address of each:

```
sortedNamesAndAddressesOn: aStream
    "Append sorted names of all members, together
    with their addresses, to aStream."
    self sortedMembers do:
        [ :p | p nameAndAddressOn: aStream ]
```

13.2.9 Polymorphism

A more useful version of method nameAndAddressOn: of the class Member would prefix the name of each member with the word Exhibitor, Delegate, or Speaker. Assuming the existence of a method prefix to derive the word, the refined implementation of the method is as follows.

```
nameAndAddressOn: aStream
    "Append prefix, name, and address of member to aStream."
    aStream nextPutAll: self prefix, ' ', name; tab.
    base addressOn: aStream
```

We implement method *prefix* by taking the name of the class.

```
prefix
    "Answer the prefix of a member."
    ^ self class name
```

This means of deriving the prefix is arguably rather poor design. It couples the specification of the program too closely to details of implementation such as class names. But should it be decided, for example, that the prefix for a speaker is not 'Speaker' but 'Presenter' then we can provide a version of method prefix in the class Speaker that overrides the version in the class Member:

```
prefix
   "Answer the prefix for an speaker."
   ^ 'Presenter'
```

13.2.10 Technical summary

We conclude this section with a summary of some technical attributes of SMALLTALK, mentioning features not previously illustrated in this brief introduction.

- All kinds of object are first-class entities. There are no pointers, or – taking an alternative view that is closer to the reality of an executing system – *all* objects are pointed to and none are embedded.

- The arity of inheritance is unity. There is no aliasing and no renaming of things inherited (*cf.* EIFFEL).

- Typing is weak but bullet-proof. By 'weak' we mean that checking takes place at time of execution rather than compilation.

- SMALLTALK does not support generic types that can be parameterized, but containers may embed objects of any type. Furthermore, classes are objects too. Exploiting this can lead to code that is both compact and of great generality.

- As its name hints, SMALLTALK is a simple language. See, for example, Figures 13.1 and 13.2 which specify its complete lexis and concrete syntax.

- The SMALLTALK class library is comprehensive. Its source is in front of the programmer's nose, always.

- The binding of message to method is dynamic, always.

- SMALLTALK is an expression-based notation.

- The scope of a variable is either its instance or its class, or is global. The scope of a method is its instance or class.

- SMALLTALK supports information hiding with variables which are private to their class – 'protected' rather than 'private' in C++ terms – and methods which are public.

- Abstract data types are the fundamental modelling concept in SMALLTALK.

- A class acts not only to define an ADT but also as the unit of modularity.

- SMALLTALK is so regular that it can take some getting used to. For example, an IF-THEN-ELSE test is not part of the language itself but is effected by sending the message 'ifTrue:ifFalse:' to an object of one of the two subtypes of type Boolean – types True and False.

- Allocation and deallocation of memory are automatic, based on collecting and recycling memory – garbage collection.

- Polymorphism is deeply ingrained.

- SMALLTALK is where the model–view–controller architecture for GUI software was invented.

- SMALLTALK supports processes, semaphores and schedulers – even on computers whose underlying operating system fails to provide such fundamentals.

- SMALLTALK is the yardstick by which to measure the 'purity' of other object-oriented languages.

13.3 Epilogue

In considering language choice, and in particular in trying to select a suitable language for teaching modern programming principles, we have visited topics managerial, practical and technical. It would be remiss to leave the subject without observing something else, and that is the observation that 'SMALLTALK shops are happy shops'.

I have visited or been part of SMALLTALK teams in Britain, mainland Europe, and the United States of America. All were notable in their relaxed atmospheres. Here were staff confident in their productivity and their ability to deliver on time. SMALLTALK programmers know that, rather than being grudgingly accepting of their endeavours, their customers are usually delighted with the finished product. Not many software environments deliver products like that or engender such feelings in their workers.

The reasons for these widespread attributes of SMALLTALK are not far to seek. Human beings enjoy doing things well. Almost all SMALLTALK projects succeed. Many projects based on other languages fail or are abandoned before completion. SMALLTALK programmers feel that the language and its supporting environment are on their side, as opposed to being things to struggle with and conquer.

Relating these experiences to teaching, the simplicity and uniformity of SMALLTALK free the novice – as they do the expert – from effort wasted in running the gauntlet of arbitrary syntactic and semantic rules. The bullet-proof language design, memory management and run-time system ensure that the programmer never has to waste time poring over hexadecimal dumps of memory or traces of register values, simply to track down a recalcitrant bug. Instead he or she can concentrate on the essentials, whether the design being made or the principle being taught. With SMALLTALK there are no more students so frustrated and wound-up by minutiae that they have exhausted their pool of concentration for learning before tuition even starts.

13.4 References

Budd, T. (1987), *A Little Smalltalk*, Addison-Wesley, Reading, MA.

Goldberg, A. (1984), *Smalltalk-80: The Interactive Programming Environment*, Addison-Wesley, Reading, MA.

Goldberg, A. and Robson, J. (1983), *Smalltalk-80: The Language and its Implementation*, Addison-Wesley, Reading, MA.

Kay, A. (1993), The History of Smalltalk, *SIGPLAN Notices*.

Krasner, G. (1984), *Smalltalk-80, Bits of History, Words of Advice*, Addison-Wesley, Reading, MA.

Krasner, G. and Pope, S. T. (1988), A Cookbook for Using the Model–View–Controller User Interface in Smalltalk-80, *Journal of Object-oriented Programming*, **1**(3), 26–49.

LaLonde, W. (1993), *Discovering Smalltalk*, Benjamin-Cummings, Redwood City, CA.

LaLonde, W. R. and Pugh, J. R. (1990), *Inside Smalltalk*, volume I, Prentice-Hall, Englewood Cliffs, NJ.

LaLonde, W. R. and Pugh, J. R. (1991), *Inside Smalltalk*, volume II, Prentice-Hall, Englewood Cliffs, NJ.

LaLonde, W. R. and Pugh, J. R. (1994), *Smalltalk/V®: Practice and Experience*, volume II, Prentice-Hall, Englewood Cliffs, NJ.

Lewis, S. (1990), *The Art and Science of Smalltalk*, volume I, Prentice-Hall, London.

Pinson, L. J. and Wiener, R. S. (1988), *An Introduction to Object-oriented Programming and Smalltalk*, Addison-Wesley, Reading, MA.

Savic, D. (1990), *Object Oriented Programming with Smalltalk/V*, Ellis Horwood, London.

Skublics, S., Klimas E. J. and Thomas, D. A. (1996), *Smalltalk with Style*, Prentice-Hall, Englewood Cliffs, NJ.

Smith, D. N. (1991), *Concepts of Object-oriented Programming*, McGraw-Hill, New York.

14 Omega

Günther Blaschek

OMEGA started as a simple and prototype-based object-oriented programming language in the spirit of SMALLTALK and SELF. This chapter describes the OMEGA language, programming environment and library. It must be noted that this description is by no means complete. It rather concentrates on the key concepts of the whole OMEGA system and tries to give the reader an impression of a typical OMEGA programming style.

14.1 Introduction and overview

The work on OMEGA started in 1990 as a research project. The original goal was to create a simple yet powerful pure object-oriented programming language in the spirit of SMALLTALK [Goldberg and Robson, 1983] and SELF [Ungar and Smith, 1987]. The idea of prototypes, as implemented in SELF, was deemed promising for the construction of object-oriented software. In a prototype-based language, new objects are created by simply cloning an existing object. A new 'class' of objects is created by creating a new object (a prototype) and defining the object's structure, behaviour and initial contents. All these properties are directly attached to the prototypical object. Classes in the sense of SMALLTALK or C++ [Stroustrup, 1986] are not needed.

Another goal of the OMEGA project was to achieve the highest possible degree of safety by means of static typing. As many programming errors as possible should be detected at compile time. Unfortunately, SELF's delegation approach and the possibility to modify the structure and/or behaviour of individual objects make static typing impossible. It was therefore necessary to find another way of implementing prototypes. The solution was to use traditional inheritance rather than delegation and to distinguish prototypes from other objects. In contrast to a 'regular' object, a prototype has a name that also serves as a type name in declarations. When a prototype's structure and/or behaviour is modified, the modification affects not only the prototypical object itself but also all existing objects that have been cloned directly or indirectly from the prototype.

As soon as static typing was implemented in OMEGA, it became apparent that some sort of genericity was needed to allow for convenient implementation of object collections. The prototype concept also influenced the way in which genericity was introduced in OMEGA. In EIFFEL [Meyer, 1988; 1992], a generic class is an incomplete class with some holes that must be filled in order to get a usable class from which objects can be instantiated. In contrast, a generic prototype in OMEGA is already a usable object with an associated default type. For example, the `Array` prototype is associated with the default element type `Object`, which means that `Array` and its clones can be filled with arbitrary objects. OMEGA's concept of genericity allows the creation of a new prototype by replacing the general default type with a more specific type. For example, `Array{Window}` and its clones can only be filled with objects of type `Window` or of any subtype of `Window`.

The language itself is rather small. The syntax of OMEGA is defined by not more than 29 EBNF rules. The language itself does not even contain operators on elementary data types or control-flow elements. In SMALLTALK-like fashion, all these 'language features' are provided by the prototype library. The library not only contains static descriptions of the prototypes but is a collection of objects (in particular, prototypes) that are stored in a workspace file (similar to a SMALLTALK image).

When working with prototypes, it is essential that prototypes can be constructed and the structure and behaviour of prototypes can be defined interactively. It is therefore not possible to separate the OMEGA language from the OMEGA programming environment. An OMEGA program consists of a set of objects within a workspace. The programming environment enables the programmer to interactively inspect and modify all parts of a workspace.

The following sections describe the OMEGA language, the programming environment and the library in more detail. It must be noted that this description is by no means complete. It rather concentrates on the key concepts of the whole OMEGA system and tries to give the reader an impression of a typical OMEGA programming style. A complete description of the OMEGA system can be found in [Blaschek, 1991; 1994].

14.2 The Omega language

The OMEGA language itself is rather small and simple. Objects, types, inheritance, assignments and messages are all that are needed to understand and teach the language proper. Of course, more is needed to actually use OMEGA in software projects. In particular, it is necessary to understand the key concepts of the library, since virtually all operations are defined in the library, not in the language. And, as OMEGA programs are developed interactively, it is also necessary to understand the workspace concept and to know how to manage the workspace by means of the programming environment. This section concentrates on the actual language features. The programming environment and the library are discussed in sections 14.3 and 14.4. The key features of the OMEGA language are:

- pure object-orientedness;
- prototypes instead of classes;
- inheritance instead of delegation;
- static typing;
- genericity;
- monomorphic types;
- conditional assignments;
- single inheritance;
- single-rooted hierarchy;
- garbage collection.

14.2.1 Reference semantics and dynamic binding

As OMEGA is a pure object-oriented language, all data is treated as objects. In contrast to most hybrid languages (such as OBERON-2 [Mössenböck and Wirth 1991; Mössenböck, 1993] and C++), OMEGA uses reference semantics only. This means that variables never contain objects but rather refer to objects. Per definition, all messages to objects are resolved by means of dynamic binding. In other words, all messages are virtual by default. There are no language elements to define a message as non-virtual. However, the compiler may choose to use static binding where this is possible and may improve the efficiency of a program.

14.2.2 Monomorphic types

In order to improve the efficiency of operations with elementary data types (such as Integer, Real, Char and Boolean), these types are defined as *monomorphic* in OMEGA. We are not allowed to derive a new type from any of these types. Consequently, a variable v of, say, type Integer is guaranteed always to contain an integer value. The compiler makes use of this knowledge to optimize operations with values of elementary types. It is noteworthy that such values are still treated as objects. In particular, Integer is derived from the most general type Object and thus inherits the methods already defined in Object. Moreover, an Integer object can be used wherever an object of type Object is allowed. This is particularly important with the generic container types. For example, a set of integers can be constructed by parameterizing the generic prototype Set with Integer. This is possible because type Integer is a specialization of the most general type, Object.

14.2.3 Messages

The syntax of OMEGA is similar to that of SMALLTALK. In particular, all operations are expressed by unary, binary and keyword messages, and every expression (including assignments and declarations) returns a value. The following examples show some typical OMEGA expressions.

```
x:=y              -- assigns the reference contained in y to x and returns this reference
x clone           -- unary message; returns a shallow copy of x
'x'*5             -- binary message; returns the string "XXXXX"
arr at:5          -- keyword message; returns the fifth element of the array arr
arr at:5 put:x    -- keyword message; puts x into the fifth element of the array arr
```

14.2.4 Declarations

As OMEGA is a typed language, every variable has to be declared and associated with a data type. There are three kinds of declarations. A fully qualified declaration takes the form v:T:=e, where v is the variable to be declared, T is its (static) type, and e is an expression that determines the variable's initial value. Both the expression and the type can be omitted. The form v:T declares v as of type T and assigns an appropriate initial value to v (zero for numeric types, false for Boolean, the null character for type Char, Nil for other types). When the type is omitted, a declaration takes the form v::=e. In this case, the variable is implicitly declared with the static type of the expression e. Table 14.1 shows some typical declarations and explains their effects.

Table 14.1   Declarations and their effects

Declaration	Type	Initial value
i::=42	Integer	42
arr::=Array{integer} copy	Array{Integer}	a new, empty array of integers
s:String	String	Nil
c:Integer	Integer	0
w:Window:=ZoomWindow copy	Window	a new ZoomWindow object

As illustrated by these examples, the fully qualified form is needed only when the variable and its initial value are to be of different static types. In all other cases, one of the shorter forms can be used. Variables can be declared anywhere within a method. They are typically not introduced at the beginning of a method, but rather at the point where they are first needed.

14.2.5 Conditional assignments

Assignment compatibility is governed by the usual rules for polymorphism. An object (or, rather, a reference to an object) can be assigned to a variable when the object's type is identical to or a subtype of the variable's type. The possible operations with a variable are determined by the variable's type. The message v m is considered legal when the method m has been defined in the variable's static type T or in a direct or indirect supertype of T. While this rule ensures correct usage of variables, it is sometimes too rigid, as it narrows the programmer's view of objects. For example, let the type T1 be a subtype of T with an additional method m1. It would be perfectly legal to assign a T1 object to the variable v of type T (e.g. v:=T1 copy). However, the message v m1 would be rejected by the compiler, because m1 has not been defined for type T. This is correct because it is not statically known that the variable v in fact refers to an object of type T1. A run-time test along with a *type cast* is therefore required to send the message m1 to the object referred to by v. In OMEGA, this is done by means of a *conditional assignment*. In a conditional assignment v:?=e, the expression e need not be statically compatible with the variable v. Instead, the compatibility of e with v is checked at run time. When the dynamic type of e is compatible with the static type of v, the assignment is performed, and the whole expression returns the value true. Otherwise, no assignment takes place, and the value false is returned. To check whether the variable v refers to an object of type T1 and, if so, send the message m1 to this object, the following statement sequence can be used.

```
v1:T1;              -- v1 is an auxiliary variable with the static type T1
(v1:?=v)            -- try to assign v to v1
    ifTrue: [v1 m1];  -- if the assignment was successful, send the message m1 to v1
```

In contrast to type casts in C++, OMEGA's conditional assignments are type-safe operations. They are possible only because knowledge about the dynamic type of objects (so-called *meta-information*) is available at run time.

14.2.6 Blocks

Like SMALLTALK, OMEGA uses blocks for flow control. A block is an expression sequence enclosed in brackets. Blocks are first-class objects and can be sent messages and passed as arguments of messages. The message do is used to execute a block object. Blocks are used in OMEGA for the construction of conditional expressions, short-circuit evaluation of boolean expressions, and exception handling. The example above shows a typical application of block objects.

In contrast to SMALLTALK blocks, OMEGA blocks can be evaluated only in LIFO order. That is, a block can be executed only as long as the method containing the block is still executing. This is enforced statically by a simple rule: blocks may be used only as receivers and arguments of messages, but they cannot be assigned to variables.

There is also a generic variant of blocks. So-called actions can be parameterized with an arbitrary type. For example, Action{Integer} represents an action that must be supplied with an Integer argument upon activation with the message doWith:. Actions are primarily used for iteration over collections of objects. For example, the code fragment

```
windowList forAll:{w:Window} [w close]
```

closes all windows contained in the array denoted by windowList.

For the sake of efficiency, both block and action are defined as *monomorphic* in OMEGA. Although all control-flow constructs are implemented as methods, the compiler can perform various optimizations on them.

14.2.7 Methods

A method consists of a sequence of expressions enclosed in square brackets. The expressions are executed from left to right, and the result of the last expression deter-

mines the value to be returned by the method. Within a method, the predefined identifier self denotes the receiver of the method. The following example shows the implementation of the Integer method factorial for computing the factorial of the
receiver.

```
[ fact::=1;
  2 to:self do:{ i:Integer} [fact:=fact*i];
  fact   ]
```

Methods with arguments must be preceded by the declaration of their formal arguments within braces. The following example shows the implementation of the Integer
method to:do: that was used in the above method.

```
{ limit:Integer; act:Action{ Integer} }
[ i::=self;
  [i<=limit] whileTrue: [act doWith:i; i:=i+1];
  self   ]
```

The formal arguments limit and act correspond to the arguments passed after the
keywords to: and do:, respectively. They are treated as read-only within a method.
It is thus not possible to return an object through a method argument. If a method is
supposed to return an object, it must be returned as the method result. If a method has
no meaningful result, it returns the receiver by convention (hence the identifier self
at the end of the above method).

14.2.8 Garbage collection

An important consequence of *reference semantics* is that OMEGA programs work with
dynamic objects only. During execution of a program, many objects are created. To get
rid of obsolete objects, the run-time environment contains a garbage collector. In this
way, a high degree of safety is achieved, and the programmer is relieved from the tedious task of keeping track of objects and determining when they can safely be disposed
of.

14.3 The programming environment

The previous section summarized the essence of the OMEGA language. The reader
may have noticed that the language does not contain any elements for the declaration
of types (*i.e.* the introduction of new prototypes) and methods. All these operations
are performed interactively in the programming environment by means of menu commands. The programming environment operates on a workspace and provides views
of several aspects of the workspace in windows, as shown in Figure 14.1. The most
important parts of an OMEGA workspace are

1. all currently existing objects;

2. the symbol table with information about

   (a) types, their inheritance and genericity,

Method
Editor

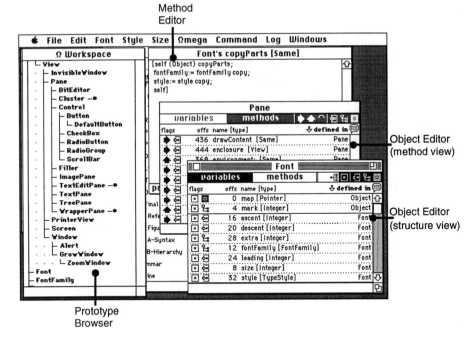

Prototype
Browser

Figure 14.1   Snapshot of an OMEGA session.

(b) the structure of all classes of objects,

(c) the interfaces of all methods;

3. the source text of all methods; and

4. the compiled methods.

In order to ensure integrity of its various parts, a workspace is always processed as a whole. It is loaded from a disk file at the beginning of an OMEGA session and saved back to disk at the end of the session. During a session, the current state of the workspace can be captured in a disk file at any time. In this way, adverse effects of programming errors can be reduced to a minimum.

14.3.1 The prototype hierarchy

The most important view of a workspace is the prototype hierarchy. It is displayed in the prototype browser. All prototype-related operations, such as creation, deletion, re-naming and reordering of prototypes, are performed directly in this window through menu commands. It is important to note that the items displayed in the hierarchy window represent types as well as prototypes. That is, every entry represents a prototypical object that can be opened for inspection in a window.

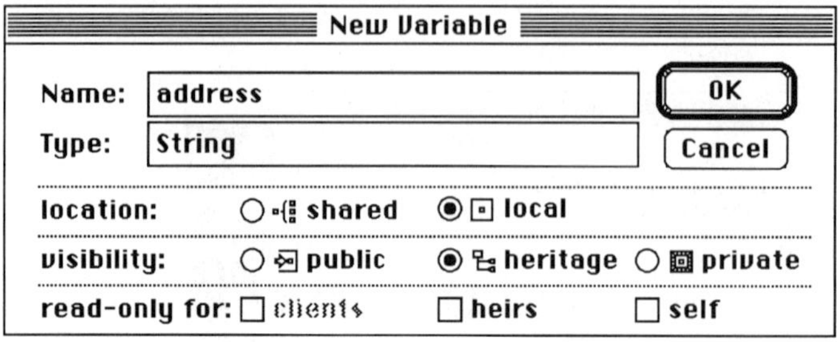

```
╔══════════════ New Variable ══════════════╗
║                                           ║
║  Name:  │address                    │  ┌─────────┐  ║
║                                        │   OK    │  ║
║  Type:  │String                     │  └─────────┘  ║
║                                        ┌─────────┐  ║
║                                        │ Cancel  │  ║
║  location:      ○ ⊶ shared   ◉ ⊡ local   ║
║                                           ║
║  visibility:    ○ ⊠ public  ◉ ⊡ heritage ○ ⊡ private  ║
║                                           ║
║  read-only for: □ clients    □ heirs     □ self  ║
╚═══════════════════════════════════════════╝
```

Figure 14.2   New Variable dialogue.

14.3.2 The object editor

An object editor window shows either the structural or the behavioural aspects of an object. In the 'structure view', instance variables of an object can be added, removed, renamed and redeclared. The menu commands Copy and Paste are used to perform assignments without having to write a single line of code. Figure 14.2 shows the dialogue that appears when the New Variable command has been issued.

When a new instance variable is defined, the following information must be supplied:

- The variable's name.
- The variable's type.
- The variable's location. A local variable is part of every object of a specific type and its subtypes. A shared variable is associated with the prototype only; it exists only once and is thus similar to a class variable of SMALLTALK.
- The variable's *visibility*. Private variables defined in a prototype P can only be accessed from within methods of P, heritage variables are also accessible in methods of P's direct or indirect heirs, and public variables may be accessed from everywhere.
- The variable's *modifiability*. A variable can be selectively defined as read-only for each scope (clients of P, heirs of P, and P itself) from which the variable can be accessed.

The 'method view' of an object shows all methods that have been defined for that object. It shows not only those methods defined in the actual type of the object, but also all inherited and overridden methods. Figure 14.3 shows the dialogue resulting from the invocation of the New Method menu command.

When a new method is defined, its name, the argument types, the result type, and the visibility of the method must be specified. It is also possible to protect a method against inadvertent overriding in subtypes. From the method view of an object editor, the source code of a method can be displayed in another window by means of a menu command.

14.3.3 Interactive execution

An OMEGA workspace consists of a collection of interconnected objects, but there is no such thing as a main program. The programming environment provides a log win-

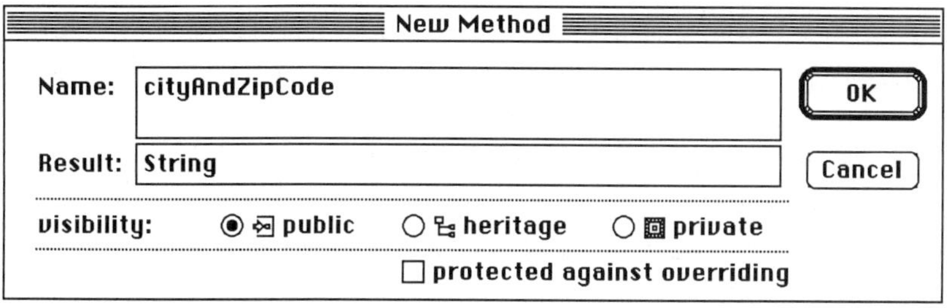

```
╔══════════════════ New Method ══════════════════╗
║                                                  ║
║  Name:  │cityAndZipCode                    │   ┌──────┐
║                                                 │  OK  │
║                                                 └──────┘
║  Result: │String                           │   ┌────────┐
║                                                 │ Cancel │
║                                                 └────────┘
║  visibility:    ◉ ⊠ public   ○ ⊑ heritage   ○ ▣ private
║
║                          ☐ protected against overriding
╚══════════════════════════════════════════════════╝
```

Figure 14.3   New Method dialogue.

dow in which arbitrary expressions can be entered and executed by means of a menu command. The result of the execution of the last expression is then displayed in the log window. The result of evaluating the expression

```
myself::=persons lookup:"Blaschek"; mySelf cityAndZipCode
```

is

```
>> A-4040 Linz
```

A special prototype Application serves as the basis for the construction of inter-active programs. A 'main program' can thus be constructed by deriving a new proto-type from Application and overriding a few methods. The programming environ-ment contains an application generator that converts such a prototype into a stand-alone application that can be executed independently of the programming environment.

14.3.4 The compiler

The OMEGA compiler is integrated in the programming environment. It operates on a persistent symbol table and compiles method sources into native 680x0 code. Since there is no module concept in OMEGA, methods are the compilation units of OMEGA. This enables the compiler to automatically recompile inconsistent methods in the background (*i.e.* during input pauses).

The compiler performs some simple optimizations. In particular, it generates efficient inline code for operations with monomorphic types. As a result, OMEGA programs are five to eight times faster than comparable SMALLTALK programs.

14.3.5 Analysis and documentation tools

The OMEGA programming environment not only provides functionality for the construction of programs but also supports inspection, debugging and documentation. These features include:

- Extensive workspace-wide search facilities.
- *'Who calls who' analysis* which delivers information about which methods can be potentially called directly or indirectly by a given expression.

- *Profiling* which tells which methods have actually been executed and how often.
- Object counts which for each type tell how many copies of that type's objects have been created during execution of an expression.
- *Traceback* which allows the user to inspect the call chain and the exact locations of the most recent exception.
- Workspace information which provides statistical information about the status of the workspace.
- *Documentation generators* which create textual information about individual objects or (parts of) the entire workspace. The resulting text files can be used as the basis of the documentation of an OMEGA program. Several options are available to control the amount and granularity of the documentation.

14.4 The Omega prototype library

Most of OMEGA's power does not come from the language proper, but rather from the OMEGA library. Currently, the library contains about 160 prototypes and 2300 methods with a total of 9500 lines of code. The most important parts of the library are:

- standard types (`Object`, `Integer`, `Char`, `Boolean`, `Block`, `Action`, `String`, `StringConstant`);
- collections (arrays, sets, dictionaries, stacks, ...);
- graphical objects (rectangles, lines, ovals, text, pictures, ...);
- file management (files, volumes, directories, streams, activation, 'passivation,' ...);
- user interface elements (menus, buttons, windows, views, ...);
- application elements (events, event handlers, framework components, ...).

Despite the small size of the library, it already constitutes a rather solid basis for the development of OMEGA programs. Of the 2300 methods, about 50 are implemented as primitive methods. They are either known to and implemented by the compiler or implemented in another programming language (in particular, PASCAL and assembly language).

As is often the case with languages that are tightly bound to their development environments, learning the language is much easier than learning how to use the library. The browsing capabilities of the OMEGA programming environment are very helpful in this respect. It is, however, first necessary to understand the concepts of the library (as documented in [Blaschek, 1994]) and to get used to a prototype-oriented programming style.

14.5 Implementation

At the time being, there is only one implementation of the OMEGA system. It runs on Macintosh computers with at least System 6.0.2 and requires about 2 Mb of memory. The programming environment and the compiler are implemented in THINK PASCAL [Symantec, 1991]. Only some parts of the run-time system (in particular, the memory

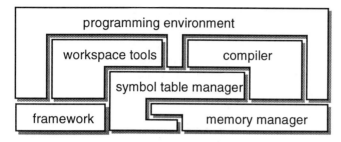

Figure 14.4   Architecture of the OMEGA system.

manager) are implemented in 68000 assembly language. The whole implementation currently consists of about 33 000 lines of code. The implementation is modular, as shown in Figure 14.4.

As OMEGA is a prototype-based language, 'living objects' play a central role. In contrast to conventional languages, objects (in particular, prototypes) must already exist when execution of an OMEGA program starts. For the same reason, the symbol table must be persistent. The memory manager is responsible for keeping track of all existing objects and for maintaining the consistency between the objects, their methods and the corresponding information in the symbol table. The symbol table manager provides routines for creation, deletion and redefinition of types, variables and methods. The compiler uses both the memory manager and the symbol table manager to generate code for the objects' methods. All interactive manipulation of the workspace is performed via workspace tools, a collection of classes that provide operations on specific views (such as the prototype hierarchy) of the workspace. Finally, the programming environment (which is based on a framework for interactive applications) glues the parts of the OMEGA system together.

14.6 Examples

In this section, two examples are presented to give the reader an impression of a typical OMEGA programming style. The first example shows the implementation of a generic stack, the second example shows part of the implementation of a set of prototypes for persons attending a workshop or conference. In order to cut down the size of the examples, elementary types and existing prototypes will be used where applicable. Both examples are, of course, developed in an object-oriented fashion. However, only some basic design ideas will be discussed here. The reader is therefore expected to have sufficient knowledge of object-oriented design.

14.6.1 Example 1 – a generic stack

A typical aspect of programming in OMEGA (and object-oriented programming in general) is re-use. An OMEGA programmer would therefore not implement their own stack but rather use the one that is already supplied with the OMEGA library. Stack is a generic prototype that can be parameterized with an arbitrary type. For example, Stack{Integer} and Stack{Person} would be two legal incarnations

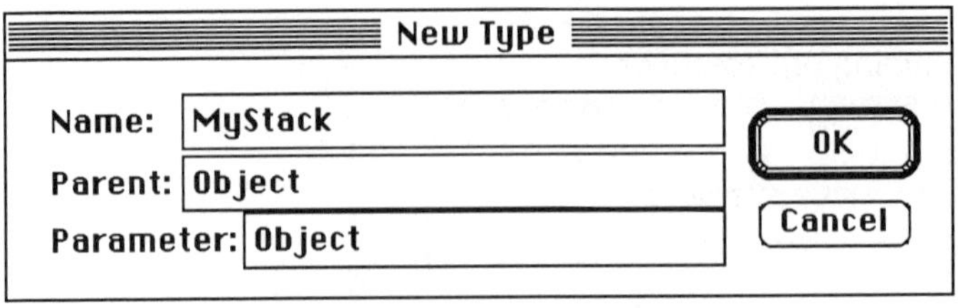

Figure 14.5   Creation of the MyStack prototype.

of Stack. In order to show how a generic stack could be implemented in a simple programming exercise, we will see the development of a new prototype MyStack. We will only implement the absolutely necessary methods and then show how such stack objects can be used.

Step 1 – Finding the proper supertype

The OMEGA library contains a subtree with the root Collection. Such collections are structured objects that can maintain (references to) several other objects. The interface of Collection already provides operations for adding and removing elements and for iteration over all elements of a collection. It is therefore tempting to derive MyStack from Collection in order to re-use these operations. This is, however, not recommended as clients of a stack should not be allowed to access elements other than the element on top of the stack. Therefore, a better solution (from the software engineering point of view) is to derive MyStack from Object and add those few methods needed to implement a stack.

Step 2 – Creating the MyStack prototype

In the hierarchy browser, we select the Object prototype, invoke the **New Type** menu command and complete the resulting dialogue as shown in Figure 14.5.

When the **OK** button is pressed, a clone of the Object prototype is created and defined as the new generic prototype MyStack. The default parameter type is Object, which means that MyStack can be parameterized with any type. As a result of this operation, MyStack appears in the hierarchy browser as a direct descendant of Object. At this point, MyStack is already globally known and can be used throughout the entire workspace, although this is not yet meaningful.

Step 3 – Defining the new type's structure

The MyStack prototype is opened in the hierarchy browser for inspection. In the variable view, an instance variable named content of type Array{Parameter} is added (see Figure 14.6). The location and visibility of the variable are defined as local and heritage, respectively. Parameter is a pseudo-type that represents the formal parameter type with which the current incarnation of MyStack is parameterized. When a new object MyStack{Integer} is created, the instance variable content is given the type Array{Integer}. Figure 14.6 shows how the object then appears in the object editor. The components map and mark are inherited from Object; they are present in each object and used by the run-time system.

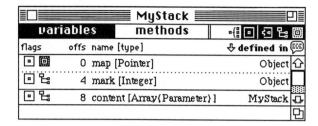

Figure 14.6   The MyStack prototype with the new instance variable content.

Step 4 – Overriding inherited methods

When creating a new prototype, we first have to consider which methods must be overridden. In the case of MyStack, we only have to override the method copyParts which is responsible for copying objects referenced by instance variables when the object receives the message copy. In the case of MyStack, a shallow copy of the array must be created using the message clone:

```
copyParts → Same
    [ content := content clone; self ]
```

The pseudo-type Same represents the type of the receiver of a message. It is similar to EIFFEL's 'like Current'. One of the uses of Same is to indicate that a method will return an object of the same (static and dynamic) type as the receiver. It is therefore used wherever a message returns the receiver (self).

Step 5 – Defining additional methods

Now it is time to implement the actual methods for manipulating the stack. We simply list the methods first; explanations of certain details are given below.

```
clear → Same
    -- initializes the stack with an empty array of elements
    [ content := Array{Parameter} copy; self ]
size → Integer
    -- returns the number of elements in the stack
    [ content size ]
push: Parameter → Same
    -- appends a new element at the end of the array
    { newElem:Parameter}
    [ content add:newElem; self ]
pop → Parameter
    -- returns the top element and removes it from the array
    [ n::=self size; top::=content at:  n; content delete:n; top ]
```

That's all there is to do to define the basic behaviour of MyStack. New elements are simply appended to the array referenced by the variable content. This is possible because OMEGA arrays are not declared with a fixed size; they rather expand and shrink as needed. When the message pop is sent to an empty stack, the variable n will have the value zero, thus leading to a range error when attempting to access the nth element of the array with the message content at:n. The exception handling mechanism of OMEGA can then be used to perform appropriate corrective actions. If a more descriptive exception is to be generated, the method pop could be implemented as follows.

```
pop → Parameter
   -- returns the top element and removes it from the array
   [ n::=self size;
     "pop only works for non-empty stacks" assertion:  n>0;
     top::=content at:  n; content delete:n; top ]
```

Step 6 – Using MyStack objects

The following code fragment shows how MyStack objects can be used. It assumes that the variable stk refers to an existing stack and uses a second stack tmp to reverse the order of the elements in stk.

```
tmp::=stk copy;   stk clear;
[tmp size>0] whileTrue:[stk push:tmp pop];
```

As MyStack inherits from Object, many predefined operations can be applied to MyStack objects without having to implement additional methods. For example, activation and 'passivation' of objects are implemented in a general way in Object. Circular references and so-called unique objects (which are supposed to exist only once) are automatically taken care of by this mechanism. In this way, MyStack objects can be written to and read from files, copied to the clipboard of the Macintosh, and sent to remote computers.

To make MyStack attractive for future re-use, a couple of additional methods would be needed. It would, for example, be convenient to concatenate stacks and to inspect their contents in a window. For this reason, the Stack prototype in the OMEGA library contains sixteen methods instead of the five methods shown above.

14.6.2 Example 2 – conference attendees

As a second example, we will consider the initial steps of the development of a set of prototypes for maintaining persons at a conference. This example is a small exercise in object-oriented design rather than a typical example of OMEGA programming style. Once adequate design decisions have been made, the implementation is quite simple and straightforward.

Step 1 – Developing the prototype hierarchy

The most important issue to settle is how to deal with attendees who have more than one role at the conference. For example, a single person could be a presenter in one session, chair in another session, and also an exhibitor. It would be tempting to use multiple inheritance to model multiple roles, but such a solution would cause more problems than it solves. Besides that, multiple inheritance cannot cope with changing roles (for example, when a speaker decides to present a poster during the conference). Fortunately, OMEGA has single inheritance only, so we have to look for another solution, anyway. We decide to develop a single prototype Person (with all unique attributes of a person) and a hierarchy of roles with an abstract root prototype Role. Figure 14.7 shows a subset of the resulting hierarchy.

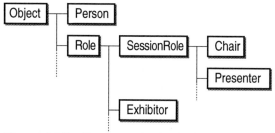

Figure 14.7   Persons and roles in the prototype hierarchy.

Instead of saying that a person is a presenter we rather say that a person has the role of a presenter. As a single person may have several roles, we include an instance variable `roles` of type `Set{Role}` in `Person`. An empty set is associated with a person who only attends the conference.

Step 2 – Defining the prototypes' structure

Next, we have to determine the interfaces and the structure of the prototypes. To simplify matters, only the most relevant instance variables and methods are listed in the sequel. In order to be practically usable (and re-usable), finer granularity and more types (for example, `Address` with subtypes for countries with different conventions) would be necessary.

Table 14.2   Definitions of prototypes

Prototype	Instance variable	Type	Initial content
Person	name	String	'unknown'
	organization	String	'unknown'
	address	String	'unknown'
	roles	Set{Role}	empty set
Role	– – – –	– – – –	– – – –
SessionRole	session	Session	Nil
Chair	– – – –	– – – –	– – – –
Presenter	title	String	'unknown'
	timeSlot	Integer	0

As Table 14.2 shows, a new type `Session` would be convenient. All roles relating to a particular session could then refer to the same `Session` object. This makes it easy to make global changes to a session (for example, to change a session's title or to shift it in the timetable).

The above definitions can all be made without implementing a single line of code. The interactive 'declaration' and initialization of these five prototypes takes no more than two or three minutes.

According to the principles of information hiding, all instance variables were defined with the visibility attribute `heritage`. This guarantees, for example, that clients cannot inadvertently access and modify the session of a `SessionRole`, but the subtypes `Chair` and `Presenter` have unlimited access to this instance variable.

Step 3 – Implementing the basic methods

What methods are to be provided depends on the context in which our objects will be used. It is certainly advisable to implement simple access methods to examine and change the instance variables. It would, of course, be easier to simply define the instance variables as public, but implementing methods for this purpose is more flexible with respect to future changes of the objects' structure. In order to avoid external references to the objects referred to by instance variables, access methods often create copies of the objects in question. The following example shows typical implementations of methods for accessing a person's name. By convention, the method with the same name as the instance variable returns the requested value, and a method ending with a colon modifies the instance variable.

```
name  →  String
-- returns the name of a person
[ name copy ]

name:  String  →  Same
-- changes the name of a person
{ newName:String }
[ name:=newName copy; self changed ]
```

The message `self` changed at the end of the `name:` method indicates that a significant change had been made to the receiver. OMEGA's change propagation mechanism then informs objects depending on the receiver (such as windows that display the contents of an object) of the change and gives these objects a chance to update themselves accordingly.

The access methods for the remaining instance variables would have a similar structure. For the sake of brevity they are not listed here.

Step 4 – Implementing additional methods

What remains to be done is to implement other methods as needed. Such methods are typically rather small and straightforward. The following example shows how a textual representation of a person (which may then be printed or displayed on the screen) can be produced.

```
asString  →  String
-- returns a textual representation of the receiver
[str::=name+String.eol+organization+String.eol+address+String.eol;
 roles forAll:  r:Role [str add:r asString+String.eol];
 str]
```

The message `asString` is implemented in `Object` with a default behaviour (it returns just the name of the object's type). It should be overridden if an object has something more meaningful to return. `String.eol` is a public *shared*, read-only variable (*i.e.* a global constant) that contains the end-of-line character(s). The `asString` method of `Person` simply concatenates the individual components and then appends the textual representations of all roles (again using the message `asString`). The following example shows what the result could look like.

```
Günther Blaschek
Johannes Kepler University
Altenbergerstraße 69, A-4040 Linz, Austria
presenter ("Omega" in Session 3, 10:00--10:30)
```

Step 5 – Using the objects

Once the prototypes have been defined, they can easily be used to create, say, an array of conference attendees. The following code fragment shows how such an array can be created, filled and printed.

```
attendees::=Array{Person} copy;
mySelf::=Person copy
   name:"Günther Blaschek",
   organization:"Johannes Kepler University",
   address:"Altenbergerstrasse 69, A-4040 Linz, Austria",
   addRole:(Presenter copy session:3, title:"Omega", timeSlot:3);
attendees add:mySelf;
...
attendees print;
```

14.7 Conclusions

The OMEGA system has already been used in various small projects. The development of the library and framework itself is a challenging project during which both the language and the programming environment have already proved themselves useful. Static typing, exception handling, garbage collection and the availability of tools contributed much to the surprisingly low number of programming errors made. Incremental compilation and direct manipulation of objects led us to an experimental and extremely productive programming style.

The OMEGA project started as a one-man project (I was the man). After two years, I was joined by another programmer. At that time, no description of the system (not even a complete language definition) was available. Despite the lack of documentation, it turned out that both the language and the usage of the system were easy to learn. However, it took much longer to get used to a prototype-oriented programming style.

Although the OMEGA system can already be used for practical projects, there is still much work to be done. At the time of writing, we have not yet completed the work on the OMEGA library (it probably never will be completed, as new demands arise constantly). In particular, we plan to include support for machine-independent user interfaces, concurrency, distributed systems and visual programming. Other tasks include the reimplementation of the OMEGA system in OMEGA, porting the system to other machines, and optimization of the code generated by the compiler. In short, the OMEGA project will surely keep us busy for the next couple of years.

14.8 References

Blaschek, G. (1991), Type-safe object-oriented programming with prototypes – the concepts of Omega, *Structured Programming*, **12**(4).

Blaschek, G. (1994), *Object-oriented Programming with Prototypes*, Springer-Verlag, Berlin.

Goldberg, A. and Robson, D. (1983), *Smalltalk-80: The Language and its Implementation*, Addison-Wesley, Reading, MA.

Meyer, B. (1988), *Object-oriented Software Construction*, Prentice-Hall, Englewood Cliffs, NJ.

Meyer, B. (1992), *Eiffel – The Language*, Prentice-Hall, Englewood Cliffs, NJ.

Mössenböck, H. (1993), *Object-oriented Programming in Oberon-2*, Springer-Verlag, Berlin.

Mössenböck, H. and Wirth, N. (1991), The programming language Oberon-2, *Structured Programming*, **12**(4).

Stroustrup, B. (1986), *The C++ Programming Language*, Addison-Wesley.

Symantec Corporation (1991), *Think Pascal, The Fastest Way to Finished Software – User Manual*, Symantec Corporation, Cupertino, CA.

Ungar, D. and Smith, R. B. (1987), Self: the power of simplicity, in *Proceedings of OOPSLA '87*.

15 Pride and prejudice: four decades of Lisp

Stuart Watt

The purpose of this chapter is to encourage those involved in choosing a language to consider LISP by dispelling any prejudice against it and by providing an overview of the language and the LISP family of languages. Thus shall the myths concerning LISP be put to rest and many years' service to computer science be recognized!

15.1 Introduction

> 'The whole of this unfortunate business', said Dr Lyster, 'has been the result of pride and prejudice.'
>
> *Cecilia*, Fanny Burney

Introducing a language like LISP is a tricky matter, as there are so many myths that surround it. It is a language that raises strong feelings on both sides. On the one hand, people who use LISP are very proud of it, and extol its virtues at every opportunity and frequently at great length. On the other hand, LISP has a reputation of being big and slow, using lots of parentheses and, worst of all, being an 'artificial intelligence' language. This was a fine description of the language twenty years ago, perhaps even ten; and although a lot has changed since then old prejudices die hard. New compiler techniques have been developed, computers are faster and cheaper than ever, and now the cost of software development is starting to be more important than hardware costs. The requirements of programming languages have changed.

LISP has a unique style among programming languages. It has kept a conceptual purity throughout its history, remaining both simple and powerful. While other languages were being deliberately shaped to encourage particular design approaches, LISP remained passive; it could mould itself around any approaches that seemed appropriate without changing in substance. It doesn't interfere with the design processes, it just offers a wider scope: programs and data can be structured so flexibly that people can express themselves in many different ways within the same framework. This makes LISP ideal as a teaching language: in many institutions SCHEME – a dialect of LISP – is taught because it allows different styles of procedural, constraint and logic programming to be used all within the same basic language [Abelson et al., 1985]. Besides this, LISP is an incremental language, so new procedures can be tried immediately they have been defined. This, together with type testing during execution and true abstraction from the underlying computer hardware, mean that it has all the qualities which make it ideal for developing both systems and programming skill quickly.

Today, LISP is still a vibrant and thriving language; indeed, it has always been pioneering new concepts and approaches. There have, however, been fundamental changes both in its design and in its implementation, and now it runs easily on desktop and laptop computers, it is fast, and is used for many different kinds of application. These changes mean that LISP can offer more than it ever has been able to in the past; many of the problems once associated with LISP are no longer applicable.

LISP has changed with the times. While the essence of the language has remained the same, its availability, portability and performance have all improved dramatically. This chapter gives an overview of LISP: a brief taste of what the language is about, and some indication of the kinds of task that LISP may be more or less suitable for than conventional languages.

15.2 What is Lisp?

LISP is an acronym for 'list processing'; the language was originally designed for applications involving manipulating patterns of symbols, for instance, symbolic differentiation and integration of algebraic expressions. It was first developed by John McCarthy at MIT with the initial implementation beginning in 1958 and ending in 1960, and the first stable version of the language, LISP 1.5, being completed in 1962. There were many variants on this language, but none really superseded LISP 1.5 until the early 1970s.

Since then, there have been many different dialects of LISP. Figure 15.1 shows the relationships between some of the more commercially successful LISP dialects, although it should be noted that in practice every dialect borrowed ideas from just about every other dialect that preceded it. Fortunately, most of these have now passed away, and many are best left in their unmarked graves. For a more detailed history, see [McCarthy, 1978] (up to 1960) and [Steele and Gabriel, 1993] (from 1960 to 1993).

The origins of LISP lie in the formal mathematics of Church's lambda calculus, although somewhat modified by contamination with procedural semantics. To this day the lambda form reflects this history. Lambda calculus is still used today, principally as a tool to formally define the semantics of other programming languages; indeed, part of the SCHEME standard [Rees and Clinger, 1992] formally defines its semant-

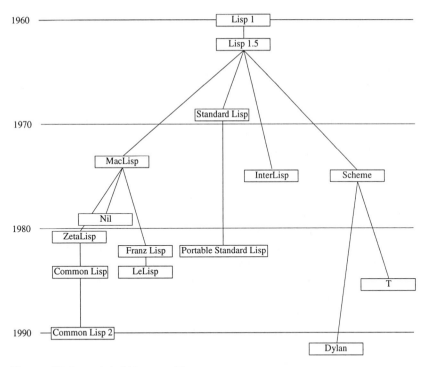

Figure 15.1   A brief history of LISP.

ics in terms of lambda calculus in just a few pages. It is this inherited flexibility that allows LISP to form programs in many different ways, without enforcing any particular principles. LISP is not so much a language as a platform on which new languages can be built, and applications are usually constructed by designing a cascade of general and increasingly special-purpose languages that eventually make the final application trivial.

There are a number of key features that remain from these original LISP dialects. First, *symbolic expressions*, a simple and almost ultimately general data structure; second, functions are first-class objects, so programs can be used as data; and third, programming in the style of function application as well as procedurally. Almost everything else in the language has changed quite fundamentally through the years. Binding has changed from dynamic to lexical, the early LISP interpreters have been replaced by fast and efficient compilers themselves written in LISP, and many new kinds of data structure, strings, arrays, hash-tables and objects have all been built into the language since. Whole new programming paradigms have been added: object-oriented programming and data-flow programming; and all this lies within the same basic framework.

LISP is normally called a 'weakly typed' language, but this is an extremely deceptive term. A far better term would be 'dynamically typed', as the truth of the matter is that in LISP the type is associated with the value rather than with the variable, and that error checking is provided at run time rather than at compile time. Of course, this is a little slower, but a good LISP compiler is capable of inferring the possible types of an object at any point in the program, and skipping type checks when they aren't needed. The advantage of this method is that it is actually stricter about the typing, as silly values will signal an error immediately, rather than letting the program run on and do something extremely nasty to the memory which may only show up later. It is also useful when abstract objects are added to the language, as they also need to have the types associated with the object rather than the variable to do proper message handling. By contrast, statically typed languages usually add abstract objects by adding a second type system: in parallel with the static types they keep object descriptions around while the program runs – leaving problems for the programmer in understanding which type system is actually being used in a particular reference.

In LISP, despite prejudices to the contrary, it is even possible to add type declarations, so that even if the compiler can't infer the types of variables, it can be told them so that further optimization and checking may be possible. In COMMON LISP, for instance, there is a 'safety switch' so that at *high safety* these declarations are checked as assertions, and at *low safety* they are used to optimize out any type-checking code that would be provided by default. Programs can be developed and tested with high safety, and when they are free of bugs the safety can be switched to generate a smaller and faster version with these additional optimizations.

These features are shared by most dialects of LISP, but standards have evolved. Today, there are just two dialects in active use: COMMON LISP and SCHEME; they differ greatly in size and even in syntax, but the most important distinction between them is in their different aims.

COMMON LISP [Steele, 1990] was intended as an 'industrial strength' language, and emerged as an attempt to create a single standard from the plethora of dialects in active use in industry in the early 1980s, most of which were variants of MACLISP. It succeeded, after some initial resistance. Today it can be used on almost every conceivable platform with good performance. COMMON LISP is a big language, although at its core there is a small one trying to get out. Taken as a whole, though, it is rather larger than ADA, and this makes it difficult for implementors, users and novice programmers alike. Learning LISP is fairly quick and the benefits are reaped soon, but the scale of COMMON LISP does make life rather hard for its users in their early days.

SCHEME [Rees and Clinger, 1992; Sussman, 1975], by contrast, was conceived almost by accident in laboratory experiments studying the connection between denotational semantics and message-passing languages. The upshot was the abandoning of the 'go to' concept, even implicitly, as part of the language, and its replacement by the more general notion of a continuation function. The result was a very small, clean language ideal for teaching. It also has carefully defined semantics: semantics which are truer to the original lambda calculus than other dialects of LISP. Many of the higher-level elements of the COMMON LISP standard, such as the object system and sorting procedures, are intentionally not part of SCHEME. This allows exploration of many different possible program structures in the learning process, much more than with most conventional languages which are generally biased towards a particular kind of organization. Besides this, it keeps the language small and means that students can understand these rather fancy elements by actually building them for themselves as part of the learning process.

Whichever dialect is being used much of the language shares the same basic principles: the principles which have kept the language alive from its early days by allowing it to adapt to changes in requirements. These early foundations provided a degree

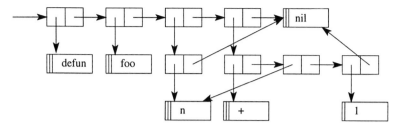

Figure 15.2   A LISP list structure.

of flexibility almost unparalleled in other languages. A large part of this flexibility was originally due to its use of symbolic expressions, a simple and flexible data-structuring system constructed from cons cells, each of which contains two pointers to other objects, called the car and cdr for arcane historical reasons associated with the original IBM hardware underlying the first implementations. Each pointer can point to either another cons cell or to something else, such as a symbol or a number, so cons cells could be daisy-chained into long pointer-linked structures, and lists were born.

Figure 15.2 shows the references for a fairly simple list structure, and how it is made up of 'conses' and atoms. The same structure could have been written in 'dotted pairs' notation (each dotted pair has the form (car . cdr)) as follows:

```
(defun . (foo . ((n . nil) . ((+ . (n . (1 . nil))) . nil))))
```

but this wouldn't make much sense to anybody. The LISP syntax abbreviates this by rewriting chains of conses as lists of elements separated by spaces and leaving out the symbol nil marking the end of the list. That is, (a . (b . (c . nil))) can be written as (a b c). The usual syntax for the structure in Figure 15.2 is therefore:

```
(defun foo (n) (+ n 1))
```

which corresponds to defining a function taking a single parameter n, adding one to it, and returning the value.

In summary, LISP is a dynamically typed language originally derived from the mathematical foundations of lambda calculus, but throughout its history it has continually been developed to be better tuned to the requirements of the time. The positive elements, such as symbolic expressions and its consistent treatment of programs and data, have been retained, but problem areas, like LISP's use of interpreters and dynamic binding, have been replaced with fast and efficient compilers using static binding. Whole new features have been added where the language was deficient, more data types such as strings and hash-tables, object-oriented programming, and powerful numeric capabilities. LISP is a survivor, and it has survived by adapting to today's needs.

15.3 Why use Lisp?

LISP today is a practical language. Its advantages in practical use lie in its core properties, its consistency, its simple general data structures, and its acceptance of functions as values. This consistency, where everything in LISP is a first-class object: numbers, lists, symbols, functions, hash-tables and so on, means that in practice LISP programs

```
(do ((list1 list1 (rest list1))     (mapcar #'list list1 list2)
     (list1 list2 (rest list2))
     (result ()))
    ((or (endp list1)
         (endp list2))
     (reverse result))
  (push (list (first list1)
              (first list2))
        result))
```

Figure 15.3   Comparison of iterative and sequence versions of the same function.

form an elegant cascade of increasingly specialized components, all bound together by the common framework of the underlying language.

For instance, the use of functions as values means there is a key difference between LISP and most other languages: the extensive use of higher-order functions. Higher-order functions are normal functions which can be passed other functions as parameters, and call them in order to calculate their result; a typical example is mapcar, which takes a function and a list of values, and returns a new list of values, created by calling the function on each value in the list. Of course, the same can be done with a looping construct, but to see the difference compare the two definitions in Figure 15.3.

In the iterative version, which uses the do form, the procedure explicitly moves down the two lists, using the functions first to get the first elements and rest to get the rest of each list. When either of the lists is empty, the function stops and returns the result. Each time round the loop, the list function is called on the two first elements, and the returned value is added to the front of the result list. Finally the returned result is reversed so that the order of the output is the same as the order of the input.

But, note, the function that is applied – in this case list – can be considered as a parameter to this function. If the two lists were of numbers we might want to add corresponding elements by using +, or multiply them by *. mapcar does exactly this: it provides a general iteration framework for free, and uses a function passed by its caller to generate values it can then combine into a result list.

Not only is this version much shorter, it is also much more reliable, because the iteration framework only needs to be written once. mapcar circumvents all the potential errors in having to write iteration frameworks all over the place. The compiler then takes the higher-order function mapcar and unravels it to generate code which will, in practice, be identical to that in the iterative version. The nastiness of the basic iterative isn't a problem, because in practice nobody would bother writing it when there is no performance advantage, but the power of the general iteration framework in do is available for exceptional circumstances.

Conventional languages such as PASCAL and C also allow higher-order functions, but their static type-checking removes much of their utility: an equivalent of mapcar could not be used with both list and +, because one returns a list and the other an integer, and these cannot be accommodated in a single function result in a statically typed language.

LISP's sequence functions can go even further than this, because they treat all the different kinds of object equivalently. It is possible to map over vectors and lists in the same way. After all, both contain an ordered sequence of values. COMMON LISP contains a key set of sequence-generic functions – functions which will operate on any kind of sequence: lists, vectors, strings, and so on. These functions can be used to find, count, or delete elements, for instance, without the programmer needing to know anything about the underlying representation. LISP provides true independence from the underlying representation, so that in a well-designed system data representations can be changed without any effect on the code that uses it, without needing to encapsulate everything so that it becomes difficult to debug.

In LISP, another common kind of higher-order function is a *macro*. Unlike conventional languages where macros operate by transforming program text at the lexical level, LISP macros are themselves written in LISP, and they work by transforming one LISP program into another. As LISP programs are just LISP lists, this is both quick and simple to do, and the effect is to give macros access to the whole power of the language. Macros are used extensively in COMMON LISP, indeed most of the control structures programmers use are actually macros, implemented in terms of a small number of primitive 'special forms' which are all that the compiler needs to worry about. SCHEME has about ten special forms, and COMMON LISP about thirty. As an example, there isn't a PASCAL-like `repeat` form in COMMON LISP, so let's write one:

```
(defmacro repeat (form predicate)
  `(loop
     ,form
     (when ,predicate (return))))
```

The new macro creates a control structure which repeatedly executes its body, and then evaluates a predicate; when the predicate is true the loop exits. The backquote (`` ` ``) syntax marks whatever follows as a kind of template: everything that follows is used literally to construct bits of program, except that forms preceded by a comma (`,`) are evaluated first and their value put in instead. From now on, the macro will be expanded when it is used in code, so the definition:

```
(let ((command ()))
  (repeat (setf command (read-command))
    (null command))))
```

will be transformed before the compilation proper into:

```
(let ((command ()))
  (loop (setf command (read-command))
    (when (null command)
      (return))))
```

Other macros in this form, notably `loop` and `when`, will then be expanded until only special forms are left, and then the compiler will be run to generate the corresponding executable code.

In the same manner whole new languages can be constructed, with entirely different syntax and semantics from those of COMMON LISP, and indeed this is a very typical way of programming in LISP. First, a more applicable (and usually quite re-usable) general purpose language is built, and then this is gradually specialized to the application in hand. LISP is a natural for writing compilers and interpreters for other languages.

```
> (defun fact (n)
    (if (= n 1)
      1
      (* n (fact (- n 1)))))
FACT
> (fact 100)
9332621544394415268169923885626670049071596826 4
38162146859296389521759999322991560894146397615
651828625369792082722375825118521091686400000000
00000000000000000
>
```

Figure 15.4   A typical REP loop display.

Often this is done by adding a *code walker*, a program which can go through the nested list structure of a segment of program code and can process it according to the semantics of the special forms it contains. This adds the whole power of a compiler to the macro facility and is often used to generate extensions to the language: this is exactly how the data-flow and nondeterministic choice extensions which will be described in sections 15.3.2 and 15.3.3 are implemented.

Some of the advantages of LISP lie not in the language itself, but in the environments which are its natural consequence. LISP's ancestry as an interpreted language lives on in its incremental nature; changes can be made to existing definitions while in the middle of testing, and, should an error occur, even in the error context itself, within the LISP error handler. The edit–debug cycle is very short in LISP compared to almost any other language.

LISP environments are usually centred around a loop, called the REP loop (for read, eval and print, the functions it calls repeatedly). This is a bit like a command-line interface: LISP repeatedly reads an expression, evaluates it, and prints the answer. Functions can be defined, functions called, or variables evaluated, all by typing in a form to be evaluated. If there is an error, for instance in the middle of evaluating a function call, the LISP error handler is invoked and this creates a new, inner REP loop. In this loop, functions and variables can be evaluated as before, but additionally local variables bound in function calls on the stack can be inspected, and even changed, before execution is continued by returning a value from one of the calls on the stack. An error caused by faulty code can be fixed in the source, the function redefined, and the program run continued without needing to quit or rebuild the system to get it back into the right context for continued testing. A new generation of C environments also provide this facility: many of the companies that supply these were once LISP houses and their environments use the same technologies and techniques which led to today's advanced LISP systems.

Figure 15.4 shows a typical top-level REP loop display from one particular LISP implementation. In this window, the function fact is first defined, and then (fact 100) called to generate the factorial of 100. It is worth noting that, unlike most languages, COMMON LISP (and also SCHEME) does *exact* arithmetic, so the answer is completely precise. Although floating-point numbers, and even complex numbers, are pro-

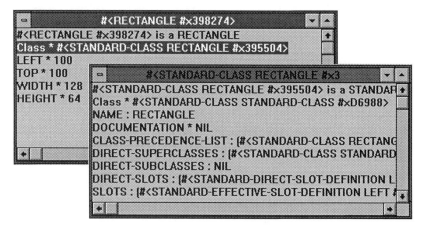

Figure 15.5   A typical inspector display.

vided, the ability to handle arbitrarily big integers and exact rationals (such as $\frac{1}{3}$) makes for easy solutions to some kinds of numeric problem.

Since LISP associates data types with values rather than with variables, and so the data type information is around at run time, LISP environments usually provide an *inspector* to allow the contents of structures and objects to be browsed and even changed. Figure 15.5 shows a typical inspector display: the upper window shows a rectangle object with its *slots* left, top, width, and height, and the lower window shows its class. The class is a first-order object describing the slots and structure of all rectangle objects, and it too consists of slots with values, just like the basic rectangle object. The power of the inspector lies in the fact that it can be used at run time to check and even change the *actual* values of variables; as such it is an invaluable debugging tool.

15.3.1 Is Lisp an object-oriented language?

LISP today is an object-oriented language, although it only started to become so after Alan Kay gave a presentation at MIT and convinced some of the LISP community how powerful object-oriented approaches could be.

As with many other programming language features, LISP was first used as an experimental laboratory for this new approach to program design, and the result was gradual emergence of a synthesis which added value in the process, without too many effects on the existing language. Object-oriented programming (OOP) wasn't added to LISP as a 'bolt-on goody'. The COMMON LISP object-oriented programming system took many years to develop, and was actually a hybrid of two existing OOP systems, *flavors*, which was part of the ZETALISP [Weinreb and Moon, 1991] environment, and COMMON LOOPS, which was part of Xerox's INTERLISP environment. After a small group of proponents from each camp had been locked in a room for several years, they emerged with the COMMON LISP Object System, or CLOS; a standard that everybody (eventually) agreed was better than any of its antecedents.

Defining a class in CLOS is simple. Like the defun form used to define functions, there is a defclass form to define classes. The following example defines the class rectangle, as shown in the inspector window example shown in Figure 15.5.

```
(defclass rectangle ()
  ((left :initarg :left)
   (top :initarg :top)
   (width :initarg :width)
   (height :initarg :height))))
```

Objects are created by calling the function make-instance, which takes a class and returns a newly created instance of that class. The following example code will create and inspect a rectangle – the display that it creates is shown in the top window in Figure 15.5.

```
(inspect (make-instance 'rectangle
             :left 100 :top 100
             :width 128 :height 64))
```

Methods can be written using defmethod, which is rather like defun, except that for each parameter there is a corresponding class. For instance, to write a function to return the right boundary of a rectangle, the slots left and width must be added. with-slots creates a local context where the slots can be used as if they were simple variables:

```
(defmethod rectangle-right ((object rectangle))
  (with-slots (width left) object
    (+ width left))))
```

These methods are bound up by CLOS into a *generic function*, which corresponds roughly to a message in SMALLTALK. Generic functions combine all the different methods together with some hidden glue so that when the generic function is called the right method is run.

By extending functions rather than using message passing as the structure to hang methods on, CLOS opened up the possibility of one of its main innovations: *multimethods*, methods which dispatch on more than one parameter. Although this has been criticized as against the spirit of message passing (which it is) and even object-oriented programming itself (which it isn't) there is no doubt that multimethods are used, and used both extensively and effectively, in real applications. For example, drawing a shape depends on both the class of the shape and the class of the device it should be drawn to. These examples (derived from [Kiczales *et al.*, 1991]) show a *generic function* draw which dispatches on two parameters, and how different methods can be defined for the different combinations. The first method will only be run if the first parameter is a rectangle and the second a bitmap-device, the second method for a rectangle and a postscript-device, and the third for a circle and a postscript-device. The generic function draw will check the types of its two parameters to decide which should be run. A standard message-passing approach can achieve a similar effect by chaining together messages, but this is not so elegant or clear a solution as these draw methods:

```
(defmethod draw ((shape rectangle) (device bitmap-device))
  ... paint pixels on display ...)
```

```
(defmethod draw ((shape rectangle) (device postscript-device))
  ... output PostScript commands ...)

(defmethod draw ((shape circle) (device postscript-device))
  ... output PostScript commands ...)
```

Because the method-combination glue is program code rather than a table, CLOS allows methods to be written on standard LISP classes, such as `list` and `string`, and on individual objects, like the number 1. We can add another `draw` method, which draws strings by dispatching on the built-in class `string`:

```
(defmethod draw ((shape string) (device postscript-device))
  ... output PostScript commands ...)
```

Much of the power in CLOS comes from the way that the different methods can be combined. For instance, we might define a class of shadowed objects which has a `draw` method like this:

```
(defmethod draw ((shape shadowed) device)
  ... set shadowed context and offset shape ...
  (call-next-method)
  ... restore original context and shape ...
  (call-next-method))
```

This shows the use of the standard function `call-next-method` which invokes the next most specific method. If we defined a new class which inherited from both `shadowed` and `rectangle` the `draw` method for `shadowed` would be run first. The method above would then set up the context to draw a shadow, and use `call-next-method` to call the `draw` method for `rectangle`. The context would then be restored and this method called again to draw a normal rectangle over the shadow. The power of the multimethod combination approach means that `shadowed` can also be mixed with other classes of shape, such as `circle`, and it will still work. Also, because this `draw` method doesn't need to be specialized to `postscript-device`, the same shadowing code can be used for many different kinds of device.

Method combination like this, multimethods, and the integration with base COMMON LISP classes give CLOS a qualitative advance over other object-oriented programming systems. Finally, if CLOS isn't enough, there is a whole metaobject protocol [Kiczales *et al.*, 1991] which allows the basic patterns of inheritance, slot access and method writing all to be specialized to provide, for instance, object-oriented front-ends to databases. All this power is there should it be needed, although most people get by with simple classes and methods.

15.3.2 Is Lisp a data-flow language?

LISP has accommodated object-oriented programming with ease, but this is not the only new programming form that has been added to LISP. The *series package* [Waters, 1989] adds a data-flow style of programming to COMMON LISP; that is, programs can be thought of as processes which operate on streams of data values, some generating them, others collecting values, and others merging or modifying them. The smart thing about the series package is that it unravels all this process-like description into something which can be executed iteratively.

Series can provide very elegant solutions to many problems: solutions which are as efficient as code which has been written iteratively but which has a style and elegance normally only possible with inefficient approaches such as lazy evaluation.

The series package is implemented as a set of macros, and using the COMMON LISP macro facility they apply the whole power of the language to analyse a user's code and to transform it by interleaving code from the component functions to create a single, although complex, iterative function.

As an example, LISP people frequently try out an implementation with an approximation to the factorial function, which is easy to define recursively as follows:

```
(defun fact (n)
  (if (= n 1)
    1
    (* n (fact (- n 1))))))
```

In words, the factorial of n is n multiplied by the factorial of $n-1$, with the special case that the factorial of 1 is 1. The same function can be written using the series macro package as follows.

```
(defun fact (n)
  (collect-product (scan-range :start 1 :upto n)))
```

The `scan-range` function generates a series containing the elements 1 to n inclusive. The `collect-product` function (which actually isn't part of series like `collect-sum`) can be trivially defined similarly to `scan-range`. (The series version of the function is shorter, and is often faster because the code that is generated is iterative rather than recursive.)

Series have a fair number of restrictions, some of which are problematic, but code which is written using series is generally both efficient and elegant. Series, as with CLOS, coexists with the rest of LISP, although it tends to supersede some aspects of the core language; `mapcar` for instance, is rather redundant because the series function `mapping` does the same kind of thing.

15.3.3 Is Lisp a nondeterministic language?

Like the series package, the Screamer macro package [Siskind and McAllester, 1993] adds a significant layer of new functions to COMMON LISP, but this time it is nondeterministic choice and backtracking that are added, rather like adding an efficient PROLOG engine to LISP. It achieves this by adding two primitive functions: `either`, a nondeterministic choice operator, and `fail` which causes backtracking to the next possible `either` value.

As an example, consider the following definition:

```
(defun an-integer-between (low high)
  (if ($>$ low high)
      (fail)
      (either low (an-integer-between (1+ low) high))))
```

This function nondeterministically returns an integer between the given bounds. The set of all possible values can be collected into a list by `all-values`, which is roughly equivalent to the `bag-of` primitive in PROLOG [Clocksin and Mellish, 1984]:

```
(all-values (an-integer-between 1 5))
⇒ (1 2 3 4 5)
```

Nondeterminism is a natural tool to apply in search problems: for instance, in a difficult scheduling task there will be two components to the problem, a search tree and a heuristic. Nondeterministic choice operators allow the search tree to be efficiently constructed. It is particularly good for solving 'constraint satisfaction' problems, where there are a number of variables which must be given values while maintaining certain constraints on the relationships between the values. This is a special kind of search problem: one which packages like Screamer can make very easy, and one that can be applied in a very natural way to solve many different kinds of task, particularly planning and scheduling problems.

In a conventional language, it might be claimed that the features of a data-flow language (like series) and nondeterminism (like Screamer) might be implemented by a library or a preprocessor, but the LISP macro package strategy is very different. In LISP, the languages are built one upon the other, so the result is a single uniform language, which has the power of the new paradigm and retains the generality of LISP. The ability to construct a whole new language is beyond the capabilities of a library in a conventional language, and using a preprocessor creates a new language rather than combining the two. It is LISP's ability to manipulate programs as data that makes packages like the series package and Screamer possible in a way they could never be in any conventional language.

Object-oriented and data-flow programming and nondeterminism aren't the whole story. Most LISP programming is done in this style, designing more specialized languages within the basic LISP framework. Production-rule languages are a common class of language, but others include constraint solvers and generic editors. It is this ability to unify many different specialized and re-usable languages within a single framework that makes LISP a uniquely flexible language.

LISP, a single language, can be programmed in many different ways. It can be programmed in traditional LISP style as a combination of procedures and function application. It can be programmed as an object-oriented language, complete with multiple inheritance. It can be programmed as a data-flow language, with nondeterministic search, or as a rule-based inference engine. All these different styles can be wrapped into a single language, so that the most appropriate style can be chosen for the problem in hand.

15.3.4 Is Lisp a user-interface language?

As with most other programming languages, LISP doesn't have a single standard graphical user interface, although there have been a number of rather ambitious at-

```
(defparameter text-item
  (make-dialog-item :widget 'lisp-text
    :box (make-box 18 35 250 60)))
(defparameter dialog-items
  (list (make-dialog-item :widget 'default-button :title "OK"
          :box (make-box 18 74 89 96)
          :set-value-fn #'(lambda (item new-value old-value)
                            (print (eval (dialog-item-value
                                            text-item)))
                            (values t t)))
        (make-dialog-item :widget 'cancel-button :title "Cancel"
          :box (make-box 177 74 250 96)
          :set-value-fn #'(lambda (item new-value old-value)
                            (values t t)))
        (make-dialog-item :widget 'static-text
          :box (make-box 18 10 250 25)
          :value "Please enter a form to be evaluated")
        text-item))
(defun evaluate ()
  (let ((dialog (cg:open-dialog dialog-items 'dialog *screen*
                  :pop-up-p t
                  :title "Evaluate"
                  :window-interior (make-box 18 34 285 142))))
    (pop-up-dialog dialog)
    (close dialog)))
```

Figure 15.6   Common Graphics code for the evaluation dialogue.

tempts. It does, however, have some natural advantages which make implementing graphical interfaces very easy.

Perhaps the most important of these is LISP's treatment of programs as data. In an interface, this means that a procedure can be installed as a 'callback', so that when the user selects something in an interface, say an 'OK' button or a 'Print...' menu item, that procedure is run to carry out the corresponding action.

Figure 15.6 shows the LISP code needed to create a dialogue interface to the LISP evaluator; this has a box where a form can be typed in, and an OK button which when pressed causes the form to be evaluated and the answer printed. There is also a Cancel button which quits the dialogue without evaluating the form. This example is written using *Common Graphics*, the user interface package used by Procyon COMMON LISP on the Macintosh and Allegro COMMON LISP under Windows 3.

The code elements beginning #'(lambda ...) are anonymous functions: they behave just as if they had been defined by defun, but as they are only needed within the dialog item, anonymous functions are fine. These are the two callback functions, called when the item value is changed (which happens when a button is selected). The first handles the OK button, and it first prints the result of evaluating whatever is in the LISP text item: *i.e.* the LISP form in the single-line text editor in the dialogue. It then returns values which cause the dialogue to exit. The callback for the Cancel button is almost the same, except that it just causes the dialogue to exit. The two other items are the LISP text item itself, and a static text item that appears as a label in the dialogue. When all these elements are combined into a single dialogue by the function evaluate, the display appears as shown in Figure 15.7.

The LISP object-oriented programming system, CLOS, also helps in the construction

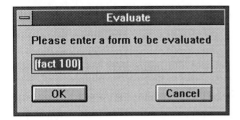

Figure 15.7   The evaluation dialogue display.

of interfaces. In the evaluation dialogue, the `open-dialog` function is passed the class name `dialog`, which specifies the class of dialogue to use. This can be overridden by defining a new subclass of `dialog` and passing the name of the subclass instead. Similarly, the dialogue items are instances of the standard Common Graphics classes `button`, `static-text` and `lisp-text`, but new classes can again be created using `defclass`, and then these new kind of dialogue item can be added and used just like the standard ones. New kinds of button, for instance, can be written and added to interfaces if none of the existing kinds has quite the right appearance or behaviour.

Even though LISP doesn't have a standard graphical user interface system, it has features which make the development of user interfaces rather easier than in many other languages. It is incremental, so interfaces can be developed bit by bit without constantly needing to rebuild everything. It treats programs as data, so callback procedures can be used to handle menu and dialogue selection, and it is object-oriented, which allows new kinds of object to be written and added to interfaces without unnecessarily duplicating or breaking what is already there. LISP is an easy and natural language for the development of graphical user interfaces.

15.3.5 Is Lisp an artificial-intelligence language?

Well, no, not really. The artificial-intelligence and LISP communities gradually split over a number of years, and by the middle of the 1980s the split between the two fields was effectively complete. Of course, artificial-intelligence people still mostly use LISP, but they consider it as just another programming language. They might well use PROLOG, or even C if it met their requirements. LISP, of course, does have many natural advantages: it is a symbolic language which makes it appropriate for implementing many AI techniques, and a lot of tedious stuff to do with memory management is handled automatically, so it has remained the dominant programming language in the field. It has, however, also had its problems.

First and foremost of these was delivery; in the early-to-mid-1980s it simply wasn't feasible to deliver a LISP application of any size on hardware that could be widely used. It required either a special card or extra memory, and this pushed the cost up too high to be commercially viable.

These problems were all solved in the late 1980s, but the relationship between the LISP and artificial-intelligence communities has remained a bit strained. There has, though, been a gradual change since COMMON LISP was introduced, and now virtually every major computer hardware supplier has endorsed one LISP implementation or another, although nowadays few suppliers mention artificial intelligence explicitly when they try to sell LISP.

Ever since artificial intelligence became a bag of tools which could be applied to solve previously hard problems, the success of LISP has grown step-by-step, as it provides exactly the right framework to implement these tools with the minimum of fuss. Although the two fields are now separate, there is still a positive feedback which benefits both.

LISP is still used by artificial-intelligence researchers, but its incremental nature has opened up a whole new range of opportunities. LISP, especially with the CLOS, has proved very powerful in human interface design, where it allows the interface to be developed step-by-step without ever leaving the LISP environment. In short, whenever some kind of language is needed, even if it isn't textual, LISP's ability to stretch into new forms incrementally has proved an immensely valuable characteristic.

15.4 What's wrong with Lisp?

It's time to be honest: there are problems using LISP, but I want to claim that these problems are not so serious as to significantly restrict its usefulness.

COMMON LISP especially is a big language, and as recently as five years ago delivering applications widely on cheap hardware was almost impossible, but as hardware costs have dropped it has become much more viable. COMMON LISP applications can and have been delivered on PCs with an 80386 processor and 4 Mb of memory under Windows 3.1 [Evertsz *et al.*, 1990], a cheap and fairly typical system configuration.

LISP does have one severe problem in real-time systems. Most languages handle memory dynamically by requiring programmers to explicitly free memory when they have finished with it. This is actually pretty difficult for the programmer, and adds significantly to the cost of development. It is usually necessary for any statically typed language, because they throw away all the type information at run time, so when a memory reference can no longer be accessed the run time environment has no information as to what to do with the memory it referred to. Dynamically typed languages keep the type information at run time, so when memory runs out, everything that can no longer be referred to can be implicitly deallocated and its space recycled. LISP usually implements this with a garbage collector. Only if memory is genuinely full of accessible data does LISP really run out of memory. This makes a programmer's life significantly easier, but means that occasionally the LISP system stops to reorganize all its memory. For real-time systems, this stopping usually isn't acceptable, and although there are complicated variations on garbage collection that allow processing to continue while the memory is being reorganized, in practice it means that LISP is rarely used for real-time systems. For a conventional interactive system, however, the occasional garbage collection isn't regarded as a problem, even by users [Evertsz *et al.*, 1990; Nurminen, 1990].

Perhaps the biggest problem with LISP, though, is the shortage of skilled people. LISP isn't used much as a teaching language (although it is on the increase), and transfer of skills from conventional languages isn't always natural, or good for developing skill with LISP. People normally take three to six months experience to have an adequate grasp of COMMON LISP, and much less for SCHEME, although their technique and style will continue to develop for many years. This may seem like a long time, but their productivity is such that even while learning LISP people can still build systems more quickly than their more skilled equivalents in a conventional language. For equivalent levels of skill and experience, LISP programmers are roughly twice as productive as C/C++ programmers, even assuming a C/C++ environment that offers the same kind of incremental development. If the environment isn't incremental, the difference is far larger.

15.5 Can I use Lisp in industry?

Industrial exploitation of LISP has always been a rather curious affair. Within most large companies there is a small set of groups using LISP to solve real problems, but the old prejudices of size and performance remain, so however hard these groups push, the result is that LISP is generally only used for prototyping.

LISP has unparalleled advantages over other languages – principally in its development time. A substantial program may take two people a few months to develop, whereas another language would require a bigger team and take longer, perhaps requiring two to five times as much effort. The resulting system need not even look like a LISP program: it could have been written in C or PASCAL as far as any of its users are concerned, so by cutting the time (and so the cost) of development it can be a very attractive language for niche applications where there is a small market and high development cost would make product development uneconomic.

One example of just such a niche application is *Syllabus* [Evertsz *et al.*, 1990] – a program to help schools construct timetables. This is a significant problem; every year a typical deputy head may spend six weeks locked away constructing a timetable, and without any guarantee that the result is consistent. Two people were able to develop a program for the Apple Macintosh to help in this process; it took a little over a person-year to build the program to the beta test stage, and then with the program's assistance constructing a timetable would typically take two days.

Syllabus was one of the first LISP applications to be delivered widely on standard hardware. At the time of its launch (1990), the minimal hardware configuration cost about £1000; today this would be about £400, or even less.

This is the kind of system LISP is ideal for. There isn't a very large market for this application, so the low development cost made the product viable. The application, however, is still valuable, and was competitive against existing products – even those which had been written in more conventional programming languages. Of course, the users of the system weren't aware of the choice of language, although some did ask; the human interface hid any evidence of the details of the underlying language anyway. All that mattered was that the program did the job.

Other LISP applications developed for use in industry are similar: applications that have fairly small markets, such as aircraft scheduling and design of analogue electronic devices, but which nevertheless are valuable tools within those markets. LISP makes the development of these products cost-effective in a way that other languages can't.

15.6 What is the future of Lisp?

New LISP dialects continue to be developed, each with a different intent. A whole bunch of dialects are currently going through the standardization process, although by far the most significant of these will be COMMON LISP and SCHEME.

Perhaps the most exciting prospect for the future is Apple's decision to define a new dialect: DYLAN [Apple, 1991]. This was motivated by the problems with COMMON LISP as an industrial language; Apple split their effort into two branches, the first concentrating on Macintosh COMMON LISP, and the second on DYLAN. The DYLAN dialect is a direct descendant of SCHEME, but incorporates an object system with the scope and style of CLOS and the consistency of SMALLTALK. All its functions, even the system primitives, are generic functions, and new methods can be written on them.

The intent behind DYLAN was to create a new, object-oriented but dynamic language which is attractive enough to entice C++ programmers to use it. Accordingly, the whole language has syntax which is closer to C++ than to traditional LISP, hopefully one more congenial to those who blanch at the sight of all those nested parentheses. Underneath, the whole power of LISP is available for rapid development. In fact, DYLAN is a language designed to be fast, small, without lots of parentheses, and to be used for developing conventional software applications – the antithesis of everything that LISP is supposed to be.

To give a hint of the correspondence between DYLAN and COMMON LISP, here is the DYLAN syntax definition equivalent to the factorial function shown on page 246:

```
define method fact (n)
   if (n = 1)
      1;
   else
      n * fact (n - 1);
   end if;
end method fact;
```

Apart from anything else, DYLAN sets out to overcome the criticisms of COMMON LISP as an industrial programming language: it is smaller, more consistent, and likely to be better in performance. Whether or not DYLAN will be a success isn't yet clear, although a strong industrial consortium has committed to its development. The signs of potential success are certainly visible, but much hangs on the first implementations and the acceptability of the alternative syntax to programmers familiar with more conventional languages.

15.7 Conclusion

McCarthy [1978] foresaw the obsolescence of LISP:

LISP will become obsolete when someone makes a more comprehensive language that dominates LISP practically and also gives a clear mathematical semantics to a more comprehensive set of features.

But then, many people, past and present, have said 'LISP is dead', or its equivalent, apparently without checking its pulse, and history hasn't borne out clear semantics or comprehensive features as the properties which are likely to determine the survival of any particular language. As LISP begins its fourth decade, a better conclusion might be that it is just maturing into a stately middle age.

And the LISP community shouldn't complain about the prejudices of people outside: this is the very force which encouraged the development of more practically useful dialects – the very force which will ensure the survival of LISP as a useful language. As Burney's character Dr Lyster went on to say, 'Yet this, however, remember: if to pride and prejudice you owe your miseries, so wonderfully is good and evil balanced, that to pride and prejudice you will also owe their termination.' Enough said!

Acknowledgements

Thanks to John Domingue, Marc Eisenstadt and Brian Meek for essential comments on the manuscript, and to Richard Gabriel for valuable insight into the differences in programmer performance between LISP and C/C++. Conjectures and errors remain all my own.

15.8 References

Abelson, H., Sussman, G. J. and Sussman, J. (1985), *Structure and Interpretation of Computer Programs*, MIT Press, Cambridge, MA.

Apple Computer Inc. (1991), *Dylan: An Object-Oriented Dynamic Language*, Apple Computer Inc., Cupertino, CA.

Clocksin, W. F. and Mellish, C. S. (1984), *Programming in PROLOG*, Springer-Verlag, Berlin, 2nd edition.

Evertsz, R., Dalgarno, M., Forster, G. A. and Watt, S. N. K. (1990), Syllabus: A Solution to the School Timetabling Problem, in *Proceedings of the First European Conference on the Practical Application of Lisp, Cambridge, UK*.

Kiczales, G., des Rivières, J. and Bobrow, D. G. (1991), *The Art of the Metaobject Protocol*, MIT Press, Cambridge, MA.

McCarthy, J. (1978), History of Lisp, *ACM SIGPLAN Notices*, **13**(8).

Nurminen, J. (1990), RFT Design System: Experiences in the Development and Deployment of a Lisp Application, in *Proceedings of the First European Conference on the Practical Application of Lisp, Cambridge, UK*.

Rees, J. and Clinger, W. (1992), *Revised Revised Revised Revised Report on the Algorithmic Language Scheme (R^4RS)*, AI Memo 848b, MIT AI Laboratory, Cambridge, MA.

Siskind, J. M. and McAllester, D. A. (1993), *Screamer: A Portable Efficient Implementation of Nondeterministic Common Lisp*, Technical Report IRCS–93–03, University of Pennsylvania Institute for Research in Cognitive Science.

Steele, Jr. , G. L. (1990), *Common Lisp: The Language*, Digital Press, 2nd edition.

Steele, Jr. , G. L. and Gabriel, R. P. (1993), The Evolution of Lisp, *SIGPLAN Notices*, **23**(3), 1–80.

Steele, Jr. , G. L. and Sussman, G. J. (1975), *An Interpreter for the Extended Lambda Calculus*, AI Memo 349, MIT AI Laboratory, Cambridge, MA.

Waters, R. C. (1989), *Optimization of Series Expressions, Part I: User's Manual for the Series Macro Package*, AI Memo 1082, MIT AI Laboratory, Cambridge MA.

Weinreb, D. and Moon, D. (1981), *Lisp Machine Manual*, MIT AI Laboratory, Cambridge, MA, 4th edition.

16 Programming and programming languages

Derek Andrews

The main foundation course of any computer science degree is the one that teaches programming. Unfortunately the issues of teaching programming and teaching a programming language are very much intertwined. This chapter will discuss a radical approach: realizing that the teaching of programming and the teaching of a programming language are different activities and, therefore, separating them. The issue of what language to teach first is similar to the choice of programming language for writing software. Issues of ease of development, simplicity of final code, and ease of maintenance should affect the choice more than issues of fashion and popularity.

Though this chapter concentrates on the choice of programming language for teaching, the issues behind the choice of language for teaching are similar to the choice of language for software development in industry – of course the final choice could be different, or the same.

In the second half-century of computing it is time to realize that programming should be taught before programming languages, that the choice of programming language need not be the main issue in the choice of syllabus for programming courses, and that there is a theory of programming. The main issue is: the teaching of programming and the teaching of a programming language are different activities.

There have been many attempts over the last 22 years to separate the two concerns of programming and programming languages, starting with [Dahl *et al.*, 1972] and continuing to this day. The many attempts to encourage a new approach to teaching the art of programming have had only a minor impact on the teaching of programming; perhaps the time has come to listen and to adopt the ideas. Some of the main contributions are listed in the bibliography; this chapter is another contribution to the debate.

16.1 Architecture is not laying bricks[1]

Because of the history of computing it is thought by many that writing code is programming. The introduction of first the online system, and then the microcomputer, both offering the possibility of direct 'hands-on' development of code, has exacerbated this problem. The software developer is encouraged to develop programs at a keyboard and screen – modern software tools encourage this approach, as witnessed by the sales of C development tools. If programmers are lucky enough to work for an 'enlightened' company they are provided with a complete program development environment including tools for writing, checking, debugging and managing code. Just as typing in text has very little (or nothing) to do with writing, coding a program has little to do with the art, or even science, of programming. Mathematical ideas have been applied to the problem of writing correct programs for over twenty years and this has produced techniques which can be applied by the average programmer to improve their programming ability.

It is worth considering again the standard parallel often quoted by teachers of computing: that of constructing a building – in the sense of building from concept to bricks and mortar. This activity is not usually started by just taking delivery of the component parts and then laying one brick on top of another, before the overall design of the building has been considered. Though those of us who live in modern houses may not believe this, some sort of design process has occurred and the result of this is used to drive the building process.

This particular analogy can be taken further. Early architects and stonemasons learnt by experience. They knew – usually by trial and error – that a particular set of strategies worked, so next time a similar building was constructed, the known strategies were used. Our early architects occasionally had major set-backs, for example, the cathedral at Chartres collapsed; it was larger than the last cathedral which had been built and unfortunately the techniques did not quite scale up to the bigger problem! The solution of course was to rebuild it using the existing strategies but extended to handle this 'larger' case. In programming one can see this technique reborn with the idea of defensive programming: the programmer doesn't quite know what is going to happen and so adds extra 'twiddly bits' to the code to deal with the unknown situations (which is more or less what the developers of the new cathedral at Chartres did). Unfortunately even the approach of the stonemason may not be used by a programmer: each new program is written from scratch, even strategies that are known to work are not used, each new 'building' is treated as a new problem.

It is rumoured that some early architects used mathematics to help design their cathedrals. In that period the mathematics that worked came from the Islamic world and, of course, was considered heretical and so had to be done in a 'dark corner' – perhaps these architects calculated the properties of their buildings before constructing them,

---

[1] Or: Programming is not writing programs

and thus would have some idea of their shape and strength before construction began. Today there is a small minority of programmers who use mathematics to develop their programs; where are the dark corners where they work to be found?

The main difference between architects of buildings and architects of computer systems is that if the former go wrong during the building process their result is a pile of rubble, for the latter the offending component is just modified. Imagine how different the history of architecture and civil engineering would be if it were possible to modify an offending part and then to have the edifice instantly rebuilt. Because engineers cannot afford to have a component fail they use the science of mathematics plus some well-established rules (strategies, experience) to help to construct buildings which do not fall down. Programmers should adopt a similar approach when building their programs.

The first software crisis occurred when computers were large and powerful enough to run programs that are bigger than one person can manage – a team of programmers that understood the development process needed to work together to produce a working computer system. Many such teams did not understand software development and the result was the first software crisis in 1968. It should be noted that the first microcomputers were about the same size and power as the old computers and the programs that ran on them were about the size that one person can manage. As microcomputers have increased in power, the lessons of writing large programs had to be learned for their full potential to be exploited. The fact that software development for microcomputers needs a team was discovered in 1984, and this led to a second software crisis. We are probably heading towards the third when the one-man programmer currently working on spreadsheet and database macros grows to a team of programmers that need to work together to develop such systems.

One point is clear from the history of programming, we are quite good at developing small programs, but terrible at writing large systems. A knowledge of the theory of programming would make us very good at writing small programs and could throw some light on the development of large systems that were correct.

Perhaps at present it is too much to expect programmers to learn all the necessary mathematics that forms the foundation of programming so that they can develop programs more effectively, but there is no reason why the teachers of programming should avoid understanding the theory of programming. It behoves us to learn the mathematical background to our subject and to extract some of the ideas to teach to the non-mathematicians amongst our students. Before teaching any specification, development, or programming techniques, the underlying mathematics should be fully worked out and understood. Too many of the program design and software development methods taught today have little or no mathematical background, or have one which has not been properly worked out.

This leads to two problems. First, the technique could be wrong, and second, when the sophistication of the people using the technique reaches a level where they wish to know the theory behind it so they can understand and use it more efficiently, they discover that this background does not exist – the cathedrals have been built on sand.

16.2 Programming versus programming languages

The previous section has tried, in perhaps a grand way, to intimate that there is a difference between architecture and bricklaying. There is a difference between programming and a programming language, thus there should be a difference between teaching programming and teaching a programming language. There is, of course, some overlap. It is difficult to teach programming without also teaching a programming language – we need to teach some sort of notation in which to express the results of the activity of programming, algorithms. This notation will have syntax (a description of the symbols that can be written down and the order in which they can be written) and semantics (what the symbols mean). Such a notation is usually called a programming language and since students will need to learn the discipline of both writing syntactically correct programs and semantically correct programs it is obvious that the programming language should be executable; the execution of an algorithm is an excellent initial test of its possible correctness – execution of a program is also necessary to address the notion of correctness through testing.

Teaching a programming language is a different activity from teaching programming and if the student already knows how to program and understands the basic ideas of programming it is a fairly straightforward activity to teach a new programming language. The first procedural or declarative or functional programming language is difficult to learn because as well as the actual language that has to be learnt there are also the program development (algorithm development) strategies that go hand in hand with the language. However, once the programming strategies are understood, learning the second language of one of these families is much easier because the student can relate their understanding to their existing knowledge. The first language to be learnt is usually difficult, the second language in the same family is easier; after that it really becomes a case of sitting down with a manual and learning what syntactic constructs are needed to express certain semantic ideas.

Before addressing the problem of teaching a foundation course in programming it is well worth writing down the objectives of such a course. Careful thought needs to be given to whether the course is mainly about algorithm development, or programming in the large, or programming in the small, or learning a programming language. Other objectives are possible but these are the main ones. These objectives are different but related. In fact it could be claimed that there is an order in which these topics need to be taught. First algorithm development, then programming in the small, and finally, programming in the large – learning a programming language is a separate activity and should be treated as such. Learning programming is the main activity, learning a language should be done *en passant*, a sort of 'oh, and by the way, this is how you express these ideas so you can run your program on a computer'.

16.3 Feed a person for a day or feed them for life[2]

A comment usually made by anyone involved with third-world problems is that if you give a man a fish you feed him for a day, but if you teach a man to fish you feed him forever. This comment should be taken into the context of education and training. Train-

---

[2] Or: Training versus education

ing is about giving a man a fish, education is about teaching a man to fish, and it is in the latter activity that universities should be involved. Before proceeding to discuss how to teach fishing, let us look at what fish can be used to practice on; or, if we are giving fish away, what fish can be presented. There is a wide choice of programming languages that could be taught; a possible (but definitely incomplete list) together with a brief reason for choosing each language, is given below.

PASCAL	Perhaps still the best teaching language – the language is almost small enough that as a teacher you may be forced to teach some algorithm development.
MODULA-2	Supports hiding and is powerful – standard MODULA-2 is large enough that you can teach all sorts of clever things like error recovery, initialization, cleaning-up and hiding, and can thus avoid algorithm development entirely.
MODULA-3	Even bigger and more powerful than MODULA-2 – even more opportunity to avoid teaching algorithm development.
BASIC	A good interactive version exists with access to windows; this will allow graphical user interfaces to be written. The student can be seduced into writing all sorts of user interfaces, and they will probably learn how to code without design by the well-known 'suck-it-and-see' approach.
COBOL	There are a large number of programs already written in this language which need maintenance.
FORTRAN	The 'standard' scientific language (but, perhaps, not any more).
APL	A small, concise language, ideal for calculations – what else do you want to do with a computer?
C	The standard language of today with weeks and weeks and weeks of clever tricks to teach.
C++	The standard language of tomorrow – even more clever tricks to teach.
OBERON-2	Small, elegant, concise, powerful – in order to fill a programming course it may even be necessary to teach some programming; however, given the windowing system it comes buried in, it may be possible to avoid this.
EIFFEL	Large, elegant, concise and powerful – the teacher can easily avoid teaching programming.
ADA	An elegant, powerful, language but with far too many features – thus these can be explained and programming avoided.

This list is not complete, but does contain the major languages which are readily available today. A conservative choice would be either COBOL or FORTRAN – the majority of the programs written in the world today are written in one of these languages and these programs need to be maintained; the usual statistic is that 80% of programming is about maintaining your old programs, thus a student knowing either one or both of these two languages could easily find a job. However, nobody would choose to teach COBOL as a first language: it can be dismissed as it is a large, 'messy', old-fashioned language. It can be dismissed on several grounds: the human mind can remember about thirty keywords, COBOL has a mere 500 to learn; its abstraction facilities are almost non-existent; it is verbose. Almost anybody could supply a list of good reasons why COBOL should not be taught. What about FORTRAN? Again, it could be said to be old fashioned, clumsy, and replaced by C – though it is worth looking at the latest FORTRAN, and if you remove or forget about those features that make it compatible with FORTRAN 88, it is in fact a rather modern, elegant, language; however, old prejudices die hard, so we will reject this one too.

Well, are there any other choices? What would be a radical choice? Many universities have made the statement that the only choice is C – this is not a radical choice but a backward-looking conservative one. It is modern, it is fashionable, it is the industry standard – students can easily get jobs writing C programs. Those who think C is modern should look at its history: it is based on a language called B, which is based on BCPL, which dates from about 1965. C is not a modern language, and does not even contain any of the ideas developed in the 1970s! There is probably a hidden agenda to the choice of C. Many of those who put C forward as the programming language to teach as the first language have as a reason that there are lots of clever tricks that can be taught, and the teacher can show how clever they are at expressing these tricks. Those who think that this is an unkind comment are asked to look at almost any textbook on C – most are nothing more than a catalogue of coding tricks, those that are not spend much time telling the students how to avoid the problem areas of the language.

One of the reasons why C is not a good language can be seen from the following example extracted from a textbook:

```
while(++size<20)
{
   foot = scale * size + offset
}
```

The textbook from which this example was taken asks the question: 'what is good about this approach?' and then goes on to state that this solution to a particular problem is more compact and gathers in one place the two processes that control the loop. Writing programs is not about writing compact programs, this is the job of the compiler, not the programmer, and 'gathering together in one place' should only be done if it makes intellectual sense.[3] More of this topic later.

If you are considering C and the above comments about its being old-fashioned are accepted, the only other choice is C++. This language is even more up-to-date, even more fashionable. It is the next industry standard. The need for people who can write C++ is tremendous – anyone who can program in C++ should have no difficulty in finding employment. But what exactly is C++? Well, for me it is C plus objects; it is about making silk purses from sows' ears! The average teacher of C++ probably doesn't really understand what exactly objects are, but they can do even more clever things. C++ allows hiding; this is a good thing – it is intellectually respectable, but it also has trapdoors that can be used to sneak through the brick walls that are there to provide the hiding mechanism. What more could a clever programmer want? There lots and lots and lots of clever things to teach, but none of these things are to do with programming. A further problem: what exactly are the semantics of C++?

---

[3] Increasing size is about establishing a variant and breaking the invariant, it is not about testing the completion of the loop!

The above debate is the wrong approach: the choice of programming language is driving the issue; it is not even about what fish to teach someone to fish for, it is a debate about what type of fish is to provide the meal of a day. The ultimate aim should be to teach programming in the large, programming in the small, and algorithm development.[4] What exactly is programming? Well, it is 'program solving', developing a program to solve a problem; and there are various aspects to this. If it is a large problem it is probably necessary to develop a system as the solution; so we can discuss programming as developing the architecture of a system, architecting the programs which make up this system, developing the algorithms that form the programs. We should be teaching the students abstraction, both data and control abstraction, and teaching them strategies for decomposition and hiding, both of which are to do with abstraction.

Surely we should teach our students how to fish, not just give them a fish? Therefore, as we are educating our students, there must be a theory behind what is being taught. This theory can either be given now or later; at the introductory level of teaching programming, it surely should be given later. It is perhaps an advanced topic, but the strategies and techniques we teach can be based on that theory even though the student may not be aware of it (the teacher of programming should be aware of the theory; if they are not they are trainers, not teachers – old dogs teaching new dogs old tricks). Consider an analogy: we teach engineers how to solve differential equations, we do not teach them all about continuity – that may or may not come later. The student may choose to understand what they are doing by taking an advanced course.

The usual technique of teaching a programming language is to teach the syntax and a ragbag of tricks, perhaps with some indication of the semantics of the language. The student is presented with a list of language constructs together with examples of their use and, if they are lucky, their semantics. The student is shown the *if-then-else* statement, the *for* statement, the *while* statement, the *repeat* statement, the *loop* statement, the *case* statement, the *goto* statement, the *exit* statement, and so on – each is explained. A list of properties, tricks and features is presented. What is the alternative? The alternative is to teach fishing, to teach algorithm development, to teach algorithm development based on a mathematical theory, so our cathedrals are not built on sand.

What is this theory? Well, there is a fairly elementary theorem to start off with, the teacher ought to know it, the students need not and perhaps should not. It goes as follows:

If $P \sqsubseteq Q$ and if F is continuous, then $F(P) \sqsubseteq F(Q)$

First of all, what is $\sqsubseteq$? It is about *satisfaction*, $P \sqsubseteq Q$ means that Q satisfies P or P is satisfied by Q; this needs to be explained. The first step is to realize that there is no difference between a specification and a program. Let us consider a specification:

Op
ext wr $w : W$
pre P
post Q

---

[4] It is assumed that algorithms make up small programs which make up large programs which make up systems.

A specification consists of a pre-condition P defining under which circumstances the program is supposed to work and a post-condition Q, which defines what the program does, together with a list of variables that can (or should) be changed to establish the post-condition. It is not necessary to teach Z or VDM-SL: pre-conditions and post-conditions can be written in English. A specification can be thought of as a possibly non-executable program, and a program can be thought of as an executable specification. We should try and forget the difference between these two aspects and think of them as just, well, specifications or programs, and use the words interchangeably. The difference between the two ideas is about execution. A specification can be economically executed in the mind and probably can't be executed (or can't be executed economically) on a computer. A program can't be executed economically in the mind, but probably can be executed economically on a computer – it is an economically executable specification. When we write $P \sqsubseteq Q$ we mean that if a customer is happy with the specification (program) P they will be happy with the program (specification) Q. The customer in fact can't tell the difference between P and Q: there is no test they can perform that will discern the difference between the two programs – or specifications, or program and specification.

What do we mean by the function F? Well, it means similar things to what is usually meant in mathematics, but instead of using operators like $+$ and $-$, we will use programming language constructs such as **if** ... **then** ... **else** ..., **while** ... **do**, the ';' combinator, function calls, *etc.* (there are some restrictions). It is best to think of $F(P)$ as a program that contains the program fragment P, and if we replace all instances of P by another program fragment Q then $F(Q)$ is also a program which in effect does the same thing as $F(P)$. This theorem is about composition, it is about re-use, it is about stepwise refinement: all of those activities that are about replacing one program fragment by another without changing the intent of the program.

What do we mean by the statement that F is *continuous*? Well, in terms of programming languages, roughly speaking it will mean that there is no possibility of side-effects – functions are functions are functions, they cannot and must not have side-effects. The main restrictions to enforce continuity are:

- no changing of global variables in functions; and

- no *pass-by-reference* – the only way you pass information to a function or procedure is by value.

The removal of side-effects also affects other aspects of a language; for example, if the programming language has a *for* statement, it should be simple, for example, like the *for* statement found in PASCAL. There are other constraints, but these are the main ones.

The main difficulty people would have with this is the restriction of no pass-by-reference; how do you get results back from a procedure? This is easy: the functions of the language are allowed to return multiple results. (There is in fact another parameter passing technique which is allowed; this is the ALGOL-W *pass-by-value-result*. However, with the possibility of functions returning multiple results there is no need for this.) We need to add to this fundamental theorem four concepts: sequence, selection, iteration and abstraction, together with the semantics of these concepts.

These are the ideas that should be taught on a programming course, and the programming language only gives support for these ideas. The four concepts turn up in control structures with the semi-colon being the equivalent of sequencing, the if-then-else statement being selection, the while statement being iteration, and the concept of procedure or function call for abstraction. In data structures these ideas turn up as the list or file sequence, the union (or the very unfortunate version in PASCAL, the variant record). Iteration, the record and abstraction embody the concept of a mapping which occurs in a very restricted way as the array. This theory and these ideas are about structured programming, they are about stepwise refinement, they are about code re-use, they are about abstraction, they are about algorithm development.

16.4 A programming language

How small can our programming language be? A possible choice is the small, simple language shown below, which is based on the programming language LEWD.[5]

dcl $x : X$ **in** A — Extend the state space with a new component named x of type X with an arbitrary initial value, then activate the statement A, and then retract the new component.

$x := E$ — Substitution: change the value denoted by x to the value of the expression E. Until further notice x has this new value – x denotes the value E.

$A; B$ — Sequencing: A and B are statements. Activate A, then activate B.

$p \rightarrow A$ — Guarding: p is a first-order predicate and A is a statement. Activate A in a state in which p is true. If p is false then we cannot activate A – our program will deadlock.

$p \mid A$ — Pre-conditioning: p is a first-order predicate and A is a statement. Activate A in a state in which p is true, otherwise do anything. The kindest thing we can do is **abort**.

$A \,\square\, B$ — Bounded choice: A and B are statements. Activate either A or B.

skip — Do nothing.

The priority of operators from low to high is:

low $\square$
        $\rightarrow$
        $;$
        $\mid$
high $:=$

Brackets can be used to turn a group of statements into the syntactic equivalent of a single statement.

One more major idea is needed: that of *totality*. All our constructs must be total, working for all possible inputs. Unfortunately guarding is not total, so we need two other constructs to make guarding total:

if A **fi** — Activate A until successful – keep looping until A is successful. (This construction is **if** ... **then** ... **else** in a clever disguise.)

---

[5] A Language by E. W. Dijkstra – also known as DTL (Dijkstra's Toy Language).

do A **od**   Activate A until not successful – keep looping until A is unsuccessful. (Just **while** ... **do** ... in a simple disguise.)

Totality is about the law of the excluded middle (see [Dijkstra, 1976] and [Morgan, 1990]).

It would also be useful to have a variant of the assignment statement – multiple assignment:

$$x_1, x_2, \ldots, x_n := E_1, E_2, \ldots, E_n$$

The semantics of this are straightforward: evaluate all of the expressions on the right-hand side and then assign the result to the variables on the left-hand side so that x_i is set to the value of expression E_i. These rules imply that all of the x_i are distinct and the evaluation of the right-hand-side expressions should have (as usual) no side-effects.

We also need datatypes: steal these from PASCAL (but at least replace variant records by unions); and functions and procedures: again steal these from PASCAL, but don't forget to add the restriction that there is only pass-by-value and to add the extension that functions can return multiple results *and must not have side-effects*. Note that (give or take a small technical point) all the above constructs are continuous!

A final construct that is needed is the specification statement, which can be stolen from VDM-SL [Jones, 1991; Dawes, 1991]:

ext rd $r : R$
    wr $x : X$
pre P
post Q

The pre-condition states what must be true in order for an operation to be defined and the post-condition defines the result of the processing that an operation carried out. The frame (the **ext** component) states what variables the operation can read, and what variables the operation can (and should) change.

16.5 A theory of program development

To develop executable code from a specification, the approach to be taken will be to break down the specification into smaller parts, each defining an easier problem. These easier problems are solved, and the resulting code is put together to produce a program that satisfies the original specification. Each of the smaller specifications is tackled in an equivalent way; these will, in turn, be broken down into even smaller specifications until we eventually reach a point where it is trivial to write the code that satisfies these specifications[6]. A further bonus will be that the techniques used to split specifications will provide the techniques to glue the code fragments together to give the final program (see Figure 16.1).

What is the 'glue' that will be used to join everything together? The 'glue' will be the

---

[6] If we were doing this in a theory of programming course some mathematical proofs would need to be done – nothing is obvious!

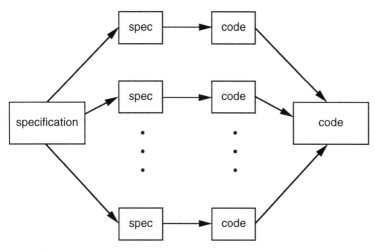

Figure 16.1   From specification to code.

programming constructs described above. Also, we will make adjustments to pre- and post-conditions without fundamentally changing the problem. These ideas will allow us to break down a single large specification into a smaller set of specifications that can be translated into code.

16.6 The rules of programming

The following rules could be expressed in terms of the little language above, and perhaps should be. But we shall stick to the more familiar *if-then-else* statement instead of the **if** ... **fi** and the *while-do* instead of the **do** ... **od**.

One of the arguments of this chapter is that we should teach problem solving and algorithm development to students and that both should be based on theory. What exactly is that theory? Well, it is straightforward, it is almost obvious – the mathematics is not difficult. Let's look at the rules of programming. The first of these rules is the equivalent specification rule:

$$\text{if} \left\{ \begin{array}{c} P \ \Rightarrow \ P' \\ P[w:=\overleftarrow{w}] \wedge Q' \ \Rightarrow \ Q \end{array} \right\} \quad \text{then}$$

ext wr w		**ext wr** w
rd r		**rd** r
pre P	$\sqsubseteq$	**pre** P'
post Q		**post** Q'

This allows us to change a specification. What it means is that we can widen a precondition, we can open up acceptable input for this piece of code, or whatever that we are specifying, the pre-condition may give a limit as to what it can do, this limit can be widened to allow more inputs. The original specification, for example, might say that w must be greater than or equal to zero. The new specification could say that any input value for w is acceptable. The second thing we can do is to narrow the post-condition. Typically a post-condition allows a choice; one of the things we can do is restrict this choice. One of the things we can do is restrict the choice to none. This, together with allowing any input, provides us with the most elegant and useful program that could ever be written. It is called *miracle* and has the following specification:

> *miracle*
>
> **pre true**
>
> **post false**

The program that satifies this specification is truly a miracle as it satisfies any specification! Fortunately it cannot be realized. We cannot write a program as an executable version of *miracle*. It is a non-executable program. We are lucky because if it could be written we would all be out of a job. One of things we must not do when changing our specification is introduce *miracle*, or worse, *miracle* in disguise. This is a technical problem which should be discussed in detail, perhaps in an advanced course. It need not worry us any more, except to say that a guarded command is a minor miracle – it provides an answer if the guard is **true**, otherwise it is *miracle*.

The next rule is about assuming the pre-condition in the post-condition:

$$
\begin{array}{ccc}
\textbf{ext wr } w & & \textbf{ext wr } w \\
\textbf{rd } r & & \textbf{rd } r \\
\textbf{pre } P & \sqsubseteq & \textbf{pre } P \\
\textbf{post } Q & & \textbf{post } Q \wedge P[w: = \overleftarrow{w}\,]
\end{array}
$$

This just means that the pre-condition is true and can be moved down to the post-condition providing we hook all the variables. It is really used for housekeeping when simplifying specifications.

The third of our rules is the assignment rule. This shows how a specification can be refined, can be satisfied by an assignment, and under which conditions this can be done:

$$
\begin{array}{ccc}
\textbf{ext wr } w & & \\
\textbf{rd } r & & \\
\textbf{pre true} & \equiv & w := E \\
\textbf{post } w = E[w: = \overleftarrow{w}\,] & &
\end{array}
$$

If we have a programming language in which all the constructs are continuous, the assignment statement has an interesting meaning. If we write $x: = E$ in our program it means from this point on we can replace all occurrences of x by E until further notice, up to and including the right-hand side of the next assignment statement that has x on the left-hand side. Except for the limitation about 'up to the next assignment statement' this is what functional programming is about. There is little difference between a continuous procedural language and a pure functional language. Semantically they are almost identical; thus the procedural versus functional argument is almost a non-argument when we are dealing with continuous languages.

Now we move on to the next rule, the first of the problem-solving rules. If in order to solve a problem, a (hopefully) easier problem can be found whose solution establishes an intermediate step M, then solving the initial problem to establish M and then

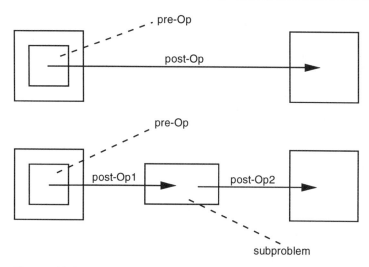

Figure 16.2   'Divide and conquer' used to establish a subproblem.

using M to get to the final solution is a good problem-solving strategy. This technique allows a large problem to be divided into smaller subproblems that can each be solved so that each contributes to the solution of the original large problem. This is depicted in Figure 16.2 in terms of the post-condition, post-Op, of an operation (the 'large' problem) being achieved by the post-condition that results in a subproblem, post-Op1, and the post-condition of the subproblem, post-Op2. The 'mid-rule' is an encapsulation of this strategy:

For any M that does not contain hooked identifiers other than $\overleftarrow{x}$

$$
\begin{array}{ccc}
 & & \textbf{ext wr } x \\
 & & \quad \textbf{rd } r, w \\
 & & \textbf{pre } P \\
\textbf{ext wr } w, x & & \textbf{post } M \\
\quad \textbf{rd } r & & ; \\
\textbf{pre } P & \sqsubseteq & \textbf{ext wr } w, x \\
\textbf{post } Q & & \quad \textbf{rd } r \\
 & & \quad \textbf{rd } c \\
 & & \textbf{pre } M[\overleftarrow{x} := c] \\
 & & \textbf{post } Q[\overleftarrow{x} := c]
\end{array}
$$

The rule involves introducing an extra variable c that cannot occur anywhere in the final code, but can be used in proofs.

A typical application of this rule might be that we are given a specification to satisfy, if we had a more restrictive, less general, stronger, pre-condition, it might be easier to establish the post-condition. We now have a subgoal, an intermediate step: to establish this more restrictive pre-condition. An alternative application of this rule might be to weaken the post-condition, that is, establish part of it. Now we have two problems: the first is to establish the weaker post-condition and the second is to establish the full post-condition from this weaker one. Either of these two approaches gives us a way of decomposing one large specification into two smaller ones. This is nothing more than traditional stepwise refinement, but with a mathematical rule to back it up! In each case the intermediate subgoal is defined by M.

The mid-rule can be extended when we know one of the components is assignment. The three rules shown in Figure 16.3 are really just special versions of the mid-rule. They show that if by doing an assignment part of a problem can be solved, then it is possible to calculate what is left of the problem to solve. This must have an effect on the way we think about programming sequences of statements; if it does not we are not teaching programming in a reasonable way. These rules are not needed for program development, but they do provide further understanding.

The following assignment rule:

$$
\begin{array}{ccc}
 & & \textbf{ext wr } w, x \\
\textbf{ext wr } w, x & & \textbf{rd } r \\
\textbf{rd } r & & \textbf{pre } P \\
\textbf{pre } P & \sqsubseteq & \textbf{post } Q[x := E] \\
\textbf{post } Q & & ; \\
 & & x := E
\end{array}
$$

The leading assignment rule – 1:

$$
\begin{array}{ccc}
 & & x := E \\
\textbf{ext wr } w, x & & ; \\
\textbf{rd } r & & \textbf{ext wr } w, x \\
\textbf{pre } P[x := E] & \sqsubseteq & \textbf{rd } r \\
\textbf{post } Q[\overleftarrow{x} := \overleftarrow{E}] & & \textbf{pre } P \\
 & & \textbf{post } Q
\end{array}
$$

where $\overleftarrow{E}$ is equivalent to $E[w, x := \overleftarrow{w}, \overleftarrow{x}]$

The leading assignment rule – 2:

$$
\begin{array}{ccc}
 & & x := f(y) \\
\textbf{ext wr } w, x, y & & ; \\
\textbf{rd } r & & \textbf{ext wr } w, x, y \\
\textbf{pre } P & \sqsubseteq & \textbf{rd } r \\
\textbf{post } Q & & \textbf{pre } P[y := f^{-1}(y)] \\
 & & \textbf{post } Q
\end{array}
$$

Figure 16.3   Three assignment rules.

The next rule is about selection; it is about domain partitioning (depicted in Figure 16.4). The problem has a domain in which the statement of the problem is valid. Can this domain be partitioned into two (or more) parts so that in one part of the domain

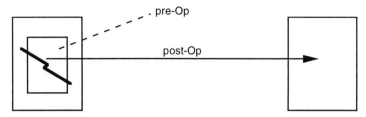

Figure 16.4   Case analysis – domain partitioning.

there is a smaller and easier problem to solve, and in the other part of the domain there is also an easier (and different) problem to solve? This is again a good problem-solving strategy and the selection rule encapsulates this:

$$
\begin{array}{l}
\textbf{ext wr } w \\
\quad \textbf{rd } r \\
\textbf{pre } P \\
\textbf{post } Q
\end{array}
\quad \sqsubseteq \quad
\begin{array}{l}
\textbf{if } cond \textbf{ then} \\
\quad \textbf{ext wr } w \\
\qquad \textbf{rd } r \\
\quad \textbf{pre } P \wedge cond \\
\quad \textbf{post } Q \\
\textbf{else} \\
\quad \textbf{ext wr } w \\
\qquad \textbf{rd } r \\
\quad \textbf{pre } P \wedge \neg\, cond \\
\quad \textbf{post } Q \\
\textbf{end}
\end{array}
$$

To apply this rule to a specification we need to discover some restriction to the pre-condition such that under that restriction the problem can be solved, that is, the post-condition can be established, and under the remainder of the pre-condition the problem can be solved (another way).

A third problem-solving strategy is, given a large problem, is it possible to iterate through a series of smaller problems that, when put together, solve the large problem? This is in fact the iteration rule:

$$
\begin{array}{l}
\textbf{ext wr } w \\
\quad \textbf{rd } r \\
\textbf{pre } P \\
\textbf{post } inv \wedge \neg\, guard
\end{array}
\quad \sqsubseteq \quad
\begin{array}{l}
\textbf{ext wr } w \\
\quad \textbf{rd } r \\
\textbf{pre } P \\
\textbf{post } inv \\
; \\
\textbf{while } guard \textbf{ do} \\
\quad \textbf{ext wr } w \\
\qquad \textbf{rd } r \\
\quad \textbf{pre } guard \wedge inv \\
\quad \textbf{post } inv \wedge (0 \le V < \overleftarrow{V}) \\
\textbf{end}
\end{array}
$$

where $\overleftarrow{V}$ is equivalent to $V[w: = \overleftarrow{w}]$

This rule involves understanding what an invariant is, what a guard is, and what a variant is. It is about understanding that certain things are not changed in the body of the loop, that we need to think about loop termination, and that we need to think about guards. All of this can be done informally with pictures: students do not need to know the mathematics, but can be shown diagrams and shown what the invariant is, what the guard is, what the variant is, and thus they can learn how to develop loops correctly.

It should also be noted that the body of a *while* loop can be solved by using one of the three semi-colon rules. Students can be taught to first establish the variant and then what needs to be done to re-establish the invariant (since establishing the variant normally breaks the invariant). This approach involves forward assignment. Students can be taught to extend the invariant and then establish the variant. This approach involves the trailing assignment rule. In all these cases students are being told to decompose large problems into smaller ones – this is how programming should be taught.

Missing from our list is the rule about abstraction. It really exists but has not been stated because it is a little bit more complicated and requires introducing even more notation than has been used so far.

A programme to teach formal methods within IBM found that participants who learnt that a program can be proved correct were influenced in the way they thought about programming: bugs are programmer errors.

Now we can discuss why languages such as C are so awful – most of the time *they are not continuous*! The language C is the worst offender – almost every one of its constructs encourages side-effects, the killer of continuity.[7] Let us look at the *for* statement in C:

```
n = 0; m = 0;
for (i = 1; i <= k; i++)
{
    k:= k+i; i:= k/2; m++; n=i+k
}
```

Note that we have a starting value, a step value, a final value and a guard. Notice that we can change the control variable in the body of the loop, we can change the step size in the body of the loop, we can change the upper limit during the body of the loop. There are side-effects everywhere, so continuity is lost. What do the refinement rules look like? Well, it is difficult! It could probably be worked out because the C for loop can be translated into a while loop and the semantics (rules) given in terms of this. The result would be complicated.

> **An aside** Many years ago I taught a programming language called PL/S which was IBM's version of C. In fact it was really C, but using a PL/I-like syntax. It had a *for* statement which was as powerful (complicated) as the one in C. One problem given to the students was ten examples, each of the style of the example given above; the students were asked how many times each loop was executed, and what were the values of variables on exit from the loop. After about twenty minutes they had usually managed to do two or three examples – all but a few got the wrong answers. The students were then asked what they had learnt. The normal answer was 'well, we think we understand how the for statement works'. My response was 'The obvious lesson to learn is not to write code that changes the loop control variables or expressions!' The effect of having a complicated

---

[7] One of the current 'magic bullets' is re-usable code; the first theorem states that we need continuity for code substitution, code re-use; C is not continuous ...

language such as C can be seen by the amount of effort used to write clever debugging and tracing tools so that the programmer can debug their C program. There is a better way – don't write any programs with programmer errors[8] in the first place.

16.7 Implications

Those who push for languages such as C and C++ misunderstand or forget that writing programs is more than just programming: the code that is produced at the end of the activity of programming must be maintained, must be managed, must be debugged, and must be understood. All of these things are difficult with many of the languages used today. In fact many of them seem to be designed to make these four activities difficult or almost impossible.

Part of a programming course should be to teach the students about these four items. A major part of the course should be on how to maintain code, improve it, add new features to it, and change it; how to fix programmer errors; how to test; how to manage the process, organize all of the files, and make certain that everything fits together properly; how to write code that can be understood by other people, because in real life it will have to be. It should also be noted that if you write a program and then have a good two weeks' holiday, when you come back, as far as that program is concerned, you are another person. You have probably forgotten the concepts, ideas and strategies that are entwined in the code, and as far as you are concerned it might as well have been written by somebody else.

16.8 A programme for teaching programming

So, what to teach? This problem should be approached like all good software engineering problems, and we should separate our concerns. It should be realized that we need to teach algorithm development, programming in the small, programming in the large, comparative languages, semantics, and theory of programming. Other things could be added to this list, but these are the main items. To carry out these activities, or at least the first four, we need a programming language. What are the requirements of this programming language?

In early programming languages control dominated the design of the language and thus how it and programming were taught; there was no concept of abstraction, for either control or data. Thus, programs written in these languages have low-level control dominating and data smeared all over the program – the examination of almost any FORTRAN or COBOL program will illustrate this. The pendulum has now swung too far in the opposite direction. The modern approach to data is that data abstraction is all important and control is to be forgotten; this can be seen in modern object-oriented languages where programs written in the language have all the data 'up-front', but control is smeared all over the program. There is a need to be able to write programs to match the problem, which may be data-dominated or control-dominated. Students should be taught that both data and control are important, and that which one dominates is to do with the problem, not the solution.

---

[8] 'Politically correct' term for bug.

Another question to be faced is the issue of objects: should the language support these? The answer to this is perhaps difficult to give. On the whole, objects should be part of programming: they should be a more advanced part, and it would be useful if the first language supported objects so that a new one did not have to be taught. Following on from this is the question 'What exactly are objects?'. The semantics of those languages which support and use objects are usually given by explaining how they are implemented – this is not how semantics should be explained. If objects should be taught they should be taught with abstract semantics which do not mention pointers, and entry points, or any of the other implementation strategies. This is perhaps another subject for discussion.

When selecting a language to teach, it is often suggested that a subset of a large, good language should be taught. Unless the selection of a subset is under the control of the compiler or tool-set there will be problems of students straying into uncharted parts of the language and getting what they think is an incorrect program to work. Subsetting a language in an industrial context also has its dangers; unless subsetting is properly policed, it would effectively mean 'different languages' would be used in different groups of a large project. Worse, the maintenance group are faced with different subsets of the same language.

Given these requirements, what is the list of good languages? Well, it is empty – a sad state of affairs after over fifty years of computing. What are its requirements? It should support each of the four basic ideas in both control structures and data structures: sequence, selection, iteration, and abstraction. All its components should be continuous – otherwise we cannot teach stepwise refinement properly. It should support hiding: this is a good concept – students should know about it right from the start. Other features are luxuries which students can learn when they have understood the basics.

If there are no good languages that can be taught, how about a list of not-so-bad languages? Here we can write down a short list: OBERON-2, LEWD, PRO (see [Hehner, 1984]), PASCAL (OBJECT PASCAL that is, one of the modern variants which supports units – in other words, hiding). Of these four, PRO is almost continuous; however, it is rather large and has some strange quirkiness which therefore causes it to be demoted from good to not-so-bad. LEWD is (probably) continuous but does not support hiding, which is why it has been demoted. OBERON-2 is small, but not continuous, hence it is here in this list of not-so-bad languages.

How about a list of bad languages that really should not be taught. Well, just about everything else: they are all dismissed because they are too big, too complicated, and only address one of many issues: C is designed to be written not read. ADA to be read, not written, and has too many ways of doing things, too many tricks, and too much function. The list of why they fail is long and obvious to the enlightened. However, the main reason they fail is that they all go out of their way not to be continuous!

Another, less obvious aspect of teaching programming v. teaching a programming language is the aspect of syntax v. semantics. Learning to program in a particular language is about learning the semantics of that language. The syntax is really just something that gets in the way: it is nothing more than a mechanism for expressing the semantics. Most (procedural) programming languages share semantics, but certainly do not share syntax. Most languages have examples of the standard control constructs and data types, and on the whole the semantics of the languages are very similar. Teaching programming and semantics with syntax in the background would probably give a much better understanding of programming. The difference between syntax and semantics needs to be understood.

Problems like this are still being perpetrated by 'professionals' – the drive to standardize the *syntax* of the XBASE language used in most database packages illustrates this point; it is still thought that by standardizing syntax it would be possible to interchange programs between the various packages!

Designers of both languages and programming courses should beware of the 'syntax is semantics' idea; in many modern programming languages there is the concept of a definition module (or package) and this is its specification. Associated with the definition module is an associated implementation module (package) that gives the implementation of the functions and procedures given in the definition. However, the definition module is only syntax, it is not semantics! A definition module should be an abstraction of the semantics of a module, and the implementation module should be the refinement of the definitions (see [Morgan, 1990]). All teachers of design and programming should also beware methods and ideas that are syntax without semantics – data-flow diagrams are a classic example of syntax without semantics, though attempts are being made to give them (formal) semantics.

The general lack of understanding of programming and programming languages can be seen in the design of some of the (so-called) 4GLs and in the design of macro languages for spreadsheets. Some of these are so appalling that it is difficult to believe they were designed by computer professionals; perhaps they were dreamed up by someone who had never actually programmed a computer before. In the design of most of the 4GLs, no thought whatever was given to what kind of features a database language should have. The elegant database query language SQL has been saddled with all sorts of ill-thought-out additions so that database applications can be written; the additions have little or nothing to do with the activity of programming but are just a set of new 'features' that are thought to be of some use.

When writing a course that teaches programming, one approach would be to write the course using text macros that expanded to some non-executable (non-existing) language that contained versions of the common, useful features of many of the procedural languages. This would allow the choice of programming language to be left for as long as possible. The programming language could be chosen when the course writer is happy about what is being taught and how it is taught. This approach could even avoid choosing a particular language for ever (see [Hehner, 1984], [Dijkstra, 1976] and [Gries, 1981] for examples of this approach).

Choosing a programming language before deciding on what should be taught is putting the cart before the horse. Students need to be given a set of paradigms, techniques, models and strategies that will last: programming in the small, programming in the large, concurrency, functional programming, system architecture, abstraction both of control and data. There is no single solution. Arguments about choice of language are missing the point: any arguments should be about what are the best programming tools to teach – 'syntax is not semantics' can be used to drive this discussion.

Different programming paradigms should be taught in programming languages that specialize in that paradigm. Object-oriented programming should be taught in a proper object-oriented language such as SMALLTALK, where it is difficult not to write in an object-oriented style. Concurrency should be taught in OCCAM which demands an understanding of concurrency. Straight procedural programming should be taught in PASCAL, the declarative style should be taught in PROLOG, and the functional style in MIRANDA or SCHEME. If this approach is taken it forces students to think about the paradigm. Adopting a language that supports several styles of programming (such as MODULA-3) will mean that students will just write in their favourite style – we all know of programmers who can write FORTRAN programs in any language (probably even PROLOG!).

16.9 Other courses

It can be argued that programmers do need to know C and C++; if they know how to program correctly they can be taught how to program in C, or better, how to program correctly in C. It can be argued that students need to know C++; if they know how to program they can be taught how to program in C++. The solution to this problem is to provide a course of comparative programming languages that compares the features of languages, what is good and what is bad, how they should be used, why the additional features are there, and why the language has not stuck with just the basic four ideas of sequence, selection, iteration and abstraction. Functional and declarative languages, objects, late versus early binding and its influence on language power and performance, would all be included in the comparison. By doing this you can provide students with the knowledge of a lot of languages and, more importantly, they will at the end of the course be able to learn almost any language fairly quickly. This means that we are taught how to fish, not given a fish and fed for a day.

A more advanced course could teach semantics, probably denotational but perhaps also relational. We could also teach the theory of program development based on both data and program refinements. All of these are much easier if the student already knows how to program properly. Finally, if courses are developed together carefully enough, during a course on comparative languages, a course on the theory of semantics, and a course on the theory of programming, the student will perhaps make the link and understand what they are doing. A further course to round things off would be a course on the development side of software engineering so students know how to design and develop large systems.

The idea of the additional courses is to separate concerns and build on the students' understanding of design, development and coding, obtained from a good introductory programming course.

16.10 Summary

The bibliography of this chapter consists of those books and papers that are required reading of all who educate programmers. Those who just train programmers can continue in their ignorance – hopefully not working in a university. There is a theory of programming, and any introductory course should build on this theory. The ideas can be left behind the scenes, but they should be there. The students do not need to know the theory, but one day the students who have learnt programming the correct way may choose to take a theory of programming course and spend the whole time understanding what they have been taught – a sort of 'so that's were that idea came from' understanding. Anyone who teaches programming should have some insight – all teachers of programming should have read at least [Dahl *et al.*, 1972] and [Dijkstra, 1976]. An informal idea of the theory of programming can be obtained from [Andrews and Ince, 1991] and the full theory from [Morgan, 1990]. Perhaps a programming course should be based on either [Gries, 1981] or [Latham *et al.*, 1990].

The main thrust of this chapter has been to state that the teaching of a programming language should be separated from the other aspects of software development:

- We don't teach a programming language, but we teach how to program.
- We don't teach a programming language, but we teach how to solve problems.
- We don't teach a programming language, but we teach how to design systems.
- We don't teach a programming language, but we teach the *principles* of programming languages.
- We don't teach a programming language, but we teach a theory of semantics.
- We don't teach a programming language, but we teach the theory of programming.

The main realization is the first point: we need to teach our computer scientists how to program!

16.11 References

Andrews, D. and Ince, D. (1991), *Practical Formal Methods with VDM*, International Series in Software Engineering, McGraw-Hill, London.

Dahl, O. J., Dijkstra, E. W. and Hoare, C. A. R. (1972), *Structured Programming*, A. P. I. C. Studies in Data Processing, Academic Press, London.

Dawes, J. (1991), *The VDM-SL Reference Guide*, Pitman, London.

Dijkstra, E. W. (1976), *A Discipline of Programming*, Series in Automatic Computation, Prentice-Hall, Englewood Cliffs, NJ.

Gries, D. (1981), *The Science of Programming*, Springer-Verlag, New York.

Hehner, E. C. R. (1984), *The Logic of Programming*, International Series in Computer Science, Prentice-Hall, Englewood Cliffs, NJ.

Jones, C. B. (1990), *Systematic Software Development Using VDM*, International Series in Computer Science, Prentice-Hall, London, 2nd edition.

Latham, J. T., Bush, V. J. and Cottam., I. D. (1990), *An Introduction to VDM and Pascal*, International Computer Science Series, Addison-Wesley, Wokingham.

Morgan, C. (1990), *Programming from Specifications*, International Series in Computer Science, Prentice-Hall, Hemel Hempstead.

16.12 Appendix – Suggested glossary of programming terms

Some terms you might like to think about, below, make the start of a glossary which should be part of a course on programming. The idea is, as usual, to try and change attitudes. (This is a sort of political correctness for programming terms: less extreme, but still with the intent of changing attitudes for the better.)

a function	a piece of program to produce result – can only be used in expressions; cannot have any side-effects.
a procedure	a piece of program to carry out some activity – cannot be used in expressions; may have side-effects.
a value-returning procedure	a piece of program to carry out some activity and return a result – cannot be used in an expression, but can be used on the right-hand side of certain types of assignment statements. May have side-effects. Most programming languages incorrectly called these 'functions'.
a *for* statement	a statement that allows the reader of a program to deduce statically how many times the body of the *for* loop will be executed. Equivalent to concatenating the statements of the body together that many times. The number of times can be calculated at run time, but is known before execution starts, and doesn't change.
a *while* statement	a statement that warns the reader of a program that the number of times the body will be executed will be determined at run time during the execution of the statement. Will come with an invariant and a variant.
a *repeat* statement	a statement type no longer found in modern programming languages; tended to cause errors because the body was always executed at least once, even when it shouldn't have been.
a *case* statement	another obsolete statement type deriving from the machine-code branch table.
a default	popular way of saving work in the 1960s and 1970s, the ultimate application being in PL/I where defaults allowed meaningless programs to run and produce results.
a programmer error	in the old days, this used to be called a bug – now correctly called what it is.

17 VDM-SL as a prelude to a language

C. Pronk and P. G. Kluit

The introduction to programming and programming languages at the Faculty of Mathematics and Informatics at Delft University of Technology was changed in 1990 from a classical set-up to a set-up based upon the early introduction of a formal method (VDM-SL) and the systematic transformation of formal specifications into MODULA-2. The intention has been to create a cohesive sequence of courses during which students are trained to reason in an abstract way about specifications and programs. This chapter gives a short overview on the contents of these courses and reports on our experiences so far.

17.1 Introduction

Teaching a sound way of developing programs and teaching a first programming language have always been closely interrelated. The consequence has been that both teachers and students experienced difficulties abstracting from the details of the programming task while developing skills for abstract reasoning about programs and specifications. We present here a set-up trying to remedy that problem by giving the students an early introduction to a formal specification language before they are introduced to a programming language. The formal language we use is named S*pe*L and is a subset of VDM-SL [Dawes, 1991].[1] We use MODULA-2 [Wirth, 1985; King 1988] as our programming language.

Our new courses were introduced during a complete revision of the first and second year's curriculum which became effective in 1990. In this section the old and new courses will be described. Subsequently some constraints on the development of the new courses will be given and in section 17.3 we will give a detailed description of the programming paradigm we use. A short overview of the characteristics of SpeL and MODULA-2 will be given in section 17.4. In section 17.5 an example will be shown to further elucidate our way of teaching prior to a description of our experiences and our overall conclusions.

17.1.1 History

Before 1990 the curriculum was based upon a classical set-up. A first course named Introduction to Programming (35 hours' of teaching, 60 hours' practicals) was devoted to an introduction to PASCAL up to the level of recursion, procedures with **var** parameters and pointers.

In a second course called Data Structures and Algorithms (35 hours' of teaching, 40 hours practicals) the construction and use of data structures like stacks and queues was emphasized, together with the notions of procedure and data abstraction. Following that, searching, sorting and backtracking algorithms were developed, together with a limited notion of correctness.

A third course called Software Engineering (21 hours of teaching, 80 hours' practicals) was split in two parts. The first half concentrated on software development paradigms and costing models. The second part consisted of an introduction in a subset of VDM-SL. During the practicals, students were asked to develop a VDM-SL specification for a problem and then develop a PASCAL program from that specification. VDM-SL was used as a design notation; no use was made of the *method* in VDM, nor of any proof system.

Several problems were identified with this set-up:

- the impossibility of constructing proper abstract data types using PASCAL,

- the difficulty of raising the level of abstraction during program development in the second and third courses.

A new course set-up should handle both problems but should, in particular, introduce the notion of abstraction in an early stage.

17.2 Requirements analysis for a new method

As explained in the previous section, a new course should use both a 'method' for program development and another language for programming activity. The method should be systematic, scalable and motivating; the language should be imperative.

---

[1] SpeL, apart from being an acronym for specification language, is also a Dutch word for 'game'.

Systematic and scalable

The programming task going with an introductory course does not require a real *method* to be followed. The student typically stares at the ceiling and then types `begin`. Unfortunately this 'method' does not lend itself to large-scale program development and moreover as a 'method' it is addictive. In the next phase of a programming course, programs become more difficult, and tools for mastering complexity (stepwise refinement, procedural abstraction) are offered. Unfortunately, students seem to be very much attached to their 'method', such that they are very reluctant to change their habits for what they perceive as only a small increment in complexity. During the course on software engineering this little history repeats itself when data-flow diagrams and structure charts are introduced.

Motivation

Many students are highly motivated to type in programs and consider the debugging of their programs as a kind of adventure game. Any method requiring 'preparatory thinking' in order to reduce the dependency on the art of debugging is well known to reduce the student's motivation. It is a paradox in teaching programming that the presence of a keyboard highly motivates the student, but at the same time reduces the quality of the program composed. As the faculty is paid on a per-student basis, apart from improving teaching, motivating the student is an important means of increasing yield without compromising on quality.

Imperative language

A constraint put upon the developers of the new course is that such a course should result in students being able to program in an imperative language. Of course, in an idealistic mood we say 'within five years from now imperative languages will be obsolete' but then we are put on solid ground again when one of our colleagues from one of the technical faculties asks why we aren't teaching FORTRAN or C.

17.3 Design model

The basic framework on which our method is based is called the RFI model, RFI standing for requirements, formal specification and implementation. A pictural description of the framework is given in Figure 17.1.

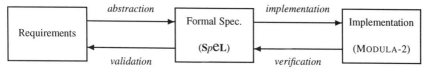

Figure 17.1   The development paradigm.

In essence, the meaning of the model is that between the informal requirements and the implementation an extra phase is needed during which a formal specification of the requirements is to be constructed.

17.3.1 Requirements analysis

The analysis of the user's requirements and the construction of a 'Software Requirements Document' [Fairley, 1985] is not part of the course. Obtaining such requirements is well known to be far from trivial. We therefore assume complete, consistent
and non-ambiguous requirements being available, albeit formulated using natural language. We realize ourselves that there is a kind of contradiction in the previous sentence,
together with some optimism. We use that contradiction to explain to our students the
value of having formal specifications.

17.3.2 Specification and abstraction

A formal specification consists of denotations for data and algorithms. Specifications
for data describe their abstract form, not the implemented structure. Specifications for
procedures describe *what* a procedure does, and hide *how* it does it. Such a specification acts as a contract between the user and the implementor of such a procedure, a
contract describing the circumstances under which the procedure may safely be called
(pre-condition) and the effect of the procedure (post-condition). Obtaining such a formal specification requires an abstraction activity during which irrelevant details are
omitted. We assert that this activity in particular contributes to the overall success of
our new course.

17.3.3 Implementation

Implementing a formal specification (expressed in **SpeL**) in an imperative language
(**MODULA-2**) sometimes requires several steps to be taken. During each step a reification takes place; the final step will lead to an executable program. Each reification
step can be verified by formal means. During our teaching, the number of reification
steps seldom exceeds two. Formal verification is shown only a few times. Extensively
discussed, however, are the so-called abstraction and representation functions given
formally in Figure 17.2. We ask the students to write down these functions during exercises.

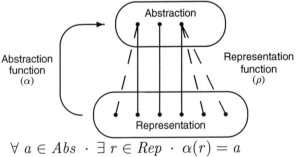

$$\forall\, a \in Abs \, \cdot \, \exists\, r \in Rep \, \cdot \, \alpha(r) = a$$

Figure 17.2   Abstraction and representation functions.

17.4 The new course

The courses developed for the new curriculum concentrate on early development of abstraction and the use of a single formal notation in the first- and second-year courses. A short overview of these courses will be given in the following subsections.

17.4.1 Programming-1

The first course, named Programming-1 (56 hours of teaching, 30 hours' practicals) starts with a short introduction on the essence of problem solving by programming. An introduction to formal notations (EBNF, syntax diagrams) and an explanation of the difference between syntax and semantics are given. The material then develops in two directions. The first direction is data types: numeric types, booleans and characters are introduced, followed by enumerations, subtypes and product types. The other direction is complexity of algorithms: simple recursive and iterative algorithms are introduced.

It is a characteristic of our course that almost no attention is being paid to syntactic details. Having been exposed to EBNF using examples from SpeL and MODULA-2 students are able to master such details themselves. They develop the necessary skills during practicals.

The introduction of the imperative features of MODULA-2 is done using an abstract model of a machine consisting of:

- an *evaluator* for calculating expressions;
- an *executor* for doing statements;
- an *environment* in which the maplets {identifier $\mapsto$ value} are registered; and
- an *agenda* containing a sequence of statements to be executed.

Developing algorithms is based upon the following strategy. Starting from an implicit specification using SpeL we search for a more explicit one (again in SpeL). This specification is transformed into a tail recursive one using accumulating parameters which is then converted to an imperative program in MODULA-2.

Programming-1 then continues with the introduction of the notion of state and operations on the state using pre- and post-conditions. During this stage their MODULA-2 equivalents, PROCEDURES and VAR parameters, are introduced. Following that, an introduction to sets, sequences and maps is given using SpeL. Their implementation in MODULA-2 is hardly discussed here; the most that can be said is that there is insufficient support in MODULA-2 for sets. For practice we offer a DEFINITION MODULE Sets containing applicable operators.

17.4.2 Programming-2

In this course (42 hours of teaching, 70 hours' practicals) the programming paradigm sketched in section 17.3 is developed. Dynamic data structures and pointers are introduced using SpeL. The course concludes with the development of ADTs and algorithms for queues, stacks and backtracking similar to a conventional CS2 course. However, as all of the development starts with SpeL, all course material had to be developed from scratch.

17.4.3 Software engineering

In teaching Software Engineering, $SpeL$ is further developed and compared to other formal and informal specification methods. During practicals students first develop a system using data-flow diagrams and Teamwork.Their second task is the transformation of a $SpeL$ specification into a working MODULA-2 program. The typical level of $SpeL$ used here is as in [Jones, 1990].

17.4.4 Other courses

The subject matter developed so far is used in other courses. The first-year course in Theoretical Informatics uses the same notation for the construction of proofs and the second-year course Introduction to Programming Languages, for which we use the books by Watt [1990, 1991], starts with the now-familiar notations for product types, union types, sets and powersets.

17.5 The Open University workshop problem

In this section we will both introduce our subset of VDM-SL, and use that subset to present our solutions to the Open University workshop problem. $SpeL$ and VDM-SL are such large languages that they cannot be covered in this chapter. Moreover, not all features of $SpeL$ are needed in the OU example.

The second part of this section will show how a $SpeL$ specification can be translated into MODULA-2. We will refrain here from presenting the Stack problem; such a presentation can be found in almost any textbook on VDM-SL [Andrews and Ince, 1991; Dawes, 1991; Jones, 1990; Woodman and Heal, 1995].

17.5.1 $SpeL$

Types

In this section we specify the types, state and operations needed for the workshop problem.

The simple data types in $SpeL$ are the numeric types, booleans, characters and enumerated types. Using type invariants we may construct (almost) arbitrary subtypes of a given type. Furthermore, types may be combined with the union construction.

$$Hours = \mathbf{N}$$

$$\mathbf{inv}\ h \triangleq h < 24$$

$$Minutes = \mathbf{N}$$

$$\mathbf{inv}\ m \triangleq m < 60$$

$$Day = \text{SEPT29} \mid \text{SEPT30}$$

SpeL has two different Cartesian product types: *records* (with named fields) and *products* (with unnamed fields). Students tend to mix these constructs up (both are mapped to records in MODULA-2), so we prefer to restrict ourselves to records. Selection of components for both constructs can be done using pattern matching. For records we have the usual field-selectors as well.

$$Time0 = Hours \times Minutes$$

$$Time :: hours \quad : Hours$$
$$minutes : Minutes$$

$$Timeslot :: date \ : Day$$
$$begin : Time$$
$$end \ : Time$$

inv $mk\text{-}Timeslot(\text{-}, mk\text{-}Time(bh, bm), mk\text{-}Time(eh, em)) \ \triangleq$
$bh < eh \lor (bh = eh \land bm < em)$

$$Timeslot0 :: date \ : Day$$
$$begin : Time0$$
$$end \ : Time$$

inv $mk\text{-}Timeslot0(\text{-}, mk\text{-}(bh, bm), time) \ \triangleq$
$bh < time.hours \lor (bh = time.hours \land bm < time.minutes)$

(Of course *Timeslot0* is a crazy type, but it serves to illustrate pattern matching and field selection.)

Next, SpeL has structured types of non-constant size: (finite) sets, (finite) sequences and maps. Maps are partial functions with finite domain. Sequences are indexed, so their recursive nature is a bit hidden. The selectors *head* and *tail* are provided, however.

$$Text = \mathbf{char}^* \text{ — dit is commentaar}$$

$$Person :: name \quad : Text$$
$$affiliation : Institution$$
$$etc \quad : \ldots$$

$$Institution = Text$$

$$Presentation :: presenter : Person$$
$$subject \quad : Text$$
$$title \quad : Text$$

$$Scheduled :: chair : Person$$
$$when : Timeslot$$

$$Schedule = Presentation \xrightarrow{m} Scheduled$$

> **inv** $sch \triangleq$
> $\forall pres \in \textbf{dom}\ sch \cdot pres.presenter \neq sch(pres).chair$

Functions

SpeL contains a functional language as a subset.

> $Before : Time \times Time \to \textbf{B}$
>
> $Before\ (b, e) \triangleq$
>   **let** $mk\text{-}Time(bh, bm) = b$ **in**
>   **let** $mk\text{-}Time(eh, em) = e$ **in**
> $bh < eh \lor (bh = eh \land bm < em)$

> $Disjoint : Timeslot \times Timeslot \to \textbf{B}$
>
> $Disjoint\ (ts1, ts2) \triangleq$
>   **let** $mk\text{-}Timeslot(day1, begin1, end1) = ts1$ **in**
>   **let** $mk\text{-}Timeslot(day2, begin2, end2) = ts2$ **in**
> $(day1 \neq day2) \lor Before(end1, begin2) \lor Before(end2, begin1)$

Using the function *Disjoint* we could (and should) add to the invariant of the *Schedule* the fact that different presentations should have disjoint timeslots.

Functions may be specified implicitly as well (using pre- and post-conditions).

The function *Schedulist* makes a list (sequence) of presentations, in the order of *Timeslot*.

> $Select : Schedule \times Day \to Schedule$
>
> $Select\ (sch, d) \triangleq$
> $\{p \mapsto sch(p) \mid p \in \textbf{dom}\ sch \cdot sch(p).when.date = d\}$

> $Sort\ (sch : Schedule)\ plist : Presentation^*$
> **pre** $\forall p1, p2 \in \textbf{dom}\ (sch) \cdot p1 \neq p2 \Rightarrow$
> $Disjoint(sch(p1).when, sch(p2).when)$
> **post elems** $plist = \textbf{dom}\ sch\ \land$
>   **len** $plist = \textbf{card dom}\ sch\ \land$
> $\forall i, j \in \textbf{inds}\ plist \cdot$
> $i < j \Rightarrow$
> $Before(sch(plist(i)).when.begin, sch(plist(j)).when.begin)$

> $Schedulist : Schedule \to Presentation^*$
>
> $Schedulist\ (sch) \triangleq$
> $Sort(Select(sch, \text{SEPT29})) \frown Sort(Select(sch, \text{SEPT30}))$

State

SpeL has a notion of state and operations (changes of the state). This notion will be used here to model the workshop as a whole.

state *Workshop* **of**
    attendees : *Person*-**set**
    schedule   : *Schedule*

  inv *mk-Workshop*(*atts*, *sch*) $\triangleq$
    $\{pers \mid mk\text{-}Presentation(pers, \text{-}, \text{-}) \in \textbf{dom } sch\} \subseteq atts \land$
    $\{ch \mid mk\text{-}Scheduled(ch, \text{-}) \in \textbf{rng } sch\} \subseteq atts$

  init *mk-Workshop*(*atts*, *sch*) $\triangleq$ ...
end

The invariant on the state assures that all persons known are attendees.

This is not a very good model. A presentation may only be added if both the timeslot and the chair are known. It is more likely that we start with presentations and later on assign a timeslot and (separately) a chair to it.

In fact, presentations are organized in sessions, and chairs are assigned to sessions. If we strictly specify things this way, however, we lose too much freedom: imagine someone only chairing half of a session because they have an appointment with their dentist during the other half.

The following model is better.

state *Workshop* **of**
    attendees   : *Person*-**set**
    presentations : *Presentation*-**set**
    chair   : *Presentation* $\xrightarrow{m}$ *Person*
    when   : *Presentation* $\xrightarrow{m}$ *Timeslot*

  inv *mk-Workshop*(*atts*, *press*, *chair*, *when*) $\triangleq$
    $\textbf{dom } chair \subseteq press \land$
    $\textbf{dom } when \subseteq press \land$
    $\textbf{rng } chair \subseteq attendees \land$
    $\{pers \mid mk\text{-}Presentation(pers, \text{-}, \text{-}) \in press\} \subseteq atts \land$
    $(\forall pr1, pr2 \in \textbf{dom } when \cdot$
        $pr1 = pr2 \lor Disjoint(when(pr1), when(pr2))) \land$
    $\forall presentation \in \textbf{dom } chair \cdot$
        $\textbf{let } mk\text{-}presentation(presenter, \text{-}, \text{-}) = presentation \textbf{ in}$
        $presenter \neq chair(presentation)$
end

We consider the possibility of abstract reasoning about such specifications as one of the big assets of our course.

Operations

The state is changed using operations. Assigning a timeslot to a (known) presentation:

    AssignTimeslot (*pr* : *Presentation*, *ts* : *Timeslot*)
  ext wr *when* : *Presentation* $\xrightarrow{m}$ *Timeslot*
    rd *presentations* : *Presentation*-**set**
  pre *pr* $\in$ *presentations* $\land$
    $\forall occupied \in \textbf{rng}\,(\{pr\} \triangleleft when) \cdot Disjoint(ts, occupied)$

$$\textbf{post } when = \overset{\textstyle\frown}{when} \dagger \{pr \mapsto ts\}$$

In VDM-SL operations may be defined explicitly using statements. In S*pe*L operations can be specified only implicitly, using pre- and post-conditions.

In VDM-SL implicitly defined operations may be composed by quotation of post-conditions. This technique is absent in S*pe*L. We accept the loss of abstraction levels resulting from that simplification.

Algorithmics

As mentioned before, S*pe*L has no statements (VDM-SL has). Therefore the only way to describe algorithms explicitly is using a functional style. As the implementation language (MODULA-2) is imperative there may be a substantial gap between specification and implementation of an algorithm.

We decided to have no higher-order functions in S*pe*L in order not to widen this gap. This decision, however, substantially diminishes the expressive power and means of abstraction of the language.

Under the rug

In S*pe*L, functions may have a pre-condition, that is, they may be partial. We do not pay too much attention to the logic of partial functions, however.

Implicit specifications and pattern matching introduce loose specification. We do not pay too much attention to that phenomenon either.

Why SpeL?

It became clear quite early in the development of the courses that approaches based on pure functional or algebraic languages would not meet our constraints and that only model-oriented languages like VDM-SL or Z would be considered. VDM-SL was chosen because some of the staff members already had considerable experience using that language and were taking an active part in its standardization.

17.5.2 Implementation and Modula-2

The implementation of simple types and record types is straightforward.

Implementation of subtypes using type-invariants is absent in MODULA-2. In simple cases we may obtain what we want using a subrange type:

```
CONST
    maxhour   = 23;
    maxminute = 59;
TYPE
    Hours     = [0..maxhour];
    Minutes   = [0..maxminute];
    Day       = (sept92,sept30);
    Time      = RECORD
                    hours   : Hours;
                    minutes : Minutes;
                END;
    Timeslot  = RECORD
```

```
        date  : Day;
        begin : Time;
        end   : Time;
    END;
```

Simple explicit function specifications can be transformed into MODULA-2 functions in a straightforward way.

```
PROCEDURE Before(t1,t2 : Time): BOOLEAN;
  BEGIN
    RETURN (t1.hours < t2.hours) OR
           ((t1.hours = t2.hours) AND (t1.minutes < t2.minutes));
  END Before;
```

Explicit function definitions involving quantifiers may be non-constructive. Implicit function definitions almost always are non-constructive. In both cases we have to design an algorithm before we can write an implementation in MODULA-2.

The structured types of non-constant size cannot be implemented in MODULA-2 in a straightforward way (MODULA-2 has a set type, but with very severe restrictions). The module-system of MODULA-2 allows us to hide this problem giving a DEFINITION MODULE for an abstract data type.

```
DEFINITION MODULE Schedules;

   FROM PresSets IMPORT ...;
   FROM SchSets  IMPORT ...;

   TYPE Schedule  =  ... ;

   PROCEDURE NewSchedule(): Schedule;
   PROCEDURE UnitSchedule(d: Pres; r: Sch): Schedule;
   PROCEDURE UnionSchedule(m1, m2: Schedule): Schedule;
   PROCEDURE OverrideSchedule(m1, m2: Schedule): Schedule;
   PROCEDURE ApplySchedule(m: Schedule; d: Pres): Schedule;
   PROCEDURE RestrictbySchedule(s: PresSet; m: Schedule): Schedule;
   PROCEDURE RestricttoSchedule(s: PresSet; m: Schedule): Schedule;
   PROCEDURE DomainSchedule(m: Schedule): PresSet;
   PROCEDURE RangeSchedule(m: Schedule): SchSet;

END Schedules.
```

The operation *AssignTimeslot* is now easily implemented:

```
VAR when : Schedule;
PROCEDURE AssignTimeslot(pr : Presentation; ts : Timeslot);
  (* ext wr when *)
  BEGIN
    OverrideSchedule(when,UnitSchedule(pr,ts));
  END AssignTimeslot;
```

Why Modula-2?

Reasons for choosing MODULA-2 as the programming language include the following:

- It is possible to construct ADTs and a module system featuring separate compilation.

- Strong typing allows early detection of errors.
- MODULA-2 is only a small step in teaching complexity from PASCAL.
- There is a wide choice of compilers for MODULA-2, both on professional workstations and on PCs.

Other candidates (ADA, EIFFEL) have been rejected as they cause a substantial overhead on teaching and/or machine processing power. Of course, several aspects of MODULA-2 such as local modules, coroutines and low-level access to the machine are not discussed.

17.6 Experiences

During the development of the course material the following – not unexpected – problems came up:

1. Educational problems:

    - As the element types of sets are not restricted to basic types in *Sp*eL there are problems mapping the more complex types onto MODULA-2. Solutions have to be found on an individual basis. Implementing sets (*etc.*) of different types would require genericity – a feature missing from MODULA-2.
    - Proper use and explanation of opaque types requires the explanation of pointers – a coupling that is unwanted.

2. Technical problems:

    - During the development process the VDM-SL syntax was not yet stable. This resulted in some changes to *Sp*eL.
    - As the VDM-SL changed, the LaTeX macros obtained from the British National Physical Laboratory [Dickinson] changed. This resulted in a somewhat different layout in the course material.
    - Beforehand, it was unclear which VDM-SL subset would be needed. The subset we use now has grown slowly.

These problems have largely been solved.

The effort students are willing to spend in order to actively master *Sp*eL seems insufficient. An important point is that students consider MODULA-2 as a serious language (because it is executable) whereas *Sp*eL is considered as a hypothetical language (because it is not). Although we (the teachers) are perfectly happy with a paper-and-pencil specification language, we feel that the availability of an interpreter or compiler for *Sp*eL would greatly enhance the students' motivation in the use of *Sp*eL. At the moment several implementations of subsets of VDM-SL exist. What we need, however, is a reliable and student-proof PC implementation of (a subset of) *Sp*eL. The only way to create such an implementation seems to be constructing it ourselves. The main problems here are the size and complexity of the language (even of our subset!). An important issue is the use of more than one syntax in VDM-SL. The *ISO 646 concrete syntax* which is needed for tool support differs in several aspects from the *mathematical concrete syntax* which is used in the written course material. For first-year students the use of more than one syntax is a serious problem.

17.7 Conclusion

At the time of writing it is slightly too early to provide a full conclusion on the project. A preliminary conclusion falls into two sections: experiences of the staff and those of the students.

Development of the new courses has been a challenging task to the university staff. Several new problems of developing motivating teaching material have been successfully solved. The construction of a mechanical checker of S*p*eL-specifications and a prototyping facility still need much attention. The development of the course material has taken up more time than expected, partly because of the need to have people with different backgrounds converging to a common view on specifications and programming.

It can't be denied that students have difficulties adapting to our 'specify before implement' paradigm. They do not reap the fruits of our method before they are solving the more complex design and programming problems. On the one hand, students understand the necessity of having a high-level formalism for abstract reasoning about specifications. On the other hand, it is clear that with the approach we use it takes longer before students are allowed to sit at the computer and experience the motivation of having constructed a working program.

17.8 References

Andrews, D. and Ince, D. (1991), *Practical Formal Methods with VDM*, Software Engineering, McGraw-Hill, London.

British Standards Institution, VDM Specification Language, Proto-Standard, BSI IST/5/-/50, BSI, London.

Dawes, J. (1991), *The VDM-SL Reference Guide*, Pitman, London.

Dickinson, I. P., Typesetting VDM-SL with V$_{DM}$S$_L$, NPL document obtainable via ftp.

Fairley, R. (1985), *Software Engineering Concepts*, McGraw-Hill, New York.

Jones, C. B. (1990), *Systematic Software Development Using VDM*, International Series in Computer Science, Prentice-Hall, London, 2nd edition.

Jones, C. B. and Shaw, R. C. F. (1990), *Case Studies in Systematic Software Development*, International Series in Computer Science, Prentice-Hall, London.

King, K. N. (1988), *Modula-2: A Complete Guide*, D. C. Heath and Company, Lexington, MA.

Watt, D. A. (1990), *Programming Language Concepts and Paradigms*, Prentice-Hall, Hemel Hempstead.

Watt, D. A. (1991), *Programming Language Syntax and Semantics*, Prentice-Hall, Hemel Hempstead.

Wirth, N. (1985), *Programming in Modula-2*, Springer-Verlag, Berlin, 3rd (corrected) edition.

Woodman, M. and Heal, B. (1995), *Introduction to VDM*, McGraw-Hill, London, 2nd (corrected) edition.

18 Initial programming language choice: a review of the factors

John Traxler

This chapter examines the factors that currently govern the choice of an initial undergraduate teaching language. In particular, it looks at two recent exercises at what was Wolverhampton Polytechnic, a typical large, modular, resource-constrained, higher-education institution, and sets out the largely non-technical and sometimes trivial factors that govern the choice of an initial programming language.

18.1 Introduction

I begin with an overview of the modular structure of computing teaching at my institution which is the context for my analysis of the factors that impact on the choice of an initial programming language.[1]

In the early 1990s the School of Computing and Information Technology at Wolverhampton Polytechnic (now Wolverhampton University) redesigned its provision of computing courses at undergraduate and postgraduate levels and this is now near to being an archetype for the higher education system of the current decade. For both undergraduate and postgraduate provision there was considerable debate about the appropriate initial programming language. This internal debate was informed by an on-

---

[1] A fuller and more formal description of the impact of modularization on our provision of computing can be found in [Traxler, 1993] whilst [Pollard, 1994] has recently looked at the modularization of computing courses.

going and wider national debate in the university sector and we drew on surveys of the national situation in [Furber, 1992] and [Jones and Pearson, 1993]. Unfortunately, this debate and these surveys dealt principally with describing or prescribing the content and delivery of monolithic computing courses or the contribution of computing (as 'service' teaching) to other monolithic courses, rather than with *modular* provision. The most recent examples of this are [Finkelstein, 1993], [Pemberton and Smailes, 1993] and [Budgen and Gibbs, 1989] (which are drawn from special issues of the *Computer Journal* and the *Software Engineering Journal*).

The school has now completely gone over to a modular, credit-accumulation provision. This means that it now offers students from across the institution a large set of discrete modules of study from which it and other schools can build courses. The fundamental building-block of the new system is the module (rather than the old-style course) and these modules are seen as the school's contribution to an institution-wide free market in modules for student registrations. Capturing or holding enrolments to modules from students within the institution is now as important as attracting recruits from outside the institution for the courses that contain the modules.

Each module is characterized by a number of parameters. A module's credit rating gives its volume of study (equivalent to a notional study-time in hours, usually 150 hours giving 15 undergraduate credits). A module's level (0, 1, 2, 3 or 4) denotes the level of intellectual skills that have to be applied and demonstrated by the students in assessment (thus the level of a module is not a function of the pace or density of delivery, the nature of the learning resource material, or the difficulty or abstractness of the material taught). Level 0 is access, level 4 is taught postgraduate. The teaching strategies are often identified in module descriptions, and there should be some progression in the learning style required as students progress.

The set of prerequisites (that is, prior skills and knowledge needed to start on the module) is given for every module, often specified as prerequisite modules. There may also be excluded combinations of modules. And, as might be expected, each module has specified aims, objectives, content and assessment strategy. There should be some clear development from aims to objectives to content that combines with the level and the credit rating to give the assessment.

The computing subject now consists of the pool of modules provided by the School of Computing, and these range from embedded real-time systems to commercial systems analysis; from level 1, first-year or introductory, to level 4, postgraduate; and from highly permeable and accessible, to highly prerequisited and constrained. Full-time students normally study eight modules per annum.

Modularity imposes an obligation to partition subjects in a curriculum into modules of a uniform, prescribed size and to then deliver the modules as advertised for fear of failing to deliver material that might act as a prerequisite for subsequent modules. This means the system is open and explicit, that is, highly documented but not always very responsive. The flexibility in the system is variable and the couplings in the system not always immediately apparent. For example, introducing MIRANDA to the third-years for a few weeks has few consequences but changing the brand of PASCAL for the first-years has very many. The actual initial programming language cannot be seen as a detail of module delivery to be left to the discretion of the module leader. There is obviously a strong, hidden coupling between the initial programming language and much of the other and subsequent computing teaching.

The volume, content and level of a module are now orthogonal. This takes some getting used to but is useful for teasing out the exact nature of the curriculum. Postgraduate (master's level) conversion courses are an acid test of one's understanding of the ideology since their modules have no prerequisites but constitute a master's programme, even the introductory programming module, and because the level of the course is a function of the level of its modules – and not vice versa – even the shortest, early module must be demonstrably conducting assessment at postgraduate level. Compared to this, introductory undergraduate programming modules are straightforward. There are no prerequisites for either undergraduate or postgraduate introductory programming so students are assumed to have no keyboard skills or file-handling experience and there are no co-requisites so students are not picking up any background information on, say, information technology, data processing or discrete mathematics.

General academic regulations concerning credits for degrees or other qualifications, modularity, and economies of scale, mean that there can only be one introductory programming module and that the language chosen must work for whoever enrols on the module and support whatever they go on to do.

In addition to these ideas of modularity and permeability, there is a philosophy of credit-accumulation and transfer which should mean a commonly understood currency of credit ratings that enables greater mobility between and within institutions and greater confidence in granting exemptions for prior learning. These factors all make it difficult to make any assumptions at all about the knowledge or experience of programming students, especially those taking the introductory programming module. Furthermore, the school attempts to use this module as a vehicle for recruiting and converting uncommitted combined studies students within the institution to a course in computing.

Alongside this formal framework, there are other new characteristics of the teaching context: the most obvious are rising student numbers, static resources and developments in teaching delivery such as 'enterprise' and resource-based learning. Increasingly students arrive via non-standard routes, often without formal school qualifications in mathematics or computer studies. Some may transfer internally from the HND (Higher National Diploma, a vocational qualification) and a minority may be 'access students' arriving, for example via a 'Women Into IT' course.

Many of these remarks are also true for postgraduate conversion-course students, many of whom have a background in arts or social sciences and are returning to study. They enrol on a very intensive course. There will not be time for them to study a second language, nor indeed an overly complex first language.

18.2 What we used to do

Previously the school ran a large self-contained degree course in computer science and contributed service teaching to other schools. The initial programming language used was Prime PASCAL (strictly speaking Sheffield PASCAL) and as students moved into their second and third years they quickly took on board a selection of DBASE, COBOL, C, assembler, some MODULA-2 and OCCAM, a little ADA, and maybe PROLOG or LISP.

Some applied-science and other non-specialist students managed to slip into the introductory programming module, but the overhead of Prime and Primos meant that many of the features of PASCAL that make it more readable or problem-oriented (such as subrange types and user-defined types) got squeezed out.

The program-development methods students use to study were initially (very informal) stepwise refinement, followed by JSP [Jackson, 1975]. Most of them then met formal specifications in Z and then branched out into MASCOT [Bate, 1986], SSADM [Central Computer and Telecommunications Agency, 1990] and JSD [Jackson, 1983]. As a consequence of this diversity, program design skills were always poor and apparently seldom transferred to other languages. Language acquisition was bottom-up and focused largely on small-grain syntax. The capacity to read code for meaning and to propose alternative design solutions was very underdeveloped. Furthermore, the software engineering and software quality assurance aspects of programming received too little attention and reinforcement as the students hurried from language to language, worrying about semi-colons and compilation errors.

During the review process of the degree scheme, there was a general feeling that we were teaching too many languages too soon in too many environments and failing to bring out anything other than surface differences between languages.

In the postgraduate conversion course, comprising mainly systems analysis (*i.e.* SSADM) and software engineering (*i.e.* ADA), the school used FOXBASE as an introductory programming language, for one month, then launched into ADA (*i.e.* ADA 83). There were continued technical and pedagogic problems with teaching ADA and its size and complexity were a considerable distraction. FOXBASE was an inadequate preparation for ADA and so, pending the revision of the entire course, ADA was eventually replaced by TURBO-PASCAL. Whilst alleviating the problems with ADA, this change made FOXBASE somewhat redundant.

18.3 Factors for choosing an initial programming language

In this section I describe the various factors that informed our choice of an initial programming language. For convenience I have divided them into those most associated with students, those to do with the institution and the particular department, and those to do with staff. Of course, in reality they interact in subtle and awkward ways.

18.3.1 What students do afterwards

In both the old monolithic undergraduate scheme and the new modular one, computing students go on to take modules that range from real-time and embedded systems to systems analysis and business information systems; they also do a group software project, an industrial placement and a final-year project. They then get jobs, usually, or go on to research. In some sense or other, the choice of an initial programming language had to underpin all these contingencies.

In terms of industrial placements, there was clear pressure for competence in C or COBOL, and maybe even DBASE or Windows programming, but we felt that these could easily be learned as second languages in the second year. Students were often given training courses during their placements anyway and so it was felt that the industrial placement dimension was not critical. The same was true in relation to their first jobs.

18.3.2 Market forces

Furthermore, it was felt that one of the major determinants of initial programming language choice must be the subsequent careers pursued by graduates. Whilst this was self-evident, it was decided it was not a simple relationship since, first, the language they first learned need not be the one they eventually work in and, second, any languages that students learn must underpin their subsequent professional development and industrial language acquisition for some considerable time into the future, not just into their first job. In immediate market terms, COBOL and C were major contenders; in the longer term ADA might join them, but on the other hand all three could give way to databases, application generators and 4GLs. So the market forces argument was not straightforward. The only easy deduction was that 'real' languages were a considerable motivator to students and that C was the best bet in this respect. If there was a way of connecting the first programming language with other vocational 'buzzwords', such as 'real-time', 'object-oriented' and 'M4 corridor',[2] then so much the better.

18.3.3 Cultural factors

Whilst not a vitally important factor, it is nevertheless true that different languages have different cultural associations. We were conscious that choosing C, COBOL or ADA would have labelled us as a specific type of institution. And, choosing a particular language would also place us at a point on a spectrum from 'academic' to 'technical' to 'commercial data processing'. From marketing and recruitment angles, these associations had to be considered in language choice.

Judging by some of the old FORTRAN apocrypha, there may also have been gender issues here that we did not explore – 'Real programmers don't eat quiche' *etc.*

18.3.4 Staff expertise

Staff expertise, as one would expect from the introduction, was diverse and uncoordinated but the responsibility for teaching initial programming rested with the software engineering section of the staff whose expertise and preference was in the PASCAL–ADA–MODULA-2 arena of block-structured procedural languages. Even if C were adopted, it was felt that staff specializing in systems programming would be inappropriate tutors.

18.3.5 Staff development

We tried to identify the staff development costs of the various major options for the software engineering staff teaching introductory programming: MODULA-2 was a

---

[2] An area surrounding the major motorway from London to the west of England and Wales which is known for the density of companies that rely on computing staff.

relatively small, smooth transition; ADA a large, smooth transition; and C or COBOL a serious discontinuity.

One aspect of this staff development was the time that would have to be invested in the development of teaching materials, lecture notes, teaching schedules and student assignments for each of the contending languages. Choosing MODULA-2 or PASCAL would enable us to exploit our existing experience of what worked and what did not. C would have been or should have been a 'green field' for us as a first language and we had experience suggesting that the size of ADA was demotivating for students unless a strictly policed subset of the language were used.

Although only a speck on the horizon at the time, the suitability of a language or environment for facilitating the computer-mediated delivery of modules may in future become a significant staff-development or course-development cost.

We felt that, at least in the long term, we should address the fact that teaching a language bottom-up is clearly undesirable in principle. One very attractive strategy for teaching MODULA-2, TURBO-PASCAL or any other modular language was a top-down approach where students were supplied with modules containing very high-level procedures that related to a specific problem-domain and their first experience of programming would merely involve sequencing and selecting these procedures to solve a problem. This would be in sharp contrast to the traditional approach where they learn their syntax word-by-word and only eventually reach the larger-scale organization involved in procedures and modules.

This strategy would have offset one other problem with MODULA-2 (and ADA), namely that novice programmers are normally forced to take a lot of 'magic' words on trust, for example EXPORT and IMPORT, but would see more of the reason for these words if they used this method. Though attractive, this approach would have involved a considerable investment in defining an attractive problem-domain and developing and maintaining the sets of modules, and so it was not pursued.

18.3.6 Paradigms and formality

Much has been written, most of it anecdotal, about new students arriving from a home-computing 'hacking' background, with an academic qualification from school (*e.g.* an A-level in computing) and a procedural mind-set. Our own informal surveys had shown many if not most students arriving with home or school experience of some micro-computer dialect of BASIC, often followed by assembler. Other institutions, especially the older universities, worried by this, have attempted outflanking techniques such as teaching functional programming and formal methods from day one. We decided to stick to procedural programming and informal program design as our initial vehicles and only introduce modest formality during semester three. Whilst we recognized the nature of the problem, we felt from early on that because of our experience of our students, we must stick with a procedural language and informal stepwise refinement for beginner programmers.

18.3.7 Generality

Our previous scheme, at its weakest, seemed to produce students who could write HELLO, WORLD programs in seven languages, whose C and PROLOG looked like transliterations of PASCAL, and who thought every new problem-domain demanded a new language. We hoped to find a very broad initial language that would not be discarded by second- and third-year lecturers wanting to demonstrate diverse domains such as commercial data processing and real-time, embedded systems. We even wondered whether ADA or C++ would give us two (or one-and-half) paradigms for the price of one but decided the students needed languages that clearly embodied one paradigm rather than badly embodying two.

Furthermore, our experience with Prime PASCAL, especially our attempts to express abstract data types and information hiding, suggested that we needed a language that enforced good practice, rather than just allowing good practice. A permissive or overgeneral language was thus unattractive. Using Prime PASCAL, students had always been supplied with code using arrays or pointers to implement stacks, for example. Because these could not be encapsulated and compiled into modules, lecturers spent hours checking this code for unauthorized access or alteration when it was incorporated using an editor into assessments.

18.3.8 Size and simplicity

Whilst there was a strong 'real-world' lobby making a case for C or COBOL and a software engineering 'purity' lobby arguing for ADA, we felt that an initial language had to be learnable. This meant a small, simple, regular language. MODULA-2 and PASCAL qualified, ADA did not. Perhaps OCCAM or DBASE should have been included for simplicity. C was interesting in this respect because although it seemed simple and compact, having a modest vocabulary, it also had complex levels of precedence, a terse, opaque style and a multitude of operators.

Standard PASCAL had the advantage that, compared to ADA with its packages, C with its 'includes', and MODULA-2 with its modules, its programs were monoliths and writing a simple program did not require 'magic' words such as 'define' or 'include'.

18.3.9 Technical issues

Deciding to stay with the procedural paradigm in effect brought us back to the big five, namely PASCAL, COBOL, C, MODULA-2 and ADA. The lobbies for C and COBOL were probably mutually cancelling and both suffered from fairly obvious technical and cultural shortcomings.

We moved on to identify what might be the major technical criteria covering both programming in the large and programming in the small. These included strong typing, separate compilation, modularity, information hiding, orthogonal operations, and so on. It seemed a foregone conclusion that ADA would exemplify best practice in most of the technical domain but was already disqualified for reasons of size, availability and textbook support.

It also seemed the case that advocates of the non-software engineering languages were reluctant to engage in debate about these issues anyway.

18.3.10 Textbooks

Trivial though it may sound, we felt that a broad base of good and inexpensive textbooks was a crucial factor in choosing a language. Specifically, the textbooks had to be addressing novices. There seemed to be very few introductory or cheap ADA textbooks (and many incorporated a heavy software engineering perspective as well) and although there were undoubtedly several good introductory C books, there were also a lot of beginners' C books that made the software engineers queasy.

18.3.11 Standards

The school had historically felt that sticking to a standard such as ISO PASCAL was important in the interests of portability and textbook choice. Unfortunately, it had become increasingly obvious that anyone who subsequently used PASCAL, and most students did not anyway, had to adapt considerably in order to use any of the *de facto* standards of industrial programming. Consequently, we decided to ignore the standards issues.

18.3.12 Environments

We were moving away from a Prime environment where even the most elementary program required some competence with an uncongenial editor and with Primos. We were looking for a relatively easy or intuitive environment – one common to several languages would have been attractive in further reducing the unnecessary learning overhead. For example, we considered both the TURBO and the JPI[3] families of products. On the other hand, there was a reluctance to being too dependent on one product or to choosing a language because of only one implementation.

Because our part-time students may be in the system for five years, we needed a fairly stable product, preferably cheap enough that part-time students could afford their own copies running on affordable machines.

18.4 Conclusions

The conclusion of the undergraduate exercise was largely negative: it was clear what should not be chosen (namely C, COBOL and ADA), but not what should be chosen.

We gave ourselves a respite of two years, in order to watch developments. In the interim we are using TURBO-PASCAL. This is proving admirable, but limited in many respects. It has certainly facilitated the gradual migration of object-oriented approaches into the early semesters and enabled a large number of precompiled units (standard data structures such as stacks) to be easily rewritten for the students. It is strongly supported by good textbooks at the right level that often come with instructors' manuals and a disk of sample programs. It has taken these two years for teaching staff to settle into TURBO-PASCAL and for the changes in style and emphasis to percolate downstream to higher-level modules. We attract a considerable number of non-computing students but they seem to sample only the one module and we will have to reconsider the function of initial programming as a recruiting agent.

---

[3] Jensen and Partners International, now Clarion TopSpeed Software.

We have now added a business information systems degree and an information systems stream to the computer science degree. The possibility of running a generic introductory programming module in two languages, C++ and FOXPRO 2, for the two different audiences, has now been considered and rejected.

Any future choice will depend on the popularity and industrial acceptance of MODULA-2, the durability and enhancement of TURBO-PASCAL, the growth of the object-oriented paradigm, and the simplification and educational acceptance of ADA. Currently, it looks as if ADA has lost ground and credibility, largely in favour of C++, and at the time of writing C++ is our most likely choice along with the early introduction of an object-oriented design notation, probably OMT [Rumbaugh *et al.*, 1991].

We have also looked at two systems for delivering programming modules with computer assistance, CLEM [Boyle *et al.*, 1994] for MODULA-2 and CEILIDH [Benford *et al.*, 1993] for C, and used CEILIDH for an introductory systems programming module. CEILIDH produced a considerable adverse reaction amongst the students, even after they discovered how to tweak the system and generate high marks!

In the revised postgraduate course, we focused specifically on information systems engineering. We have adopted FOXPRO 2 as a coursewide language and this has given considerable economy of scale (covering database and 3GL programming teaching and subsequent software development topics) whilst still allowing us to teach most software engineering principles in an accessible and realistic way given the time and scope of the course.

18.5 References

Bate, G. (1986), Mascot 3: an informal introduction, *Software Engineering Journal*, **1**, 95–102.

Benford, S., Burke, E. and Foxley, E. (1993), Learning to construct quality software with the Ceilidh system, *Software Quality Journal*.

Boyle, T., Gray, J., Wendl, B. and Davies, M. (1994), Taking the Plunge with CLEM: the Design and Evaluation of a Large Scale CAL System, *Computers and Education*, **22**, 19–26.

Budgen, D. and Gibbs, N. E. (1989), The education program of the Software Engineering Institute, Carnegie Mellon University, *Software Engineering Journal*, 176–80.

Central Computer and Telecommunications Agency (CCTA) (1990), *SSADM Version 4 Reference Manual*, NCC/Blackwell, Oxford.

Finkelstein, A. (1993), European computing curricula: a guide and comparative analysis, *Computer Journal*, **36**(4), 299–319.

Furber, D. (1992), A survey of the teaching of programming to computing undergraduates in UK universities and polytechnics, *Computer Journal*, **35**, 530–3.

Jackson, M. A. (1975), *Principles of Program Design*, Academic Press, London.

Jackson, M. A. (1983), *System Development*, Prentice-Hall, Hemel Hempstead.

Jones, J. and Pearson, E. (1993), An informal survey of initial teaching languages in UK university departments of computer science, *University Computing*, **15**, 54–7.

Pemberton, J. D. and Smailes, J. M. (1993), Educating the masses: is IT a tricky business?, *Computer Journal*, **36**(4), 335–42.

Pollard, D. J. (1994), Modularisation of first degree courses in the UK, *Engineering Science and Education Journal*, **2**(5), 209.

Rumbaugh, J., Blaha, M., Premerlani, W., Eddy, F. and Lorensen, W. (1991), *Object-oriented modelling and design*, Prentice-Hall, Englewood Cliffs, NJ.

Traxler, J. (1993), The Nature and Impact of Current Trends in Higher Education on the Teaching of Computer Science and Software Engineering, in *All Ireland Conference on Curriculum and Computing, Dublin, 1993.*

19 Programming language choice for distance computing

Mark Woodman and Rob Griffiths

Many problems exist in teaching software development in the distance learning mode. Choosing a programming language as an appropriate vehicle for teaching concepts is complicated by the breadth of topics to be covered in a stand-alone introductory course (*e.g.* from elementary programming to software project management, and from operating systems to security systems) and by practical considerations such as compiler unit cost and ease of access to structures used in a programming environment. This chapter discusses some of the issues being considered by the Open University Computing Department for its new introductory course. The agenda for its syllabus is outlined and some criteria for assessing languages and their implementations are proposed.

19.1 Computing courses in the distance mode

The distance mode in which the Open University operates has a significant impact on its syllabi and its pedagogy. Several aspects of the teaching of computing and, in particular, of the teaching of programming are more difficult in a distance-learning institution than in the conventional sector. For programming, the relative isolation of students from their peers and tutors is important; there are no 'lab' sessions to help students in their early exercises and there is often no-one on hand to resolve an ambiguity in an instruction manual. In order to understand some of the constraints which affect the distance teaching of computing and choice of language we outline the current situation.

The Open University is the United Kingdom's university for distance learning. It also offers its programmes of study throughout continental Europe and sells courses in Eastern Asia. In 1994 there were some 150 courses in the OU's undergraduate programme; a further 250 courses and packs are also offered through other programmes. In this academic year nearly 150 000 students have registered to study with the university, over half in the undergraduate programme. The degree programme is modular and there are relatively few constraints on how students can mix courses and subject areas.

The median age of students is 37 (mainly in the 25–45 age group) and the vast majority remain in employment throughout their studies. This makes courses that can be considered vocational very attractive to OU students. Computing courses are particularly popular for this reason, especially as they can be used in obtaining membership of the British Computer Society [Conway *et al.*, 1989].

Four specialist courses are currently offered by the Computing Department in the undergraduate programme (and more are planned). These courses cover a variety of topics such as programming, compiler technology, database technology, structured methods, formal methods, software project management and software quality assurance. Further topics in computing are provided by other departments. The department's courses are much in demand, with some 6000 students per year taking the four alone.

Students are taught using a supported open-learning approach which is increasingly multimedia in nature – teaching materials consist of paper and computer-based correspondence texts, broadcast television and radio, video and audio cassette programmes, and interactive network and CD-ROM packages. Non-obligatory local tuition is also offered but students often skip these classes. Mandatory residential schools are not currently run for computing courses. Unfortunately the cost of developing and updating courses is high and with multimedia is rising; it takes approximately 30 person-years to develop a full-credit[1] (440-hour) course. The investment of human resource and cost of technologies used to prepare and present courses (such as BBC production for broadcast television) has meant that courses must last for at least five years, which is too long in computing. This course longevity also means that the technology for which a course is designed may become outdated by the end of the first year of presentation.

The introductory course that began in 1987 (M205, *Fundamentals of Computing*) covers many topics in programming, software engineering, software systems, structured analysis and design, and social impact of computing. It is a second-level course which demands approximately four hundred hours of study over ten months; because it is second-level, certain assumptions are made about the ability (the self-sufficiency) of students. To some extent this meant the authors of the course were able to avoid the teaching of some elementary study skills; however, it has transpired that changing regulations and other circumstances have meant that increasingly too many students do not have such skills.

As usual with OU courses, the introductory course for computing has no prerequisite. Consequently it attracts students who have substantially different requirements of the course. For many it is the first of a number of computing courses that will build a computing profile for their degree. For others (too few, we think) the course is a diversion from arts, pure sciences, or social sciences; in other words it serves almost as an

---

[1] A full credit is rated at 60 points in the Credit for Academic Transfer System (CATS).

appreciation course. The consequence of this mix and the variable level of study skills is that any replacement will have to be accessible to a wide diversity of students and will have to lead to different academic careers.

M205, like its predecessor, uses U. C. S. D. PASCAL [Clark, 1981] under the p-System [Woodman, 1988]. The use of this language was almost a side-effect of choosing the p-System which was originally selected because of its portability; at the time it was not clear what microcomputer technology would succeed in the domestic market and a portable operating system allowed course development to proceed independently of the microcomputer market. (The OU's Academic Computing Service implemented the p-System first under the DECsystem-20 operating system, TOPS-20, and later under VAX VMS.) The language itself is suitable for general-purpose programming and systems programming [Willner, 1983]. The main strength of U. C. S. D. PASCAL for introductory programming and for modular design is its separate compilation units; it also has extensions for string handling and random-access files.

Our experience of the U. C. S. D. dialect of PASCAL is quite favourable, although it does not fully support concepts we would expect to be in a course for the 1990s. Most of the problems we have encountered are to do with the p-System development environment which is isolated from the host operating system (currently we use MS-DOS) and which has failed to keep pace with innovations in programming systems. A replacement course will inevitably involve replacing the programming language.

19.2 Concepts supported by programming languages

19.2.1 Starting point

The academic basis of the new introductory course is a conviction that it is legitimate to distinguish between theoretical computer science and practical software engineering[2] [Thomas, 1992], and that as a department we are more engaged in teaching the latter than the former. Furthermore, an introductory course will have to substantially cover the breadth of computing and not just software engineering.

Inevitably, our courses are designed making assumptions about the needs of our consumers – the specialist skills they wish to acquire and the educational credits they need in order to progress academically. For a modular degree programme in a distance-learning institution careful consideration must be given to current views on professional development, and what is relevant to or applicable in commerce and industry.

As implied above, students who wish to achieve a degree with a computing profile starting with our introductory programming course could be expected to meet concepts such as specification, design and coding before proceeding to courses containing more 'advanced' notions of computing mathematics, abstract data types, software project management, *etc.* While this type of course structure is unavoidable and, in general terms, desirable, we are convinced that more of the concepts from advanced courses should be introduced early, albeit in an appropriately simplified form. This has implications for language and implementation choice. For example, to teach project management from an early stage [Woodman, 1993a] is likely to involve student use

---

[2] The term 'software engineering' is one which has connotations that may deter some students; we prefer the term 'software development'.

of course-team supplied software components as well as separately developed student components. A language that allows separate compilation and an implementation that has facilities for handling 'projects' would be desirable.

At the time of writing the specific content of the new introductory software development course is still being discussed. However, many objectives have been agreed (see section 19.6.1) and an agenda for deciding a syllabus has been set (section 19.6.2). Some of these are outlined next.

19.2.2 Building with components

One of the simplest notions in engineering is the use (and re-use or adaptation) of components. In traditional programming courses this idea is often taken for granted or promoted as simply a matter of reducing coding effort, saving storage or improving performance. In order that advanced software development courses can be viable when based soundly on component re-use (see [Adigun, 1989]), we believe that novice programmers must be taught the notion explicitly. Given a suitable abstraction and an appropriate programming language, the idea of components can be introduced from the outset [Woodman, 1993b]. As mentioned, U. C. S. D. PASCAL is adequate for components, but is probably ruled out because of the p-System. ADA, MODULA-2, MODULA-3, OBERON-2 and EXTENDED PASCAL would all provide a usable platform for realizing these concepts.

19.2.3 Abstraction

A significant problem in teaching software engineering is the lack of abstraction skills among students. Our experience has been that students fail to learn how to abstract despite carefully structured materials both in the introductory computing course and in later courses. At the introductory level they frequently become absorbed by the detail of a problem and miss structural similarities. They also tend to think in terms of the concrete data structures of a programming language rather than in more general terms. In more advanced courses the situation is repeated; students studying, for example, the Vienna Development Method (VDM) [Jones, 1990] fail to notice similarities between problems (*e.g.* between a simple database and a simple stock-control system) and have extreme difficulty with notions of refinement and reification.

In order to improve the abstraction skills of students, a number of strategies should be employed, and we have proposed some [Woodman *et al.*, 1992]. Suitable language support for abstraction is an important criterion for choosing a programming language; unsurprisingly, the same languages that would be suitable for teaching component-based construction would be suitable candidates for supporting notions of abstraction.

However, the picture becomes complicated by object-oriented programming.

19.2.4 Object-oriented programming

While object-based analysis and design could be supported by many languages, particularly those with facilities for information hiding, full object-oriented programming would demand a language that supports at least classes and inheritance. It is doubtful that the most powerful features of languages like C++ and EIFFEL would be needed in an introductory course; for example, single inheritance would probably suffice for teaching object-oriented programming.

Furthermore if object-oriented programming is to be taught, what is the best vehicle? A hybrid object-oriented language, such as ADA 95, C++, OBERON, *etc.* or a 'pure' object-oriented language such as SMALLTALK? We perceive a number of problems in using a hybrid language as conceptually the approach is potentially complex for the beginning student. Beginners must be exposed in one course to a series of diverse, subtly differing, and partially redundant concepts. For example:

- both reference and value semantics for assignment;

- both basic data types and objects (and their type incompatibilities);

- both polymorphism and overloading;

- in many hybrid languages the use of pointers for references is too apparent (and explicit dereferencing is needed);

- in many hybrid languages, there is no provision for automatic garbage collection.

On the other hand we perceive a number of advantages in adopting a pure object-oriented language.

Conceptual simplicity: a very small number of concepts are required compared with a traditional approach (but see [Jones, 1994] for a contrasting view).

Intellectual power: the traditional imperative–store approach may be viewed as a conceptually simple subset of a pure object-oriented approach – the reverse is not true.

Concrete support for abstraction: this approach is excellent for teaching abstract data types and good principles of modularity since ADTs are concretely supported.

Engineering merits: excellent support is provided for good software engineering and modularity.

Student motivation: this approach has good re-use properties allowing students to build substantial programs very early.

Good environments: excellent and easy-to-alter graphical environments are available (at least for SMALLTALK).

Avoiding bad habits: avoidance of the 'C++ syndrome' where students write 'object-oriented programs' with just one class!

One interesting claimed advantage for teaching a 'pure' object-oriented language to novice programmers is that programmers who learn a traditional imperative–store approach first appear to have more difficulty absorbing an object-oriented outlook than complete beginners. The converse does not appear to be the case.

Such considerations of wealth of facilities and complexity are likely to dominate the choice of an object-oriented language for distance teaching. The size and performance of implementations of large languages would be a significant factor when buying 10 000 licences or more.

19.3 Non-language criteria

In this section we briefly examine criteria that are not directly to do with how well a language supports the concepts academics might wish to teach. The points are summarized in a questionnaire for implementors which is given in section 19.7.

19.3.1 Market-driven choice

Arguments on the choice of a programming language often generate more heat than light. This is often due to an unclear view of the abstraction a language makes concrete (see [Ambler *et al.*, 1992]) and an absence of rational criteria for judging languages. Counting the frequency of job advertisements demanding experience of a particular language may be appropriate if it is desired to fulfil specific needs. For example, it would probably have made commercial sense to teach C in the late 1980s and early 1990s. Later in the 1990s C++ looks like a better bet, and with the 1995 standard, ADA could be more attractive; if an application area, such as safety-critical systems, were targeted, MODULA-2 might be the obvious choice [Cullyer *et al.*, 1992]. If developments in the financial sector are anything to go by, then SMALLTALK could be tomorrow's language.

To be market-sensitive like this would only be feasible if it were possible to revise courses frequently – not an option yet available for predominantly print-based courses. Therefore, issues such as standards and the qualities of implementations come to the fore.

19.3.2 Standardized languages

A stance which can be argued is that to adhere to an engineering view of software development, we must know precisely what our tools do. In the case of a programming language this means that it should be properly specified. It is not of importance that beginning students will not be able to understand or provide rigorous proofs. However, if one wants to promote an engineering view of software development, then it is extremely important that students believe that such proofs are possible and necessary in certain circumstances. While proprietary languages could satisfy the specification criterion, it is more likely that a standardized language could do so – simply because language standards are drafted in accordance with the engineering view. The vocational and professional development uses of distance-learning courses demand that the chosen language have relevance to the industry. This precludes experimental languages and favours the operational store–imperative paradigm.

A clear advantage of choosing a standardized language is that dependence on proprietary products is reduced or eliminated. For the OU situation this is not just important during the life of the course during which an implementation may have to be replaced. It also has an effect on course development; choosing a standardized language would allow development of teaching material in advance of choosing an implementation – as long as the pedagogy did not need to exploit facilities of a particular programming environment.

If standardization is important then ADA, C, PASCAL and EXTENDED PASCAL would be immediate candidates. (Although they are standardized and much used,

BASIC, FORTRAN, COBOL and PL/I are of no interest for introductory teaching.) MODULA-2 will be an International Standard and the international standardization of C++ is in progress. An ANSI committee is working on SMALLTALK. Although there are *ad hoc* groups trying to shape the developments of EIFFEL and OBERON, there appears to be little prospect of standards for them.

19.3.3 Criteria relating to implementations

In the end, a language may be chosen because of the qualities of its implementation. The language products of Borland and Microsoft, for example, have demonstrated the usefulness of relatively cheap integrated programming environments. Compilers that may be objectively judged to be of very high quality (say in terms of conformity to a standard, exception reporting, or code quality) are often overlooked because they are not integrated in a programming environment.

The OU operates a personal computer policy by which it advises students of the specification of the computer academics may require. In this way students can plan how they obtain access to a computer and whether they should take courses requiring one. For introductory computing our specification (devised in 1994 for use in 1997) is for a system equivalent to a 66 MHz Intel 80486 PC with 8 Mb RAM, at least 340 Mb disk, colour monitor, mouse, modem and printer. This was already a small computer by 1994's professional standards and if the course team for the introductory computing course cannot justify a higher specification, the capacity limitations will have a significant impact on the criteria for choosing a language and implementation. Consequently, the RAM required by an implementation, the suggested processor speed, the disk storage needed, are all very important for language choice.

19.3.4 Implementations and tools

The availability of supporting tools will also be an important consideration if many of the topics we expect to teach are pursued. The provision of a tool interface – access to the internal stuctures of an implementation – is likely to be crucial. Ideally, we would like to cover all development activities by providing tools for at least the following:

- tutorial support (*e.g.* CLEM for MODULA-2 [Boyle *et al.*, 1994]);

- animation of abstract descriptions (*e.g.* [Woodman *et al.*, 1992]);

- animation of specifications (*e.g.* [Winstanley, 1990]);

- documentation and maintenance (*e.g.* [Knuth, 1992; Sametinger and Pomberger, 1992]);

- provision for configuration management, program complexity analysis, and programmer's workbook (*e.g.* [Woodman, 1993a]);

- prettyprinting and maybe style analysis (*e.g.* [Oman, 1990]).

These need not be elaborate tools. Indeed they should not be elaborate; students on an introductory course will not have time for everything. However, there must be time for simplified versions of important software engineering ideas.

19.4 Conclusion

The choice of programming language for a distance-learning course that is accessible to students with a wide variety of backgrounds and academic needs, which is being designed in 1994–5, and which must be defensible in 2001 is fraught with danger. Consequently we have examined what changes are in train in conventional universities, what students want, what changes are perceptible in the computing industry, and how various experts are expecting software development to evolve in the next decade. In conventional universities we see a gradually accelerating movement towards object-oriented programming. In general, this means students beginning to program abstract data types (usually with C++), with more advanced object concepts being introduced later (*e.g.* [Lee and Stroud, 1996]). In industry, the adoption of object technology is clearly evident with object-oriented concepts gaining increasing importance. Furthermore, the continuing preoccupation with maintenance and reverse engineering and recent reports of development with re-use yielding significant increases in productivity and quality have led us to consider a component-based perspective to be extremely important. While components are not synonymous with objects, the latter are effective realizations of the component concept. For the above reasons, choosing an object-oriented language for the course does seem to assist our particular problems of longevity.

However, in selecting a particular object-oriented language, the merits or demerits of a language may be completely outweighed by the non-language criteria outlined:

- reduced reliance on proprietary products;
- wide choice of implementations;
- rich source of teaching material;
- availability of tools, or tool interfaces.

We believe that these factors could be the primary criteria for choosing a language for distance courses in software development. However, speculation about the market-relevance may inevitably be fruitless. Maybe academics should concentrate on what concepts need to be taught and in what order, and then decide on the most appropriate programming language. For our purposes the language that best suits our pedagogical agenda would seem to be SMALLTALK.

19.5 References

Adigun, M. O. (1989), A framework for teaching programming with reuse, *Software Engineering Journal*, **4**(3), 159–62.

Ambler, A. L., Burnett, M. M. and Zimmerman, B. A. (1992), Operational versus definitional: a perspective on programming paradigms, *IEEE Software*, 28–43.

Boyle, T., Gray, J., Wendl, B. and Davies, M. (1994), Taking the Plunge with CLEM: the Design and Evaluation of a Large Scale CAL System, *Computers and Education*, **22**, 19–26.

Clark, R. and Koehler, S. (1981), *The U. C. S. D. Pascal Handbook: A Reference and Guidebook for Programmers*, Prentice-Hall.

Conway, D. E., Dunn, S. C. and Hooper, G. S. (1989), BCS and IEE accreditation of software engineering courses, *Software Engineering Journal*, **4**(4), 245–8.

Cullyer, W. J., Goodenough, S. J. and Wichmann, B. A. (1991), The choice of computer languages for use in safety-critical systems, *Software Engineering Journal*, **6**(2), 51–8.

Jones, A. (1994), *Smalltalk – An Educator's Dream?*, Technical Report, University of Wales, College of Cardiff.

Jones, C. B. (1990), *Systematic Software Development Using VDM*, International Series in Computer Science, Prentice-Hall, Hemel Hempstead, 2nd edition.

Knuth, D. E. (1992), *Literate Programming*, CSLI Lecture Notes (Number 27), CSLI, Stanford.

Lee, P. A. and Stroud, R. J. (1996), C++ as an Introductory Programming Language, in *Programming Language Choice: Practice and Experience*, M. Woodman (ed.), International Thomson Computer Press, London, Chapter 5, (this volume).

Oman, P. and Cook, C. (1990), Typographic Style is More than Cosmetic, *Communications ACM*, **33**(5), 506–20.

Sametinger, J. and Pomberger, G. (1992), A hypertext system for literate C++ programming, *Journal of Object Oriented Programming*, 24–9.

Thomas, M. (1992), Computer Science or Software Engineering, in *Proceedings of Workshop on Computing Curriculum, The Open University, 1992*, R. Weedon (ed.), 18–23 (available from OU Computing Department, Milton Keynes, UK).

Willner, E. and Demchak, B. (1985), *Advanced U. C. S. D. Pascal Programming Techniques*, Prentice-Hall, Englewood Cliffs, N. J.

Winstanley, A. C. and Bustard, D. W. (1991), EXPOSE: an animation tool for process-oriented specifications, *Software Engineering Journal*, **6**(6), 463–75.

Woodman, M. (1988), The p-System, in *Operating Systems: Communicating with and Controlling the Computer*, L. Keller (ed.), Prentice-Hall.

Woodman, M. (1993a), Making Software Quality Assurance a Hidden Agenda?, in *Proceedings Software Quality Management '93, Southampton, March 1993*, BCS SQMSG.

Woodman, M. (1993b), Software Engineering Concepts for Distance Learning, in *Proceedings TeleTeaching 93, Trondheim, Norway, August 1993*.

Woodman, M., Robinson, H. and Griffiths, R. (1992), Learning industry-oriented software development via exploration using hypertext courseware, in *Proceedings of East-West Conference on Emerging Computer Technologies in Education, Moscow*.

19.6 Appendix – M206 aims and objectives

The main aim of the course is to extend the students' knowledge of computing and their computing skills by exploring the processes in software development. In particular, the practical nature of computing will be emphasized by using a sophisticated programming environment and the global and sociological context will be stressed by using modern networked computing (e-mail, conferencing and the World Wide Web), both as an integral part of course delivery and tuition and by syllabus topics. The software development approach taken is object-oriented (the language used is SMALLTALK); however, students will be taught to reflect on software development processes and paradigms (including issues to do with language choice). To enhance their understanding of software engineering, the course also aims to provide students with experience of working in a group project.

19.6.1 Main course objectives

Having successfully studied the course students should:

- have a general understanding of computing and software, including an extensive vocabulary;
- have obtained practical, generally applicable skills in using software, including the use of telecommunications and multimedia software;
- have sufficient knowledge of the object-oriented paradigm to: (i) analyse artefacts and problems in terms of it, (ii) sketch the design of a software system and make design choices, and (iii) complete or extend an application;
- be capable of using SMALLTALK to develop small applications, including their graphical user interface;
- be able to understand and describe the issues involved in large-scale software development including those due to group work;
- understand the need for user-interface design (*i.e.* HCI) and be able to describe and analyse user interfaces;
- appreciate the benefits and risks associated with global networked computing.

19.6.2 Pervasive themes

The following are the pervasive knowledge themes of the course:

- abstraction;
- the 'language' of computing and software;
- the structure of software;
- software development as a rational engineering process;
- dynamic program behaviour;
- that software uses a multiplicity of views;
- that objects are significant software structures.

The following are the pervasive skills themes:

- analytical skills;
- debugging;
- reading programs;
- reasoning about programs and program behaviour.

19.7 Appendix – Programming language implementation questionnaire

The following is a sample of a questionnaire which can be used to document properties of a language implementation according to the criteria discussed earlier in this chapter. It has been developed in a simple text format to facilitate dissemination and receipt via electronic mail.

```
PROGRAMMING LANGUAGE IMPLEMENTATION QUESTIONNAIRE
-------------------------------------------------------
Your name/address/telephone/fax number/e-mail id/URL:


Are you? developer [   ] or vendor [   ]

-------------------------------------------------------
Language:

Name of Implementation:


Is the implementation multi-platform? [   ]
If Yes, then please list platforms:



-------------------------------------------------------
Minimum Disk Capacity Required:

Recommended Disk Capacity Required:

Minimum Memory Required:

Recommended Memory Required:

Minimum Processor and Speed:

Recommended Processor and Speed:

-------------------------------------------------------
Is a debugger available with the implementation?
If so, please describe in three lines or less:



Is a help system available with the implementation?
If so, please describe in three lines or less:



Is a tutorial  available with the implementation?
If so, please describe in three lines or less:



Enumerate other tools available with the implementation:
```

List other tools available from third-party suppliers
(no endorsement is implied):

Is an interface to the data structures of the
implementation provided? (i.e. Is it straightforward
to build tools to use with the implementation?)

List extensions that distinguish the
implementation from others:

List library facilities that distinguish
the implementation from others?

Please list user guides/reference manuals
available with implementation:

Does implementation conform to a standard?
If Yes, then which?

Has implementation been validated? [   ]
If Yes, what level of conformance?

List Books/Papers/Reports on which implementation
is based (give editions):

Price band (A/under 100, B/100-200, C/200-300,
D/300-400, E/over 400): [   ]

Site Licenses available: [   ]
If Yes, then at what cost (specify currency)?

Support arrangements (Hotline, BBS etc):

----

20 Standardization and language proliferation

Brian Meek

This contribution is aimed at all faced with the problem of language choice – both academics and those in the commercial and industrial world. The chapter considers the world of language standardization and the issue of language proliferation. However, academics may find this of more practical use than commercial people. Business imperatives often determine choice of programming language for you, though you may still be faced with a proliferation problem. Also businesses do not have to look far to find good reasons for adopting a local (company) standard, that is, one or two languages, and for using well-standardized versions of the language or languages of importance to them. (Some companies admittedly seem not to do any looking, but that is because, depressingly, IT is not always run very professionally; professionals in all disciplines take the importance of standards for granted.) Business users may still find useful pointers in what follows, however: for example, that they'll get better work out of people whose experience is not confined just to one language, and who are aware of standards and their importance.

20.1 The languages scene

Nowadays there are a large number of books, varying in approach and style, on comparative programming languages (*cf.* Herbert Klaeren's chapter [1996]). This was not always the case. Comparative programming languages as a subject for study began, like so much else, in the 1960s, no doubt because in that decade there were invented many of the main programming languages that we still have today.

To many of my generation, the key event in this regard was the publication in 1967 of Bryan Higman's classic, *A Comparative Study of Programming Languages* [1967]. It changed the way that I for one looked at languages, permanently and (I think) for the better. It did more than just show me ways of looking at languages as things warranting study in their own right. It turned me, not overnight but in due course, from someone tending to be partisan for a particular language or language style, into one better able to recognize (rather than just dismiss as unimportant) the shortcomings of languages I tended to like, and appreciate the virtues of those that generally I found uncongenial. Eventually this developed into a scepticism about all languages, but Bryan Higman cannot be blamed for that: it is the result of an inborn character trait, defect if you like, fed by continual encounters with those who remained partisans.

I hope that I shall not be the only sceptic to contribute to this volume, since a discussion of choice of programming languages, consisting only of contributions by enthusiastic partisans of particular choices, is likely to prove as sterile as the ALGOL versus FORTRAN confrontations of a quarter of a century ago. The world has become somewhat more mature now. Many courses include comparative programming languages, and not all of them are based on persuading the students that the lecturer's pet choice is the best. However, maturity, regrettably, is as yet not universal.

20.2 Partisanship

Partisanship – not just partiality – for one language is a common trait. There are one-language communities, COBOLers speaking only to COBOLers and the like. In a book review a decade after his book appeared, Bryan Higman remarked [1978] that he found the parallels with natural languages fascinating. He likened FORTRAN and ALGOL-60 to Latin and classical Greek in medieval times, the one a 'brutish archaism' but also a *lingua franca*, the other 'the language of philosophers, mathematicians and artists' but seldom of the common people. COBOL was a 'barbarian tongue' akin to Anglo-Saxon. I shall draw a veil over what he said of PASCAL. Higman remarked on the way that 'languages determine cultures', and was also aware of the way that some latch on to languages as expressions of separate identity.

You cannot push analogies too far, of course; there are many traces of Latin as well as of Greek in modern natural languages, whereas in modern programming languages the traces of FORTRAN are minimal (apart from in FORTRAN), but those of ALGOL-60 are still clearly visible (including in FORTRAN). Nevertheless partisanship, as well as the phenomenon of one-language communities, do have their analogues, such as the militancy of some speakers of Welsh and of *Québecois*, the official promotion of Gaelic in Ireland, simply that people get emotionally involved and feel the language to be part of them: attack my language, and you attack me. Dialects, and the evolution of languages over time, also carry over, as does the sheer number of languages.

Many of the same features are found in another familiar analogue, that of religion. There is no point in risking upsetting sensibilities by exploring this too much, but clearly the programming language world too has its simple ceremonies and its elaborate rituals, the ornate and the ascetic, its fervent converts, its evangelists, its militant fundamentalists.

20.3 Dependence

However, the analogy I'd like to explore here is that programming languages are like drugs. As with drugs, people can become dependent on them, in part physically and in part emotionally. Likening programming languages to drugs may be regarded as extreme or distasteful, but there are parallels.

People obviously *depend* on natural languages to communicate, but many are *dependent* on a religion in a somewhat different, non-physical sense. People can become dependent, in a similar sense, emotional if not spiritual, to other things too: on another person, on political beliefs or a political movement, on an organization, even on a job. The parallel is that people get dependent both physically and emotionally on drugs. With programming languages, they do depend on them to communicate, but they can also get so emotionally involved that they get dependent in the other sense as well – they get hooked.

Note also that the parallel is not with natural drugs like nicotine, cannabis, or opium – though some might find analogies for strychnine! It is more with *designer* drugs – and I hasten to add I do not just mean the LSDs and the Ecstasies, but legitimate medical drugs which are beneficial in treating certain conditions, but can also become habit-forming. Can anyone suggest a parallel for Valium?

The point is the designers of languages share some at least of the ethical responsibilities of designers of drugs; and those who decide on what languages to teach, share some at least of the ethical responsibilities of those who prescribe or dispense drugs – and could also share similar ethical responsibilities to drug pushers! Computing services like the one I work for are dispensers, though like good pharmacists we do try to counsel our users about what the various things we have in stock are best used for, and how to avoid misuse. Those who decide what languages students should use are the prescribers. The moral from this analogy is exactly this: lecturers in that position need to take special care that they *are* acting as prescribers, and not as pushers!

20.4 Proliferation

There is an enormous variety of drugs, all designed for particular purposes, some very specific, some more general. There are so many, because of the many different conditions needing treating, and the richness of organic chemistry making possible the continual invention of new products. They are *tools* to achieve certain effects. The designer drugs are *human artefacts*, and they are almost all *complex artefacts*. How does this compare with languages?

The factors leading to the existence of so many languages are well known, but they are worth reviewing and analysing. Programming languages also are *tools* to help in carrying out tasks in IT environments, and there are many because of the many different tasks needing to be tackled, and the inherent richness of language making possible the same limitless invention. They also are *human artefacts*, and they also are *complex artefacts*. In addition, unlike drugs they are *abstract artefacts*. All four characteristics tend to promote proliferation of languages and, since they are related, they reinforce one another.

The IT environments in which programming languages are used as *tools* are themselves complex human artefacts, and are also to a large extent abstract. Hence the tools are needed for a myriad of different tasks, and these tasks in turn are often extremely complex. This helps to increase the demand for new tools to suit particular tasks. If you list properties that a language might have, then place a priority ordering on them, and then use the ordering to design a language, the orderings will differ greatly from task to task and hence the resulting languages are likely also to differ.

It also generates a tendency to make the tools (languages) more *complex*, the reason being that complexity can widen expressiveness and so increase the range of tasks a tool can be used for. Complexity can also help to make the tools match more closely particular kinds of tasks, or particular kinds of environment, but it also increases the cost of acquiring, learning and applying the tool. Thus, when another task comes along, existing tools may be seen not to meet the needs of that particular task as well as they might, since they are tailored to somewhat different kinds of tasks. Alternatively, if any are suitable, they may be found to contain many extra features which are having to be paid for but will not be used. Both of these factors create further pressure towards proliferation.

The *abstract* nature of these languages-as-tools means that there is no natural limit to their complexity, or to adaptability of their design to particular needs. There are no visible constraints to 'why shouldn't it …'; indeed the only limits are those of human ingenuity, a point made elsewhere [Meek, 1990] as being applicable to all software. This characteristic of being abstract is the most important of the four, because it greatly reduces the constraints that might otherwise oppose the pressures from the other three, as well as itself naturally encouraging variation, even in the absence of such pressures. Inventing new language – if not a whole new language – is quite literally child's play. The perceived threshold to inventing new syntax and semantics, even a whole new language, is very low considering its complex nature, and can often appear to be less trouble – and certainly more appealing – than trying to apply a less-than-ideal tool to a particular task.

Of course, the apparently addictive qualities of programming languages, discussed earlier, is in a sense a factor working in the other direction – once people are 'hooked' on one, they don't want to move on. There's plenty enough evidence of that; and even if they aren't irredeemably hooked, those of a more conservative or more cautious disposition (or less irresponsible, if you like!) may prefer to stick with a language of which they are sure of their mastery, rather than to venture into something else even if it is more suitable to the task ahead. However, people, even programmers, come in many varieties, some more adventurous, some incorrigibly innovative; they are the ones to produce new languages, while the more conservative ones also contribute to proliferation by ensuring that old languages don't easily die! So conservatism in fact does not work *against* proliferation, but rather to help promote it.

The multiplicity of programming languages for different tasks has for at least a quarter of a century been likened to the Tower of Babel, itself another instance of likening programming to natural languages. The Babel analogy (though it is not really an analogy) brings us to the fact that these tools, like natural languages, are *human* artefacts. If it were simply that they are therefore subject to human errors, both plain mistakes and what Mike Sykes has beautifully termed 'design infelicities', it would not matter too much. However, it means that they are also subject to human traits like experimentation, 'fiddling', dissatisfaction with things as they are, flights of fancy, likes and dislikes, vanity, greed ... Complexity tends to encourage these, abstraction allows them free rein. Priority ordering by objective criteria already leads to proliferation, as noted earlier. If you add to these the subjective criteria (such as readability versus conciseness), and the many different subjective orderings of these and the objective criteria, you can see that the pressures towards proliferation are increased manifold.

20.5 The role of standardization

The title says 'Standardization and language proliferation' almost as if standardization was supposed to *cause* language proliferation! (I have actually heard arguments in favour of that proposition, though I do not know how seriously they were intended!) In fact the role of standardization in relation to proliferation is rather specific.

Standardization is sometimes discussed as if it were a means to control proliferation of new languages, at least successful ones. This was a theme right from the earliest days of language standards. Even before the formation of the ISO and US language standards committees, Stanley Gill, at the first British Computer Society conference in 1959 [Gill, 1959], talked about 'Standardization of programming language' (note the singular) as being 'the most controversial topic', and remarked that 'there are many reasons why existing notations differ, and many of these reasons will no doubt continue to exist for a long time ... there are obvious advantages to be gained ultimately from standardization, which will enable programmers to follow each others' programs ...'. Clearly he was thinking of just a single language. Interestingly, he was clearly also thinking of standardization meaning portability of programs *between people*, rather than (or rather than just) between machines.

Three years later, with the committees active, 'proliferation' had become an issue [Shaw, 1962], and it has cropped up from time to time ever since. However, the earlier analysis shows that proliferation is inherent in the nature of languages, not just endemic, and there is nothing that standardization can do about it. In all important respects, proliferation of languages is essentially uncontrollable, and it would be vain to try. So this issue is of significance only when people mistake or misrepresent the role of standards. That role is rather different.

There are in fact two kinds of proliferation, not one. The pressures towards producing new languages also apply to producing new *versions* of languages, otherwise known as dialects, which have already been mentioned. A new task may call for a language quite like an existing one, so why not adapt that, by extending its syntax and semantics? It is a seductive halfway house between using a perhaps adequate but not quite ideal tool, and making a whole new tool. Emotional attachment to, or simply familiarity with, an existing tool, is also a factor. You can like, or even deeply love, another person, without thinking they are perfect in every way, and still want them to be with you even for something they are not suited to. Indeed you may be tempted not to accept them as they are, but to change them. I am sure we can all think of instances.

It is this form of proliferation that standards address, though it is not their only role. For each language, a standard provides for that language community an aid to coping with the problems that dialects present. Though the pressures towards proliferation of dialects may be just as intense, the commonality of the base language narrows the realm of discourse sufficiently that standards can be agreed and be effective; and, even more important, it creates a community with sufficient common interest that the need for a standard is much more evident. The proliferation of languages has led to a continuing stream of demands for further language standards, as new languages become established and gain a constituency large enough for the need to be recognized and acted upon. This proliferation of language standards has been a matter of legitimate concern to the standards committees, but it is an inevitable consequence of proliferation of languages and the need for newly formed language communities to obtain the benefits of standardization already experienced by the older groups. Some who sneer at standards, whether through academic snobbery or adherence to some purist 'free market' doctrine, regard standards bodies as foisting standards on an unwilling community. Much more common in fact, at least with languages, is the community begging for a standard.

The primary benefit of a standard is usually seen to be portability of programs from one standard-conforming platform to another. In the past this has sometimes been regarded as being its only purpose, and were that the case there are plenty of people who might say that this is of no interest or value to them, so they gain no benefit – though even there, such an attitude can often prove to be shortsighted, for example when their old system needs replacing and they suddenly find that the dialect they are used to has disappeared.

However, the benefits of standards are greater than this – and could be much greater still. Portability of *people* has now come to be seen as an important feature, both for organizations (in reducing retraining costs) and for the people themselves. (As noted earlier, Gill was already there, or nearly so, in 1959.)

Even if that doesn't interest you, standard conformance gives you somewhat greater assurance of what you are getting for your money: what you can rely on. With the better standards, this is not just the syntax and semantics of the standard language, but flagging or rejection of non-standard usages, minimum criteria for things like supported ranges of values or sizes of data structures, the assured presence of certain aspects of error handling, and so on. The standards vary in that respect, and even the best could do much more, but the tendency is in that direction: for example, the ISO committees have guidelines now which give things that they should at least *consider* for inclusion in their standards.

Standards can never give you everything, and I am not saying that non-conforming implementations may not have their virtues. But the benefits to language users of standards and standard-conforming implementations are real and tangible, not just something theoretically desirable. Users in the academic world, both lecturers and students, have something to gain from using them, as we shall see.

20.6 Proliferation, standards and choice of languages

This discussion provides a number of lessons relating to the theme of the choice of programming languages. One is that it definitely *should* be choice of *languages*, not of *a programming language*. Proliferation is with us and is inherent, so students should understand the phenomenon and be able to cope with it. The first step to that is knowing several – at least two, from a very early stage, so their minds do not get cast in a particular mould; hence of just two, the two should be very different in kind. I and many others have discovered, without being taught, from our own development and from teaching others, that the *second* language is the most difficult one to learn.

(Note that, by the same token, in a commercial or industrial context it is unwise to recruit and train staff who know only one language, be it COBOL, ADA, C++ or whatever. Recruit people who are, to some extent at least, programming linguists; they are likely to be more adaptable, and there's a good chance they'll be better programmers too.)

Next, students should be dissuaded from trying to classify languages into 'good' or 'bad', rather than better suited or not to a particular task. Rather should they learn to assess the virtues and limitations of any language or any 'paradigm', that dreadful word used here for the only time![1] Indeed, they should be encouraged to be sceptical, and suspicious of partisans for any specific language or approach.

The dialect phenomenon and the role of standards also need to be understood. Students should be aware of standards: what they do, what they cannot do, what they could do but don't: the limitations of standards, the deficiencies of standards, as well as their importance. The problems that result from ignoring standards should form an important element of this.

Problems of lack of standardization are omnipresent, so they equally come into play with the choice of languages! Certainly, if a language has a standard then it should be taught as defined in the standard, not as a dialect. In fact, a good way of teaching about dialects and standards is to choose such a language as one to be taught, using it as an illustration. A valuable aid would be an implementation which is standard-conforming and has the property of being able to flag or reject non-standard usages, as mentioned above. Not all standards, regrettably, require this feature for conformance, but many reputable suppliers provide it anyway.

Lecturers benefit from the improved chances of importing teaching material or exporting their own, and being less reliant for their teaching on a particular version from one supplier on a particular platform. They have a definitive basis to work from, and usually a wider range of available but mutually compatible textbooks. It may be easier to spread the student practical load over more than one system. The students in turn benefit from better knowing what information sources are appropriate or not, and if they have access to some outside facility, whether it will be suitable. They also know that they are acquiring a skill, of possible benefit later, not specific to a particular compiler or system; in later life they may well appreciate having used a standardized language – or resent that they were not, nor given enough grounding in transferring skills between systems and languages or the role of standards.

There may be people who are uncomfortable with some of this. It may be thought to smack too much of a 'training workers for industry' approach to undergraduate teaching. I assure you that I am far from sympathetic to such an attitude. In fact, I do not even need you to subscribe to the attitude, though this is one with which I do have sympathy, that the needs of all students should be catered for in a course, not just those of

---

[1] Marian Petre's contribution to this debate [Petre, 1996] is the one instance I know of the word being given some sort of validity – and I'm not sure I'm pleased at that!

the brightest. My arguments are relevant even for anyone whose only interest is in finding and rearing potential Ph.D. students, while treating the rest as rejects. It is certainly true that the average graduate will be better equipped for the world with a good grasp of standardization issues, and no one can properly be regarded as a computing professional without it. The point is that this applies inside as well as outside our institutions; it applies to someone who enters the academic world as an undergraduate and leaves it as a professor emeritus, just as it does to someone who scrapes a third and then lands a lucrative job as an IT specialist with a firm of financial consultants.

Any choice of languages to teach is necessarily going to involve a balance between intellectual needs and practical needs, and this often hurts – I know! The point is that ignoring standards risks students (and you) encountering problems that almost always serve no purpose and simply form a distraction from the main issues. This applies as much to academic work as it does to commercial and industrial activities. Coping with incompatibilities resulting from lack of adherence to standards wastes time anywhere. The problems are quite indiscriminate about where they strike; the academic world, whether in teaching or in research, is not immune. Using standards can give you more time to concentrate on what really matters.

Throughout, I have not argued that you should *always* use a standardized language rather than an unstandardized one, or even that you should *always* use a standard-conforming implementation rather than one that is not. I am simply asking that standardization issues be given adequate weight when you come to a decision. As I said, the benefits are real, and should not be lightly disregarded.

20.7 Conclusion

Bryan Higman ended the review already cited [1978] by saying 'If lack of a common language can fragment a culture, possession of the right one can prevent fragmentation in a curriculum.' Even then, I think I would have argued for common *languages*, a multicultural environment if you like, and that it is the right choice (in your context) of those who would prevent fragmentation. Today I would argue that the stable basis provided by standards must form an important part of that multicultural environment.

Acknowledgements

This chapter has drawn considerably on material written originally as part of a UK paper on language proliferation, intended for submission to the international programming languages standards committee ISO/IEC JTC1 SC22, and also on a history of programming language standardization which is currently being written. I am grateful for comments from Peter Lee on the version presented at the 1993 Open University workshop, which suggested some useful additional points.

20.8 References

Gill, S. (1959), Current theory and practice of automatic programming, *Computer Journal*, **2**.

Higman, B. (1967), *A Comparative Study of Programming Languages*, Computer Monographs No. 2, Macdonald, London (and Elsevier, New York).

Higman, B. (1978), [Book review], *Times Higher Education Supplement*, **15**.

Klaeren, H. (1996), Programming languages: a framework for comparison and choice, in *Programming Language Choice: Practice and Experience*, M. Woodman (ed.), International Thomson Computer Press, London, chapter 2, (this volume).

Meek, B. (1990), Problems of software standardization, *Computer Standards and Interfaces*, **10**(1), 39–43, (also reprinted in *User Needs in Information Technology Standards*, ed. C. D. Evans, B. L. Meek and R. S. Walker, Butterworth-Heinemann 1993, 177–183).

Petre, M. (1996), Programming paradigms and culture: implications of expert practice, in *Programming Language Choice: Practice and Experience*, M. Woodman (ed.), International Thomson Computer Press, London, chapter 3, (this volume).

Shaw, C. J. (1962), The language proliferation, *Datamation*, 34–6.

21 The role of documentation in programmer training

Johannes Sametinger

A longer title for this chapter would be: *The Role of Documentation in Programmer Training from Conventional Documentation to Literate Programming, Hypertext and Object-oriented Documentation*. It is not 'just' about documenting programs or training programmers to document their work: high quality-software documentation reduces the maintenance burden and improves productivity by enhancing re-usability. To a great extent documentation is neglected in software education and training; neither are documentation skills taught, nor are well-documented systems used for learning purposes. This chapter explores the issues and suggests how tools for hypertext, literate programming and object-oriented documentation can be used, thus having an impact on programming language choice.

21.1 Introduction

Software engineering is the practical application of scientific knowledge for the economical production and the useful and economical employment of reliable and efficient software [Pomberger, 1993]. The need for documentation is obvious for software maintenance and software re-use. But we also have to direct our attention to the role of documentation in programmer training. The availability of programming tools already plays a major role in choosing a programming language for software education. Usually and unfortunately, neither the availability of documentation tools nor the availability of documentation support in programming tools have an impact on this choice. Well-documented software systems are also needed for students to learn from the designs and implementations of experienced engineers.

Furthermore, conventional documentation does not seem to be very suitable or attractive for learning and teaching. This chapter outlines how concepts like literate programming, hypertext and object-oriented documentation can be combined to improve software documentation quality and accessibility. This can result in a more effective education of our future software engineers.

Maintenance plays a key role in software engineering. It consumes the greatest proportion of expenses in the software life cycle [Arthur, 1988]. The most difficult problem in modifying software systems is understanding the intent of the original programmers. Although tools that support program comprehension at source-code level are of great help, adequate documentation is the most obvious and effective way to support this comprehension process. Software documentation is a necessity to enable maintenance, and increasingly attention is being paid to it in practice.

Object-oriented programming is the programming paradigm of the 1990s. Typically, object-oriented systems are not built from scratch, but rather class libraries and application frameworks are extended. However, efficient re-use of existing components is possible only when documentation is available that makes it possible to identify re-usable components in a certain context and to actually re-use them by providing all necessary information.

One of the key skills for a good software engineer is the ability to devise excellent designs for software systems. Besides practice, the only way to considerably improve one's ability to design software systems is to study existing designs. This requires the availability of well-designed software systems and their corresponding well-written documentation. Without documentation it is difficult to duplicate the chain of reasoning of the original author of a complex system. Thus documentation is crucial not only for maintenance and re-use but also for software education. Excellently designed and well-documented software systems also prove extremely useful in the education of software engineers.

The study of both good-quality design and documentation is inexcusably neglected in programmer training. This is partly due to the fact that most of the source code is proprietary and the documentation, if available, is inadequate. Nevertheless, there is enough well-designed and publicly available source code around that can be used for the purpose of knowledge transfer from experienced software engineers to fledgeling ones.

We need more attention to software documentation education to change the role of documentation from an awkward appendage to a matter of course. Additionally, concepts and tools are needed that help in analysing and learning from existing good software architectures and documentation for educational purposes.

So far, writing documentation has not been practical when a software system is frequently changing. Yet, particularly when a software system is frequently changing, documentation is required to facilitate these changes. This apparent contradiction can be resolved by using technologies like literate programming, hypertext and object-oriented documentation, as will be shown in this chapter.

21.2 Conventional documentation

Conventional documentation is simply a linear text that possibly contains some graphics and is physically separated from the program text. Typically it is written after finishing the source code of a software system. Nowadays this kind of documentation is typical, and it is almost always incorrect, inconcise, incomplete and inconsistent.

When writing software documentation is taught at all, then typically students are first instructed in the possible structure and contents. Then they have to write parts or all of the documentation for an example application that they had to program. In many cases, practical programmer training stops at the point when development of a software system is finished. As a result, documentation is hardly ever written and also is not really needed – except for getting good marks when it is required by the teacher!

Public-domain software could be used for studying existing designs, but it hardly ever comes with adequate documentation. So even if the software contains good design examples, they are not really useful for educational purposes. And even if suitable documentation is available, it is hard for students to use it, because conventional documentation is organized linearly. This handicaps selective reading and writing. Besides, there is no connection to the program text. This separation makes it difficult to check the completeness and the consistency of the documentation. Additionally, it is difficult to find the corresponding location of some source code, such as the description of a certain procedure or method.

The separation of source code and its related documentation is one of the key determinants for the neglect of documentation in education. Programming and documenting seem to be two totally different activities. Of course, the more important one – programming – is done first. Unfortunately, there appears never to be sufficient time available for the latter – documenting. This separation is also one of the main reasons for the absence of well-documented sample programs. Students could benefit from programs that are well documented, but such programs hardly exist. Literate programming promises to provide a solution to this dilemma.

21.3 Literate programming

Programs are written to be executed by computers rather than to be read by humans. Ideally, it should be the other way round. When writing programs, we should not try to instruct the computer what to do, but rather we should try to tell humans what we want the computer to do [Knuth, 1992]. The idea of literate programming is to make programs as readable as ordinary literature. The primary goal is not to get an executable program but to get a description of a problem and its solution (including assumptions, alternative solutions, design decisions, *etc.*).

With the idea of literate programming Knuth also developed the WEB system to support his paradigm. WEB programs consist of a series of documentation sections which contain documentation text and source code. Each section describes a certain aspect of the software system and has references to related sections. For compilation, the source code is extracted from the sections.

The original WEB system supports the programming language PASCAL. Other implementations have been made for C, MODULA-2, LISP and FORTRAN. In order to make WEB available to a much larger audience, a tool was developed to construct instances

3. Here is an outline of the entire Pascal program:

program sample;
    var <Global variables 4>
    <Random number generation procedure 5>
    begin <The main program 6>
    end.

4. The Global variables M and N have already been mentioned; we had better declare them. Other global variables will be declared later.

     define M_max= 5000 {max. value of M}

<Global variables 4>∫
M: integer;   {size of the sample}
N: integer;   {size of the population}

See also Sections 7, 9, and 13.
This code is used in Section 3.

Figure 21.1 Sample literate program [Knuth, 1984].

of the WEB tool from a language description [Ramsey, 1989]. Object-oriented programming languages are supported as well: for example, literate programming environments have been developed for C++ [Sametinger, 1992] and SMALLTALK [Reenskaug and Skaar, 1989].

Figure 21.1 contains two sections of a literate program taken from [Knuth, 1984]. For every section the WEB system generates hints about where the code in this section is used and which sections refer to its code.

The integration of source code and documentation makes a positive influence on the correctness, consistency and completeness of documentation. Besides, programming with documentation rather than with pure source code is a major step towards better program comprehensibility and thus maintainability. Well-documented examples, like [Knuth, 1986], are of great value to students as they provide all necessary information for studying both the architecture of existing software systems and their corresponding documentation.

Unfortunately, too few examples are available because literate programming has not been a success in practice. So, what are the disadvantages? Despite the glorious idea of integrating source code and documentation, the WEB system and its successors are rather useless to practitioners because they impose parallel and linear development of source code and documentation. This is realistic only when one has a good idea of the program to be developed. But usually, experiments and redesigns are needed because the structure of a system is not clear from the very beginning. This scenario of evolutionary, exploratory and incremental software development characterizes many projects (especially student projects) and must be supported by methods and tools for documentation as well.

In order to benefit from the advantages of literate programming we have to overcome the linear and parallel development but adhere to the integration of source code and documentation. This is where hypertext comes on to the scene.

21.4 Hypertext documentation

Usually documentation is stored in text files that are flat; that is, they are organized in a linear way. This linear organization is not adequate. The documentation of a software system should be interleaved with the source code, and there need to be many possible paths to read the available information, depending on the interests of the reader. A hypertext enables nonsequential writing and reading. It consists of a set of nodes where each node contains some amount of information (some text, a picture, or even a video sequence). These nodes are connected by links and form a directed graph. Navigating through a hypertext means following these links. As each node can have several outgoing links, there are many possible sequences in which to inspect the nodes of such a network. This gives the user the feeling of free movement through the available information (see [Smith and Weiss, 1988; Nielsen, 1990]).

Vannevar Bush was the first to describe the ideas of hypertext [Bush, 1945]. Although at that time there were no adequate computers available, Bush had a vision of organizing information as in the human mind, which operates by association. He introduced (but never implemented) MEMEX, an online text and retrieval system for browsing and making links and notes. About 20 years later Bush's ideas influenced the work of Douglas Engelbart, who then developed NLS (oN Line System). NLS was an experimental tool for storing specifications, plans, designs, programs and documentation and for doing planning, designing, debugging, *etc.* [Engelbart, 1963]. More and more hypertext systems have emerged with the evolution of cheaper and more powerful computers (see [Conklin, 1987; Shneiderman and Kearsley, 1989]). Possible applications of hypertext systems include dictionaries, encyclopedias, product catalogues, technical documentation, help systems and software engineering tools.

Hypertext tools are the new generation of documentation tools. Non-sequential reading and writing is extremely useful for software documentation, but the concepts of hypertext can also be applied to source code and – even more important – it can be used for the integration of source code and documentation. The possibility of selectively reading parts of the source code and the documentation is crucial for the comprehension process. With documentation organized as hypertext and tools providing the above features, it is much easier for both students and practitioners to explore software systems. Sample software systems and good-quality documentation – if available – can more easily be studied and checked for consistency and completeness.

The motivation to write documentation increases with hypertext, because it becomes possible to write down ideas and design decisions and connect them with the corresponding source-code locations without the need to create separate documents. Completing a web of ideas and design decisions that were written down during the development phase is far easier and less tedious than writing documentation from scratch after development. The fact that software systems change during development becomes less serious because the corresponding documentation parts are easily available and can thus be kept consistent.

The nodes and links in a hypertext documentation have to be well structured. This is a major factor that determines how easy it is to use and update the documentation. Additional features like indexes (for looking up information alphabetically), searches (*e.g.* keyword search), filters (for limiting the displayed information), bookmarks (for

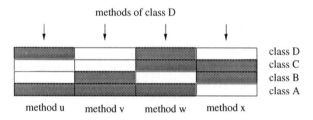

Figure 21.2   Inherited and overridden methods of a class.

marking specific locations), and path histories (for keeping track and going back), further enhance the opportunities of hypertext.

Arbitrary nodes and links can be defined when writing a hypertext, and there exist numerous possible ways through a hypertext when reading it. Unfortunately, too much freedom can cause difficulty with both reading and writing. We need predefined structures and guidelines that help in producing documentation and lessen the danger of getting lost in a complex information web. Object-oriented documentation, described in the next section, defines a suitable structure for object-oriented software systems. Additionally, it takes the enhanced reusability and extensibility of the object-oriented programming paradigm into account.

21.5 Object-oriented documentation

Class libraries and application frameworks must provide extensive documentation in order to facilitate their use in education. This documentation has to be integrated and re-used in the students' documentation just as the prefabricated software components are integrated in their source code. Object-oriented programming improves the reusability of software components. In order to increase the productivity in documenting and to make the structure of documentation better suited for object-oriented software systems, I suggest that object-oriented technology be applied to the documentation, too. This makes it possible to re-use documentation by extending and modifying it without making copies and without making any changes to the original documentation. Additionally, easy access to relevant information can be given by using the inheritance mechanism. Object-oriented documentation is another step towards integrating source code and documentation, and a way of providing non-linear access to relevant information about a software system.

The re-use of object-oriented software components is facilitated by the inheritance mechanism. Inheritance can be viewed as both extension and specialization [Meyer, 1987]. A class D directly or indirectly inherits from one or more superclasses A, B and C. The features of the superclasses are a subset of the features of class D; that is, D inherits whatever A, B and C provide and includes its own extensions. On the other hand, inheritance is used to realize an *is-a* relation. For example, a rectangle (D) is a special visual object (A) with the features of a visual object but specialized behaviour (specialization). Of course, specialization may also be achieved by disabling methods in subclasses.

Figure 21.2 graphically represents the inheritance mechanism. In this example class A provides three methods, u, v, and w. Class B (a subclass of A) overrides v and adds a method x. Class C is a subclass of B and overrides the methods w and x. Finally, class

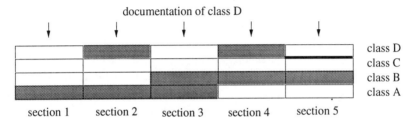

documentation of class D

Figure 21.3   Inherited and overridden documentation sections of a class.

D overrides the methods u and w. The grey and white boxes in Figure 21.2 indicate the availability of methods. Class D provides the methods u and w of its own, method v inherited from class B, and method x inherited from class C. Overriding a method means either replacing the overridden method or extending it, that is, invoking the overridden method in the overriding one. However, from the class's users' point of view there is no difference between an overriding and an extending method.

As with the source code, a class should inherit the documentation of its superclasses. However, the benefits of inheritance would not be worth the effort when applied only to a class's documentation as a whole. Therefore, I suggest dividing it into (arbitrary) sections. A section is a portion of documentation text with a title. The sections can be defined by the user (programmer) and used for inheritance in the same way as methods. Similarly to methods, sections are left unchanged, removed, replaced, or extended in subclasses (Figure 21.3). Examples of such sections are: short description, conditions for use, instance variables, instance methods. I further suggest defining a basic set of sections that has to be provided for each class (*e.g.* those listed above). Depending on the classes, other sections have to be added, such as event handling and change propagation.

Figure 21.3 contains the structure of the documentation of the classes A, B, C and D. The documentation of class A consists of three sections, and classes B and C have five documentation sections, whereas class D has only four. Class D inherits sections 1 and 3 from the classes A and B, respectively, has section 2 and 4 of its own, and removes section 5. Removing documentation sections is important when a specialized behaviour is realized in subclasses, such as object list and sorted object list. Please note that the documentation of class C consists of five parts, though not an extra line of documentation has been written for this class. For more details about object-oriented documentation see [Sametinger, 1994].

Object-oriented documentation is built according to the inheritance structure of a software system and offers both easy extensibility and easy re-usability. The simple structure helps students to find their way through the information more easily. The well-defined structure of object-oriented documentation can be combined with hypertext and literate programming to achieve high flexibility and higher integration with the source wherever it is wanted.

21.6 Experiences

Many of our students who write their thesis use the public-domain application framework ET++ for their programming work (see [Weinand *et al.*, 1989]). ET++ consists of hundreds of classes and thousands of methods. Documentation text for the most important classes and methods is available, but is stored in separate files and thus not easily accessible. For beginners it is even rather cumbersome to get relevant information about certain classes and methods out of the source code because the data is usually spread over the descriptions of several classes because of inheritance.

The use of application frameworks and class libraries is inherent to object-oriented programming. But so far such frameworks and libraries represent a hurdle to be surmounted by beginners only with great effort. This is due to the usually enormous complexity, and also to the lack of good documentation. Thus, despite the fact that these frameworks and libraries have been developed by very experienced engineers, their experience hardly ever finds its way to software engineering beginners.

We have built a programming environment prototype, which combines the concepts of literate programming and hypertext [Sametinger, 1991]. The tool automatically creates hypertext links for the source code, such as from classes to superclasses and from identifier uses to identifier definitions. This provides useful browsing capabilities and supports the comprehension process enormously. Additionally, documentation text can be integrated with the source code via hypertext links in the sense of literate programming [Sametinger and Pomberger, 1992]. We have also divided the existing documentation into sections and applied the inheritance mechanism as described in the previous section [Sametinger, 1994].

The students rate the tool as being very useful for getting familiar with an unknown class library. They like the object-oriented access to the library's documentation and the hypertext and literate programming features they can use for writing their own documentation. Unfortunately, no hypertext links are established for the library documentation and no source code is integrated in the sense of literate programming. But once such tools are widely available appropriate documentation will hopefully come with the libraries. Then we will be able not only to re-use the source code but also to fully exploit the knowledge that went into building those libraries.

21.7 Conclusion

Documentation is important not only for software maintenance and re-use, but also for the education of future software engineers. We have to train our students to write good-quality documentation. This does not mean that they should be able to write novels, but rather that everyone must be able to sketch design decisions and implementation details and to organize them in a well-structured way, so that it is readily understandable and useful for others. On the other hand, well-documented, high-quality systems can and should be used as examples in education in order to transfer design knowledge. These goals cannot be achieved with conventional documentation. We need concepts like literate programming, hypertext and object-oriented documentation plus the corresponding tools in order to improve the quality and also the availability of documentation, and to profit from it in education again.

21.8 References

Arthur, L. J. (1988), *Software Evolution: The Software Maintenance Challenge*, Wiley, Chichester.

Bush, V. (1945), As we may think, *Atlantic Monthly*, 101–8.

Conklin, J. (1987), Hypertext: an introduction and survey, *Computer*, **20**(9), 17–41.

Engelbart, D. C. (1963), A Conceptual Framework for the Augmentation of Man's Intellect, in *Vistas in Information Handling, Vol. 1*, Spartan Books, London.

Knuth, D. E. (1984), Literate programming, *Computer Journal*, **27**(2), 97–111, also contained in [Knuth 1992].

Knuth, D. E. (1986), *Computers and Typesetting*, Addison-Wesley, Reading, MA.

Knuth, D. E. (1992), *Literate Programming*, CSLI Lecture Notes (Number 27), CSLI, Stanford.

Meyer, B. (1988), *Object-oriented Software Construction*, Prentice-Hall, Englewood Cliffs, NJ.

Nielsen, J. (1990), The art of navigating through hypertext, *Communications ACM*, **33**(3), 297–310.

Pomberger, G. (1993), Software engineering education – adjusting our sails, *Education and Computing*, **8**, 287–94.

Ramsey, N. (1989), Literate Programming: weaving a language-independent WEB, *Communications ACM*, **32**(9), 1051–5.

Reenskaug, T. and Skaar, A. L. (1989), An Environment for Literate Smalltalk Programming, in *Proceedings of OOPSLA '89*, 337–45.

Sametinger, J. (1991), *DOgMA: A Tool for the Documentation and Maintenance of Software Systems*, Technical Report, University of Linz, (available via anonymous ftp from ftp. swe. uni-linz. ac. at).

Sametinger, J. (1994), Object-oriented documentation, *Journal of Computer Documentation*, **18**(1), 3–14.

Sametinger, J. and Pomberger, G. (1992), A hypertext system for literate C++ programming, *Journal of Object Oriented Programming*, **4**(8), 24–9.

Shneiderman, B. and Kearsley, G. (1989), *Hypertext Hands–on: An Introduction to a New Way of Organizing and Accessing Information*, Addison-Wesley, Reading, MA.

Smith, J. B. and Weiss, S. F. (1988), An overview of hypertext, *Communications ACM*, **31**(7), 816–9; special issue on hypertext.

Weinand, A., Gamma, E. and Marty, R. (1989), Design and implementation of ET++, a seamless object-oriented application framework, *Structured Programming*, **10**(2).

22 (Re)presenting the p-word: paradigmatic discourse on programming languages

Hugh Robinson

This chapter is a reflection on the workshop that was the genesis of this book and an analysis of the verbal discourse at the workshop. At one level this allows the reader to gain a feel for what being at the workshop was like. Its more serious aspect is a contibution to the research into the social contruction of computing and in particular into research into how computer scientists debate issues to do with programming language choice. The commentary and analysis provided is an example of how software professionals should reflect on how they analyse their strategic problems and how they discuss options that address them.

22.1 Introduction

The work described in this chapter is part of a programme of research which addresses questions about the nature of computer science – about what it is that computer scientists know and how they know it. The term 'computer science' is used here as a catch-all to cover the range of activities covered by terms such as 'information systems', 'software engineering', 'computing', 'computer studies', *etc.* No implication is made that these activities are necessarily 'scientific'. Indeed, the research disputes the straightforward response to such questions, which conceives what computer scientists know as some form of received scientific knowledge and how they produce this knowledge as some variant on the scientific method (as in [Milner, 1986] or [Hoare,1984], for example). The research utilizes (and, in part, is motivated by) the belief that a large part of the answer to the question 'What is the nature of computer science?' is served by the answer to the question 'What do computer scientists do in practice?'. The research seeks answers to this latter question from empirical studies of computer scientists carrying out the business of computer science. The particular business of computer science described in this chapter is that of the two-day workshop on the choice of programming language (often for the teaching of computer science) and papers from the workshop that were the basis of many chapters in this book.

The workshop afforded an opportunity to gain insight into the way in which participants present and utilize notions of programming languages and the processes by which they lay claim to assertions about programming languages. Such insight into the way in which computer scientists debate issues of programming language choice amongst themselves is valuable in its own right and is a resource for any investigation of the way in which such issues are presented to students in the business of teaching.

The empirical data underpinning the work is naturally occurring data, consisting of video recordings of the workshop (essentially, presentations of papers and discussion), supplemented by field notes. Most of the presenters' papers were made available to delegates at registration but had not been available beforehand. Presenters did not assume that delegates had read the papers – now edited as chapters in this book – and they are therefore not analysed significantly in this chapter.

22.2 The approach

Given that the work centres around issues of what computer scientists do in practice, the research methodology used in analysing the data is one taken from ethnography and discourse analysis, two approaches which have recently been successfully used in studying the nature of software engineering and information systems development [Cooper, 1991; MacKay, 1994; Robinson, 1990, 1993]. Ethnography ([Hammersley and Atkinson, 1983], for example) is:

> a style of research in which the observer adopts the stance of an anthropologist coming upon the phenomenon for the first time. One takes the perspective of a stranger as a way of highlighting the taken-for-granted practices of the natives under study.

> [Woolgar, 1988]

Such an approach is particularly useful in revealing specific, concrete material practices which compose the moment-to-moment, day-by-day work of occupational life and has been used in Suchman's formative study of human–computer interaction [Suchman, 1987]. Discourse analysis ([Potter and Wetherell, 1987], for example) sets out to detail the tacit, organized procedures which inform the production and recognition of naturally occurring discourse (talk, written materials, *etc.*) and has been used as a natural complement to an ethnographic approach.

Carrying out ethnography with discourse analysis brings certain ethical considerations. Whilst the ethnographer will have negotiated access to the site (in this case, the workshop) for observational studies, nevertheless the ethnographer is present amongst the 'members' (the technical term employed to denote the 'natives' – the workshop participants) as an 'outsider', with an agenda that is different from that of the members.

And, of course, the ethnographer wishes to take findings from the site of study back to the 'outside'.

Furthermore, some of those findings will be examples of discourse, verbatim transcriptions of what has been said for one purpose (that of the members) but is now portrayed for another purpose (that of the discourse analyst). There is an equivocation here, where the ethnographer is both at an advantage and at a disadvantage. This is made more poignant when, as is the case in this work, the ethnographer is, in another guise, potentially one of the members and where the findings of the study are liable to publication in journals and books that are part of the members' intellectual discipline – in this case, computer science. In recognition of these considerations, extracts from the transcription of the discourse are reproduced with changes that attempt to preserve the anonymity of individuals. No such protection, however, is afforded to the various programming languages, which were also 'participants' in the discussions.

22.3 The workshop

The aims of the workshop, as advertised, were:

> to develop criteria and techniques to judge the suitability of languages for particular uses. It is primarily for those involved in higher education but will be of relevance to practitioners in industry and commerce; the relevance of standards and implementations will be explored.
>
> [from the invitation to delegates]

The workshop took place over two days and comprised 21 substantive presentations, each lasting some 20 to 30 minutes, with a final plenary session of over one hour. The presentations covered various programming languages (C, C++, MODULA-2, MODULA-3, ADA, ML, EXTENDED PASCAL, OBERON, TURING, EIFFEL, SMALLTALK, LISP, OMEGA and COOL) as well as issues relevant to the choice of programming language, such as the role of documentation in software engineering education. There were some 84 delegates to the workshop. All but 7 of these delegates came from institutions whose main business was that of higher education. Although the event was termed a 'workshop', it operated, for all intents and purposes, as a conventional academic conference and relied on the inclination of the participants to talk to each other during breaks (particularly during the dinner on the first evening).

22.4 The p-word(s)

An accepted and received feature of discourse on programming languages and the choice of programming language is an association with the term 'paradigm'. This invokes a belief that a programming language can stand for what is seen to be a revolution in thinking about software and the business of developing software to meet the needs of users. For instance, much of the recent activity in object-oriented programming languages is frequently couched in just such terms. By way of example, Cox [1990] claims that the object-oriented approach is:

> a paradigm shift – a software industrial revolution based on reusable and interchangeable parts that will alter the software universe as surely as the industrial revolution changed manufacturing.

Indeed, for Cox, this 'software industrial revolution' is deemed to be more significant than an industrial revolution since it is conceived as a profoundly intellectual revolution – comparable with the Copernican revolution in cosmology. In this sense, 'programming paradigm' is regarded as carrying the full authority of the 'world view' of a Kuhnian paradigm [Kuhn, 1962]. That is, a programming paradigm determines all aspects of some context, from what counts as the acceptable given facts to what counts as acceptable ways of moving from given facts to 'new' facts: it constitutes not just a way of producing a solution to a given problem, but a way of conceiving the problem in the first place. Examples similar to (but perhaps not so stridently expressed as) Cox's abound, such as [Coad and Yourdon, 1992] or [Smith, 1991], and typically make claims that a programming *paradigm*, enshrined in a language that expresses solely that paradigm, prescribes certain (and acceptable) behaviour: 'It (the hierarchy of definitions) forces thinking about structure early in the design process. It forces thinking about generality and concepts' [Smith, 1991, p. 7].

What does an analysis of the data say about this accepted and received notion of programming paradigm? Perhaps surprisingly, in terms of the discourse at a workshop devoted to the choice of programming language, there is little evidence that members' (that is, presenters' and delegates') discourse oriented to, or could be accounted for in terms of, such a notion of paradigm. This is not to say that the term 'paradigm' was not used in discourse. It was, notably by one presenter who, as the second presenter on the first day, directly addressed evidence disputing the cognitive utility of the above notion of paradigm in explaining the behaviour of expert programmers. The presenter immediately following marked this impact with the introduction[1] of the term 'p-word':

> PH: I congratulate /the previous speaker/,[2] if that's the right word, on making the first shot, in my knowledge, of giving respectability to that vile word 'paradigm'. Uhm, I'm not sure if she should be thanked or condemned for that by the way. I will try not to use the p-word if I can avoid it ...

Rather, the claim that discourse did not orient to such a notion of paradigm is shown by the way in which members made and accepted a move from one supposed paradigm to another without comment or justification. A typical presentation would describe the range of languages considered by the presenter, covering examples from the imperative, object-oriented and functional paradigms, without any sense in the discourse of moving from one world view to another (as might be expected, say, if one were moving from a Ptolemaic cosmology to a Copernican cosmology). Similarly, the final choice of language was accounted for in terms that made no appeal to a notion of paradigm. Rather, appeal was made to the contingent and situated circumstances of the presenter's teaching context. Discourse such as the following was typical.

> TM: We decided very early on that we wanted an imperative language as opposed to a functional approach or any other approach as primarily the pragmatics of the set of students we are dealing with ...
>
> ... We briefly considered SMALLTALK just to say we had briefly considered it. ...

---

[1] Given that there was no 'p-word' in the original printed paper, it is tempting to conclude that this was an impromptu introduction.

[2] The notation used in reporting discourse is, hopefully, self-explanatory but it is useful to note that text between slashes is that of the author or editor, for the purpose of providing some immediate context.

... CLU was only really there as a place holder for ADT evaluation. It was never a serious candidate. But I'd used CLU and I like CLU ...

... It's nice if you can continue to use the language for second- and third-year computer science courses. It's not an absolute requirement but it's nice. I don't know about the rest of you, but we are finding that the students these days are lazy beggars (audience laughter). They don't want to learn, they don't want to go off and experiment. And if we want to switch to a new language in the second year, we've got to teach it. ...

...And the only way we made a decision was by me saying 'Right, we've got to go for C++.' (audience laughter)

Another example is as follows.

OS: /on ML/ ... and it has the practical advantage that everyone starts equal, it's a great leveller on the students as they come in.

Paradigmatic irrelevance is well summarized by one presenter's straightforward utterance:

PH: If you are lying awake at night wondering which language to choose, stick a pin in something and see what you get. You'll probably manage.

and by a series of jokes, which work at the nominal expense of students but also at the expense of the notion of programming paradigm as a prescription. Various versions of the joke were told but it essentially revolved around the fact that for many students with prior experience of an 'undesirable' language, such as BASIC or C, no matter how much of a 'desirable' language, such as ADA or MODULA-3, they were taught they 'continued to write BASIC using MODULA-3'.

It is useful here to juxtapose what I am claiming is present in the discourse with that from other sources. As has been mentioned, one of the presenters discussed evidence disputing the cognitive utility of Kuhnian paradigms in explaining the behaviour of expert programmers. In its own terms – as a piece of cognitive science – that presenter's argument rejects paradigms. In contrast, the account given above from the discourse does not seek to reject paradigms. Clearly, it could not: members' discourse displays use of the term 'paradigm', both at this workshop and elsewhere. Rather, the account seeks to explore the social utility of the notion of paradigm – what work is being done by members' use of paradigm-centred discourse and what that discourse achieves. What I am claiming from the workshop discourse is that the use of the term 'paradigm' cannot be accounted for in Kuhnian terms. That is, discourse does not proceed in a fashion that might be expected where members held different (and conflicting) views as to what, in fact, was the case (that is, differing world views). This still, of course, leaves open the question as to what is achieved by 'paradigmatic' discourse, an issue which is deferred until some other salient features of members' discourse have been described.

22.5 Pariahs

Whilst members' discourse is not accountable in terms of Kuhnian paradigm, it is accountable in terms of programming *pariah*, in the sense that the discourse reveals that several programming language artefacts can acceptably be considered to be undesirable without recourse to any justification or explanation. Such languages were the butt of jokes (as above), irony and ridicule that was clearly accepted, understood and participated in by the audience. Here are four examples:

> AC: /shows a slide of usage of programming languages and interacts with the audience by getting them to guess the entries./ ... The next one we come right down to 12%. (audience offers inaudible suggestion:) FORTRAN? Yes, that's absolutely right (inaudible). The next one's close to 'FORTRAN', it's 11%. (audience offers inaudible suggestion) No. Imagine what was top of the charts 30 years ago. (offer from audience of:) 'Its PL/I' (inaudible, followed by audience laughter) Time's running out, it's assembler. Still 11% of the world's code is written in assembler.

> SN: We see all sorts of anachronisms, people still programming away in BASIC, FORTRAN or SQL. Why? (audience laughter) For goodness' sakes, why?

> FR: /displays a slide from a recent MIT job advert, which reads as follows:/ 'Applicants must have extensive knowledge of C and Unix, although they should also have sufficiently good programming taste not to consider this an achievement.' (audience laughter when this is shown)

> OS: It is, I fear, necessary to expose our students to C at some point. It is, after all, a universal assembly code for most computers. ...

> ... and COBOL because the British Computer Society insist on it for their accreditation. We can think of no rational justification. (audience laughter)

It takes a brave questioner from the audience to challenge utterances such as this and the only significant occasion where this took place was where the questioner pointed out that the British Computer Society required, in fact, systems analysis rather than COBOL. Having made this point, the questioner then showed shared acceptance of the pariah status:

> FR: You shouldn't make that kind of (inaudible) with COBOL. (audience laughter)

Perhaps the best evidence for this notion of an anti-paradigm pariah comes from one presenter who was accounting for the choice of a language that, whilst not regarded as a full-blown pariah, was certainly discussed in a way that accepted that it had what members would take to be undesirable qualities.[3] This led to much shared and mutual irony and mirth between presenter and audience:

> TM: And the kind of things we were looking for in the language features, apart from the standard things like, er, (inaudible) strong typing, all those obvious things, clearly we wanted support for ADTs, er, we thought we wanted support for exception handling ... /and then moves through a list/ ... minimum pitfalls ...remember what we finished up with. (audience laughter) These are the ideals we strived for. (audience laughter) But in true academic sense we threw away our ideals. (audience laughter)

To labour the obvious, this shared humour can only work where members implicitly already accept the nature of the language choice that is being justified.

---

[3] The language was C++.

Underlying this notion of pariah status is a particular rhetoric about industrial and commercial practice, a rhetoric which, in its gentler forms, might be termed a 'rhetoric of disdain' and, in its stronger form, might be termed a 'rhetoric of contempt'. Instances of this rhetoric are present in the above extracts (for example, it is hard to see how the utterance '… and COBOL because the British Computer Society insist on it for their accreditation. We can think of no rational justification.' would have caused the audience response it did without COBOL having quite the industrial and commercial prominence that it enjoys. Occasionally, his rhetoric of contempt is quite exposed:

> SN: /on talking through an OHP entitled 'What do we see in industry?' and coming to the second point:/ We see a surprising amount of movement to C++. Devastating really because if you ask them why, they haven't got a clue, (audience laughter), not a clue. We see all sorts of anachronisms, people still programming away in BASIC, FORTRAN or SQL. Why? (laughter) For goodness' sakes, why? …

> … This next one is one I rather cherish and I guess this is what I really took from L /another presenter's first name/ when he first started teaching some of this stuff. You know, if it compiles, it must be right. That's absolutely rampant, that is. And when you consider some of the rubbish they are using to compile with – compiler writers in the audience, please forgive me, it's not your stuff (momentary pause) uhm, (audience laughter) perhaps. That's just tragic that is. It shows a fundamental lack of understanding of what is going on. You really worry.

22.6 The unquestioned, the unjustified

The discourse is a useful source for understanding some of the ways in which computer scientists lay claim to assertions about programming languages, ways which relate to the (mis)notion of programming paradigm discussed above. Whilst an analysis of the discourse does not reveal the argument, the questioning and justification that would be symptomatic of the utilization and advocacy of programming paradigm, it does reveal a set of tenets about programming that were universally shared by members. Many presenters gave lists of desirable features of a programming language. Whilst some features were argued for and justified, other features – forming a distinctive set – were not so supported, and this was true across presenters. The features that were argued for and justified were actively termed 'non-technical'[4] and can be characterized as contingent and contextual, dependent on the nature of the particular institution and the particular aims and aspirations of the curriculum. The explication of these features took time in the discourse and frequently began with pronouncements such as:

> OS: I want to tell you a little about the arrangements for our computer science course in D, the way it's constructed …

and even when the case for a feature had been made, it was still worth remarking on:

> TM: Real-world acceptability is something I guess we didn't used to give a toss for, right?

---

[4] As characterized by one presenter: 'Critical factors are usually non-technical.'

In contrast, a set of 'technical' features was repeatedly invoked across presenters without any significant work in the discourse to justify or argue for these features.[5] In a strong sense, these features required no further explanation: they were both incontestable and unremarkable. Here is one example:

> TM: And the kind of things we were looking for in the language features, apart from the standard things like, er (inaudible), strong typing, all those obvious things ...

and another:

> QW: The obvious things that were missing were modules and separate compilation.

Indeed, the absence of some feature from a presenter's list was a remarkable occasion, one for chiding:

> SH: The other thing I find amazing about the discussion this morning is that no one mentioned concurrency. Does that mean that it's a dead topic as far as academics are concerned?

Or status is displayed as so sufficiently incontestable that, rather than be justified, the feature can safely be joked with:

> OS: We also believe in strong typing – strong typing for weak minds, as they say.

Associated with these central tenets of programming were a series of assertions by presenters in the general form of 'language X having/not having (desirable) feature Y'. These assertions were routinely made with little or no justification, despite the assertions being contradictory across presenters in several cases. One presenter went so far as to explicitly argue for this lack of justification, for the desirability of not representing evidence:

> TM: If we start getting into any technical discussion of technical aspects of this language versus any of the other ones, we'd be here all day – so I don't really want to do that ...

22.7 The absence of argument

Whilst the assertions just discussed were not accompanied with justification, the contradictory nature of the assertions was commented on:

> SH: We heard that, uhm, from M that ADT support was going to be poor in ADA. I don't quite understand that.

and separately:

> MB: I couldn't understand either why QM, for example, er, felt that some of the languages couldn't implement abstract data types and I felt that perhaps we were talking about different things when we were talking about abstract data types. Because we felt that EIFFEL actually implements abstract data types very well.

---

[5] These features were manifested in various ways: modularity, data hiding, data abstraction, abstract data types, strong typing, safe and separate compilation, exception handling and concurrency support.

Furthermore, in question sessions the contradictions were the subject of direct questions. What is interesting is that both such comments and direct questions never led to any significant debate or marshalling of evidence for and against a position. It was sufficient for the protagonists to reaffirm their (contradictory) positions, in a way that is akin to reaffirming opinions rather than facts. Such interchanges were typically concluded with a humorous remark or similar device that generated audience laughter (and not any resolution of the dispute).

For example, one presenter (LQ) was questioned about his advocacy of MODULA-2 as being good for abstract data type support. The questioner (TM) began by making the point that LQ claimed that MODULA-2 offered good support for abstract data types, whereas QM's institution had rated MODULA-2 as being the worst language in this respect. LQ's ironic response is

> LQ: I was surprised by that! (audience laughter)

and offers nothing further. TM persists, however, by taking the line that MODULA-3 offers even better abstract data type support, so why didn't LQ consider MODULA-3? LQ's response is that MODULA-3 is a 'poorly designed language':

> LQ: ... designed by a committee, except that committee happened to be one person. (considerable audience laughter)

and this concludes the 'dispute'!

In a similar vein, TM attempts controversy with QW:

> TM: Just to, uh, add a sort of controversial observation. Uh, I really sort of feel that this is a waste of time, right. I mean, PASCAL had its day and trying to add all the bells and whistles on it to get it to be modern, I suspect is really the wrong way of doing it. (inaudible) Just cut it off, throw it away and start again.

But QW's response defuses this by immediately generating audience laughter, enabling a change of topic:

> QW: Well, (pause, followed by audience laughter) some people feel like that but if you are saying that you want to throw away all your existing investment ... I'm not necessarily arguing that this language is the thing you want to teach first in computer science ...

My contention here is that, in the face of an invitation to debate or controversy, the response of a resort to mirth or humorous irony (endorsed by the audience with their laughter), followed by a change of topic is, in effect, declining the invitation. On occasion, this declining of the invitation can be quite spectacular:

> /Following a presentation that discussed, amongst other things, tools for software testing, the following exchange took place between an audience questioner (AC) and the presenter (TL)./
>
> AC: When Fignon said that testing can only prove the presence of bugs and not their absence, which I thought was self-evident, was he ... is, hopelessly wrong?
>
> TL: I've always thought, ... I've always thought that Fignon was a complete and utter pillock. (audience laughter for 8 seconds) There are a whole lot of things that he never understood. I've, uh, I've had numerous sessions with Laurent and usually what I find with him is he says something really controversial, uhm, because he's actually got a cracking sense of humour. The trouble is because he's able to say it with a dead-pan expression, people believe it ...

Despite the ridiculing of 'Laurent Fignon' (an extremely eminent academic computer scientist), the invitation to debate and argument has been declined, for there is no further discussion of Fignon's views on software testing.

It is tempting to characterize this lack of debate as being typical of this kind of academic workshop, rather than being indicative of computer science *per se*. However, this temptation should, perhaps, be eschewed since the lack of evidence and argument was commented on by the plenary session chair (who was a cognitive scientist rather than a computer scientist):

> FM: People were saying things like 'my language is clearly defined and simple', 'you can teach people to think in concepts', 'programming in X is very natural'. All these are anecdotal – OK, fair enough, I say things like this too. I felt, I was a bit worried about this, this made me feel like I was back in California somehow. These were all – what I can say to this group, because this is a group of hardcore scientists and hardcore scientists should not be making casual anecdotal statements like this at a workshop like this. ... We can do better ...

Such admonishment was treated in the discourse in much the same way as the object of its criticism – it was regarded as a casual, anecdotal statement. No one took up the invitation: it was declined.

22.8 Concluding remarks

What am I suggesting here? Essentially that computer science, as represented in this discourse, does not proceed in quite the simple fashion of clear paradigms and rational argument that might be imagined from a characterization as 'hardcore science'. Rather, it is a more subtle and sophisticated achievement involving a set of shared and unquestioned beliefs, which can be displayed without contestation, as well as a group of programming language artefacts which are its own creation, yet are largely inadmissible in public academic discourse. There is a lack of argument and evidence for assertions, a lack of desire for disputes, that suggests that it is not straightforward facts that are being displayed but a more complex rhetoric that justifies decisions and positions that are invested as much with personal and institutional context, which is both mutable and contingent, as with the purely immutable logic of a technical rationale.

One way of approaching the fine grain of this detail is via the notion of interpretative repertoires: recurrently used systems of terms used for characterizing and evaluating artefacts, events, processes and other phenomena.[6] [Gilbert and Mulkay, 1984], in a detailed analysis of biochemists' discourse, identified two repertoires: the empiricist and the contingent. The empiricist repertoire:

> predominated in the context of formal research papers. In this discourse the experimental data were given both chronological and logical authority.
>
> [Potter and Wetherell, 1987, p. 149]

A characteristic of the empiricist repertoire is the presentation of evidence, argument and results with an impersonal, dispassionate and objective rhetoric that divorces what is being said from the scientist who is saying it ([Locke, 1992] gives a powerful account of this repertoire).

---

[6] I am grateful to Margie Wetherell for suggesting this approach.

In contrast, the contingent repertoire:

> portrayed actions and beliefs as heavily dependent on speculative insights, prior intellectual commitments, personal characteristics, unspecifiable craft skills, social ties and group membership.
>
> [Potter and Wetherell, 1987, p. 149].

Typically, an empirical repertoire is used to assert, argue for, or report on what is taken to be the 'facts' by a research scientist, whilst a contingent repertoire is used to deny, argue against, or dispute what another research scientist mistakenly believes to be the case – the 'non-facts'. As might be expected, the empirical repertoire dominated in formal research papers, whilst the contingent repertoire dominated in more informal discourse settings.

As such, it is useful to suggest that the discourse that has been analysed in this chapter is predominantly a computer scientist's version of a contingent repertoire (call it, say, the 'informal repertoire'), contrasting with the more formal accounts to be found in the presenters' papers (and, indeed, in the chapters of this book), coming from a computer scientists' version of an empirical repertoire (call it, say, a 'formalists' repertoire'). This does, in fact, seem sustainable. For example, the choice of C++ at one institution was described at the workshop as:

> .../showing a summary OHP/ So we tried ticks and crosses but that didn't quite work ... And the only way we made a decision was by me saying 'Right, we've got to go for C++'.

In contrast, it is described in the paper as:

> The recommendation for C++ was not made lightly. Indeed, most if not all of those concerned with making the recommendation would have bet money at the start that their recommendation would not have been for C++. A decision to recommend C++ was initially considered only reluctantly, but we came to realize that some of our initial prejudices were false and that, on balance of all of the issues, C++ was the best compromise. It was recognized that this choice was not without risk, and that there are criteria against which C++ does not turn out to be the best candidate, but nevertheless our recommendation stood.

There are clear elements of an informal/formalists' repertoire split here. However, even in the formal paper, the informal repertoire persists. The account is 'mutably imprinted with social, economic or personal concerns' [Nye, 1990, p. 4]: 'initial prejudices were false', 'on balance', 'not without risk', 'best compromise', *etc.* Indeed, it is tempting to speculate whether computer science does, in fact, have a truly mature formalists' repertoire. This is one way of explaining the lack of response to the cognitive scientists call for evidence and argument.

This informal/formalists' repertoire split is also useful in explaining the social utility of programming language paradigms. The notion of programming language paradigm seems to be used in both repertoires. Within the formalists' repertoire, the notion of programming language paradigm is deployed with its full Kuhnian authority, invoking all the cachet of diamond-hard-scientific truth to the cause of establishing the utility of a particular linguistic artefact. Within the informal repertoire, the notion of programming language paradigm seems to be a way of celebrating and affirming shared beliefs and attitudes as academics, of demarcating the area of professional expertise and competence that is occupied by the tribe that calls itself 'computer science'. And, of course, part of the business of reinforcing tribal membership is to be clear about where that membership is ambivalent. Every tribe has its pariahs, not formally part of the tribe but inextricably defined by the tribe. So too, computer science needs to have its CO-BOL.

22.9 References

Coad, P. and Yourdon, E. (1992), *Object-oriented Design*, Yourdon Press Computing Series, Yourdon Press, Englewood Cliffs, N. J.

Cooper, G. (1991), *Representing the user: a sociological study of the discourse of human computer interaction*, PhD thesis, The Open University.

Cox, B. J. (1990), There is a silver bullet, *Byte*, **15**(10), 209–18.

Gilbert, G. N. and Mulkay, M. (1984), *Opening Pandora's Box: A Sociological Analysis of Scientists' Discourse*, Cambridge University Press, Cambridge.

Hammersley, M. and Atkinson, P. (1983), *Ethnography, Principles in Practice*, Tavistock, London.

Hoare, C. A. R. (1984), Programming: sorcery or science?, *IEEE Software*, 5–16.

Kuhn, T. S. (1970), *The Structure of Scientific Revolutions*, The University of Chicago Press, Chicago, 2nd edition.

Locke, D. (1992), *Science as Writing*, Yale University Press, New Haven.

MacKay, A. H. (1994), Systems analysis as a social process, in *Social Perspectives on Software*, S. Woolgar and F. Murray (eds), The MIT Press, London.

Milner, R. (1986), *Is Computing an Experimental Science?*, Laboratory for Foundations of Computer Science, University of Edinburgh.

Nye, A. (1990), *Words of Power*, Routledge, London.

Potter, J. and Wetherell, M. (1987), *Discourse and Social Psychology*, Sage, London.

Robinson, H. M. (1990), Towards a sociology of human-computer interaction: a software engineer's perspective, in *Computers and Conversation*, P. Luff, N. Gilbert and D. Frohlich (eds), Harcourt Brace Jovanovich, London, 37–49.

Robinson, H. M. (1993), A philosophy of computing? – the case of sociology and computing, *Journal of Intelligent Systems*, **3**, 189–216.

Smith, D. N. (1991), *Concepts of Object-oriented Programming*, McGraw-Hill, New York.

Suchman, L. (1987), *Plans and Situated Actions*, Cambridge University Press, Cambridge.

Woolgar, S. (1988), *Science: The Very Idea*, Tavistock, London.

Index

4GL 203, 273, 295
68000 225-7
80386 250

absent 208
abstract types (ML) 152
abstract data type 51, 303, 305
   COOL 51
   C++ 66-76, 81-2
   EIFFEL 181-9, 196-7
   discourse 337-338, 340-1
   MODULA-2 108-11, 114-5, 120,
     123-4
   MODULA-3 158, 161, 162
   paradigms 36
   SMALLTALK 213
   TURING 91-2, 98
   VDM 278, 281, 287
abstract concept 19
abstract generic type 155
abstract root prototype (OMEGA) 230
abstraction 41-2, 304-6
   ADA 37, 127-8, 131-2
   building 40
   COOL 51, 55
   C++ 65-6, 74, 76, 78
   EIFFEL 196
   discourse 340
   formal 259, 261-3, 270-4
   MODULA-2 113
   MODULA-3 167
   OBERON 172
   paradigms 41, 42
   skills 40
   solution strategy 40
   standards 317
   strategies 32
   structure 39

VDM 278-81, 286
academic language 295
acceptance grammar 37
access to other languages 194
ACM (curriculum) 108
activation (OMEGA) 230
ADA 12, 14-8, 20, 24, 125-34, 293-9
   ADA 83 128-9
   ADA 95 5, 125-30, 132, 305
   array subscripts 126
   broad-spectrum language 128
   C++ 68-9, 72, 74
   call back 129
   cheap compiling technology 129
   class 130-1
   compilation 126
   compiler 125-6, 129, 132
   concurrency 128
   conference example 130
   COBOL 126-7
   COOL 47
   critical systems 132
   data abstraction 127
   data type 128
   database applications 129
   default initialization 128
   defects 126
   dereferencing 125
   detection of errors 126
   dynamic binding 128
   dynamic semantic checks 125
   efficient code 126, 128
   embedded 129
   encapsulation 126
   escape mechanisms 126
   discourse 335, 337
   event 130
   exception handling 132

extension programming 132
extension *see type extension*
external interfacing 129
fixed-point arithmetic 126
floating-point arithmetic 126
formal aspects 259, 272
generics 130–2
GNU 129
'Green' proposal 127
hardware representation 127–8
hardware 129, 133
high-assurance software 132
ideal programming language 125
imperative language 126, 132
information hiding 127
insecurities 129
large program construction 126
large projects 132
LISP 238
MODULA-2 113
MODULA-3 168
machine orientation 128
'make' 132
mathematical routines 129
object-oriented design 128
object-oriented programming 128, 130–2
operating system 127, 129
OS/2 129
package 127
paradigm 3, 39, 127–8
PC 126, 129
physical representation of data 126
pointer 125, 128, 129
portability 133
Posix 129, 133
private type 128
procedural abstraction 127
programming paradigms 126
re-use 132
readable code 126
record 130–2
run-time checking 126
run-time system 129
safety and security applications 129
safety 132
secure abstraction 128
secure code 126
security 132
separate compilation 132
SPARC workstation 129

SQL binding 129
standardization 129
standards 319
static semantic checks 125
strong typing 125,128
syntax 132
tagged types 128, 132
teaching 132, 304, 306
text books 132
type extension 130
type system 132
user-defined types 128
variant records 132
VDM 126, 288
Windows 129
ADT *see abstract data type*
advanced concepts 17
ALGOL *see Algol-60*
ALGOL-60 12–14, 16–18, 68, 88, 126, 314
ALGOL-68 12, 16–18, 24
ALGOL-W 262
algorithm
   C++ 64, 66, 72, 74
   EIFFEL 196, 258
   formal aspects 259, 261, 263, 265, 271
   formal development 261
   ML 150
   MODULA-2 115–6, 120
   MODULA-3 157, 167
   VDM 278, 280–1, 286–7
aliasing
   EIFFEL 189
   SMALLTALK 213
Allegro 248
allocation (of memory) 213
analysis and design methodologies 196
analysis tools 225
ANSI C
   C++ 71
   COOL 61
ANSI Committee X3J20 (SMALLTALK) 204
ANSI-X3 137
anti-paradigm pariah 338
APL 14–6, 18, 30, 259
application generator 225, 295
applicative languages 14
apprentice software engineers 66
arguments (OMEGA) 222, 224

arity of inheritance 208, 213
array
  bounds (C++) 75
  C++ 72–5, 79
  COOL 49, 55
  indexing (C++) 70
  formal aspect 263
  LISP 237
  MODULA-2 114, 120
  MODULA-3 158
  OBERON 172
  OMEGA 218, 221, 226, 229, 233
  SMALLTALK 203, 210
  subscripts (ADA) 126
  TURING 85, 97
artificial intelligence
  LISP 249
  EIFFEL 195
assertions
  EIFFEL 187, 193
  LISP 238
  OBERON 176
  TURING 98
AT & T 72
atoms 239
attributes 187
A/UX 77

B 260
backtracking 246
bad languages 272
bad programming 37
base COMMON LISP 245
basic type
  C++ 73
  COOL 49, 59
  EIFFEL 188–9
  VDM 288
BASIC 8, 18–9, 30
  discourse 337–9
  factors in higher education 296
  formal aspects 259
  ML 151
  TURING 85, 89–91
BCD arithmetic 59
BCPL 260
beginners 150
behaviour (of a class) 187
BETA 23
binary message (OMEGA) 219
binary search tree 120

binary/octal/hex constants 144
binding of internal variables 136, 142
bindings 17
BIT (EIFFEL) 188
bit substring (TURING) 99
blacksmith principle 35
block-structured procedural languages
  295
blocks (OMEGA) 221
BON see business object notation
BOOLEAN (EIFFEL) 188
Borland 84, 307
British Standards Insititution (BSI) 135
BRANDED (MODULA-3) 163
broad-spectrum language 128
business information systems 299
business object notation 182, 196

C 8, 14–5, 9
  C++ 71
  documentation 325
  discourse 335, 337
  factors in higher education 294–7
  formal aspects 259–60, 270
  LISP 240, 242, 249, 251, 253
  non-continuity 270
  paradigms 34
  programmer 36, 75
  TURING 84–5, 94
C++ 8, 9, 11, 12, 16, 18, 23, 63–81, 297,
  299
  A/UX 77
  abstract data types 66–76, 81–2
  abstraction 65–6, 74, 76, 78
  ADT see abstract data type
  algorithm 64, 66, 72, 74
  ANSI C 71
  apprentice software engineers 66
  array 72-5, 79
    bounds 75
    indexing 70
  AT & T 72
  basic type 73
  C 71
  C comparison 71
  C programmer 75
  Cfront Release 3 72
  choice of programming languages 67
  class 66–7, 72–4, 76–80
  compactness of notation 72
  compiler 68, 71–2, 75

computer science 64, 66–7, 69, 71, 73, 78
computing 64, 67–8
control abstraction 68, 73
COOL 47
copying semantics 71
CS1 64–6
data representation 76
data structure 64
data structure 72–4, 76–7
data type 69
debugging 75
de facto standard 78
dereferencing null 75
design goal 71
design-through-abstraction 66
discourse 335, 337–9, 343
documentation 326
dynamic binding 66
encapsulation 66, 71
environment 72, 77
error checking 74
error message 75
exception 70, 75
exception handling 68, 70, 75
experiences using C++ 73
extensible I/O 71
formal aspects 259–60, 271, 274
functional abstraction 65
functional language 66
functional approach 66
for loop 75
garbage collection 73
generic 74
GNU 72
hardware 68–9
if statement 75
imperative language 64, 66, 78
inheritance 66
initialization 71
interfaces in header file 79
linked list 74
LISP 251–3
list 74, 79, 81
logic programming 66
longevity 68
Macintosh 72, 77
MacOS 77
member function 80
message 75
MODULA-2 109

MODULA-3 168
object-oriented 66, 69–70, 78
objects 66–7, 70, 72–3, 82
OMEGA 217, 219, 221
operator overloading 71
orthogonality 68
paradigm 66
parameterized types 68, 70, 74
PC 72
pointer 64, 74, 75
pointer semantics 74
programmers 37
protected 211
public 211
queue 74
re-use 76
real-world 71, 75, 78
recursion 74
representation on screen 76
run-time checking 68, 72, 74–5
searching 74
single-paradigm language 70
software engineering 66, 71, 73, 78
sorting 74
stack 69, 74–5, 79, 82
stack example 79
stack traceback 75
standardization 78, 319
string 72–5, 81
strong type checking 71
subset of a language 71
substitute classes 74
syndrome 305
syntax 70
teaching 63, 72, 78, 304–6
template 74, 81, 93
textbooks 71–2
TURBO C++ 77
TURING 84, 93–4
type checking 75
Unix 68, 72, 77
value semantics 71
X11 77
CAD/CAM 195
call-back
   ADA 129
   LISP 248
case statement 276
C. A. S. E. tools (SMALLTALK) 203
categories of language *see classification*
CEDAR 157, 172

Ceres 174
CEILIDH 299
chaining messages 244
change propagation 329
cheap compiling technology 129
choice of programming languages
   C++ 67
   formal aspects 261–73
Clarion TopSpeed Software 298
class 304
   COOL 50, 55, 59
   ADA 130–1
   C++ 66–7, 72–80
   documentation 324, 328–30
   EIFFEL 181, 185–96
   LISP 243–5, 249
   MODULA-3 157
   OBERON 177
   OMEGA 217–9, 223–4, 227
   SMALLTALK 200–13
   TURING 85, 87, 92–3, 99–101
   versus type 208
class library
   SMALLTALK 200, 202, 208, 213
   TURING 87
class method 210
class variable 206–7, 211
classic PASCAL 136
classification of languages
   as concurrent 45
   as real-time 45
   as special-purpose 45
   COOL 45
   Klaeren's schema 23
   Rechenberg's 24
   Sammet's 23
   Shearing's 208
CLEM 299
client–server systems (SMALLTALK)
   200
client–supplier contract (EIFFEL) 184–5
clone (OMEGA) 228
CLOS 23, 243–6, 248, 250–2
cluster (EIFFEL) 194
CLU 15–6, 18, 68, 70–1, 337
commercial practice 339
COBOL 14–9
   ADA 126–7
   discourse 338–9
   factors in higher education 293–8
   formal aspects 259–60, 271

ML 151
   paradigms 41
   standards 314, 319
COMMON LISP 238, 240–50, 252
COMMON LISP Object System see
   CLOS
code walker 242
CoLibri 59
collections of objects 221
collections 226
commercial data processing language
   295
commercial research laboratories 167
commercial systems analysis 292
Common Graphics 248
communication 16
compactness of notation 72
comparisons
   C++ with C 71
   evaluation of ML 156
   ML and MODULA-3 160
   PASCAL with TURING 90
   see also main discussions of
      langugaes where others mentioned
compilation units 58
compilation
   ADA 126
   OBERON 175
compile time errors (OMEGA) 218
compiled method (OMEGA) 223
compiler 21
   ADA 125–6, 129, 132
   COOL 48, 61, 68, 72, 75
   EIFFEL 194
   discourse 339
   formal aspects 260, 272
   LISP 235, 237–42
   ML 152, 157
   MODULA-2 109–11, 113–4, 288
   MODULA-3 159–60, 166
   OBERON 173–6
   OMEGA 219–21, 225–7, 233
   SMALLTALK 203, 208
   standards 319
   teaching 302
   TURING 84, 86–7, 89–90
compiler-writing (SMALLTALK) 202
completeness 151
complex numbers
   EXTENDED PASCAL 147
   LISP 242

complexity of algorithms 281
computer science 299, 303
   C++ 64, 66–7, 69, 71, 73, 78
   discourse 333–4, 337, 39, 341–4
   formal aspects 255
   ML 149
   MODULA-2 107–9, 114, 116
   OBERON 171
   TURING 83–4, 86, 89
computer scientists 334
computer studies 333
computing mathematics 303
computing professionals 320
computing teaching 292
computing 291–3, 298, 301–4, 307
   C++ 64, 67–8
   discourse 333
   formal aspects 255–6, 272 .
   ML 149–50
   paradigms 30
concatenation operator (SMALLTALK)
   211
concepts 18–9, 303
conceptual models 8
conciseness 317
concurrency 14
   COOL 56
   discourse 340
   ADA 128
   EIFFEL 195
   ML 151
   MODULA-3 158
   SMALLTALK 213
   TURING 85
conditional assignment (OMEGA)
   219–21
conference example
   ADA 130
   COOL 50–9
   EIFFEL 190
   ML 155
   MODULA-3 164
   OBERON 178
   OMEGA 230
   SMALLTALK 205
   TURING 100
   VDM 282
consistency with commonly used
   notations 21
constant expressions (EXTENDED
   PASCAL) 143

constrained parameters (EIFFEL) 186
constraint (LISP) 236
construction and maintenance of large
   systems 157
container classes (COOL) 55, 59
contingent repertoire 343
continuation function (LISP) 238
continuity 270
continuous languages 262, 266
control abstraction
   C++ 68, 73
   OMEGA 218, 221
   formal model 271
control constructs 272
COOL 45–62
   abstract data type 51
   abstraction 51–5
   ADA 47
   ADT *see abstract data type*
   ANSI C 61
   array 49, 55
   availability 61
   basic type 49, 59
   BCD arithmetic 59
   C++ 47
   classification 45
   class 50, 55, 59
   CoLibri 59
   compilation units 58
   compiler 48, 61
   concurrency control 56
   container classes 55, 59
   CoOMS 57
   data abstraction 49
   data programming 49
   data structure 51
   data-intensive applications 47
   database schema 56
   development scenario 60
   design criteria 47
   design goal 46–7
   dialog object interface 61
   discourse 335
   dynamic binding 53
   dynamic type 53
   efficiency 48
   encapsulation 59
   environment 46, 54, 59–62
   event 50
   exception handling 54
   exception 47–8, 54, 58–9

extensions 51
foreign imports and exports 59
functional language 45
garbage collection 49, 61
generic object type 55
genericity 53, 55–6, 61
graphical user interfaces 59
implementation module 58
INFORMIX 61
inheritance 47, 51, 60
instance variable 49–52, 57
interface classes 61
ITHACA 46
language binding 59
large-scale programming 47
libraries 59
list 59
maintainability 46–7
MaX 60
member functions 49
memory of objects 49
message 48, 50, 53–4
method 49–55, 60
modules 58
Object Management Architecture 49
object state 49
object type 47–53, 55–8, 60–1
object type interface 61
object orientation 45, 47, 49, 51, 53,
    60–1
object 47–54, 56–7
OMG 49
OODBMS 56–7
openness 48
operating system 47
ORACLE 61
orthogonality 47–8
OSF X/Motif 61
persistence 56, 62
persistent declaration 57
pointer 60
polymorphism 53
print object interface 61
productivity 46
programming environment 46
programming in the large 46
protected method 50, 52
prototyping 46
quality 54
re-use 47, 51–2
read lock 57

readability 46–7
record 49, 60
redefined method 52
relational database 59, 61
reliability 48
run-time error 48
selector 50
separate compilation 58
SINIX 61
software quality 46
software reliability 54
source-code debugger 60
specification module 58
SQL 56, 61
SQL object interface 61
stack 55–6
static type 53–4
string 49, 59
strong typing 54
subtype 50–3
supertype 51–2
template 55
test object interface 60
transaction 56–7
transaction blocks 56
transaction roll back 57
transient declaration 57
TRY 54
type system 48, 59
types 49
unique clause 57
version V2.0 62
version V3.0 62
write lock 57
X/Motif 61
Unix 54, 60–1
CoOMS 57
copying semantics 71
coroutines 15, 17
correctness 258
corruption of code 158
creation clause (EIFFEL) 189
creation procedure (EIFFEL) 188
creation (OMEGA) 223
criteria for language selection 172, 307
critical systems 132
cryptoquote 121
CS1 64–6
culture 4, 8, 29–30, 32, 36–42, 295, 314,
    320
curriculum cycle 83

dangling pointer
  OBERON 175
  TURING 91
data abstraction 11
  ADA 127
  COOL 49
  formal 271
data encapsulation 136–137
data members (in C++) 49
data programming 49
data representation 76
data structures 23, 298
  C++ 64, 72–4, 76–7
  COOL 51
  EIFFEL 191
  formal aspects 263, 272
  LISP 237, 239
  ML 150, 152–3
  MODULA-2 111, 114–6, 120
  MODULA-3 158, 167–8
  OBERON 174–6
  teaching 304
  TURING 84, 87, 91, 93
  VDM 281
data type 23
  ADA 128
  C++ 69
  discourse 341
  formal 272
  LISP 239, 243
  ML 157
  OMEGA 218–20
  VDM 281, 282
data-flow language 247
data-flow programming 237, 245
data-intensive applications 47
database applications 129
database schema 56
databases 195, 203
date and time procedures 145
DBASE 293–4, 297
deadlock 263
deallocation (of memory) 213
debug statements (EIFFEL) 196
debuggers (SMALLTALK) 204
debugging
  C++ 75
  EIFFEL 195
  LISP 243
  OMEGA 225

DEC Alpha 175
DEC PASCAL 136
DEC's Systems Research Center 167
declaration schemata 140
declarations
  OMEGA 220
  TURING 97
declarative (style) 33–4, 258, 274
'decode'/'encode' 142
DECstation 175
DECsystem-20 303
de facto standard 109
default initialization 128
defects 126
deferred class (EIFFEL) 191
deferred features (EIFFEL) 190
de jure standard 109
deletion (OMEGA) 223
denotational semantics 238
dereferencing
  C++ 75
  EIFFEL 188
  ADA 125
design model 279
design criteria 47
design criterion (COOL) 47
design documentation 157
design goal
  C++ 71
  COOL 46, 47
  MODULA-3 157
  OBERON 177
design-through-abstraction 66
detecting errors 126
development team 202
dialects (of LISP) 238
dialog object interface 61
dictionaries (OMEGA) 226
difficulties with C and C++ 93
digital logic 150
Digitalk 200
Dijkstra's guarded commands 18
direct manipulation 87
direct-access I/O 143
discourse analysis 334
discourse on programming languages
    333–44
  absence of argument 340
  abstract data type 337–8, 340–1
  abstraction 340
  ADA 335, 337, 340

ADT *see abstract data type*
anti-paradigm pariah 338
BASIC 337–9
C 335, 337
C++ 335, 337–9, 343
COBOL 338–9
COOL 335
compiler 339
computer science 333–4, 337, 339,
    341–4
computer scientists 334
computer studies 333
computing 333
concurrency support 340
contingent repertoire 343
CLU 337
COBOL 338
data type 341
documentation 335
empiricist repertoire 342
ethnography 334
exception handling 338, 340
expert programmers 337
EIFFEL 335, 340
EXTENDED PASCAL 335
formalists' repertoire 343
functional paradigm 336
FORTRAN 338–9
hardcore science 342
human–computer interaction 334
imperative 336
industrial and commercial practice
    339
informal repertoire 343
information systems 333
Kuhnian paradigm 336
LISP 335
ML 335, 337
modularity 340
MODULA-2 335, 341
MODULA-3 335, 337, 341
OBERON 335
object-oriented 335–6
OMEGA 335
p-word(s) 335
paradigm 335–7, 339, 342–3
paradigm-centred discourse 337
paradigm shift 335
pariahs 337
PASCAL 341
rhetoric of contempt 339

rhetoric of disdain 339
separate compilation 340
SMALLTALK 335–6
software engineering 333–5
software industrial revolution 336
SQL 338–9
strong typing 338, 340
TURING 335
unjustified 339
unquestioned 339
workshop 335
discrete mathematics 150
distributed parallel 18
documentation
    C 325
    C++ 326
    change propagation 329
    class 324, 328–9, 330
    completeness 326
    conventional documentation 325
    EIFFEL 196
    environment 326, 330
    ET++ 329
    event handling 329
    evolutionary software development
        326
    exploratory software development
        326
    extensibility 328
    FORTRAN 325
    generators (OMEGA) 226
    hypertext 324, 327
    incremental software development
        326
    inheritance for extension 328
    inheritance for specialization 328
    inheritance 328–9, 330
    instance variable 329
    is-a relation 328
    linear and parallel development 326
    LISP 325
    literate programming 325
    maintainability 326
    MEMEX 327
    method 325–6, 328–30
    MODULA-2 325
    object-oriented documentation 324,
        328–30
    object-oriented programming 330
    OMEGA 225
    overriding 329

paradigm 325–8
PASCAL 325
productivity 323, 328
programming paradigm 324
re-usability of software 328
re-use 323–4, 328, 330
SMALLTALK 326
software engineering 323–4, 330
software engineering tools 327
software maintenance 323
source code 325
specialization 328
student projects 326
subclass 328–9
superclass 328–30
WEB 325
DOS 136
DTL 263
DYLAN 252
dynamic array
TURING 98
EXTENDED PASCAL 140
dynamic binding
ADA 128
C++ 66
COOL 53
EIFFEL 189, 191–3
LISP 237, 239
OMEGA 219
SMALLTALK 211
dynamic semantic checks 125
dynamic type
COOL 53
LISP 237
OBERON 179
OMEGA 221

early history (of languages) 13
easy of learning 21
efficiency 21, 23
ADA 126, 128
COOL 48
EIFFEL 182
MODULA-3 167
OBERON 175
OMEGA 219, 221
paradigms 38
SMALLTALK 208
TURING 85, 89
EIFFEL 12, 18, 23, 181–98, 304
abstract data type 181–9, 196–7

abstraction 196
access to other languages 194
ADT see abstract data type
AI 195
algorithm 196
aliasing 189
analysis and design methodologies 196
assertion mechanism 187, 193
attributes 187
basic type 188–9
behaviour (of a class) 187
BIT 188
BOOLEAN 188
BON see business object notation
building a class using inheritance 189
business object notation 182, 196
C++ 68, 70, 72, 74
CAD/CAM 195
changing export status 190
CHARACTER 188
check 187
class 181, 185–96
client 184
client–supplier contract 184–5
cluster 194
compilation 194
compiler 194
concurrency 195
constrained parameters 186
copy operation 189
creating objects 188
creation clause 189
creation procedure 188
data structure 191
databases 195
debug statements 196
debugging tools 195
deferred class 191
deferred features 190
dereference 188
discourse 335
documentation 196
DOUBLE 188
dynamic binding 189, 191–3
efficiency 182
exception mechanism 193
ensure 187, 196
entity 188
environment 194–5, 197
discourse 340

exception 193, 194, 197
exception handler 193
export policy 192
extensibility 182
failure history 196
feature 187
formal aspects 259
functional paradigm 182
functions 187
generic 184–5
generic parameter 186
graphics 195
hidden features 190, 192
hybrid language 182
imperative paradigm 182
implementations 195
implementing ADTs 185
index clause 196
information hiding 182, 197
inheritance 189–92, 197
INTEGER 188
invariant clause 187
ISE 195
language definition 196
library 185
linked list 185, 188
list 187, 191, 193
logical paradigm 182
loop invariants 187
loop variants 187
message 193
method 197
MODULA-2 109
multiple inheritance 190
name clash 192
NICE 195
N-version programming 194
object sharing 189
object-oriented programming 188
object-orientedness 181–2
objects 183, 187–94
old 187
once functions 193
openness 182
paradigm 182
parameterized ADT 184
persistence 194
pointer 188–9
polymorphism 185, 191–2
portability 182
post-condition 184, 187, 193

pre-condition 184, 187, 193
predicate calculus 187
procedures 187
production-level language 182
programming principles 187
programming by contract 193
'pure' object-orientedness 182
raising an exception 193
re-use 182, 185, 192, 197
REAL 188
redefining features 192
redefinition 190
relational 187, 195, 197
renaming 190
repeated inheritance 190–2
repeatedly inherited features 192
require 187, 196
retry 194
robotic real-time 195
robustness 182
role in industry 195
run-time environment 194
select clause 192
sharing objects 188
SMALLTALK 208
software engineering 182
specifying an ADT 183
stack 184–8, 190, 193
Stack ADT 183
standardization 195
strong typing 185
subtype 185, 189, 193
supertype 185
supplier 184
support needed for implementing
    ADTs 185
teaching 195
telecommunications 195
textbooks 196
time and data management 195
VDM 288
X-Windows 195
Unix 195
elementary concepts 17
embedded systems 16, 129, 292
empirical studies (of programming) 38
empiricist repertoire 342
encapsulation
    ADA 126
    C++ 66, 71
    COOL 59

formal aspects 267
engineering view (of software development) 306
ensure (EIFFEL) 187–8, 196
environment 303, 307
   C++ 72, 77
   CooL 46, 54, 59–62
   documentation 326, 330
   EIFFEL 194–5, 197
   factors in higher education 294, 296, 298
   formal aspects 256
   ML 150–1, 156
   LISP 242–3, 250–1
   MODULA-2 109–14
   MODULA-3 167–8
   OBERON 171–6
   OMEGA 218–9, 222–5, 233
   paradigms 32–3, 41
   SMALLTALK 199, 202, 204, 214, 320
   TURING 84–90, 100
environmental enquiries 144
error message 75
error-proneness 37
escape mechanisms 126
ET++ 329
ETH 171–7
ethnography 334
EUCLID 15, 157
evaluation of languages 69, *see also classification and comparison*
evaluation (of ML) 156
evaluation (MODULA-3) 167
event handling 329
event
   ADA 130
   CooL 50
   discourse 342
   OMEGA 226
   SMALLTALK 206, 209
evolutionary software development 326
example code
   ADA 130–1
   C++ 79
   EIFFEL 185–90
   EXTENDED PASCAL 137–48
   MODULA-2 110–2, 118
   OBERON 177
   OMEGA 227
   SMALLTALK 205

   see also conference and stack examples
exception handling 15, 17
   ADA 132
   C++ 68, 70, 75
   CooL 54
   EIFFEL 193
   discourse 338, 340
   EXTENDED PASCAL 137
   ML 151
   OMEGA 221, 229, 233
exception 15, 307
   C++ 70, 75
   CooL 47, 48, 54, 58–9
   EIFFEL 193–4, 197
   LISP 240
   ML 153–6
   MODULA-3 157, 158, 162, 168
   OMEGA 226, 230
   SMALLTALK 202
   TURING 99
executable code units (OBERON) 175
experiences
   using C++ 73
   with documentation 329
   with VDM 288
experimental language extensions 173
expert programmers 33, 337
experts 150
exploratory software development 326
exponentiation operators 147
export policy (EIFFEL) 192
export status 190
exports (MODULA-3) 157
expression language 211
expression (OMEGA) 219
expression sequence 221
expressivity 23, 174
extensibility 21, 328
   EIFFEL 182
   OBERON 172, 174, 176
extensible I/O 71
extension programming 132
extension (ADA) 130
external interfacing (ADA) 129
EXTENDED PASCAL 135–48
   ALPHA 136
   ANSI 137
   appending to files 143
   binary/octal/hex constants 144
   binding of internal variables 136, 142

British Standards Insititution (BSI)
    135
classic PASCAL 136
COMPLEX numbers 147
constant expressions 143
data encapsulation 136–7
date and time procedures 145
DEC PASCAL 136
'decode'/'encode' 142
declaration schemata 140
direct-access I/O 143
discourse 335
DOS 136
dynamic arrays 140
Edinburgh Portable Compilers 136
environmental enquiries 144
exception handling 137
exponentiation operators 147
exported variables 147
extensions to CASE statements 145
extensions to record variant parts 145
features 137
FOR...IN statement 146
function result variable 143
functions of any type 143
future developments 137
HALT procedure 147
history 135
implementations 136
initial-value specifiers 143
International Standards Organization
    (ISO) 135
internationalization 137
investment 136
ISO PASCAL 135–6
legacy code 136
modularity 136
modules 137
object orientation 137
OS/2 136
parameterized type 136
PASCAL 135–7
PASCAL-E 136
PASCAL Validation Suite 135
PC 136
Prospero compiler 136
protected parameters 147
relaxation of declaration rules 143
RESTRICTED 139
separate compilation 138
short-circuit logical operators 145

stack 138–9
standards 137
STRING 141
string 137, 141
structured value constructors 143
SUCC/PRED 146
type inquiry 140
type-secure separate compilation 137
underscore in identifiers 146
VAX (VMS) operating system 136
Windows NT 136
zero field width output 146
Unix 136
MODULA-2 136
OBERON 136

factors (in higher education) for
    choosing a language 3, 291–300
4GLs 295
academic language 295
ADA 293–9
application generators 295
array 297
BASIC 296
block-structured languages 295
business information systems 299
C 294–7
C++ 297, 299
CEILIDH 299
Clarion TopSpeed 298
CLEM 299
COBOL 293–8
commercial data processing language
    295
commercial systems analysis 292
computer science 299
computing 291–3, 298
cultural factors 295
data structure 298
DBASE 293–4, 297
de facto standard 298
embedded real-time systems 292
environment 294, 296, 98
formal methods 296
FORTRAN 295
FOXBASE 294
FOXPRO 2 299
functional programming 296
home computing 296
industrial acceptance 299
industrial programming 298

information hiding 297
initial/introductory programming
    language 291–2, 294
ISO PASCAL 298
JPI *see Topspeed Clarion*
JSD 294
JSP 294
LISP 293
market forces 295
MASCOT 294
method 294
MIRANDA 292
MODULA-2 293, 295–7, 299
modularity 297
object-oriented paradigm 295, 298–9
OCCAM 293, 297
OMT 299
orthogonal operations 297
paradigm 296–7
PASCAL 292–8
pointer 297
problem domain 296–7
procedural paradigm 297
PROLOG 293, 296
programming in the large 297
programming in the small 297
real-time 295
real-world 297
separate compilation 297
simplicity 297
software engineering 294, 298
software quality assurance 294
SSADM 294
stack 297–8
staff development 295
staff expertise 295
standard PASCAL 297
standards 298
strong typing 297
technical issues 295, 297
textbooks 298
TURBO-PASCAL 294, 296, 298–9
Windows 294
Z 294
failure history 196
fast compilers 21
feature (EIFFEL) 187
file management (OMEGA) 226
finite bijection 121
first-order predicate 263
fixed-point arithmetic 126

floating-point arithmetic
    ADA 126
    LISP 242
for statement 75, 276
foreign imports (COOL) 59
foreign exports (COOL) 59
form (LISP) 248
formal mathematics 236
formal method 2, 270, 296, 302
    SMALLTALK 207
    VDM 277
formal specifications 211
formalism 31, 35, 289
formalists' repertoire 343
FORTH 18–9, 36
FORTRAN 9, 14–6, 18–9, 21, 37, 150
    ADA 127
    discourse 338–9
    documentation 325
    factors in higher education 295
    formal aspects 259–60, 271, 274
    ML 150
    standards 314
    VDM 279
fully qualified declaration (OMEGA) 220
function 276
function result variable 143
functional language 45, 51, 108, 258
functional paradigm 182, 336
functional programming 12, 15, 284,
    296
functional style of programming 150,
    157, 211, 266, 273, 274, 286

garbage collection
    MODULA-3 158
    OMEGA 222
    C++ 73
    COOL 49, 61
    LISP 250
    ML 151
    MODULA-3 157, 167
    OBERON 176
    OMEGA 219, 233
    SMALLTALK 213
    teaching 305
garbage collector
    LISP 250
    ML 157
    MODULA-3 161
    OMEGA 222

general-purpose language 41
generality 21, 23, 296
generic editors (LISP) 247
genericity
    ADA 130, 132
    C++ 74
    classes (SMALLTALK) 209
    container types (OMEGA) 219
    COOL 53, 55–6, 61
    EIFFEL 184–5
    function (LISP) 244
    implementation (MODULA-3) 163
    LISP 244, 252
    ML 152, 154–5
    MODULA-2 109, 113
    MODULA-3 158, 162–3, 167
    object type 55
    OMEGA 218–9, 222, 227
        prototype 218, 219, 228
        variant of block 221
    paradigms 40
    parameter (EIFFEL) 186
    stack
        MODULA-3 165
        OMEGA 228
        SMALLTALK 199
    SMALLTALK 209–10
    TURING 87, 93
    types
        MODULA-2 111
        SMALLTALK 213
    VDM 288
global constant (OMEGA) 232
global variables
    OBERON 176
    SMALLTALK 207, 210
glossary of terms 275
GNU
    ADA 129
    C++ 72
    MODULA-3 167
    SMALLTALK 201
good languages 272
'go to' concept 238
graph algorithms 116
graphical objects 226
graphical user interface
    LISP 249
    COOL 59
    MODULA-3 167
    SMALLTALK 202, 205, 213

graphics (EIFFEL) 195
group-working 203
guard 263, 269

habits 8
HALT procedure (EXTENDED PASCAL)
    147
hardcore science 342
hardware representation 127–8
hardware
    ADA 129, 133
    C++ 68–9
    language implementations 307
    LISP 235–6, 239, 249–51
    ML 156
    MODULA-2 109, 111
hash-tables 237
HASKELL 126
heapsort 116
hidden features (EIFFEL) 190, 192
hiding internal information 157
high safety 238
high-assurance software 132
high-level languages 20, 94, 174
higher-order function (LISP) 241
history of programming languages 17
    EXTENDED PASCAL 135
    HOPL-II conference 20
    SMALLTALK 199
    VDM 278
home-computing 296
human–computer interaction 334
hybrid language 109, 182, 305
hyper-link 101
hypertext 324
hypertext documentation 327

IAL see International Algebraic
        Language
IBM RS 6000 89, 175
IBM SMALLTALK 200–1
ideal software machine 13
if statement 75
image (SMALLTALK) 201
imperative paradigm 18, 182
imperative programming language 18
    ADA 126, 132
    BASIC 151
    C 151
    C++ 64, 66, 78
    EIFFEL 182

discourse 336
MODULA-2 108–10, 114
MODULA-3 149, 162
OBERON 174
PASCAL 151
paradigms 33
VDM 278–81, 286
implementation
    MODULA-2 286
    OMEGA 226
    VDM 280
implementation module (COOL) 58
implementations (of languages)
    and hardware requirements 307
    and tools 307
    of EIFFEL 195
    of EXTENDED PASCAL 136
implementing ADTs (EIFFEL) 185
import list (TURING) 93
incremental software development 326
index checks (OBERON) 176
index clause (EIFFEL) 196
'industrial strength' language 238
industry
    acceptance 299
    commercial practice 339
    ML 151
    OBERON 174
    programming 298
    relevance (of OBERON) 174
    training 150
informal repertoire 343
information hiding 297
    ADA 127
    EIFFEL 182, 197
    MODULA-2 108, 110–1
    OMEGA 231
    SMALLTALK 211, 213
    teaching 304
    TURING 92, 94
information systemse 333
INFORMIX 61
inheritance 328
    C++ 66
    COOL 47, 51, 0
    documentation 328–30
    EIFFEL 189–92, 197
    for extension 304
    for specialization 328
    LISP 245
    ML 151

MODULA-3 158
OMEGA 218–9, 222, 224, 230
SMALLTALK 208
TURING 85, 93
initial programming language 291–2, 294
initial value (OMEGA) 220
initial-value specifiers (EXTENDED PASCAL) 143
initialization 71
    C++ 71
    EXTENDED PASCAL 143
    MODULA-3 160
    OMEGA 220, 231
initialized while loop 19
inorder traversal 120
input–output 23
insecurities (ADA) 129
inspection (OMEGA) 223
inspector (LISP) 243
instance method (SMALLTALK) 210
instance variable
    COOL 49–52, 57
    documentation 329
    OMEGA 224, 228–9, 231–2
    SMALLTALK 206, 210–1
integrated development environment
    (TURING) 84, 86
interactive execution (OMEGA) 224
interface class (COOL) 61
interface
    C++ 79
    COOL 61
    TURING 99
    MODULA-3 157
INTERLISP 243
intermediate language 34–5
International Algebraic Language 12
internationalization 137
introductory language 149, 294
introductory programming courses 63, 72, 78, 174, 303
invariant 269
    EIFFEL clause 187
    TURING 98
is-a relation (documentation) 328
ISE 195
ISM 13
ISO PASCAL 135–6, 298
iteration 263, 272
iterative algorithm 281

ITHACA 46

JPI 298
JSD 294
JSP 294

keyword message (OMEGA) 219
Kuhnian paradigm 30, 336–7

lambda calculus 236, 239
language *see programming language*
language binding 59
language choice 21
language criteria 172, *see also
    evaluation, classification,
    comparison and individual
    languages*
language design 20, 172, *see also
    individual languages*
language features *see individual
    languages*
language model 34
language standards *see standardization*
language-independent concepts 18
large programs 297
    ADA 126, 132
    COOL 46–7
    ML 150–1
    MODULA-3 157
law of the excluded middle 264
lazy evaluation 246
LCF proof system 151
legacy systems 203
LEWD 272
lexical binding 237
libraries 59, 151
lightweight processes (MODULA-3) 157
linear development 326
linked list
    C++ 74
    EIFFEL 185–8
    MODULA-2 114, 120, 123
    MODULA-3 161, 163
    TURING 92, 100
Linux 89
LISP 12, 14–6, 18, 235–54
    80386 250
    ADA 238
    Allegro 248
    array 237
    artificial-intelligence 249

assertions 238
atoms 239
backtracking 246
base COMMON LISP 245
C 240, 242, 249, 251, 253
C++ 251–3
call-back 248
CLOS 243–6, 248, 250, 252
COMMON LISP 238, 240–6, 248–50,
    252
COMMON LISP Object System *see*
    CLOS
chaining together messages 244
class 243–5, 249
code walker 242
compiler 237, 235, 238–42
Common Graphics 248
complex numbers 242
constraint 236
continuation function 238
data structure 237, 239
data type 239, 243
data-flow language 247
data-flow programming 237, 245
debugging 243
denotational semantics 238
dialects 238
documentation 325
DYLAN 252
dynamic binding 237, 239
dynamically typed 237
environment 242–3, 250–1
discourse 335
exception 240
factorial 246
factors in higher education 293
floating-point numbers 242
formal mathematics 236
form 248
garbage collection 250
generic editors 247
generic function 244, 252
'go to' concept 238
graphical user interface 249
hardware 235–6, 239, 249–1
hash-tables 237
high safety 238
higher-order function 241
'industrial strength' language 238
industry 251
inheritance 245

inspector 243
integration 236
interpreters 237
INTERLISP 243
lambda calculus 236, 239, 246
lexical binding 237
LISP 235–53
list 239–42, 245, 247–8
logic programming 236
low safety 238
MACLISP 238
Macintosh 248
macro 241
message 238, 244
message-passing 244
message-passing languages 238
method 244–5, 252
method-combination 245
MIT 236, 243
multimethod 244–5
multiple inheritance 247
nondeterministic choice 242, 246
nondeterminism 247
object-oriented programming 237
object-oriented 239, 243–5, 24–9, 252
objects 237–9, 243, 245
optimization 238
paradigm 34, 37, 40, 37, 247
PASCAL 240–1, 251
PC 250
pointer 239
procedural semantics 236
procedural 236
production-rule languages 247
productivity 251
PROLOG 246–7, 249
prototyping 251
rationals 243
real-time 250
rule-based inference engine 247
run-time 237, 243
    check 243
    environment 250
safety switch 238
scheduling 247
SCHEME 236, 238, 241, 242, 250, 252
Screamer 246
semantics 236
sequence functions 240
sequence-generic functions 240
series package 245

slot access 245
slots 243
SMALLTALK 244, 252
sorting 238
stack 242
standardization 252
standard 236, 238, 243
static binding 239
static type 238, 240
streams 246
string 237, 239, 241, 245
subclass 249
symbolic differentiation 236
symbolic expressions 237
teaching language 236
template 241
type system 238
type testing 236
type-checking code 238
vector 241
weak typing 237
Windows 3 248, 250
ZETALISP 243
list
    C++ 74, 79, 81
    COOL 46, 59
    documentation 329
    EIFFEL 187, 191, 93
    discourse 339, 340
    formal aspects 259, 263, 270–1
    LISP 239–42, 45, 247–8
    ML 150, 152–4
    MODULA-2 114, 119–20, 123
    OMEGA 229
    SMALLTALK 209
    TURING 83, 100
    VDM 284
list constructor operator (ML) 153
literate programming 325
little-endian 152
LITTLE SMALLTALK 201
living objects (OMEGA) 227
local variables (SMALLTALK) 207
logic 18
logic programming 66, 236
logic-oriented 18
logical paradigm 182
LogicAL (EIFFEL) 195, 197
LOGO 16, 90
longevity 68, 302
loop invariant 187

loop termination 270
loop variants 187
low safety 238

machine orientation 128
machine independence 21
machine-level programming (OBERON)
    172, 174
Macintosh
    C++ 72, 77
    LISP 248
    OBERON 175
    OMEGA 230
    SMALLTALK 200
    TURING 84, 89
MACLISP- 238
Mac OS 77
macro language 273
macro (LISP) 241
maintainability
    CooL 46–7
    documentation 326
managerial matters 199
map (TURING) 93
market forces 295, 306
MASCOT 294
MathCad 150
mathematical basis (ML) 150
mathematical routines (ADA) 129
MaX 60
melting ice 205
member function 49, 80
MEMEX 327
memory addresses (TURING) 94
memory manager (OMEGA) 227
MESA 15, 157
message
    C++ 75
    CooL 48, 50, 53–4
    EIFFEL 193
    LISP 238, 244
    MODULA-2 119, 121
    OMEGA 219–21, 229, 232
    SMALLTALK 203, 210–3
    TURING 86
message-passing languages 238
META 203
meta-information (OMEGA) 221
method result (OMEGA) 222
method
    CooL 50–5, 60

discourse 333
documentation 325–6, 328–30
DYLAN 252
EIFFEL 197
factors in higher education 294
LISP 244–5, 252
MODULA-3 158, 162–7
OBERON 172
OMEGA 219–32
SMALLTALK 201, 203, 210–3
TURING 99
VDM 278–9, 282, 289
method-combination 245
methodology 31
METHODS 200
Microsoft 307
    Excel 150
    Windows 89
    Word 150
mid-rule 267
MiniTunis 86
MIRANDA 14, 18, 30, 33, 292, 274
MIT 236, 243
ML 16–18, 151–7
    abstract types 152
    abstract generic type 155
    algorithm 150
    BASIC 151
    beginners 150
    big numbers 152
    C++ 151
    COBOL 151
    comparison with MODULA-3 160
    compiler 152, 157
    completeness 151
    computer science 149
    computing 149–50
    concurrency 151
    construction and maintenance of large
        systems 157
    data structure 15, 152–3
    data type 157
    digital logic 150
    discourse 335
    discrete mathematics 150
    environment 151, 156
    evaluation 156
    exception 151, 153–6
    experts 150
    functional 150, 157
    FORTRAN 150

garbage collection 151, 157
generic 152, 154–5
hardware 156
hiding internal information 157
imperative language 149–51
industrial training 150
industry 151
inheritance 151
introductory language 149
large systems 150
large-scale programming 151
LCF proof system 151
libraries 151
list constructor operator 153
list 150, 152–4
LISP 151
little-endian 152
MathCad 150
mathematical basis 150
Microsoft Excel 150
Microsoft Word 150
ML 151
MODULA-3 149–51, 157–62, 164,
    168
object-oriented 154
objects 151
OBLIQ 151
PASCAL 151
pattern matching 152–3
PC 156
polymorphism 152
PROLOG 151
proof of their correctness 150
PYTHON 151
re-usable code 151
record 154–5
recursion 153
run-time 153–4
spreadsheet 150
stack 154–6
static scoping 152
string 154–6
strong typing 150
symbolic mathematics 150
TCL 151
type inference system 154
type system 150, 153
type-checking 157
type-safe exception 152
word processor 150
model–view–controller 202, 213

modifiability 224
MODULA-2 10, 15–9, 24, 117–124
    abstract data type 108–15, 120, 123,
        124
    abstraction 113
    ACM curriculum 108
    ADA 113, 126, 128
    ADT see abstract data type
    algorithm 115–6, 120
    array 114, 120
    binary search tree 120
    C 10
    C++ 68, 70, 72, 109
    compiler 109–11, 113–4
    computer science 107–9, 114, 116
    cryptoquote 121
    data structure 111, 114–6, 20
    de facto standard 109
    de jure standard 109
    discourse 335, 341
    documentation 325
    environment 109, 14
    EIFFEL 109
    EXTENDED PASCAL 136
    factors in higher education 293,
        295–7, 299
    finite bijection 121
    formal aspects 259
    functional 108
    generic typing 109, 111, 113
    graph algorithms 116
    hardware 109, 111
    heapsort 116
    imperative language 108–10
    information hiding 108–11
    inorder traversal 120
    linked list 114, 120, 123
    list 114, 119, 120, 123
    message 119, 121
    MODULA-3 157
    modularity 123
    multiple inheritance 109
    OBERON 171–2, 174, 176
    object-oriented features 108–9, 113
    objects 110, 113, 15
    one-to-one, onto function 121
    opaque type 110, 124
    operating system 109, 111
    PASCAL 113–4
    permutation 121
    persistence 110

PL/I 113
pointer 114, 120
post-condition 124
pre-condition 124
priority queue 116
program engineering 108
programming in the large 115
queues 114
quicksort 116
radix sort 116
re-use 113
record 114, 120
recursion 114
reverse inorder traversal 120
single inheritance 109
software engineering 108
sorted linked list 120
sorting 116, 119–20
stack 110, 113–4, 124
standardization 109
static type-checking 108, 110
string 122
string algorithms 116
strong typing 108, 113
structured programming 108
teaching 304, 306–7
textbooks 109
type checking 108
type-safe compilation 108
undergraduate course 111
weaknesses 111
Unix 109, 114, 120, 122, 24
VDM 277–83, 286–8
SMALLTALK 109
TURING 84
MODULA-2+ 157
MODULA-3 157–70
    ADA 168
    workshop database 164
    abstract data type 158, 161–2
    abstraction 167
    ADT separate interface 161
    algorithm 157, 167
    alternative implementations 158
    applications 167
    array 158
    BRANDED 163
    C++ 68, 70, 168
    CEDAR 157
    class 157
    comparing with ML 160

compiler 159–60, 166
concurrent processes 158
corruption of a program's code 158
data structure 158, 167–8
DEC's Systems Research Center 167
design documentation 157
design goal 157
discourse 335, 337, 341
efficiency 167
environment 167–8
EUCLID 157
evaluation 167
exception 157–8, 162, 168
exports 157
functional 162
garbage collection 157–8, 167
garbage collector 161
generic 158, 162–3, 167
generic implementation 163
generic stack 165
GNU 167
graphical user interfaces 167
imperative programming 162
inheritance 158
initialization 160
interfaces 157
large program 157
lightweight processes 157
linked list 161, 163
MESA 157
method 158, 162–7
ML 149, 151, 158, 159, 160, 162,
    164, 168
MODULA-2 157
MODULA-2+ 157
modularity 167
module imports 157
multiple inheritance 168
OBERON 157
OBJECT PASCAL 157
object type 158, 162, 168
objects 157, 167
opaque type 163–4
operating system 167
overriding 158, 165
partial revelation 163
partially opaque type 158
PASCAL 157
PC 167
persistent systems 168

pointer 158–60
polymorphism 158
private data field 163
productivity 168
prototyping 168
rationale 157
re-use 167
real-time communications 167
record 160–2, 164, 166
repeated assignment 160
robustness 157
run-time 158, 160, 166–7
safety 158
single inheritance 167
software engineering 167
stack of 164, 166
stack 161–7
storage 'leaks' 158
string 161, 164–6
strongly typed 158
subtype 158, 164
systems programmers 168
teaching 304
template 158
textbook 157
threads 157–8
type system 157–8, 168
type unique 163
Unix 167
unreachable heap storage 161
unsafe error 158
unsafe features 157
Xerox 167
X-Windows 167
MODULA-3 157
modular design 303
modularity 23
  discourse 340
  EXTENDED PASCAL 136
  factors in higher education 297
  MODULA-2 123
  MODULA-3 167
  SMALLTALK 213
modules 85, 91
monitor (TURING)
monomorphic types (OMEGA) 219
MS-DOS (OBERON) 175
multimethod 244–5
multiple inheritance
  EIFFEL 190
  LISP 247

MODULA-2 109
MODULA-3 168
OMEGA 230
MVC (SMALLTALK) 202

name clash (EIFFEL) 192
networks 203
NEWSPEAK 132
NeXT 89
NICE (EIFFEL) 195
non-language criteria 306
non-technical features 339
nondeterminism 247
nondeterministic choice 242, 246
nondeterministic language 246
not-so-bad languages 272
numeric types (OBERON) 172
N-version programming 194

OBERON 171–80
  abstraction 172
  Amiga 175
  array 172
  assertions 176
  availability 175
  big applications 174
  CEDAR 172
  Ceres 174
  class 177
  commercial implementations 174
  compilation 175
  compiler 173–6
  computer science 171
  conference example 178
  criteria for language selection 172
  dangling pointer 175
  data structure 174–6
  DEC Alpha 175
  DECstation 175
  design goal 177
  discourse 335
  dynamic type 179
  efficiency 175
  environment 171–6
  ETH 171–2, 174–7
  examples 177
  executable code units 175
  experimental language extensions 173
  expressivity 174
  extensibility 172, 174, 176
  fun 176

garbage collection 176
generic stack 177
global variables 176
high-level languages 174
HP-PA 175
IBM RS/6000 175
imperative 174
implementations 175
index checks 176
industrial relevance 174
introductory programming courses
    174
language criteria 173
machine-level features 172, 174
Macintosh II 175
method 172
MODULA-2 171–2, 174, 176
MS-DOS 175
numeric types 172
OBERON-2 172–3
object-oriented 174
operating environment criteria 174
operating system 172
parameterized stack 177
parameterized types 177
PASCAL 171–2
pointer 172
PowerPC Macintosh 175
productivity 174
program editor 175
programming course design 173
programming language design 172
programming systems 173
receiver 179
record 172, 177–8
record type extension 172
robustness 175
run-time checks 175
Silicon Graphics 175
rize of a language 173
SMALLTALK 172
software quality 174
stability 173
stack ADT 177–8
static program analyser 176
static type-checking 174–5
statically bound procedures 177
statistical profiler 176
string 172
subclass 177
SUN Sparc 175

template 177
textbooks 173
tools 176
TURBO-PASCAL 172
type guards 176
type-bound procedures 172, 177, 178
variant record 172
Windows-NT 175
Windows 175
OBERON-2 172–3, 219, 259, 272, 304
object counts (OMEGA) 226
Object Management Architecture
    (COOL) 49
object editor (OMEGA) 224, 228
object sharing (EIFFEL) 189
object technology 308
object
    ADA 131
    C++ 66–67, 70, 72–3, 82
    cloning (OMEGA) 218
    COOL 47–57, 60–1
    EIFFEL 183, 187–4
    formal aspects 260, 272
    LISP 237–9, 243, 245
    ML 151
    MODULA-2 110, 113, 115
    MODULA-3 15, 158, 162, 167–8
    OMEGA 217–30
    paradigms 32, 36
    SMALLTALK 203, 206–7, 210, 213
    TURING 93, 99–100
object's state (COOL) 49
object orientation
    abstraction 128
    ADA 130, 132
    C++ 66, 69–70, 78
    COOL 45, 47, 49, 51, 53, 60–1
    design 128
    documentation 328–30
    EIFFEL 181–2
    discourse 335–6
    EXTENDED PASCAL 137
    factors in higher education 295,
        298–9
    formal considerations 2, 273
    general concepts 11–2, 15, 18
    languages 18, 271, 305
    LISP 239, 243–9, 252
    ML 154
    MODULA-2 108–9 ,113
    OBERON 174

Object-oriented TURING 83
OMEGA 217, 219, 227, 230
paradigm 29, 32, 34, 36, 299
programmers 11
programming in
   ADA 128
   COOL 47
   documentation 330
   EIFFEL 188
   LISP 237
   MODULA-2 109
   paradigms 34
   TURING 84–5, 89, 92
   SMALLTALK 204, 208, 214
   style 273
   TURING 85, 92, 93, 100
OBJECT PASCAL 157, 272
OBJECTWORKS (SMALLTALK) 201
OBLIQ 151
OCCAM 14, 16, 18, 41, 273, 293, 297
older languages 14
OMEGA 217–34
   68000 227
   680x0 code 225
   abstract root prototype 230
   activation 230
   analysis tools 225
   application generator 225
   argument types 224
   arguments 222
   Array 218
   array 221, 226, 229, 233
   tools 233
   binary message 219
   blocks 221
   C++ 217, 219, 221
   checks (at run time) 221
   class 217–9, 223–4, 227–8
   Collection 228
   collections 221, 226
   compile time errors 218
   compiled method 223
   compiler 219, 221, 225–7, 233
   conditional assignment 219–21
   conditional expression 221
   conference example 230
   control flow 218, 221
   creation 223
   data type 218, 220
   debugging 225
   declarations 220

deletion 223
dictionaries 226
documentation generators 226
documentation tools 225
dynamic binding 219
dynamic type 221
efficiency 219, 221
EIFFEL 218, 229
environment 218, 219, 222, 224–5, 233
event 226
examples 227
exception 226–30
exception handling 221, 229, 233
expression 219
expression sequence 221
file management 226
fully qualified declaration 220
garbage collection 219, 222, 233
generic 218–9, 222, 227
generic container types 219
generic prototype 218–9, 228
generic stack 228
generic variant of block 221
global constant 232
graphical objects 226
information hiding 231
inheritance 218–9, 222, 230
inherited 224
initial value 220
initialization 231
inspection 223
instance variable 224, 228–9, 231–2
interactive execution 224
keyword message 219
library 226, 228
list 229
living objects 227
Macintosh 230
main program 224
memory manager 227
message 219–21, 229, 232
meta-information 221
method 219–32
method result 222
modifiability 224
monomorphic types 219, 221
multiple inheritance 230
OBERON-2 219
object counts 226
object editor 224, 228

object orientation 217, 219, 227, 230
cloned objects 218
Object prototype 219, 228
objects 217–30, 232
optimization 221
overridden 224
overridden 232
overriding 225
PASCAL 226
passivation 230
polymorphism 220
primitive method 226
profiling 226
programming environment 218–9,
    222, 225–6
programming style 230
prototype 217–9, 222–1, 233
prototype browser 223
prototype hierarchy 223
prototype library 226
prototype-oriented programming
    226–33
prototype-related operations 223
pseudo-type 228
pure object orientation 217, 219
re-use 227–8, 230
read-only variable 232
read-only 222
receiver 222, 229
reference semantics 219, 222
reference to an object 220
renaming 223
run-time system 221–2, 226, 228
safety 217, 222
SELF 217–8
Set prototype 219
sets 226
shallow copy 229
shared 232
short-circuit evaluation 221
single inheritance 219
single-rooted hierarchy 219
SMALLTALK 217–9, 221, 224–5
software engineering 228
source text of all method 223
stack 226–30
static typing 217–21, 229, 233
statically compatible 221
subtype 218, 220, 224, 231
supertype 220
system 233

THINK PASCAL 226
traceback 226
type cast 221
unary message 219
variable 220
visibility 224
workspace 222
'who calls who' analysis 225
OMG 49
OMT 299
once function (EIFFEL) 193
one-to-one, onto function 121
OODBMS 56–7
OOT see Turing
opaque type
    MODULA-2 110, 124, 288
    MODULA-3 163–4
openness
    CooL 48
    EIFFEL 182
operating environment criteria
    (OBERON) 174
operating system
    ADA 127, 129
    CooL 47
    MODULA-2 109, 111
    MODULA-3 167
    OBERON 172
    paradigms 36
    SMALLTALK 200, 213
    teaching 301, 303
    TURING 90, 93, 94
operating systems 84
operator overloading (C++) 71
optimization 238
    LISP 238
    OMEGA 221
ORACLE 61
orthogonality 297
    C++ 68
    CooL 47, 48
OS/2 136, 200
OSF X/Motif (CooL) 61
overriding (of methods)
    documentation of 329
    MODULA-3 158, 165
    OMEGA 224–5, 232
    TURING 99

p-System 303
p-word(s) 335

package (ADA) 127
paradigm shift 335
paradigm 4, 8, 9, 18, 24, 273–4, 297
   abstraction 32, 37, 39–42
   abstraction building 40
   abstraction skills 40
   acceptance grammar 37
   ADA 37, 39, 127–8
   BASIC 30
   ADT 36
   blacksmith principle 35
   C 34
   C programmer 36–7
   C++ 66
   COBOL 41
   computing 30
   corpus of programs 38
   culture 29–32, 36–42
   declarative 33–4
   documentation 325, 328
   dynamic execution 32
   efficiency 38
   EIFFEL 182
   empirical studies 38
   environment 32, 33, 41
   discourse 335–7, 339, 342–3
   expert programmer 33
   expert use 29–42
   formalism 31, 35
   FORTH 36
   FORTRAN 37
   functional 30, 34, 35
   general-purpose language 41
   generic 40
   imperative 33
   implications for teaching 39
   intermediate language 34, 35
   Kuhnian paradigm 30
   language model 34
   LISP 34, 37, 40, 237, 247
   message 36
   methodology 31
   method 42
   MIRANDA 30, 33
   object-oriented 29, 32, 34, 36
   OCCAM 41
   operating system 36
   PASCAL 36–7, 40
   post hoc rationalization 34
   PROLOG 33–5
   programming culture 35, 39
   programming paradigms 31
   programming style 36
   re-use 32
   real world 30, 39
   reasoning model 34
   SCHEME 37
   secondary notation 37
   standards 319
   store–imperative 36
   superstructure 35
   VDM 278, 281, 289
paradigm-centred discourse 337
paradigm-switching 31
parameterized type
   C++ 68, 70, 74
   EIFFEL 184
   EXTENDED PASCAL 136
   OBERON 177
ParcPlace 200
pariahs 337
partial revelation (MODULA-3) 163
partially opaque type (MODULA-3) 158
partisanship 314
PASCAL 14–9
   ADA 126, 128
   C++ 63–78
   discourse 341
   documentation 325
   factors in higher education 292–8
   formal aspects 259, 262–4, 272, 274
   ML 151
   EIFFEL 181
   EXTENDED PASCAL 135–7
   implementationss 136
   LISP 240–1, 251
   MODULA-3 157
   MODULA-2 113–4
   OBERON 171–2
   OMEGA 226
   paradigms 36, 37, 40
   PASCAL-E 136
   PASCAL Validation Suite 135
   standards 314
   teaching 303–4
   TURING 84–5, 89–1, 97, 100
   VDM 278, 288
pass-by-reference 262
pass-by-value-result 262
passivation (OMEGA) 230
pattern matching (ML) 152–3
PC

ADA 126
C++ 72
EXTENDED PASCAL 136
LISP 250
ML 156
MODULA-3 167
OS/2 (ADA) 129
SMALLTALK 200
TURING 84, 89, 97
pedagogy 23
permutation 121
persistence
  COOL 56, 62
  EIFFEL 194
  MODULA-2 110
persistent declaration (COOL) 57
persistent systems (MODULA-3) 168
physical representation (ADA) 126
PL/I 12, 14–6, 18, 24, 113, 270, 276
PL/S 270
pointer semantics 74
pointer variables (SMALLTALK) 207
pointer 297, 272
  ADA 125, 128–9
  C++ 64, 74–5
  COOL 60
  EIFFEL 188–9
  LISP 239
  MODULA-2 114, 120
  MODULA-3 158–60
  OBERON 172
  SMALLTALK 213
  TURING 91, 93
  VDM 278, 281, 288
polymorphism (COOL) 53
  COOL 53
  EIFFEL 185, 191–2
  MODULA-3 158
  ML 152
  OMEGA 220
  SMALLTALK 212
  TURING 85
pool dictionaries (SMALLTALK) 207,
  210
portability 23
  ADA 133
  EIFFEL 182
Posix 129
post-condition 267
  EIFFEL 184, 187, 193
  MODULA-2 124

TURING 98
post hoc rationalization 34
POSTSCRIPT 9
PowerPC Macintosh 175
pragmatics 10
pre-condition 263
  EIFFEL 184, 187, 193
  MODULA-2 124
predicate calculus 187
primitive method (OMEGA) 226
Primos 293, 298
print object interface (COOL) 61
priority queue 116
private data field (MODULA-3) 163
private type (ADA) 128
PRO 272
problem-domain 296–7
problem-solving 266
procedural abstraction 127
procedural paradigm 297
procedural programming 274
procedural semantics (in LISP) 236
procedural versus functional 266
procedures 187, 276
process model 202
processes (in SMALLTALK) 213
production-rule languages 247
productivity
  COOL 46
  documentation 323, 328
  LISP 251
  MODULA-3 168
  OBERON 174
  SMALLTALK 214
profiling 226
program editor (OBERON) 175
program engineering 108
program reading 40
programmer errors 271, 276
programme for teaching 271
programming
  ADA applications 126
  by contract 193
  course design 173
  culture 35, 39
  in the large 46, 89, 115, 297
  in the small 297
  paradigms 126 see also paradigm
  principles in EIFFEL 187
  rules 265
  style 35

versus programming languages 258
programming environment 306–7
  CooL 46
  OMEGA 219, 222, 225–6
  TURING 83, 85, 94–5
programming language design
  goals
    Hoare's 21
    Horowitz's 21
    Wirth's 21
  OBERON 172
programming languages 8, *see also
  individual entries*
  4GL 203
  ADA 125–134
  APL 14–6, 18, 30, 259
  B 260
  BCPL 260
  BETA 23
  C 8, 14–5, 9
  C++ 63–82
  CEDAR 157
  CLOS 23, 243–6, 248, 250–2
  CLU 15–6, 18, 68, 70–1, 337
  COBOL 14–9
  CooL 45–62
  continuous 266
  design 21
  discourse 333–44
  distance teaching 301–12
  documentation 323–30
  EIFFEL 181–98
  DYLAN 252
  EXTENDED PASCAL 135–48
  factors in higher education 291–9
  formal aspects 255–76
  FORTH 18–9, 36
  FORTRAN 9, 14–6, 18–9, 21, 37, 150
  HASKELL 126
  history 12–3
  LISP 235–54
  ML 151–57
  MESA 15, 157
  MIRANDA 14, 18, 30, 33, 292, 274
  MODULA-2 117–124
  MODULA-2+ 157
  MODULA-3 157–70
  OBERON 171–80
  OBJECT PASCAL 157, 272
  OMEGA 217–34
  paradigms 31–42, *see also discourse*

PASCAL 14–9
SETL 16
SIMSCRIPT 14
SIMULA 67 8, 13–4, 16, 18, 71
SMALLTALK 199–215
SNOBOL 15–6, 18
standards *see standardization*
standardization 313–20
TURBO C++ 77
TURBO-PASCAL 84, 90, 172, 294,
  296, 298–9
TURING 83–106
THINK PASCAL 226
U. C. S. D. PASCAL 303
VDM 277–90
programming linguistics 13
programming paradigm *see paradigm*
project management (SMALLTALK) 203
proliferation 84, 315, 318
PROLOG 14–8
  ADA 126
  factors in higher education 293, 296
  formal aspects 274
  ML 151
  paradigms 33–5
  LISP 246–7, 249
proof of correctness 150
Prospero 136
protected parameters (EXTENDED
  PASCAL) 147
protected method (CooL) 50, 52
protected identifiers 211
prototype browser (OMEGA) 223
prototype hierarchy (OMEGA) 223
prototype (OMEGA) 217–33
prototype-oriented programming 226,
  233
prototyping
  CooL 46
  LISP 251
  MODULA-3 168
  SMALLTALK 201, 203, 205
  VDM 289
provability 21
pseudo-code 89
pseudo-type (OMEGA) 228
'pure' object-oriented language 182, 305
'purity' 214
public identifiers 211
PYTHON 151

quality
  C++ 74
  CooL 54
  MODULA-2 114
  TURING 87, 93, 99
  VDM 278, 281
quicksort 116

radix sort 116
raising an exception (EIFFEL) 193
rapid development 203
rationale (MODULA-3) 157
rationals 243
re-use 335
  ADA 132
  C++ 76
  CooL 47, 51–2
  documentation 323–4, 328, 330
  EIFFEL 182, 185, 192, 197
  formal aspects 262–3, 270
  ML 151
  MODULA-2 113
  MODULA-3 167
  OMEGA 227–8, 230
  paradigms 32
  teaching 304, 308
  TURING 87, 93
read lock 57
read-only variable 232
readability 21, 46–7, 126, 317
real-time
  communications 167
  factors in higher education 295
  LISP 250
  projects 204
  systems 16
real-world 30, 39, 71, 75, 78, 183, 297
reasoning model 34
receiver
  OBERON 179
  OMEGA 222, 229
record constructors 162
record
  ADA 130, 132
  CooL 49, 60
  formal aspects 263, 264
  ML 154–5
  MODULA-2 114, 120
  MODULA-3 160–4,166
  OBERON 172, 177, 178
  TURING 85, 87, 92, 93,97

VDM 283
record type extension (OBERON) 172
record types 286
recursion
  C++ 74
  ML 153
  MODULA-2 114
  VDM 278
recursive algorithms 281
redefined method 52
redefining features 192
redefinition 190
reference semantics (OMEGA) 219, 220,
    222
references 275
reflective programming 38
relational database 59, 56, 61, 187, 195,
    197, 274
relaxation of declarations 143
reliability 21, 48
renaming
  EIFFEL 190
  OMEGA 223
  SMALLTALK 213
repeat statement 276
repeated assignment (MODULA-3) 160
repeated feature inheritance (EIFFEL)
    191, 192
representation (on screen) 76
require (EIFFEL) 187, 196
requirements analysis 278, 280
retry (EIFFEL) 194
reverse inorder traversal 120
rhetoric of contempt 339
rhetoric of disdain 339
robotic real-time 195
robustness 157, 175, 182
RS/6000 97
rule-based inference engine 247
run time
  ADA 129
  C++ 68, 75
  checking 72, 126, 160, 175, 243
  environment 194, 250
  error 48, 91
  error-checking 74
  EXTENDED PASCAL 140
  formal aspect 276
  LISP 237, 243
  ML 153–4
  MODULA-3 158, 166–7

OMEGA 221–2
SMALLTALK 208, 214
system 91, 226, 228
TURING 86, 90, 97, 99
type-checking (SMALLTALK) 209
run-time landscape (TURING) 87

safety 21
  ADA 129, 132
  LISP 238
  MODULA-3 158
  OMEGA 217, 222
satisfaction (formal) 261
schedulers (SMALLTALK) 213
scheduling 247
SCHEME 13, 14, 17–8, 37, 236, 238,
    241–2, 250, 252, 274
scope (in SMALLTALK) 213
Screamer 246
searching
  C++ 74
  SMALLTALK 211
  VDM 278
SECD machine 14
'sealed' type 177
secondary notation 37
secure abstraction 128
secure code 126
security 21, 129 132
segmentation faults 94
select clause (EIFFEL) 192
selection 272
selector
  CooL 50
  SMALLTALK 202
  VDM 283
SELF 23, 217–8
semantics 10, 236, 261
semaphores (SMALLTALK) 213
separate compilation
  ADA 132
  CooL 58
  discourse 340
  EXTENDED PASCAL 138
  factors in higher education 297
  teaching 303–4
  TURING 90
  VDM 287
separate interface 161
sequence functions 240
sequence 272

sequence-generic functions 240
sequencing 263
series package 245
SETL 16
SGI MIPS 89
SGI (TURING) 97
shallow copy (OMEGA) 229
short-circuit evaluation
  EXTENDED PASCAL 145
  OMEGA 221
Sig Computers (EIFFEL) 195
Silicon Graphics (OBERON) 175
simplicity 21
SIMSCRIPT 14
SIMULA 67 8, 13–4, 16, 18, 71
single inheritance
  MODULA-2 109
  MODULA-3 167
  OMEGA 219
  SMALLTALK 208
  teaching 305
  TURING 99
single-paradigm language 70
single-rooted hierarchy 219
SINIX 61
size and simplicity 297
size of a language 173
slot (LISP) 243, 245
SMALLTALK 14–8, 23, 199–215
  4GL 203
  ADT 213
  aliasing 213
  allocation (of memory) 213
  ANSI Committee X3J20 204
  appropriateness 202
  arity of inheritance 208, 213
  array 203
  Array class 210
  availability 201
  built-in types 208
  C. A. S. E. tools 203
  categories of language 208
  class 200, 203–4, 206–13
  class (versus type) 208
  class library 200, 202–3, 208–9, 213
  class method 210
  class variables 207, 211
  classification of languages 208
  client–server systems 200
  collection classes 209
  compiler 203, 208

compiler-writing 202
concatenation operator 211
concurrency 213
conference example 205
databases 203
deallocation (of memory) 213
debuggers 204
development team 202
Dictionary class 210
Digitalk 200
discourse about 335
distance teaching 305–6, 308
documentation 326
dynamic binding 211
efficient code 208
EIFFEL 208
environment 199, 202, 204, 214
event 206, 209
exception 202
discourse 336
expression language 211
formal aspects 273
formal method 207
formal specifications 211
functional style of programming 211
garbage collection 213
generic classes 209
generic stack 199
generic types 213
genericity 209–10
global variable 207, 210
graphical user interface 205, 213
group-working 203
GUI see graphical user interface
GNU-SMALLTALK 201
help facilities 204
history 12, 199
IBM SMALLTALK 200–1
image 201
information hiding 211, 213
inheritance 208
instance method 210
instance variable 206, 210–11
legacy systems 203
LISP 244, 252, 209
LITTLE SMALLTALK 201
local variables 207
MODULA-2 109
Macintosh 200
managerial matters 199
melting ice 205

message 203, 210–13
Meta 203
method 201, 203, 210–13
METHODS 200
model–view–controller 202, 213
modularity 213
MVC see model–view–controller
networks 203
OBERON 172
object-oriented
    languages 214
    principles 208
    programming 204
objects 203, 206–7, 210, 213
OBJECTWORKS 201
OMEGA 217–21, 224–5
operating system 200, 213
OS/2 200
ParcPlace 200
PC 200
performance 201
pointer variables 207
pointer 213
polymorphism 212
pool dictionaries 207, 210
practical matters 199
process model 202
process of programming 210
processes 213
productivity 214
project management 203
protected 211
prototyping 201, 203, 205
public variable 211
'purity' 214
rapid development 203
real-time projects 204
renaming 213
run-time
    error 214
    system 208
    type checking 209
schedulers 213
scope 213
searching 211
selector 202
semaphores 213
Set class 210
single inheritance 208
SMALLTALK AGENTS 201
SMALLTALK Store 201

SMALLTALK/V 201
SMALLTALK/X 200–1
stack 209–11
stream 211
string 202–3, 207–8
subclass 206–8, 210
subtype 213
superclass 207
technical matters 205
temporary variable 206
textbook 204
transaction processing 204
TURING 84, 87
type (versus class) 208
types 208
user interfaces 203
version control 203
VISUALAGE 201
VISUALWORKS 201
VISUAL SMALLTALK 201
weak typing 208, 213
Windows 200, 204
Xerox Corporation 199
SMALLTALK AGENTS 201
SNOBOL 15–6, 18
software architecture (TURING) 94
software development 303
software development methods 257
software engineering
    C++ 66, 71, 73, 78
    documentation 323–4, 330
    documentation tools 327
    EIFFEL 182
    discourse 333–5
    factors in higher education 294, 298
    formal 274
    MODULA-2 108
    MODULA-3 167
    OMEGA 228
    teaching 302–4, 307
    TURING 84, 90
    VDM 282
software industrial revolution 336
software maintenance 323
software project management 303
software quality assurance 46, 174, 294,
    302
software reliability 54
sorted linked list 120
sorting
    C++ 74

LISP 238
MODULA-2 116–20
VDM 278
source code 325
source text 223
source-code debugger (COOL) 60
SPARC workstations 129
specialization 328
specification 280
specification module (COOL) 58
SpeL 282
spreadsheet (ML) 150
SQL 56, 61, 129, 273, 338–9
    ADA binding 129
    object interface (COOL) 61
SSADM 294
stack
    C++ 69, 74–5, 79, 82
    COOL 55–6
    EIFFEL 183–90, 193
    EXTENDED PASCAL 138, 139
    factors in higher education 297–8
    LISP 242
    ML 154–6
    MODULA-2 110, 113–4, 124
    MODULA-3 161–7
    OBERON 177–8
    OMEGA 226–30
    SMALLTALK 209–11
    TURING 86–7, 92–3
    VDM 278, 281
stack traceback 75
standardization 5, 306–7, 317–20
    abstraction 317
    choice of languages 318
    compiler 319
    computing professional 320
    conciseness 317
    culture 314, 320
    environment 320
    factors in higher education 298
    languages scene 313
    paradigm 319
    partisanship 314
    programming language 313–18, 320
    proliferation 315, 318
    readability 317
    role 317
    VDM 286
standards
    ADA 128, 306, 319

ALGOL-60 314
BASIC 307
C 306
C++ 78, 307, 319
COBOL 307, 314, 319
EIFFEL 195, 307
EXTENDED PASCAL 306
FORTRAN 307, 314
LISP 236, 238, 243, 252
MODULA-2 109, 307
OBERON 307
PASCAL 306
PL/I 307
SMALLTALK 307
static scoping (ML) 152
static semantic checks 125
static binding 239
static typing 233
static program analyser 176
static type
 COOL 53–4
 LISP 238, 240
 OBERON 174
 OMEGA 220, 221, 229
 type-checking 110, 175
static typing
 MODULA-2 108
 OMEGA 217–9
statically bound procedures 177
statically compatible 221
statistical profiler 176
Steelman report 20
stepwise refinement 262
storage 'leaks' 158
storage 17
store–imperative paradigm 2, 36, 306
stream
 SMALLTALK 211
 LISP 246
string algorithms 116
string handling 303
string
 C++ 72–5, 81
 COOL 49, 59
 EXTENDED PASCAL 137, 141
 LISP 237, 239, 241, 245
 ML 154–6
 MODULA-2 122
 MODULA-3 161, 164–6
 OBERON 172
 SMALLTALK 202–3, 207

TURING 85, 94, 97–9
strong typing
 ADA 125, 128
 C++ 71
 COOL 54
 EIFFEL 185
 discourse 338, 340
 factors in higher education 297
 ML 150
 MODULA-2 108, 113
 MODULA-3 158
 SMALLTALK 208
structured programming 108
structured methods 85
structured value constructors 143
student projects 326
subclass
 documentation 328–9
 LISP 249
 OBERON 177
 SMALLTALK 206–8, 210
substitute classes (C++) 74
substitution 263
subtype
 COOL 50–3
 EIFFEL 185, 189, 193
 MODULA-3 158, 164
 OMEGA 218, 220, 224, 231
 SMALLTALK 213
 VDM 281–2, 286
SUN Sparc 175
Sun/4 89, 94, 97
superclass
 documentation 328–30
 SMALLTALK 207
superstructure 35
supertype
 COOL 51–2
 EIFFEL 185
 OMEGA 220
symbolic differentiation 236
symbolic expressions 237
symbolic mathematics 150
synchronization 16
syntactic 'sugar' 19
syntax 10
 ADA 132
 C++ 70
 versus semantics 273
systematic programming 176
systems methods (TURING) 85

systems programmers 168
systems programming 84, 93

tagged types (ADA) 128, 132
taxonomy of languages *see
classification of languages*
TCL 151
teaching 132, 236, 261, 275, 301
technical issues 205, 295, 297, 340
telecommunications 195
template
  C++ 74, 81, 93
  COOL 55
  LISP 241
  MODULA-3 158
  OBERON 177
temporary variable (SMALLTALK) 206
test object interface (COOL) 60
textbooks 298
  ADA 132
  C++ 71–2
  MODULA-2 109
  MODULA-3 157
  OBERON 173
  SMALLTALK 204
  VDM 282
threads 157–8
THINK PASCAL 226
tool integration 84
tools 176
TOPS-20 303
totality 263
Toy Language 263
traceback 226
transaction
  blocks 56
  COOL 56–7
  processing (in SMALLTALK) 204
  roll back (in COOL) 57
transient declaration (COOL) 57
TURBO C++ 77
TURBO-PASCAL 84, 90, 172, 294, 296,
  298–9
TURING 83–106
  abstract data type 91–92, 98
  ADT *see abstract data type*
  array 85, 97
  assertions 98
  basic programming 84
  bit substring 99
  BASIC 85, 89–91

Borland 84
broad language support 85
C 84, 85, 94
C++ 84, 93–4
C++'s template 93
class library 87
class 85, 87, 92–3, 99–101
compiler 84, 86–90
computer science 83–4, 86, 89
concurrency 85
consistent user interface 87
current practice 83
curriculum cycle 83
dangling pointer 91
data structure 84, 87, 91, 93
declarations 97
difficulties with C and C++ 93
direct manipulation 87
discourse 335
dynamic array 98
dynamically generic 93
efficiency 85
efficient implementation 89
environment 84–90, 100
Excelerator 84
exception 99
genericity 93
generic 87, 93
high-level languages 94
hyper-link 101
IBM RS6000 89
import list 93
information hiding 92, 94
inheritance 85, 93
integrated program development
  environments 84
integrated tools 86
interface 99
invariants 98
language features 90
linked list 92, 100
Linux 89
list 83, 100
LOGO 90
low-level detail 94
Macintosh 84, 89
map 93
memory addresses 94
message 86
method 99
MiniTunis operating system 86

Modules and abstract data types 91
MODULA-2 84
modules 91
monitor 85
NeXT 89
object 92–3, 99–100
object orientation 84, 85, 90, 92–3, 100
object-oriented programming 84, 85, 89, 92
Object-oriented TURING *see OOT*
OOT 83, 89
OOT environment 85, 90, 94, 101
operating system 84, 90, 93–4
overriding 99
PASCAL 84–5, 89–91, 97, 100
PC 84, 89, 97
pedagogical experience 89
pointer 91, 93
polymorphism 85
efficient and portable implementation 89
post-conditions 98
programming environment 83, 85, 94–5
programming in the large 89
proliferation of programming language 84
pseudo-code 89
queue 87, 93, 99
re-use 87, 93
record 85, 87, 92–3, 97
RS/6000 97
run-time error 91
run-time system 86, 90, 91, 97, 99
Run-time Landscape 87
segmentation faults 94
separate compilation 90
SGI/SGI MIPS 89, 97
single inheritance 99
SMALLTALK 84, 87
software architecture 94
software engineering 84, 90
stack 86–7, 92–3
statements 97
string 85, 94, 97–9
structured methods 85
Sun/4 89, 94, 97
systems methods 85
systems programming 84, 93
tool integration 84

TURBO environment 84–5
TURBO PASCAL 84, 90
TURING PLUS 85, 89
type coercion 99
undergraduate curricula 84
Unix 84–6, 89–90, 97
visualization 87
Windows 89
X-Windows 89
TURING PLUS 85, 89
type (versus class) 208
type cast 221
type checking (MODULA-2) 108
type coercion (TURING) 99
type conversion 128
type extension (ADA) 130
type guards (OBERON) 176
type inference system (ML) 154
type inquiry 140
type system
    ADA 132
    CooL 48–9, 59
    LISP 238
    ML 150, 153
    MODULA-3 157–8, 168
    SMALLTALK 208
type testing 236
type unique 163
type-bound procedures (OBERON) 172, 177–8
type checking
    C++ 75
    LISP 238
    ML 157
type-safe compilation 108, 137
type-safe exception (ML) 152

U. C. S. D. PASCAL 303
unary message (OMEGA) 219
undergraduate provision 84, 111, 291
uniformity 21
unique clause (CooL) 57
Unix
    CooL 54, 60, 61
    C++ 68, 72, 77
    EIFFEL 195
    EXTENDED PASCAL 136
    MODULA-2 109, 114, 120, 122, 124
    MODULA-3 167
    TURING 84–6, 89–90, 97
unreachable heap storage 161

unsafe error (MODULA-3) 158
unsafe features (MODULA-3) 157
user interface 203, 247, 259
user-defined types (ADA) 128

value semantics (C++) 71
value-returning procedure 276
values 17
variable (OMEGA) 220
variant record 132, 172, 269
VAX VMS 136, 303
VDM 277–90
    abstract data type 278, 281, 287
    abstraction 278–81, 286
    ADA 288
    ADT *see abstract data type*
    algorithm 278, 280–1, 286–7
    basic type 288
    compiler 288
    complexity of algorithms 281
    conference problem 282
    data structure 281
    data type 281–2
    EIFFEL 288
    formal method 277
    formalism 289
    FORTRAN 279
    functional language 284, 286
    genericity 288
    imperative language 278–81, 286
    implementation 280
    iterative algorithms 281
    list 284
    method 278–9, 282, 289
    MODULA-2 277–83, 286–8
    opaque type 288
    paradigm 278, 281, 289
    PASCAL 278, 288
    pointer 278, 281, 288
    programming language 277–8, 287
    prototyping 289
    queue 278, 281
    record 283
    record types 286
    recursion 278
    recursive algorithms 281
    requirements analysis 278, 280
    searching 278
    selector 283
    separate compilation 287
    software engineering 282
    sorting 278
    specification 280
    SpeL 282
    SpeL data types 283
    stack 278, 281
    standardization 286
    subtype 281–2, 286
    textbook (on VDM-SL) 282
VDM-SL 126, *see also VDM*
vector 241
version control 203
Vienna Development Method *see VDM*
visibility (OMEGA) 224
VISUAL SMALLTALK 201
VISUALAGE 201
visualization 87
VISUALWORKS 201

weak typing
    LISP 237
    SMALLTALK 208, 213
WEB 325
well-definedness 23
while statement 276
Windows
    LISP 248, 250
    EXTENDED PASCAL 136
    ADA 129
    factors in higher education 294
    OBERON 175
    SMALLTALK 200, 204
word processor (ML) 150
workshop example *see conference example*
workshop discourse 335
write lock (COOL) 57

xBASE 273
X-Windows
    EIFFEL 195
    MODULA-3 167
    TURING 89
X/Motif 61
X11 77
Xerox
    SMALLTALK 199
    MODULA-3 167

Z 294
zero field width output 146
ZETALISP 243

Author index

Abelson, H. 236
Ader, M. 46
Adigun, M. O. 304
Al-Hadda, H. 196
Allen, R. 16
Ambler, A. L. 306
Andrews, D. 255, 275, 282
ANSI-X3 137
Apple Computer Inc. 87, 252
Arblaster, A. T.
Arthur, L. J. 324
Atkinson, M. P. 56
Atkinson, P. 334
Austing, R. H. 107

Backus, J. 8, 9, 11
Bailey, P. J. 56
Barnes, B. H. 107
Barnes, J. G. P. 128
Bate, G. 294
Benford, S. 299
Bergin, J. 113
Blaha, M. 299
Blaschek, G. 217, 218, 226
Bobrow, D. G. 244, 245
Boehm-Davis D. A. 31
Bonnette, D. T. 107
Booch, G. 21
Boyle, T. 299, 307
Brooks, F. P. 20, 31
Brown, M. 167
BSI 135, 136
Budd, T. A. 78, 204
Budgen, D. 292
Burke, E. 299
Burns, A. 16
Bush, V. J. 307, 327
Bustard, D. W. 307

Cardelli, L. 18, 157
Cargill, T. 75, 79
Cater, S. C. 107, 115,116
CCTA 294
Chi, M. T. H. 39
Chisholm, K. J. 56
Church, A. 236
Ciechanowicz, Z. J. 135, 136
Clack, C. 151
Clark, R. G. 16
Clark, R. 141, 303
Clements, P. C. 34
Clifton, J. M. 84
Clinger, W. 236, 238
Clocksin, W. F. 126, 247
Coad, P. 236
Coar, D. 114
Cockshott, P. W. 56
Conklin, J. 327
Connelly, E. M. 31
Conway, D. E. 302
Cook, C. 307
Cooper, D. 111
Cooper, G. 334
Coplien, J. O. 78, 79
Cottam., I. D. 275
Cox, B. J. 32, 335
Cullyer, W. J.
Currie, I. F. 132
Curtis, B. 38

Dahl, O. J. 255, 275
Dalgarno, M. 250, 251
Davies, M. 299, 307
Davies, S. P. 37, 40
Dawes, J. 126, 264, 278, 282
Deitel, H. M. 78, 79
Deitel, P. J. 78, 79

Demchak, B. 303
Department of Defense 20, 128
DeRemer, F. 12, 16, 46, 115
Dershem, H. L. 18
Détienne, F. 32
Dickinson, I. P. 288
Dijkstra, E. W. 18, 22, 38, 255, 264,
    273, 275
Donahue, J. 157
DuBoulay, B. 37
Dunn, S. C. 302

Eddy, F. 299
Ellemtel 75
Emms, J. 183
Engel, G. L. 107
Engelbart, D. C. 327
Evertsz, R. 250, 251

Fairley, R 280
Feltovich, P. J. 39
Feuer, A. R. 14, 22, 23
Findlay, W. 132
Finlay, B. 17
Finkelstein, A. 292
Fischer, A. W.
Flon, L. 37
Forster, G. A. 250, 251
Foxley, E. 299
Friedman, F. L. 78, 79
Friedman, Da. P. 13
Furber, D. 292

Gabriel, R. P. 236
Gamma, E. 329
Gehani, N. 14, 22, 23
Gelernter, D. 13
Ghezzi, C. 15
Gibbs, N. E. 292
Gilbert, G. N. 342
Gill, S. 317
Glaser, R. 39
Glassman, L. 157
Goguen, J. 182
Goldberg, A. 87, 200, 217
Goodenough, S. J. 306
Gordon, M. 151
Graham, N. 78, 79
Granger, M. J. 84
Gray, J. 299, 307
Green, T. R. G. 31, 32, 37, 38, 40

Greenfield, S. 113
Gries, D. 273, 275
Griffiths, L. 10, 23
Griffiths, R. 301, 304, 307
Grodzinsky, F. S. 18
Gutknecht, J. 114, 172, 173

Hammersley, M. 334
Hammond K. 126
Harbison, S. 157
Harper, R. 151, 152
Haynes, C. T. 13
Heal, B. 282
Hehner, E. C. R. 272, 273
Helman, P. 111
Henry, P. 11
Hetherington, G. A. 136
Higman, B. 314, 320
Hoare, C. A. R. 11, 20, 21, 172, 255,
    275, 333
Holt, R. C. 83, 86, 95
Holt, R. W. 31
Hooper, G. S. 302
Horning, J. J. 157
Horowitz, E. 14, 15, 21
Howlett, J. 13
Hudak P. 18
Hughes, J. 17
Hume, J. N. P. 96

Ichbiah, J. 127
IEC/SC65A/Secretariat 122 132
Ince, D. 275, 282
ISO/IEC 128
ISO/IEC JTC1/SC22/WG13 110
ISO/IEC 76, 79, 135, 136
ITC 84

Jackson, M. A. 11, 294
Jagannathan, S. 13
Jazayer, M. 15
Jensen, K. 135, 157
Jipping, M. l. J. 18
Jones, A. 305
Jones, C. B. 264, 282, 304
Jones, J. 292
Jordan, M. 157
Joslin, D. 135, 136

Kalsow, B. 157
Kay, A. 200, 243

Kearsley, G. 327
Kiczales, G. 244
King, K. N. 86, 1, 278
Kingston, J. H. 111
Klaeren, H. 7, 9, 313
Kluit, P. G. 277
Knuth, D. E. 13, 307, 325, 326
Koehler, S. 141, 303
Koffman, E. B. 78, 79, 107, 113
Krasner, G. 200, 202
Kristensen, B. B. 18, 23
Kron, H. K. 12, 16, 46, 115
Kuhn, T. S. 30, 336, 337, 343

LaLonde, W. R. 204
Lampson, B. W. 157
Landis, P. J. 13
Latham, J. T. 275
Ledgard, H. 40
Lee, P. A. 308
Lee, J. A. N. 12
Levin, R. 157
Lewis, S. 204
Lippman, S. 78, 79
Locke, D. 342
London, R. L. 157
Lorensen, W. 299
Louden, K. C. 18
Ludewig, J. 9, 15

MacKay, A. H. 334
MacQueen, D. 151
Madsen, O.L. 2
Manasse, M. 167
Mancoridis, S. 83, 95
Marcotty, M. 40
Marty, R. 329
Maybury, W. 157
McAllester, D. A. 246
McCarthy, J. 236, 252
McMahon, S. 46
Meehan, J. 167
Meek, B. 313, 316
Mellish, C. S. 126, 247
Mesegeur, J. 182
Metropolis, N. 13
Meyer, B. 78, 79, 182, 195, 196, 205,
    218, 328
Miller, P. L. 107
Milner, R. 151, 333
Mitchell, J. G. 157

Moan, G. 33
Moller-Pedersen, B. 2
Moon, D. 243
Morgan, C. 264, 273, 275
Morrison, R. 56
Mössenböck, H. 173, 219
Mulkay, M. 342
Müller, G. 46, 60
Myers, C.

Nurminen, J. 250
Nelson, G. 157, 167
Nerson, J. M. 182, 195, 196
Nielsen, J. 327
Nierstrasz, O. 46
Nye, A. 343
Nygaard, K. 2

O'Shea, T. 37
Object Management Group 49
Oman, P. 307
Østerbye, K. 18, 23

Pardo, L. T. 13
Parnas, D. L. 34
Paul, D. 8
Paul, R. J. 114
Paulson, L. 151
Payne, S. J. 33
Pearson, E. 292
Pemberton, J. D. 292
Penny, D. A. 83, 86, 95
Perlis, A. J. 7, 9
Petre, M. 9, 29, 31, 32, 33, 34, 35, 37,
    40, 319
Pinson, L. J. 204
Plödereder, E. 9
Pollard, D. J. 291
Pomberger, G. 307
Pomberger, G. 323
Poon, E. 151
Pope, S. T. 202
Popek, G. J. 157
Potter, J. 334, 342, 343
Powell jr., J. H. 113
Pratt, T. W. 15
Premerlani, W. 299
Pröfrock, A. K. 46
Pronk, C. 277
Pugh, J. R. 204

Ramsey, N. 326
Rechenberg, P. 24
Reenskaug, T. 326
Rees, J. 236, 238
Reiser, M. 157, 172, 173
Rentsch, T. 29
des Rivières, J. 244, 245
Robinson, P. 149, 168
Robinson, H. M. 183, 304, 307, 333, 334
Robson, J. 200, 217
Rota, G.-C. 13
Rovner, P. 157
Rumbaugh, J. 299

Sametinger, J. 307, 323, 326, 329, 330
Sammet, J. E. 12, 14, 21, 22, 23
Savic, D. 204
Schultz A. C. 31
Scott, T. J. 115
Sebesta, R. 17
Sedgewick, R. 78, 79, 157
Sethi, R. 16, 18
Shaw, C. J. 317
Shaw, R. C. F. 282
Shearing, B. 199
Shertz, J. 39
Shneiderman, B. 87, 327
Sime, M. E. 37
Siskind, J. M. 246
Skaar, A. L. 326
Smailes, J. M. 292
Smith, D. N. 204, 336
Smith, J. B. 204
Smith, R. B. 217
Steele jr., G. L. 236, 238
Stemple, D. 107
Stokes, G. 107
Stroud, R. J. 63, 308
Stroustrup, B. 8, 71, 78, 79, 217
Suchman, L. 334
Sussman, G. J. 236, 238
Sussman, J. 236
Sutcliffe, A. 2
Sweet, R. 157
Switzer, R. 196
Symantec Corporation 226

Taylor, J. 34
TDI 114
     ⁀pl, J. 171
     ⁀, M. C. 84

Tennent, R. 14
Thomas, M. 303
Thomas, P. 183, 196
Traxler, J. 291
Tucholsky, K. 11
Tucker jr., A. B. 15, 23, 107

Ullman, J. D. 151
Ungar, D. 217

Veroff, R. 111

Wadler, P. 30
Wadsworth, C. 151
Walden, K. 182, 196
Wand, M. 13
Wardle, C. E. 107
Waters, R. C. 245
Watt, D. A. 10, 11, 17, 132, 282
Watt, S. N. K. 250, 251
Weber, M. 45
Weedon, R. 181, 196
Wegner, P. 14, 18
Weinand, A. 329
Weinreb, D.
Weiser, M.
Weiser Friedman, L. 17, 24
Weiss, S. F.
Wellings, A. 16
Wendl, B. 299, 307
Wetherell, M. 334, 342, 343
Wexelblat, R. L. 12
Wichmann, B. A. 125, 129, 132, 135, 136, 306
Wick, J. 157
Wiener, R. S. 204
Wikström, Å. 151
Willner, E. 303
Wilson, L. B. 16
Winder, R. 30, 31, 34, 37
Winstanley, A. C.
Wirth, N. 7, 11, 12, 20, 21, 22, 90, 110, 135, 136, 157, 171, 172, 173, 19
Woodman, M. 1, 282, 301, 303, 304, 307
Woolgar, S. 334

Yourdon, E. 336